PASSAGE TO UNION

PASSAGE TO UNION

How the Railroads Transformed American Life, 1829–1929

SARAH H. GORDON

Ivan R. Dee

CHICAGO   1996

Library of Congress Cataloging-in-Publication Data:
Gordon, Sarah, 1950–
    Passage to Union : how the railroads transformed American life,
1829–1929 / Sarah H. Gordon.
        p.   cm.
    Includes bibliographical references and index.
    ISBN 1-56663-138-6 (alk. paper)
    1. Railroads—United States—History.   2. United States—Economic
conditions.   3. United States—Social conditions.   1. Title.
HE2751.G64   1997
385′.0973—dc20   96-28259

This book is dedicated to

Patricia Dearborn Jencks Gordon Pollock

Herbert Chermside Pollock

Ann Dexter Gordon

Peter Lane Gordon

David Jewell Gordon

Daniel Edward Marketti

Julie Ann Gordon

Megan Lane Gordon

and, in particular, to

Joseph Donald Gordon (1988–1995)

Preface

THE SEARCH FOR improved transportation from the eastern United States to the interior, in order to promote trade and unite the country's geographic regions, led to profound and unforeseen changes in the economic, legal, and social structures of American society. By raising hopes that trade and travel would bring economic betterment and unite a far-flung society, the railroads uprooted and reorganized populations, changed the size, structure, and purpose of towns, altered the distribution of wealth, created new national hierarchies, and ultimately raised a great many questions about the terms on which a diverse people would tolerate national unity.

Each of these consequences engendered considerable civil conflict. Townspeople felt the loss of control over their land and the welfare of their citizens; the South fought the loss of states' rights as they pertained to control over railroad corporations; and rural dwellers fought the tendency of the urban Northeast to drain the countryside of its wealth without adequate recompense. In their new relationship, passengers and railroad companies sought their own philosophy of unity. Should disturbing elements be excluded? Or were the boisterous drunks, gamblers, confidence men, ladies of the night, hoboes, and others who found a home in the new public crowd all parts of the American democratic system?

The nation's distant parts were in fact brought into closer community, but in the process traditional units of social organization and established legal relationships lost much of their power to regulate the behavior of the American people. Transient crowds of strangers replaced local communities as a defining social experience. National markets and organizations with national membership replaced small, local markets and institutions as the cornerstones of social order. The size of the country, and an economy rooted in trade and exchange, determined the large role played by railroads in shaping the structure of American society and its institutions; all echoed the theme of trade and exchange.

This book had its origins in a paper I wrote while a sophomore at Smith College. Using the collections of Smith's Neilson Library and of the local history room at the public library in Springfield, Massachusetts, I wrote "The Connecticut River Railroad: Its Evolution in the Connecticut Valley" for a course on the Gilded Age taught by Professor David Allmendinger. My first thanks, therefore, go to him. I picked up the thread of my interest in railroad history at the University of Chicago, in a seminar on the history of transportation in the United States taught by Professor Neil Harris. With the excellent resources of the university's Regenstein Library, I wrote a paper entitled "Ladies' Train Travel, 1848 to 1890: The Problem of Appearing in Public."

Neil Harris later became my adviser for a dissertation entitled "A Society of Passengers: Rail Travel 1865–1910," which I completed in 1981. I owe a great debt to him and to Professor Stanley N. Katz for reading and editing that manuscript. During my years in Chicago I also consulted material in the holdings of the Chicago Historical Society and the Newberry Library, and went to many of the city's antique stores to take pictures of luggage. Indeed I received help on the history of luggage from the family of Charles T. Wilt, one of the oldest luggage makers in Chicago. Material on train conductors I found in the Baker Library at Harvard University, and I had access to the proceedings of the General Ticket Agents' Association in the collection of the John Crerar Library, now at the University of Chicago. Others who provided substantial help to me during my years in Chicago include the late Robert Rosenthal, director of special collections at the Regenstein Library, who, among other things, introduced me to Romaine's guide to trade catalogs; Vera Aronow, who has periodically sent me clippings and even alerted me to the presence of some very old trunks and suitcases waiting on a New York sidewalk for the trashmen; and Professor Martin J. Hardeman, whose knowledge of American history is apparently boundless and whose support for more than twenty years has been unflagging. Mary Ann Johnson, the curator at Jane Addams's Hull House, gave me much information about immigrants who came to Chicago by train, and she alerted me to an important book on railroad planning in the city. She also made it possible for me to present my research on women's train travel to the Chicago Area Women's History Conference. Beth Durham shared my endeavors in learning about nineteenth-century heating and ventilating, and photocopied letters on train travel from her own research. Robert Siedle brought me stacks of books about railroads. My sister, Ann D. Gordon, kept me supplied with information about the history of luggage from all points of the compass. Finally, Fannia Weingartner, who published one chapter of my dissertation in the Henry Ford Museum *Herald*, encouraged me to persevere as a writer of history at a time when few opportunities existed for me to do so.

This book took many years to write, largely because it required the collection of so many bits and pieces of information from so many different fields of historical scholarship. In providing a publishing contract and the editorial support I needed, Ivan R. Dee has made this book possible. In taking me to sales of used and rare books in many parts of Connecticut and Massachusetts, librarian William K. Finley enabled me to write a much more complete and accurate book. James Goodwin, engineer for both the Valley Railroad and the Connecticut Central Railroad, introduced me firsthand to the technical side of railroading. And my brother, David Gordon, an authority on train routes and schedules, not to mention computers, has had answers for any number of questions. I also consulted materials in the Yale Law Library, the Seelye Mudd Library at Yale University, the Sterling Memorial Library at Yale, the Library of the Court of New Haven, the State Library of Connecticut, the Connecticut Historical Society, the New York Public Library, and public libraries throughout Connecticut. Requests for information have been answered by the Railroad Museum of Pennsylvania in Strasburg and the Virginia State Library in Richmond.

Annette Hise provided information about railroad stations in Connecticut; John H. White, Jr., supplied prices of freight cars; Kathy Murphy, Pam Euerle, and the entire Lyons family provided years of moral support. Among those who have read and commented on portions of the manuscript are Stanley N. Katz, Elizabeth Blackmar, Walter Licht, James Goodwin, Patricia Hipsher, Mark Johnston, Kathy Deierlein, Lynne Hodgson, Mark Wenglinsky, Neil Nelan, Rachel Ranis, and David Stineback.

Finally, my parents, Patricia Gordon Pollock and Herbert C. Pollock, supported my work throughout the writing of this book.

S. H. G.

North Haven, Connecticut
July 1996

Contents

PASSAGE TO UNION

Introduction

MANY HISTORIANS have credited the railroads with unifying the United States by overcoming two situations not usually discussed in American history textbooks. The first was the lack of communication among towns even along the Atlantic seaboard during the colonial and early national periods (1607 to 1846). At the time of the American Revolution, post roads for carrying the mail from Boston through Washington and into the South provided the only unifying means of land transport in the new country. Coastwise vessels carried on a sea trade from port to port and took on passengers only as space permitted. On interior rivers, keelboats carried a trade in manufactured goods and frontier products such as animal hides and lumber. Otherwise the United States had no ties of unity at all. Indeed, throughout the nation's history, efforts to secure and strengthen the bonds of union have met with stiff resistance.

The second situation not clearly defined in standard recountings of American history concerns the frequent threats of secession that dogged the country between 1781 and 1861, when the Southern states finally did secede. Familiar events such as Shays's Rebellion in Massachusetts, and the Whiskey Rebellion, both against taxes, take on their full significance in the context of a very loosely organized country without sufficient means—military, political, or economic—to hold itself together. The Virginia and Kentucky Resolutions of 1796, which attempted to place the power of the states over that of the federal government in determining the constitutionality of federal laws; the threat of federalist secession in New England; the South Carolina nullification crisis of 1832, which challenged the power of Congress to determine tariffs paid by all states; and the Southern land speculation that sought to create a new country in Louisiana—all contained at their root the threat of secession. In surmounting these threats the advocates of union depended in some measure on the suppression of local and regional interests.

The fragility of the government as a unifying force deeply concerned men such as George Washington, Alexander Hamilton, and James Madison, all of whom suggested in their writings that a program of internal improvements—meaning improved transportation to the interior of the country—would provide unity and at the same time increase prosperity by allowing more trade between the interior and the Atlantic coast. Thus was born an alliance between the new nation's trading interests and the interests of government.

This alliance faltered, however, when federal grants to local internal improvement projects were opposed as promoting private commercial interests rather than the general welfare. State governments therefore took over the task of chartering and helping to finance local internal improvements, including canals, bridges, and harbors but particularly railroads, and the drive for national unity came to have almost exclusively local origins and brought uncounted local interests to bear on the problem. The states then had to find a legal way to select and promote those private commercial interests they thought would benefit the public.

Under the guiding philosophy of the United States Supreme Court, state governments refashioned the legal system to accommodate an overwhelming interest in private commercial construction and investment. Between 1800 and 1840, governments made major changes in the laws affecting transportation and corporations: states began eliminating the charter requirement in favor of general laws of incorporation, because obtaining a charter required time and money for both the legislatures and those entrepreneurs who frequently represented the interests of small towns and cities hoping to enrich themselves through trade; states, following the lead of the Supreme Court, divested themselves of the right to take control of corporations they had legally created, making businesses completely private and subject to much less government control; and state courts in all parts of the country provided railroads with all the land they needed, under the doctrine of eminent domain.

These and other changes dramatically accelerated the construction of railroads and contributed to unification. But in the process they unleashed a storm of civil conflict between those who benefited from the old legal, social, and economic order and those who gained from the new. The railroads' need for legal help became legendary as townspeople and farmers fought to preserve their land and their own safety from the loud, dangerous, and apparently unstoppable steam engines. Passengers too sought redress for personal injuries and in-adequacies. The social aspects of this new commercial service fell far short of people's needs and expectations.

The conflict raged on other levels as well. Long before the Civil War it had become evident that towns were incapable of regulating the operations of railroads beyond their own borders. Different towns passed different laws, creating a patchwork of regulation without uni-formity or consistency. While the states tried to regulate railroad ser-vices before the Civil War, the low quality of services widened the gap between townspeople and the railroad corporations.

Sectional differences also emerged. Southern states did not wish to connect their railroads with those of the North. In fact, proponents of states' rights would not allow any railroad corporation to control track in more than one state, since this would diminish the power of the state. As railroad lines grew longer and longer in the North, and by 1857 connected the Atlantic coast with the Mississippi River, the South was guided by its sectional beliefs. In 1861 no track connected railroads north and south of Washington, D.C., and the Ohio River. True to the concerns of the founding fathers, the Union broke almost precisely along this line.

Train travel uprooted people from all regions and generated the crowds that became a new and permanent feature of the American social order, eclipsing the old bulwarks of community, family, and church. Cultural and social differences in crowds of Northerners, Southerners, and Westerners, rich and poor, black, white, and Indian, all worked to create a society at once more united and diverse, but also one fraught with conflict over social and cultural standards. The experience of social diversity on the train and in once-distant regions fascinated travelers, but deep rifts persisted. Observing the behavior of the rural poor, slave society, Indians, or others did not translate into an acceptance of them as equals.

Finally, cutthroat competition among the railroad companies worked both for and against the principle of national unity. In the name of competition, the stronger roads rapidly bought out the weaker. While this consolidation helped to unify services, the railroads' competitive stance prevented them from cooperating. Although the ideal of a railroad system connecting all parts of the country in orderly fashion had emerged by 1850, the railroads never adhered to this ideal unless forced to do so by law.

The nation's rush toward unification screeched to a halt in the late 1850s, once the railroads had reached the Mississippi River. The South, holding to a states' rights doctrine, refused to allow Northern lines to dominate expansion into the West. This slowed Western development markedly and contributed directly to the outbreak of the Civil War in 1861.

During the war the railroad became the central institution that promised order amidst chaos, signaling a sea change in the relationship between social order and mass transportation. As a supply line the railroad kept armies fed and clothed, and withdrew the wounded from the field of battle. It brought the essentials of civilization, in portable form, to armies in the field. In the havoc of war, the train, despite its dangers and poor services, seemed orderly indeed. The Northern victory assured Northern railroad interests that they would dominate the drive to connect the sections and the two coasts by rail, using the railroad as their new standard of union and social order. Epitomizing the principle of exchange, of people as well as goods, railroads could lead the effort to settle the West and rebuild the South through the medium of trade with the North. But the local conflicts that had accompanied this expansion before the Civil War were later transformed into state and national struggles.

After the war the trains moved west, carrying hundreds of thousands of passengers to settle the land. The railroads, cumbersome for the transport of small groups, were ideally suited for the large numbers of immigrants and farmers heading west. Investment money poured in from Europe as well as the eastern United States, and railroad building preoccupied Northern business interests more than any other single economic project. More than 300,000 miles of track were laid between 1865 and 1917, much of it in the South and West. While population grew in both regions, social order remained a question because as a new institution the railroads operated largely outside the bounds of the law. The states responded with a flood of laws regulating the quality and safety of rail service. But for the railroads themselves, the guiding principle was commercial exchange; their role as a social institution with a fixed legal identity was secondary.

With the increasing dominance of interstate railroads, state commissions strove to apply uniform standards to the operation of the roads because they could see no other way of making the laws stick. But railroads crossing state lines constitutionally fell under the jurisdiction of the federal government. In 1887 Congress passed its earliest railway regulation with the founding of the Interstate Commerce Commission, a small solution to a very large problem.

By this time even the railroad owners had begun to realize that order and uniform standards of service might increase their efficiency and lower their operating costs. The population had grown too large and too commercially interdependent to rely on local or regional standards of service. While they might exacerbate local conflicts over railroad operations, standard time, standard gauge, and standard design of cars did improve the efficiency of national service. They made cars interchangeable from line to line, and scheduling of service became a national rather than a local affair.

But civil conflict persisted on a national stage after 1865. Lawsuits involving property damages, personal injury, and inadequate service increased rather than declined after needed laws were on the books. Railroad barons enriched themselves with excessive grants of land and money from the federal government, which wanted to see the West drawn into the Union as quickly as possible. Efforts by the railroads to eliminate competition concentrated the ownership of the roads under a few men from the major urban centers of the North. Crowds of travelers swamped the cities, drawn to the centers of the

greatest wealth. The cities quickly grew to unprecedented and un-
manageable proportions just as the population and wealth of smaller
towns began to stagnate. Cities welcomed the crowds, which translated into profits for stores, restaurants, theaters, and hotels, but they
did little to control crowd behavior or protect the weak from the
strong in crowds of strangers.

Despite these unsettling aspects of an emerging mass society, a
corresponding growth in national institutions with national member-
ships came to depend on the railroads to carry large groups of people
from long distances. The wealthy followed established paths of travel
from city to city, and even liked to vacation together in fashionable resort areas. The middle class traveled to the early political conventions
held before the Civil War; to schools that drew students from all parts
of the country; to professional gatherings in law, medicine, teaching,
and library work; to national meetings of retailers, women's clubs, and
suffrage associations. The poor, who could not afford long-distance
travel, affiliated with groups that met closer to home. In each case the
railroad continued to provide a unifying and even orderly influence
which aided the country's rapid growth, but only by providing services
that reflected the social and economic divisions among their passengers.

After the Civil War, railroads financed by Northern money expanded quickly into the predominantly rural South and West, severely
limiting local control of railroad service in those regions. Despite the
financial panic of 1873, the South and West were drawn into the national rail net by 1890. But both regions had serious grievances. Their
expectations of large-scale commercial development that would follow on the heels of railroad service were largely unmet. In the absence
of local control of the railroads, profits traveled eastward and northward to the controlling interests rather than enriching the patrons.

By the close of the nineteenth century the drive to expand the railroad network to every conceivable location of business opportunity
had begun to slow. New railroads continued to be built, particularly
in the West and South, but the number of lines in the country far exceeded need. The era after 1890 was more notable for further centralization, with Harriman, Gould, Morgan, and a few others
controlling most of the country's track mileage. Population became

more and more concentrated in the urban areas of the Northeast, as the South and West failed to build the industrial base that would attract people looking for jobs. Wealth too gravitated to the urban Northeast, and, as international trade grew, American trade became more centralized in the major port cities, leaving smaller ports such as Portland, Portsmouth, Providence, and New Haven without the booming business they had hoped for.

With the centralization of wealth in Northern cities and the reduction of rural areas to second-class economic status came a new philosophy of business which emphasized efficiency in the pursuit of profit. Speed became the watchword in both the production and delivery of services, and railroads sought to move as many people and as much freight as quickly as possible. Speeding trains vied to reduce travel time between the country's major economic centers, delivering passengers, goods, stock quotations, and business mail. To save time the roads reduced the number of stops at small stations that provided the least economic return.

Rural train service, lacking any specific need to race the clock, continued at the pottering pace it had known for decades. With fewer passengers and fewer profits, rural lines were the first to be discontinued when railroads began facing competition from automobiles. The economies of small towns and rural railroads depended on each other; they collapsed together as the wealth and the means of attaining wealth became ever more centralized.

Thus the centralization of wealth and services advanced the national economy but left behind many individuals, towns, and even states. Even among those individuals who migrated to the cities were some who could not find a secure living and became permanent drifters in urban America. By the 1920s, when investments and social habits began to favor the automobile, a new railroad culture emerged, one which stressed the terrible loneliness of the declining countryside, the migration from hometowns, or the hobo's niche in an urban train yard. In the drive for national unity and prosperity, some were left behind and unable to go home. In a commercial society, home was no longer a fixed abode, rooted in social and legal protections, but merely a resting place along the road.

PART ONE

"Called Forth by the Urgency of Some Local Want"

UNION THROUGH EXPANSION, 1829–1861

In 1832 Matthias Baldwin built one of the first locomotives in the United States for the Philadelphia, Germantown and Norristown Railway. True to the style of the earliest trains, the passenger cars resembled stagecoaches. (HISTORICAL SOCIETY OF PENNSYLVANIA)

1

||||||||||

E Pluribus Unum

The entire population, both slave and free, west of the mountains, reached not yet half a million; but already they were disposed to think themselves, and the old thirteen states were not altogether unwilling to consider them, the germ of an independent empire, which was to find its outlet, not through the Alleghenies to the seaboard, but by the Mississippi River to the Gulf. . . . Nowhere did eastern settlements touch the western.
> —Henry Adams, *History of the United States of America*, 1889[1]

At the last session of the legislature of New York in 1836, no less than forty-two new railroad companies were incorporated. . . . The state of New York alone, therefore, will in a few years have ninety-two railroads, facilitating the intercourse of its principal towns and villages, or connecting them with the railroads of other states in order to establish lines of communication with the southern, western, and eastern parts of the country.
> —Francis J. Grund, *The Americans, in their Moral, Social and Political Relations*, 1837[2]

IN 1889, WHEN the historian Henry Adams published his six-volume *History of the United States of America*, he devoted the first chapter

to a description of the transportation problems encountered by
Americans in 1800. Roads were so few, stagecoaches so slow, and
sailboats so occasional that statesmen and merchants feared for the
stability of the Union. More than two-thirds of the American people
lived within fifty miles of the Atlantic Ocean, and they had almost
no contact with settlers who had crossed the Allegheny Mountains
to the Northwest Territory, Kentucky, and Tennessee. By 1845
more than half the population lived west of the Alleghenies; by
1900 the western frontier of open land was closed all the way to the
Pacific.

Adams was not alone in identifying transportation as crucial to the
success of the new American nation. George Washington, James
Madison, and Alexander Hamilton, three of the Federalists who had
sheperded the Constitution into place in 1788, favored cooperation
between business and government to advance the cause of internal
improvements: the development of transportation routes over land
and water. The interests of business would be served by opening the
West and making it accessible to the commercial centers of the East.
And the interests of government would be met by putting the West,
South, and Northeast in closer touch with one another, thus strength-
ening the weak and untested political bonds of a rapidly growing nation.[3]

Before 1800, long-distance travelers usually followed water routes.
Up and down the coast from Maine to the port of New Orleans, the
coastwise trade of food, ice, and other local products was frequently
accompanied by small numbers of passengers. Early settlers to the interior almost always followed the course of rivers. Eastern colonial
settlements dotted the shores of the Connecticut River, the Hudson,
the Delaware, and other waterways. To reach points further west,
travelers headed for the Ohio River, which had its headwaters in
western Pennsylvania and followed a western course until it emptied
into the Mississippi River at the site of present-day Cairo, Illinois.
Further south, pioneers followed the course of the Cumberland and
Tennessee rivers, while others took boats north from New Orleans up
the Mississippi all the way to Illinois.[4]

By 1800 the river routes had been supplemented by roads constructed for military purposes and by three wagon roads, all of which

facilitated travel to the Ohio River: the Wilderness Road, the Knoxville Road, and the Old Walton Road.[5] But construction of these roads was hampered by disagreement over the appropriate role of the federal government, so that the impulse for internal improvements came to reside more and more with state governments. By 1830 state legislators had successfully backed the construction of several thousand miles of canals, including the Erie Canal which connected the Hudson River to the Great Lakes, and the Ohio canals which scored that wide, flat state from the Great Lakes south to the Ohio River. Emigrants followed these water routes at a speed of about four miles per hour to find and claim open land.

Even as newspapers hailed canals as the solution to America's transportation problem, both state legislators and the federal government began receiving appeals from entrepreneurs who sought special considerations for the construction of railroads. During the early 1820s Congress took an interest in marine railways for bringing ships into dry dock. Small railways with horse-drawn wagons were used to haul freight. The Quincy Railroad in Massachusetts hauled granite; the Mauch Chunk gravity railroad in Pennsylvania brought coal down to water's edge, then brought its cars back up to the mine with animal power.[6]

By 1830 railroads in New York, Maryland, and South Carolina had begun providing regularly scheduled services for passengers, carrying them in a train of cars pulled by steam locomotive. During the next thirty years business and state governments cooperated, awkwardly but effectively, to construct 30,626 miles of railroad between the Atlantic coast and the Mississippi River.[7] Railroads evolved from local lines serving local interests, to regional lines with service that first connected bodies of water, then towns, cities, and states. In many respects this construction helped to realize the hopes of those who supported internal improvements. Trade and transport emerged as unifying forces, promoting the exchange of people and goods among the nation's regions.

Despite a professed goal of national unity that encouraged state legislatures to charter railroads, a close look at the relationship between state governments and business reveals a highly complex relationship that was not always successful. Eastern cities and states pursued their plans for railroads in order to gain the advantage in fierce economic competition. The plum they each sought was trade that extended beyond their immediate boundaries to distant communities and eventually to the undeveloped West, with its lure of wealth in natural resources.

New York, which had taken the lead in developing the Western trade with the opening of the Erie Canal in 1825, began to face stiff competition for that trade when Baltimore opened its Baltimore and Ohio Railroad about five years later, and when Boston began to build its Western Railroad, connecting the city with Albany and the Erie Canal. When railroads proved more efficient and cheaper than canals, New York retaliated against Baltimore and Boston by beginning construction on the Erie Railroad, a railroad that would eventually connect the Hudson River to the Great Lakes. Pennsylvania had entered the competition with a combination of trains and canals connected in patchwork fashion across the state. But this system could not compete with the railroads either, and Philadelphia fell behind New York and Baltimore in its Western trade. Portland, Maine, tried to bypass strong competition to the South by connecting its railroads with Canada, but in the long run this proved almost fatal to the success of Portland's railroad system and Maine's economy.

In the South the earliest railroads connected port cities with cotton and tobacco fields to the west. But because of relatively few towns and low populations, railroading in the South developed slowly and remained chiefly a state enterprise until after the Civil War.

Railroad building generated competition and conflict in other ways as well. Canal owners and operators resented the railroads as unfair competition, disallowed by their state charters. Technically the canal owners were right, and the law was changed to accommodate state economic interests. Stagecoach drivers also objected, as did tavern owners and farmers who did not want tracks across their land. Local farmers did not want produce shipped to their cities from a distance, and townspeople would not allow locomotives within city limits. The list of protesters was a long one, but exhortations for prosperity and national unity eclipsed individual considerations.

States issued the charters and helped raise the funds that made railroad construction possible. Under traditions of state law, anyone who wished to start a business such as a railroad had to obtain a charter from his state legislature or the United States Congress. The system of issuing state charters for business ventures allowed state governments close control over their economies, and railroads were no exception. In the public interest the charters placed legal restrictions on the operation of railroads, regulating such matters as fares, the nature of services, the location and condition of the track, and train speed.[8]

Between 1820 and 1860, however, business chafed at these restrictions, which limited the building of railroads, the time allowed to build them, and their potential for profit. Because it took time and money to apply for a charter and push it through the legislative process, only the rich could afford to obtain charters—or so reasoned the frontiersmen and other relatively poor people who sought to open their own businesses in undeveloped regions. By the 1840s changes in the law and in Supreme Court interpretation of the law helped railroads and other business ventures throw off many legal controls and operate in a "wilderness" of law as well as geography.[9] By 1860 the economic promise of railroading had brought about fundamental changes in state laws, all of which reduced the authority of the states to control and regulate business and speeded national economic development.

One such change, occurring over several decades, ended the issuance of charters by special act of the state legislatures. This made it much easier for any individual or group to found a public corporation such as a railroad, and eliminated the need for state legislatures to debate the terms of each incorporation. Railroad interests played a central role in pressuring many state legislatures to eliminate the charter system and open transportation routes to competing lines, a change which sometimes resulted in two, three, or more railroads serving the same routes, and eventually brought the country far more railroads than it really needed.[10]

Another change in the law ended state power to confer a monopoly of business. The Erie Canal, for example, by the terms of its state charter, retained a monopoly of the transportation business between the Hudson River and Lake Erie. Monopolies of this type were intended to limit wasteful duplication of services and ensure that canals, railroads, and toll bridges operated in a manner consistent with the public interest. But the monopoly provision became difficult to maintain as the railroad proved to be a faster and more efficient carrier than a canal boat. Supreme Court decisions, particularly the Charles River Bridge case, finally ended the early power of states to confer monopolies on the canals and early railroads through charters.[11]

A third change involved the degree of authority the state retained when it issued a charter. Many state legislators of the 1820s and 1830s assumed that when they chartered a business, they retained the authority ultimately to repossess it and run it themselves. The Supreme Court had called this authority into question in the famous Dartmouth College Case of 1819, asserting that any business, once chartered, was a separate and private entity, to be run by those who received the charter and not by those who granted it. In the long run the authority of the state succumbed to the interests of private enterprise.[12]

Some states, even before these changes, did not allow railroads to operate as separately chartered businesses. They put them under the control of a state internal improvements commission. Pennsylvania was one of the first states to do this. By this tactic its state legislature hoped to promote orderly railroad building, without overlapping services, in a manner consistent with the public interest. No such state-controlled railroad remained solvent, however, and within years states sold their railroads to individuals who incorporated them as businesses and ran them for profit.[13]

The internal improvements commission appointed by the Pennsylvania state legislature was originally established to oversee the state's canal traffic. It took on responsibility for the state's railroads during the period 1827 to 1842. During the late 1820s the commission authorized geographical surveys for a railroad to head west from Philadelphia, which became known as the Philadelphia and Columbia Railroad. The commission determined the location of all early railroad lines in the state, sold the bonds that funded construction, and oversaw the building of the roads. It also had responsibility for regulating traffic on the lines, because the railroad cars themselves

were privately owned. An early compilation of canal and railroad regulations reveals some of the conditions that governed freight and passenger traffic on Pennsylvania's state-owned transportation system.
The state controlled such matters as the speed of trains, tolls to be
charged for use of the track, safety considerations such as the need to
enclose all lamp and lantern flames, and the order of priority of different types of trains using the track.[14]

The state-appointed Superintendents of Transportation of Motive
Power also determined each train's time of departure, and decided
which trains would be allowed to pass on the single track while others waited on a siding. Mail cars were given priority, followed by passenger cars and "burden" or freight cars, in the "starting, passing and
turning out of trains." The Superintendents required these different
types of trains to obey different speed regulations. Mail and passenger trains could not legally exceed a speed of eighteen miles per hour;
the slower burden trains were limited to a speed of ten miles per
hour. All trains had to proceed even more slowly when crossing
wooden bridges and viaducts, notorious for their weakness in
pre–Civil War America.[15]

The owners or their appointed "conductors" had to accompany the
railroad cars and take responsibility for them. These early conductors,
not in the pay of a railroad company at all, took responsibility for col-
lecting fares and state tolls for the use of track, submitting these receipts to the state commission, and for keeping order in the cars. A
single train might consist of several sets of privately owned cars, each
under the authority of its own conductor.[16]

The Pennsylvania commission's agents set railroad fares that varied
according to the age of the passenger and the weight of luggage or
freight. Any passenger over twelve paid a penny a mile; children aged
six to twelve paid half a penny per mile. Weight considerations were
important because the load had to be sufficiently light for the lightweight steam locomotives to haul. Nevertheless, the commission determined that "Fifty pounds of baggage will be allowed to each
passenger free of charge." Every twenty-five pounds beyond that
limit cost one mill (a tenth of a cent).[17]

"Freight" carried by train frequently consisted not of products for market but of heavy and unwieldy "agricultural implements, carts, wagons, sleighs, ploughs and mechanics' tools" which emigrants needed to earn a living. When accompanied by the owner, each thousand pounds of this type of freight cost one cent per mile. All other items except glassware cost less than two cents per mile per thousand pounds.[18]

In the state of New York, railroads were operated by businessmen, not by the state. But a debate raged nevertheless—mostly in the 1840s—as to the extent of state control over businesses it chartered. In the end, the state backed off, allowing railroad entrepreneurs a much freer rein in the location of track and the quality of transportation services.[19]

One of the first three states to boast a passenger railroad, New York saw the opening of its Mohawk and Hudson line in 1831, connecting the Hudson and Mohawk rivers west of Albany. By 1841 seven short lines formed a "continuous chain" from the Hudson to Lake Erie. While none of these lines seriously compromised the monopoly of the parallel Erie Canal, together they had the potential to take away canal business. And each of the railroads had been granted a monopoly by state charter over transportation in its separate region.[20]

Over the objections of canal interests, the state compromised by allowing the short lines to carry only passengers while the canal retained a monopoly over freight business. This expediency worked as long as small, lightweight locomotives and cars were unfit to carry anything of great weight, such as the lumber or barrels of grain that canal boats carried east during the 1830s. Frustration remained, however, because the canal froze during winter months, leaving manufacturers with no western market within the bounds of New York. New York felt the pressure of competition as other states chartered and built railroad routes westward.[21]

By 1845 the New York legislature had again redrawn the lines of monopoly to allow railroads to carry freight during the winter months when the Erie Canal lay useless. This policy shift led to the recognition that railroads could handle freight more cheaply and efficiently than the canals. The final irony came when the state granted a charter to the Erie Railroad, the first long-distance or "through" railroad in the Northeast, along a route that paralleled the Erie Canal. This irritated both the holders of the canal charter and the owners of the small railroad chain that had been pursuing canal profits.[22]

After 1845 the concept of monopoly came under attack from a number of different directions. The Supreme Court had already declared in the Dartmouth College case that charters did not imply a monopoly of business. Now newspapers began to suggest that monopolies did not invariably act in the public interest, as intended, because the absence of competition resulted in poor service and high fares. Finally, the number of entrepreneurs who wished to charter railroads continued to increase to the point where the state legislature could not practically debate the merits of each application for charter or grant monopolies without offending a great many rejected applicants.[23]

Given these pressures, the state of New York passed a law in 1848 that has come to be known as a general incorporation law. The legislature no longer required a state charter for corporations. Instead, one set of rules applied to all businesses seeking to incorporate. By filing these articles of incorporation with the state, a corporation could be established without demonstrating any public benefit, and without debate or consideration by the New York state legislature.[24]

Other states followed New York's lead, but not before a lengthy public debate in each state on the best means for founding railroads and running them at a profit. Massachusetts, for example, like Pennsylvania, had an internal improvements commission, but the first railroads, including the Boston and Lowell and the Boston and Worcester, were under private ownership from the very beginning. The commission regulated the roads but did not attempt to run them.[25] These early Massachusetts roads owned their own cars as well but would tow the cars of others for a fee.

Despite sparse population and commerce in the interior states, they did not delay in planning railroads within their own boundaries. By the 1830s businessmen and legislators in Michigan and Illinois realized that within a matter of years the tracks heading west from New York, Philadelphia, and Baltimore would reach them, opening avenues for trade. In 1832, even before Michigan became a state, the territorial council began chartering railroads, anticipating the state's position on the route between New York and Chicago. Michigan's business community hoped to garner profits from this through traffic. In 1837, after Michigan became a state, it began an extensive program to build both railroads and canals. The state itself began construction of three railroads, one of which was the Michigan Central, which cut across the state from east to west. The state program slowed, however, during the panic of 1837. Like Pennsylvania, Michigan could not make a profit in the railroad business and sold all its lines to businessmen in 1846. Even so, the Michigan Central did not reach Chicago until 1852.[26]

Chicago interests, representing a city just founded in 1830, organized the Illinois and Michigan Canal Commission and became the center of railroad construction in the state because its location on Lake Michigan assured it of contact with the East through the Great Lakes and the Erie Canal. Businessmen dominated railroad building in Illinois and obtained a charter in 1836 for the state's first railroad, the Galena and Chicago Union, which privately built the state's first two hundred miles of track. None of the railroad track in Illinois was built by the state.[27]

While each railroad and each state had its own tale of founding and control, nationally the balance of power shifted steadily away from the states and toward private enterprise. Yet regulation of the roads did not entirely cease. In most states every railroad company, whether or not it had actually laid track, had to submit an annual report to the state, detailing its operations. Many states compiled these reports for all railroads and published them under one cover. Such reports revealed income and expenditure, and included inventories of freight cars, passenger cars, and locomotives. Some lines also reported the rates charged and an accounting of accidents, for safety became a concern within only a few years after the inauguration of passenger services.[28]

Those railroads that still operated under special charters also had to submit to inspection by a commissioner or commission, assigned to this duty in the text of each charter. In Connecticut, for example, each chartered railroad had its own commissioners, named by the state legislature to consider complaints brought against the company. In 1832 the charter of the Boston, Norwich and New London Railroad, recorded under the private acts of the state legislature, included the requirement that "there shall be a board of commissioners consisting of three persons . . . who shall not be interested in any way whatsoever in said corporation" to hear conflicts pertaining to damages arising from the taking of land for railroad tracks. Other railroads operated under similar restrictions. In the late 1840s Connecticut passed a general incorporation act like New York's, placing all legal restrictions on railroad operations in the standard text of the articles of incorporation. Then, in 1853, the state established a general railroad commission to regulate all roads in the state.[29]

While states retreated from close oversight of the railroads and allowed competition among numerous lines and overlapping service, they began to enact statutes protecting the life and property of passengers. The first such statutes became law at about the same time that the general incorporation acts were passed. In Connecticut a statute of 1848 held railroad companies liable for lost baggage, while another permitted a local court to regulate passenger fares within the bounds of the city.[30]

These state statutes regulating rail service signaled an increasing awareness that letting go of the charter system had resulted in a serious legal vacuum. The railroads did not create a systematic passenger or freight service but rather a great many services that competed for dollars at the expense of reasonable accommodations. Only a few statutes defined what passenger service ought to be. And because early railroads were not always regarded as common carriers, they fell outside a large body of regulatory law. For the remainder of the nineteenth century the relationship between the law and the railroads' services would remain problematic and steeped in political conflict.

The effort to unify the country by rail, in order to stabilize the Union and promote trade, was from the beginning a conflicted process. Trade was based on competition, the idea of union was based on cooperation. The two forces never coexisted peacefully, and the rail service became an amalgam of both: the network of rails that brought distant communities together, and the agent of cutthroat competition that drained the public purse (through state bonds and other considerations) for private gain. And even when distant communities came into contact with each other, common interest was not always the result. The most notable example of this was in the South, which rejected both the philosophy of industrial trade competition and the idea of a strong federal union.

2

||||||||||

The Lay of the Land

Rail road travelling is getting all the go,
All you got to do is to get a board on,
Fust they break your back, and then they throw you off the track,
And they land you on the other side of Jordan.

—Railroad Song[1]

IF COOPERATION BETWEEN business and government was uneasy, an even more unsettled relationship prevailed between railroad technology and the geography of the country. While promoters hoped to render mountains, rivers, deserts, storms, and seasons irrelevant to transportation, in fact the railroads' journey to the Pacific included many precarious and hazardous feats.[2]

Even the most sophisticated transportation of the 1820s could not afford to ignore the weather or the changing seasons. Canals in the Northern states froze in winter and leaked in all seasons, requiring constant maintenance. Steamboats too had to limit their service to the warm months of the year in order to avoid ice. In summer a

drought might lower the water level on rivers sufficiently to make
steamboating difficult or impossible. Both steamboats and canal boats
had cabins to accommodate passengers during a storm, but traveling
a river in storms reduced visibility and made accidents common.[3]

While steamboats had advanced transport by traveling upriver at a
constant rate of speed, the technology that made this possible—the
steam boiler—presented hazards even more lethal than storms or low
water. The boilers had a habit of blowing up, and steamship companies had a large order in minimizing this risk and counteracting neg-
ative nationwide publicity.[4]

The faster a steamboat proceeded, the more water the boiler
consumed, and the greater the likelihood of an empty boiler—and
disaster. Yet passengers wanted speed, especially over long distances
up and down the Hudson, Ohio, and Mississippi rivers. The steamboat could achieve greater speeds over longer periods of time than
any other mode of transportation. Canal boats, on the other hand,
traveled very slowly, moving only four to five miles an hour, as mules
or other beasts of burden pulled them along in a deliberate fashion.
Still, transport by canal cost less than transport by steamboat, and carried people who otherwise might not be able to afford any transportation other than a wagon or walking.[5]

The introduction of several short railroads in the period 1827 to
1831 did little to challenge a national reliance on water travel. Yet
within twenty years the technology of railroading had advanced to the
point where trains could successfully negotiate mountains, storms,
seasons, and long distances more successfully than either steamboat
or canal boat, and could cross most of the Eastern rivers. Much of this
progress, however, came not by rendering nature irrelevant but by es-
timating how technology could best be adapted to the American landscape.

The adaptation of railroad technology to the terrain took place in
stages, and in most cases change came as a consequence of equipment failure. The earliest inventors put down track extending a few
miles over level ground, then tested the track by running a horse-
drawn carriage or a locomotive over it. These tests attracted much
public attention as onlookers lined the tracks to witness and judge the
results.[6]

Edward Lamson Henry's painting *The First Railway on the Mohawk and Hudson Road* captures the excitement of the 1831 opening. Note the scrap from the hasty construction project just completed. Henry submitted this work for display in the Transportation Building at the 1893 Columbian Exposition in Chicago. (ALBANY INSTITUTE OF HISTORY AND ART)

The merchants of Baltimore, anxious to establish a connection between their port city and the Ohio River, organized a railroad company in 1827, before they even knew whether a railroad would accomplish their goal. In May 1830 the Baltimore and Ohio Railroad opened its first few miles for business, but it had no steam locomotives. A horse pulled the first ceremonial brigade of cars twenty-six miles out to Ellicott Mills and back. When the use of horsepower proved less than satisfactory, the company tried both sail power and an engine motivated by a horse on a treadmill. Finally it found an American-built locomotive called the "Tom Thumb," which pulled cars at an exhilarating eighteen miles per hour. After that, the B&O expanded at an ambitious rate to become one of the first "trunk" or long-distance railroads in the United States.[7]

In a parallel achievement, the merchants of Charleston, South Carolina, chartered a railroad in 1828 and opened it for business in November 1830, only a few months after the trial runs of the B&O. The South Carolinians gained the advantage, however, by ordering a steam locomotive, the "Best Friend of Charleston," built at the West Point Foundry in New York, while the B&O was still debating its type of motive power. The Charleston locomotive could travel thirty-five miles per hour when not pulling cars. The South Carolina Railroad, also planned as a trunk line, ultimately connected the port of Charleston with Augusta, Georgia.[8]

The Delaware and Hudson Canal Company of New York watched a demonstration of the English engine "Stourbridge Lion" on its tracks in 1829, but New Yorkers did not enter the railroad competition successfully until 1831 with the opening of the short Mohawk and Hudson Railroad, connecting the Mohawk and Hudson rivers. By that time the operations of the B&O and the South Carolina Railroad had encouraged dozens of merchants in East Coast towns to seek railroad charters.[9]

These new companies began raising money to build tracks despite the fact that trial runs and daily service had exposed numerous flaws in the technology of railroading. Horatio Allen, the inventor who brought the "Stourbridge Lion" to America, found his engine too heavy for the track, and he abandoned the use of that engine after his first trial run. The tracks themselves, built of wood with strips of iron nailed on top, warped after exposure to extremes of temperature and damp. Exposure and wear caused the iron strips to come loose from the wooden track, curl upward, and poke into the bottom of the train, often causing injury to passengers. The ride on track without suspension or cushioning was extremely rough, causing passengers to lose their seating and cars to bounce off the track entirely.[10]

The steam locomotive posed even greater dangers. The "Best Friend of Charleston" exploded on one of its first runs when a fireman closed a steam valve and sat on it. The fire required for steam power created a constant risk because parts of the early locomotives, and most of the early cars, were built of wood. The pressure of the steam needed constant attention to avoid building to the point where an explosion occurred in the engine itself. A stream of burning cinders flew out of the engines' smokestacks and left burns and holes in the cars and in the passengers' clothing and hair. On longer journeys the locomotive required periodic stops to take on wood for fuel and water for the steam boiler; but stopping was problematic for a locomotive because it had no brakes and was shifted into reverse in order to slow its progress.[11]

The first train cars, a motley collection of designs which resembled stagecoaches, omnibuses, or simply flat platforms, were lightly built and offered little protection in bad weather, since they had no windows, and in collisions, which occurred even during the very first ceremonial rides, when livestock strayed onto the tracks. The cars were linked together only by lengths of chain, so that when the locomotive started, the cars jolted badly into motion, and when they stopped, they ran into one another. The only brakes on passenger cars had to be applied by hand, and each car braked separately. Finally, cars had almost no capacity to negotiate curves, and they frequently tipped over in the process.[12]

Natural obstacles slowed early railroading. Bridges, made chiefly of wood, rotted or collapsed in floods and heavy snows; track washed out in heavy rains; snow and ice stopped service altogether. But the chartering of railroads proceeded anyway, partly because, despite these drawbacks, the railroad could move more quickly than any other mode of land transport. The demand for railroads also grew among merchants seeking to expand their markets and among passengers who found land travel transformed by the railroad from a tedious, dirty, slow, and hazardous enterprise to an experience of comparatively greater speed, predictability, and convenience.[13]

By the mid-1830s, after a second wave of experimentation, provisional solutions had been found for many of the earliest problems in railroad technology. In place of the wooden track with iron strips came the iron rail—more expensive, but heavier and more durable. Under the track, railroads inserted ballast, usually composed of pebbles or broken stone, which gave the track more resilience and provided a drainage area for water.[14]

The locomotive now gained a cowcatcher, an iron wedge attached to the front of the engine to prevent ever-present livestock from rolling under the train and making it impossible to proceed. The cowcatcher pushed the livestock ahead of the train until the animals could be removed from the track, dead or alive. A whistle and a lantern were added to the front of the locomotive to prevent all too common collisions with livestock, with pedestrians who found the track easier for walking than most roads, and with tree limbs, rocks, and other natural obstacles. Some railroad companies put spark arresters on top of the smokestack to minimize the damage of flying cinders. Most important, progressive increases in the size of the steam boiler made the locomotive more and more powerful, enabling it to pull longer trains and bigger cars. Yet both locomotives and cars remained of relatively lightweight construction.[15]

Before the mid-1830s the passenger car evolved into an elongated shape with a central aisle. This "American style" passenger coach made it possible for conductors to collect tickets while the train was in motion. European conductors collected tickets in the station and did not mind the private compartments that opened directly to the outside. Americans, who built few stations in the wilderness, or in centers of low population, and frequently adapted old buildings, such as taverns or inns, did not have the facilities, staffing, or organization to collect tickets at the station. Furthermore, many passengers simply jumped off and on the train as it passed by, without observing the formality of the station.[16]

Passenger cars gained in comfort, with windows, ventilators to introduce fresh air, and coal- or wood-burning stoves to provide warmth in the cold months. The better cars had padded seats and curtains or painted woodwork to suggest the look of a contemporary hotel.[17]

Mechanical improvements of the 1830s included the wheel "truck," which placed four wheels instead of two at each end of the passenger car and put the wheels on a swivel rather than attaching them directly to the bottom of the car. This arrangement, worked out by a number of American inventors, enabled the wheel truck to accommodate turns in the track without upsetting the equilibrium of the passenger car. The coupling between cars evolved from the unsatisfactory and unsafe chain to a link-and-pin design. A solid loop of iron on each end of each car overlapped a similar loop on the next car, and a metal pin, inserted through the loops by hand, held them together.[18]

All these adaptations increased the reliability of train service and made it less hazardous. But at this same time, roughly 1829 to 1835, inventors were struggling with the more difficult question of whether a railroad train could go over mountains. Before the advent of the passenger train, coal trains had gone up and down steep grades, both in the mines of England and from the mines down to the river's edge in both England and America. The small coal cars ran downhill by gravity, controlled by a brake or rope; the uphill journey proceeded under the power of a person, frequently a child, or a horse, pulling the wagon under harness. Two early industrial railroads in the United States fit this description. The Quincy Railroad outside Boston, which started operations in 1827, pulled cars uphill by horse or mule, to be filled with granite, then let the cars descend by force of gravity. The Mauch Chunk coal railroad of Pennsylvania, opened the same year, pulled rail cars up to the coal mines by horse, then sent the full cars gliding downhill without any motive force other than gravity.[19]

Even some of the early steam locomotives attached a horse or mule to help in the uphill climbs. The descents required constant braking of the cars, which stopped the wheels from turning but did not always slow the train. On early railroads in Pennsylvania, the places where a horse had to pull the train uphill were known as inclined planes, or ramps. Their use led to many accidents when the rope between the horse and the train broke.

As early as 1814, English trials of steam locomotive power had demonstrated that an engine could pull "nine loaded wagons up a twelve-foot grade." Americans nonetheless surveyed and built rail routes on as flat a surface as possible. The general belief persisted that if a locomotive went uphill it would slide backward due to insufficient friction between the wheels and the track. In 1836, however, an American mechanic named William Norris built an engine that weighed over seven tons and drove it up a plane more than a mile long. He then repeated the experiment successfully with the engine hauling a train of cars. After 1836 railroad builders stopped asking whether a train could drive through mountains and started wondering about the limits of length and steepness of each hill, and the size of the locomotive that would be required to surmount it. Even today, railroads coming through the Rocky Mountains are drawn by the most powerful locomotives in use.[20]

The first decade of experimentation with railroads also required experimentation with bridges. Pennsylvania railroads, which ran through a much more rugged and mountainous terrain than the Mohawk and Hudson, the South Carolina Railroad, or the B&O, had constructed wooden bridges across streams, rivers, ravines, and other deep depressions in the landscape. These bridges retained many of their characteristic problems, even though they were now being built by engineers. Without precise engineering guidelines, builders constructed bridges of wood without knowing how much weight or stress the bridge could withstand. By state law, Pennsylvania trains were required to proceed more slowly over bridges than over any other part of the route, to minimize stress. Even quite late in the nineteenth century, railroad bridges wobbled, bent, and broke under the weight of a train.[21]

Weather conditions also shortened the life of bridges. Snow or ice that remained on a bridge for a long period of time caused the bridge to sag or break. Melting snow and rain caused the wood to rot—and, of course, so did the waters in which bridge supports stood. Excessive heat dried the wood, causing it to crack and weaken or catch fire.[22]

Like any wooden structures, bridges were a fire hazard, and sparks from the engine set a great many blazes, both on the bridge itself and in surrounding woods. The spark arrester helped alleviate this problem but did not entirely resolve it. From the very first years of railroading, states also had to pass laws prescribing penalties for vandals who deliberately set fire to bridges.[23]

For bridging large rivers, such as the Connecticut or the Delaware, wood was not a successful material. Partly this was because of wood's weight-bearing limits, and partly because wooden railroad bridges were supported by numerous posts which obstructed river traffic. Mechanics, or "mechanical engineers" as they were coming to be known, turned to iron as a bridge-building material. In 1840 William Howe of Massachusetts patented a new bridge-building technique that relied on iron rather than wood. This new type of bridge was supported by iron trusses which extended from the upper part of piers set into the bottom of the river. In 1841 one of the first Howe truss bridges opened in Springfield, Massachusetts, enabling trains to cross the Connecticut River. The Howe Truss did not, however, guarantee bridge safety, nor did it remove the issue of railroad bridges as obstacles to navigation. Each major bridge built in the nineteenth century was celebrated as a major achievement, but many communities and railroad companies could not afford to build the best bridge possible, and accidents over wooden bridges and flawed metal bridges remained common for the remainder of the century.[24]

In other respects train travel remained subject to characteristics of the landscape. For example, steam trains never outgrew their need to stop for fuel and water; not until the twentieth century were they replaced by diesel power. Before the construction of water towers and coal shutes, the engineer stopped the train wherever wood and water appeared within reach. At first the crew did not even bother to inquire whose wood and water it was, but as schedules were regularized, wood piles and water were placed at intervals along the track. Steep hills remained steep hills, and even the largest engines had to strain to surmount parts of the Alleghenies. Rain, wind, sleet, and other bad weather took their toll of trains as of every other structure, natural or man-made.[25]

After the 1830s, railroad technology stalled. Passenger cars, tenders, and locomotives grew bigger and more powerful, lights more reliable, cowcatchers stronger, and track of heavier metal. But in many respects the train of 1860 had no major characteristics different from more primitive forms of twenty years earlier.[26] Patents multiplied, but railroad companies began to focus on increasing the distances trains could travel, rather than their safety or comfort. As a consequence, some technological hazards remained common and left their signature on railroad travel as much as did technological innovation.

The brakes of the 1860 train differed little from those in 1840. Brakemen, riding on top of the cars, applied the brakes on each car individually by turning a metal brake wheel atop the car. Locomotives remained without brakes, and air brakes, an invention of Westinghouse in the early 1860s, were not universally installed even after the turn of the century.[27] The wooden passenger car, with its wood-burning stove, remained a standard design because of the availability of wood, but also persisted as a fire hazard and a cause of death well into the twentieth century.

Surmounting longer distances in shorter periods of times became an obsession, overshadowing the need for a technology aimed at comfort and safety. First in the planning of longer and longer roads, then in the running of more, bigger, and faster trains, the railroads entered a race to build and left behind their cautious, experimental approach. In this way technological innovation lost its focus on specific characteristics of the landscape and was applied instead to all types of landscapes—across mountains, through swamps, and between towns and cities of every state, and every size.[28]

The recognition that a railroad could be put down anywhere and draw investment funds to any region coincided with the election of James K. Polk in 1844, a president remembered for his policy of Manifest Destiny—the idea that the United States had a destiny to extend its sovereignty all the way to the Pacific and into Canada. In pursuit of this ideal Polk waged a war with Mexico which brought the entire Southwest, from Texas to California, into the United States. He settled a treaty dispute with Britain which brought the Oregon Territory into the Union. It was in the first year of the Mexican War, 1846, that Asa Whitney of Michigan first petitioned the United States Congress for permission to build a railroad from Michigan to the Pacific Ocean. Congress dutifully debated the petition and finally sponsored army surveys of Western lands during the 1850s. But sectional strife, notably between slave and free states, made it impossible to settle on a Western railroad route that would suit the conflicting commercial interests of both North and South.[29]

The passing of general incorporation laws occurred in the wake of Polk's westward drive, making it possible to create a railroad corporation without the expensive and time-consuming task of obtaining a charter. The Western states pushed hardest for these laws because they put incorporation within the reach of the "common man," i.e., the Westerner with less capital or political influence than his Eastern counterparts. The general incorporation laws were to railroads of the 1850s what the starting gun was to the Oklahoma land rush. Railroad companies were founded by the hundreds in the Midwest as well as the East, without regard for need or the expense of construction.[30]

What had begun during the 1830s as a close scrutiny of circumscribed land and the application of technology required to surmount its obstacles and climate, shifted dramatically during the 1840s to include all the land of the continent.

The race for more track and bigger profits was on.

3

||||||||||

Leaving Home for the West

I liked the town because it was somewhat faded; in an undecided state of transition; uncertain whether to accept the insidious advances of the proposed branch from a remote main line of railway in a friendly spirit, or simultaneously close its shutters and emigrate west in a compact body, to grow up with the place. It was attractive to me, because it was a sulky coaching chrysalis, determined not to develop into the railway butterfly without a severe struggle.

—Stephe Smith, "Fogeyville and the Branch,"
in *Romance and Humor of the Rail,* 1873[1]

THE ADDITION OF railroads to the drive for internal improvements transformed the national effort to settle the West and bring it into closer communication with the established regions of the country. While keelboats and canals took small groups of settlers and entrepreneurs along the water routes that connected the nation's sections, and steamboats brought larger groups to the same areas, the trains carried wholesale crowds of settlers across New York, Pennsylvania, and Virginia, opened land for settlement at a distance from rivers, lakes, or canals, and promised limitless access to the wilderness with its vast natural resources.

But the construction of railroads also created a social revolution among Eastern communities. More people of every social level traveled more often and journeyed increasingly greater distances from home. People who had concentrated on cultivation of the land and the local transaction of business began to investigate the world beyond these traditional horizons. As national commerce thrived through travel and the long-distance transit of goods, the local boundaries of daily life began to lose their meaning. As citizens in all parts of the country found opportunities to travel, observe, meet, and trade with one another, the legal and governmental boundaries that distinguished one town from another were routinely crossed and recrossed. With trade as the measure of wealth, it seemed that home might be anywhere that promised opportunity. But many older towns lost their economic strength and social identity in the face of this compulsion to travel; and many new towns failed to develop into stable communities in the incredible rush to go anywhere and do anything in the search for economic security.[2]

Before the 1830s even the well-to-do of cities such as Boston worked and lived within a small radius year round. Farmers stayed close to their land and merchants close to their commercial interests. Although merchants depended on the arrival of imported goods for their livelihood, and farmers depended on urban markets more than ever before, in general they did not undertake long trade journeys themselves but left them to the specialized skills of middlemen, sailors, and sea captains.[3]

Those most likely to travel were migrants: those who sought a permanent improvement in home or income. Even during the colonial period, farmers and land speculators moved across the Appalachians. They settled the Kentucky of Daniel Boone and Abraham Lincoln's family, the Tennessee of Davy Crockett, and the lands of the Northwest Territory. The poor, seeking greener pastures, began their migrations westward to escape the dominance of the Eastern merchant "aristocracy" who looked down upon the lives of farmers and craftsmen, and to find more and better farmland than could be had along the East Coast.[4]

For the most part, this early migration followed rivers and waterways. Those who walked over the mountains found in the river valleys a way to avoid the peaks and a guide to avoid getting lost. Others took to the keelboats and flat boats that plied Western waters. In 1806, after Robert Fulton successfully piloted his steamboat *Clermont* upstream on the Hudson River, boatmen on the Mississippi, Ohio, and other Western rivers saw the great benefit of having steamboats on Western waters as well. Their introduction hastened the course of Western settlement and brought elegance to the river towns of the West. With their comforts and amenities, they announced that travel would bring more than migrants to the West; it would also bring the standards of Eastern cities and put down new cities just as elegant as New York or Philadelphia. Steamboats would bring more people to the West more often than any other form of water transport, and they would run regularly, to the pulse of trade, not just migration and settlement. The size of the largest steamboats made it possible to carry hundreds of passengers at once, rather than the dozen or so which fit snugly aboard a canal boat or riverboat.[5]

This transformation made Western travel so much easier that it brought changes in the types of passengers on Western rivers. Steamboats still carried migrants, just as the keelboats had, though frequently these migrants were to be found encamped in the saloon or on the deck rather than observing the amenities suggested by their surroundings.[6] But men and women of a higher social station were also traveling. Passengers on the Mississippi and the Ohio were not just looking for a land to farm but for financial opportunities in the ports and river towns that had begun to spring up after the first migrants had established themselves.

River towns in the West, such as Cincinnati and St. Louis, and lake ports such as Cleveland and Chicago, provided markets where settlers could buy Eastern manufactured goods and sell farm produce, lumber, and other Western products. Regardless of the distances settlers had to travel in order to reach town, they kept in touch with these centers of commerce to exchange their surplus homemade goods for the vital manufactured tools, bricks, ironwork, and house-

hold items that would bring their style of living up to a level com-
mensurate with the wealthier Eastern society.[7]

Railroads took this revolution further. In the wilderness extending
back from Western rivers, the idea of improving transportation between farms and port towns proved as popular as it was in the East,
and by the early 1830s the states of Ohio, Michigan, Illinois, Kentucky, and Tennessee had added railroads to their lists of necessary
internal improvements. Ohio's Mad River and Lake Erie Railroad
connected Lake Erie, the terminus of the Erie Canal and of the new
parallel chain of short New York railroad lines, to Springfield, Ohio, a
town far south of Lake Erie near Cincinnati and the Ohio River.
Ohio's Little Miami Railroad then connected Springfield to Cincinnati itself, on the Ohio River.[8]

North of Ohio, in Michigan, railroad plans predated the state's ad-
mission to the Union. The territory chartered two lines: the
Detroit and St. Joseph in 1832, and the Erie and Kalamazoo in 1833.
The first was intended to connect Detroit, on Lake Erie, with St.
Joseph, on the shores of Lake Michigan. The other was to connect
Toledo, on Lake Erie at the point where Michigan and Ohio meet,
with the Kalamazoo River, which runs into Lake Michigan.[9]

The ambitions of Westerners, however, were frustrated by scanty
capital resources. They had nothing like the number of investors the
East could bring together to fund internal improvements. In Michigan only parts of their two rail lines were built before 1837 when
Michigan became a state. In that year the new state legislature re-
newed the commitment to railroad construction and began to build
the state-controlled Michigan Central Railroad. But 1837 was also
the year of a financial panic brought on when President Andrew Jackson, champion of the West and the common man, left office. Sources
of bank credit dried up, especially in rural areas with few banks, and
this slowed the building of Western institutions in general. Midwesterners, with a small, widely distributed population of farmers, also
lacked the local capital that Easterners could generate from a denser,
wealthier, and more established urban population. Michigan's railroads, like those in Pennsylvania, lost money under state ownership
and had to be sold into private hands, a process not completed until
1846. Illinois also began an internal improvements program in 1837

but laid little track before the 1850s, by which time Easterners were well on their way to buying up many local Midwestern lines. Thus the Midwest depended on canals and steamboats longer than did the Northeastern states.[10]

South of the Ohio River, entrepreneurs also wanted railroads to connect the interior rivers with ports on the Atlantic and Gulf coasts. But like the Midwest they moved more slowly than the East, for they could call on less capital, a smaller population, and fewer urban centers. Nevertheless, short lines in Kentucky and Tennessee were laid out with the aim of connecting Charleston and Savannah on the Atlantic coast with the Mississippi River. The Memphis and Charleston line put Tennessee in contact with the port of Charleston through connections with other railroads. And further south, a track was laid from Savannah and Macon in Georgia west to Montgomery, Alabama. Montgomery was itself a port on the Alabama River which emptied into the Gulf of Mexico at Mobile.[11]

Both Southern and Western states sought to tie their rural areas to markets and port towns before the Civil War. In addition, states both north and south of the Ohio looked forward to connecting their railroad lines with the Atlantic coast and the nascent network of Eastern railroad commerce. Michigan, for example, saw itself as a vital link on the route between New York and Chicago, the beneficiary of trade passing across its land.[12] Yet Michigan settlers also feared Eastern capitalists who might buy out their local railroads and strip them of any profits.

Southern railroaders especially feared the Northeastern capitalists who might compromise state control of the lines. Southerners therefore developed their railroads according to a distinctive plan. In the South each state sought to retain control of its own railroads by preventing any one road from operating across a state line. Thus the states' rights doctrine that produced sectional antagonism as early as the 1820s also motivated Southerners to keep their railroads out of the control of any corporation outside the state. This applied to neighboring Southern states as well. Railroad tracks might cross state lines, but corporate control of these lines had to separate within each of the states. The rule also applied to any connection between the Southern states and the railroads of the North. Southerners made no effort to connect their railroads with those north of the Ohio River, despite numerous plans put forth by Northern capitalists to connect Ohio to Mobile, and Philadelphia to Baltimore and Charleston.[13]

In the Northeast, rapidly growing rail lines tied towns to rivers and Western markets but also made it much easier for Easterners to leave home and seek opportunity elsewhere. A major social crisis took shape as Eastern farmers moved west, individually and in large groups, to farm Western lands or build towns and railroads on the frontier. Simultaneously the introduction of factories in the Northeast drew groups of laborers to factory towns. The newcomers were usually poor, and many lived without their families. They could not afford to buy land and settle into the communities vacated by those moving west. They lived in rental accommodations, and the factory was frequently their only tie to the community in which they lived. These two trends completely changed the character of Eastern towns.

Transplanted Easterners found hope in Western plans to build railroads and bridges, dig canals, and construct wagon roads. In the 1830s and 1840s the distinction between labor and capital was not clearly drawn, and many young men who took jobs as laborers hoped to join the ranks of the capitalists and investors who controlled emerging transportation companies. River towns were expanding rapidly and needed laborers of all kinds to build everything from factories and warehouses to government buildings, hospitals, schools, and churches.

LaFayette Stone grew up in North Oxford, Massachusetts, and worked on Nathan Hale's new Boston and Worcester Railroad before deciding to migrate west in 1840. He hoped to become a capitalist and intended to start by seeking employment on one of the Western railroads that was already laying track. He traveled to Cincinnati, where he found work laying track for the Little Miami Railroad. He lived in boardinghouses and spread his few belongings among several of them along the length of the rail line. When his sister, who remained at home in North Oxford, wrote to inquire about his living arrangements, he replied:

> . . . you ask me if I have a pleasant boarding house the fact is I have none my business is over the whole line of the Road consequently I

WANTED!
3,000 LABORERS
On the 12th Division of the
ILLINOIS CENTRAL RAILROAD

Wages, $1.25 per Day.

Fare, from New-York, only - - $4)5

By Railroad and Steamboat, to the work in the State of Illinois.

Constant employment for two years or more given. Good board can be obtained at two dollars per week.

This is a rare chance for persons to go West, being sure of permanent employment in a healthy climate, where land can be bought cheap, and for fertility is not surpassed in any part of the Union.

Men with families preferred.

For further information in regard to it call at the Central Railroad Office,

173 BROADWAY,
CORNER OF COURTLANDT ST.

NEW-YORK.

R. B. MASON, Chief Engineer.

Before the Civil War the population of Illinois was so sparse that the Illinois Central Railroad could not find sufficient workers to lay track. The company distributed flyers in New York City and other urban areas in order to attract workers who might also buy land along the tracks and settle.

stop at all places a Cap in Cin.—a Trunk—Carpet Bag and washing at
Montauk [?] cottage—a Trunk—Books & writing at Morrow—my
sword at Xenia and a hat at Springfield . . . [14]

Stone's sister wrote monthly and expressed constant concern that
he was among strangers. But Stone did not return until after the Civil
War, and then stayed only for a visit. He remained a wanderer all his
life, holding many jobs, mustering for the Mexican War, and later
working in Texas. He pinned his hopes on various speculations to
make him a man of leisure, but he remained single, relatively poor,
and rootless. This was the nature of frontier life for many people who
migrated seeking their fortunes and then moved again and again
when wealth failed to materialize.[15]

Cincinnati in 1844 was a city of travelers, and businesses that
catered to travelers, as LaFayette wrote in a letter to his sister.

> If you could remove to Cincinnati for one week and see the amount of
> emigration you would be astonished there are from two hundred to a
> thousand leave here daily for the far west and I saw an account in a St.
> Louis paper the other day stating that a company of four hundred men
> about leaving for Oregon. . . . the Little Miammi [sic] Rail Road the
> Miammi Canal & the Whitewater Canal are the only works of internal
> improvement which have their terminus in this city . . . at the steam-
> boat landing you will find six to twenty steamers and twice that num-
> ber of flat boats which are continually arriving & departing. . . . since
> I have been here I have visited the Gas works, Water works, Distil-
> eries—Brewery—Flour Mills Linseed Oil mills Land oil mills &
> Foundries . . . [16]

The numbers of people migrating westward diminished the able-
bodied population of New England even before President Polk
waged war against the Mexicans in 1846. But after that time enormous wagon trains headed northwest to Oregon and southwest into
Santa Fe and southern California. Then, in 1848, gold was discovered
near San Francisco, further accelerating the migration west and the
construction of railroads.

In the 1850s railroads that had begun laying track in the Mississippi
River Valley began to advertise for laborers in Eastern newspapers

and in Europe. Not enough able-bodied men lived in the Midwest to enable the track to be laid within a reasonable period of time. The Illinois Central Railroad, which started building southward from Chicago in 1851, saw a need for more workers if the road was ever to be built, and more settlers if the road was to survive economically. The company distributed flyers in New York for men to work in Illinois at $1.25 a day. This ad brought thousands of men into Illinois, including many immigrant Irish and Germans who laid track across the state. The railroad also began advertising the land bordering its tracks for sale at bargain rates designed to attract immigrants.[17]

Illinois Central agents traversed the Northeast and the South in an effort to interest farmers in settling the lands adjacent to the IC lines. The company printed and distributed emigrant guides for those who wished to journey west to gain larger acreage and more fertile lands than they owned in the East. The towns of Northampton, Massachusetts; Gilmanton, New Hampshire; and Conway, Massachusetts, each sent a large contingent of residents westward to settle in Illinois. Once again, New England began losing so much population to the West that farm prices in that region dropped by an estimated 40 percent.[18]

Not only did the railroads entice large groups from single New England communities, but new emigrant associations recruited people in large numbers to move westward together. The Vermont Emigrant Association and the Working Man's Settlement Association recruited in New England; the American Emigration Association from Louisville, Kentucky, went west to investigate living conditions before recommending settlement in Illinois. Encouraged by its success, the Illinois Central began sending agents to Europe to recruit settlers. From 1855–1861 the railroad sold almost 1.5 million acres of railroad lands and was the greatest factor in swelling the state's population by 101 percent during the 1860s, to 860,481.[19]

LaFayette Stone's sister, Martha Elvira Stone, still living in North Oxford, Massachusetts, in 1854, wrote to her brother describing how one of the emigrant groups in her area made plans to leave for the territory of Nebraska, in reaction to the passage of the Kansas-Nebraska Act that year. The act specified that the slavery issue would be determined in the Kansas and Nebraska territories by popular vote. So parties from both Northern and Southern states headed west to populate these areas and contribute their votes to the decision. Elvira wrote that their brother Jeremiah wanted to

> go beyond Ohio he even itches to the new Territory of Nebraska; there are companies forming in many of the free States to settle in there in order to neutralize the odious effects of its admission into the family of States with its slave facilities; in Worcester there is a company of one hundred men about forming; they meet in the City Hall in Worcester the 18th. instant to make the preliminary steps.[20]

Among the many groups that promoted mass migrations westward was the Children's Aid Society, newly founded in 1853 and head-quartered in New York City. The Society began to assemble young children without homes, and children whose parents could not support them, for relocation in Michigan, Illinois, Indiana, Ohio, and Missouri. The process was called placing out, and resembled the placing out of colonial times by which children were brought up in homes other than their own. In the year of its founding, Children's Aid "placed" children first in New England to work in the mills, and in rural environments throughout the Northeast. In 1854 the Society sent its first group of orphans west to Michigan. Wrote Marilyn Holt, author of *The Orphan Trains*, "The first site for western placement has no explanation other than the presence of transportation, the Michigan Central Railroad," and the scarcity of labor in the West.[21]

While the railroads did not create the high degree of mobility in pre–Civil War America, they did carry hundreds of thousands of people—more than any other type of transport—from place to place in search of economic opportunity. Farmers and land speculators were first over the Appalachians, followed by speculators who hoped to buy and sell other products in the West. The growth of new towns and their institutions followed, helped along by laborers who also moved west for economic gain. Then internal improvements programs, especially in railroads, opened a floodgate of migration for men who could not make a living in the East. Finally, urban Easterners, beset by serious economic dislocations in the cities, sent children to this supposedly healthier Western environment.

Many of these migrants, however, like LaFayette Stone, never found a stable society or economy in which to settle. They remained on the move, looking for the next speculation, the next break, that would deliver them from poverty. Separated from families and communities, they found their new frontier neighbors to be as transient as themselves. The economy of the West was based on travel and the need to advance the frontier almost as much as it depended on farming.

As mobility increased, the older New England towns lost their self-sufficiency and their distinct social identities. The Western Railroad and the Boston and Worcester Railroad both helped people come and go from North Oxford with greater ease and frequency, and in greater numbers, than ever before. Mills and other factories transformed the appearance of North Oxford and many other New England towns, and factory owners hired outside laborers to do the work. Railroads, which affected the economic and social order in virtually every American community, took away local people who had to move in order to support themselves. Strangers began to replace the web of family relationships that distinguished each community. Undercut were the distinctively local patterns of town and farm life which emphasized loyalty to family, land, and town institutions. In their place came a new emphasis on mobility, capital, investment, and industry.

The Hometowns
Left Behind

. . . Two thirds of a generation has passed away since you left, and almost
all things are strange to you here, as in almost every other place.
 —Martha Elvira Stone to Joseph
LaFayette Stone, October 25, 1863[1]

THE UPROOTING AND REDISTRIBUTING of the population had a considerable impact on the traditions of established Eastern towns. Historically few strangers entered the towns' legal boundaries, and few
local residents left. Local governments and institutions developed
over two hundred years proved capable of imposing authority on
long-term local residents and providing the protection they needed.
The opportunity for increased mobility that railroads brought right to
the heart of towns gradually shifted the focus of individual lives from
local concerns to regional or national interests. Local institutions
began to lose their sway over the lives of citizens and strangers who
daily passed in and out of town jurisdiction.

Commercial interests saw the advantage of this influx of strangers and supported the construction of railroads. More people in town meant more customers to buy goods and patronize local inns, taverns, and stables. But in the long run, commercial relationships began to supersede older community ties and lines of authority, to the regret of those who still lived by an older set of rules.

Before the construction of railroads in New England, travel beyond the boundaries of a hometown or region was uncommon. Edward Everett Hale, born in Boston in 1822, spent most of his youth in the familiar streets of that city. While ships came and went regularly from the wharves, the arrival of strangers by land rarely passed unnoticed. Those few who did come through had the taverns at their disposal and the tavern stables for their horses and wagons.[2]

Hale termed the traveling of 1833 "retail," as compared with the "wholesale" arrivals and departures of train passengers in 1893. Even his father, a Boston newspaper editor, ardent advocate of internal improvements, and first president of the Boston and Worcester Railroad, rarely went even as far as New York. Hale recalled:

> In 1832 my father went to Schenectady to see the Albany and Schenectady Railroad, and, I believe, to order some cars for the Boston and Worcester road. He also went to New York City on the business of that road. I think he had been to that city but once since 1805, when he went there on his way from Northampton to Troy.

Edward Everett Hale's childhood travels included numerous family excursions to the wooded areas on the edges of Boston, a well-remembered family outing on the Middlesex Canal, and finally the exciting rides on his father's Boston and Worcester Railroad.[3]

One of the most significant changes in Boston social life between 1833 and 1893 was, in Hale's view, the fact that the vast majority of inhabitants in the earlier period did not maintain summer homes outside of Boston. They lived in Boston year round. Only later did the seashore north and south of town develop summer colonies of second homes for the well-to-do of Boston.[4]

Bostonians who could travel for pleasure rode in carriages drawn by horses. Only the wealthier could afford to own carriages or the opportunities they created for leaving town. This genteel, individual form of transport had an etiquette and history of its own, requiring the walking Hale children to bow whenever a carriage passed them by on the road. Of this period, Hale remarked that "although people no longer offered prayers for their friends when they were going to New York, still a journey to New York was a comparatively rare business."[5]

Ringed by sea and woods, Bostonians lived in relative isolation from inland towns despite the city's large population. They read newspapers, kept in touch with the world by sea, and caught up with the railroad boom a few years after its beginnings. Inland, midway between Worcester and the Connecticut border, lay the small town of North Oxford, Massachusetts. Here, even more than in Boston, one family could easily know the movements of all other inhabitants, and saw the larger world only through the pages of newspapers, magazines, and books. Births, marriages, and deaths, illnesses, bankruptcy, arrivals, and departures all took place within a group bound by family ties and by many generations of lifelong acquaintance.[6]

Martha Elvira Stone, who lived in North Oxford in her father's house all her life, was one such resident. She stayed in touch with her neighbors daily, and with the world beyond North Oxford chiefly by mail and by the exchange of books and newspapers with correspondents. She had received sufficient education to read and write well, and taught school for a number of years. When her brother LaFayette left town to seek his fortune working on the railroad in Worcester, and then on the Ohio frontier, she kept in touch with him by monthly letters written over twenty-five years until the end of the Civil War. "Come home" was her repeated message to him. She saw the dangers of traveling too far, without the supports of home.[7] Her life remained stable, and she followed the traditions of homemaker that her mother and grandmother had practiced. After her early days as a teacher, she took on more and more family responsibility in nursing her father, nephews, neighbors, and relatives through illness, in many cases until their deaths.

Despite the tendencies of residents in both places to organize their lives around local traditions and family ties as old as the town itself, one difference remained. Many North Oxford residents still earned their living from the soil, while in Boston, trade had predominated for more than a century. All members of the North Oxford family had to help with the family farm and with the processing of food. Small though it was, the acreage around Elvira's family house produced their fruit supply, their dairy products, chickens and eggs, and garden vegetables. Elvira's descriptions of nature at her doorstep, and her concern with the success or failure of crops, derive from this dependence on the soil.[8] North Oxford was a poor town.

Bostonians had long since abandoned farming as their primary vocation. Food came to Boston in horse-drawn wagons from farms surrounding the town and from ships that docked in port. While Edward Hale kept a small garden in the family's tiny yard, he saw little of farming in his youth.[9] When the railroad came to Boston, it only extended the area from which food could be brought to tables in town. Boston was wealthy compared with North Oxford. And the impetus for a railroad, when it came, was from Boston entrepreneurs who saw in it a way to expand the trade that already governed their economy. North Oxford's gain came from its location near a station stop on that first train line.

When the railroad came to Boston it owed its arrival largely to the political and financial backing of Nathan Hale, Edward's father. While merchants still looked to the sea, supporters of internal improvements saw the potential of the railroad in connecting outlying towns and markets with the city. Nathan Hale tried in town meeting to suggest the magnitude of the change that railroading would bring to Boston. In 1831 he declared in public meeting "that if people could come from Springfield to Boston in five hours an average of nine people would come every day." At the time the prospect of nine strangers coming to town daily seemed an impossibly high number.[10]

But Hale persevered, and in 1833 the Boston and Worcester Railroad began carrying passengers daily between the two cities. Boston roused itself to the new interest, and every afternoon eight cars went out to Newton and back, drawing many who wanted nothing more than the experience of a ride on the new railroad.[11]

Young Hale saw no immediate social revolution with the opening of the Boston and Worcester line. At first the local population found ways of adapting their habits to this new convenience. Horse-drawn carriages and wagons were not left in the stable but carried along, tied into position on a flatbed train car. Hale also pointed out that even as late as 1845, the number of passengers who *needed* to go from Boston to Worcester remained very low. Established trade customs saw only minor modification in the 1830s. As passing trains slowed from a top speed of fifteen or twenty miles an hour to only about ten miles an hour on steep hills, "Farmers, berry-pickers, and girls with country produce would station themselves . . . and pass their wares to the conductor, who would sell the articles in the city." Hale found the improvements of train service informal and personal in nature. When he needed to send a parcel to New York, he simply handed it to a conductor he knew on the Boston and Worcester. The conductor, named Harnden, made certain the package reached its destination. Only a few years passed before Harnden started American Express, the first package-delivery company in the country. He was soon followed in this business by Adams Express Company and others.[12]

After the railroad came to nearby Worcester, Elvira Stone's travel also widened gradually. But in keeping with Hale's perceptions about Boston, the earliest changes she experienced were informal and personal. Only the absence of her brother LaFayette and other relatives who had left for the West signaled the beginnings of major social change. During the early 1840s most of Elvira's daily visiting remained within the small circumference of North Oxford and neighboring towns. She walked or rode on horseback. Seldom did she use a carriage, let alone take a train. She traveled as far as Webster, Massachusetts, where she attended school. From there in 1845 she wrote to LaFayette, "I have been home once, went in the cars."[13] This was the first time she mentioned riding the train herself.

After Elvira's brother Jeremiah married and moved to the nearby town of Clinton, her travels extended there. On occasion, when her domestic obligations and finances allowed, she began to take "the cars" further afield, as a tourist. Her travels took her east to Boston in the spring of 1845, on the Boston and Worcester. She visited the Atheneum, the Boylston Market, the Bunker Hill monument, and the state prison, where one of her relations was an inmate.[14]

After this trip Elvira began to dream of traveling even farther away from home. She began to write to her brother about going west to be with him, but she feared giving up the family property because she might not succeed financially in the West. She also worried about her aging father who would have no one to care for him if she left home. After much consideration, she decided against a move to Ohio.[15]

During the 1850s Elvira found more opportunities to see the world outside North Oxford without giving up her home. In the summer of 1851 she took advantage of a railroad excursion group fare to visit Niagara Falls, near Buffalo. The half-price ticket cost her $16.50 round trip. The views of Massachusetts mountains moved her to write that LaFayette would have shared her delight "with the *beautiful, grand* scenery. . . ." The towns of Springfield and Pittsfield she found "truly New England, with the word *Puritan almost written* upon every corner. . . ."[16]

At Albany she stayed in the Standwick Hall hotel, "within speaking distance of the Western R.R. Depot." After browsing through a museum of stuffed birds and seeing a play, the group boarded a steamer on the Mohawk River and set out for Oswego, New York, on Lake Ontario. They continued westward to Lewiston, where they "took the cars (drawn by horse power for five miles). . . ." This roundabout route took three and a half days. Once again, in 1855, Elvira rode west in the cars for a visit to relatives in Brattleboro, Vermont, and for views of the Adirondacks.[17]

The widening range of travel away from New England towns was not the only sign of change illustrated in North Oxford. Elvira Stone reported on her cousin Stephen Barton's efforts to build and run factories in the town. This involved the recruiting of laborers from outside the town, and resulted in the opening of numerous boardinghouses for these unattached workers. Jeremiah Stone, the brother who did not go west, opened and ran a boardinghouse in Clinton for laborers. When one of Stephen's factories burned down, the workers drifted off and some of the boardinghouses lost their business. The presence of the railroad in town made this kind of wholesale transition possible.[18]

Stephen Barton relocated to North Carolina where he started a new set of factories and founded the town of Bartonsville. But these factories also failed because of the poor climate and consequent illness among the workers. Among Stephen's workers were some of his own relatives, who trickled back to Massachusetts when they lost their jobs.[19]

Elvira herself finally found a compromise between the old local way of life and the new shift to regional and national interests. In 1857 she became the postmistress of North Oxford, thanks to the efforts of her cousin in Washington, D.C., Clara Barton.[20] She spent hours every week hearing the news from people picking up and dropping mail; she pored through the newspapers and magazines that came through the mail, writing letters and occasionally ordering a book that she would share with family and friends. But she never joined the procession westward or to the city.

Many New England towns had more success than North Oxford in adapting water and steam power to the production of goods for regional, national, or even international markets. But like Boston, they had taken an interest in trade before the coming of the railroad, and they adapted to train transport as a way of extending the reach of existing trade routes. Also like Boston, they began to see some of the effects, first personal and then corporate, of connecting their towns to outlying districts and to Boston by rail. Towns such as Lowell, Lawrence, and Newburyport, on the Merrimack River, imported workers for their textile factories and built housing for them even before the coming of railroad service. Amoskeag Mills, in Manchester, New Hampshire, sent its woolens and cottons to Boston via the Middlesex Canal or by ox cart before the coming of the railroad. Textile companies transformed the towns in which they stood, opened schools and banks, and at the same time increased the towns' dependence on other towns and foreign ports.[21]

But the coming of the railroad fundamentally undercut local control in a way that previous modes of transport had not. Even the railroad promoters and investors did not foresee this change. Railroad investors in Northampton and Springfield, Massachusetts, were typical of many local railroad supporters who lost control over their investment.

Businessmen in Northampton and Springfield sought to construct a railroad between the two towns to revive the sagging fortunes of the area economy and thus keep young men from going west to seek their fortune. In 1845 two existing lines between the two cities were consolidated to form the Connecticut River Railroad. "This extension of the road," predicted the railroad's annual report that year,

> will command yet more fully the business of the main and tributary vallies. . . . Capabilities for supporting population, and rewarding agriculture and mechanical industry are pre-eminent, and will be rapidly developed under the fostering hand of internal improvement. Its transportation business has enriched all who have hitherto been engaged in it, and we doubt not will abundantly reward us.[22]

Paralleling the Connecticut River, this new line superseded much of the river traffic. But in the long run the coming of the railroad involved a loss of local control. Offices and operations were centered in Northampton until Springfield men gained control and moved offices to that town. This was the first step in a series of financial decisions that weakened the hold of either community on the railroads.[23]

The second step toward loss of local control stemmed from the unexpected profitability of the road itself, which attracted investment from businessmen who did not live in the area. Finally, in 1892 the Connecticut River Road was absorbed into another railroad corporation altogether, the Boston and Maine, with headquarters in Boston.

At the same time outsiders were seeking to invest in the Connecticut River Railroad, local railroad leaders were creating financial portfolios that included businesses at a distance from either Northampton or Springfield. The widening gyre of the transport network led Chester Chapin, first president of the Connecticut River Railroad, to invest in the Boston and Albany Railroad, the New York, New Haven and Hartford, the New York and New Haven Steamboat Company, and the Western Union Telegraph Company, in addition to his home railroad company.[24] This pattern of investment overrode both local interests and geographical boundaries. The capitalist no longer represented any one local interest. In the long run this crazy-quilt pattern of investment subordinated local interests to the interests of investors who might live anywhere but who frequently could be traced to the financial centers of Boston or New York. Long before the Civil War, the total capital value invested in these companies far

surpassed the total capital value of either Northampton or Springfield.

This economic imbalance affected Massachusetts and towns outside New England as well. Of Massachusetts, the *Merchants' Magazine* for 1848 reported that "The amount of capital invested in
railroads now exceeds the banking capital of the state." Baltimore also
found that the value of its railroad exceeded the fiscal resources of
the city. The capitalization of railroads gradually weakened rather
than strengthened the finances of the towns and cities they had been
built to serve. While some towns grew and prospered in the wake of
railroad connections, railroads themselves generally had more capital
and income than any one town.[25]

As money left, so did opportunities for work. New England suffered the consequent loss of many young men. While the process of
industrialization temporarily revived New England's economy, in the
long run the towns lost much of their economic position and their independence after they constructed railroads intended to tie them to
the growing national economy.

In retrospect it appeared to local historians that town leadership had given the railroad its financial strength, honesty, and good
service. Each member of the board had had a stake in other community institutions. These communities, rather than the railroad,
were intended to be the beneficiaries of railroad service.[26] While
the population and cumulative wealth of Springfield and Northampton rose, most of the benefit accrued to a small group of private investors.

From the hindsight of 1923, a letter writer to the *Springfield
Republican* expressed his regret at the loss of local control over the
Connecticut River Railroad. Benjamin Cook stated that the local
leadership were

> men whom the stockholders knew and had every confidence in, [and]
> the road was what it should be today. . . . I have been on crowded
> trains, with people standing, to Springfield, three times within a
> month, paying 64 cents from Northampton to Springfield, when they
> ran for years the same distance for 20 cents.[27]

In light of the experience of Northampton and Springfield, it becomes possible to understand why most New England towns did not experience the renaissance that took place in the towns where investors' money tended to collect: Boston and New York. Towns like North Oxford were ill-equipped to profit from railroad traffic. They had few stores and, despite the efforts of Stephen Barton, not much surplus of any product to sell in distant markets. The solution of LaFayette Stone, to go west, seemed the best option at the time. His sister Elvira, who stayed home, recorded the meager attempts of her hometown to participate in the industrial and trade revolutions. In the end, her closest relatives and friends either joined the exodus west or died of old age.

5

The Legal Conflict Between Railroad and Government

In a large covered terminus, a train of cars was drawn up, ready to start with a locomotive at their head across an open street; and the whole set off without any other protection to foot-passengers than that which might be imparted by the warning sounds of a bell attached to the top of the engine. And so onward, through town and country, here intersecting a village, and there crossing a highway, did the train pursue its way, with no other trace of protection for the public, than the very useful bit of advice—"Look out for the locomotive when the bell rings!"—painted in large characters on sign-boards at every point of danger.
        —William Chambers, *Things as They Are in America,* 1857[1]

THE COMING OF THE RAILROAD created other conflicts of interest reflected in the evolution of the law. These conflicts led first to the abandonment of the charter system as the chief means of regulating railroads, and then found expression in local and state court cases, ordinances, and statute law. Before the Civil War neither landowners, town governments, nor individuals received their traditional legal protections when they confronted the new realities defined by railroads running through their fields, roads, and front yards, and then across borders that limited the jurisdiction of local law. And in the long run the law favored the railroads and the commercial interests they represented over the more traditional property and personal protections customarily associated with the hierarchy of government.

The abandonment of the charter system for railroads grew directly out of a desire among legislators and entrepreneurs to develop commercial interests more quickly, as they were central to establishing civilization on the frontier and to promoting trade between the frontier and the East Coast. Charters were written and issued just one at a time, and it took too long for the state legislatures to debate and write each one individually. But the abandonment of charters also led to an overall reduction in the level of business regulation, because the charters had been the traditional vehicle of regulation.[2]

When a legislature debated the terms of a charter, it had the power to specify the geographic area where the railroad could lay track; the amount it must pay in compensation to landholders losing their land to the railroad; where it could erect buildings; how much land on each side of the track it could claim; the speed at which the trains could travel; the types of services the railroad could provide; the rates it could charge; and whether it had exclusive or monopoly right to provide transportation in the area it served. The legislature also appointed railroad commissioners for each railroad to ensure compliance with the law. Historically many businesses, including roads and canals, had by the terms of their state charters been granted state monopolies on the services they provided. But in 1837 the Charles River Bridge case led to a decision by the U.S. Supreme Court that state charters could not grant monopolies. This was the opening salvo in a transformation of traditional law to meet the needs of an emerging industrial nation. Traditional monopoly protections were abandoned in favor of competition: any number of businesses might vie for patrons, whether the business was a bridge, a toll road, a canal, or a railroad.[3]

In the state of New York, railroad interests were the moving force behind the effort to pass general articles of incorporation, under which anyone, not just those with the time and means to lobby for a charter, could incorporate a business. The New York legislature agreed to the new plan but at the same time passed a statute providing for uniform regulation of all railroads in the state. Other Eastern states followed a similar course, making speed and fare requirements uniform within each state. States also appointed railroad commissioners whose duties were to make certain that all railroads in the state operated safely and complied with the law. In the Midwest the fewer numbers of railroads reduced the need for state intervention on a uniform basis and left the roads freer of government regulation until after the Civil War.[4]

The transformation of laws that accompanied the rise of industry and the railroads has been interpreted differently by legal historians. Some, including Lewis Haney, have concluded that the state and federal governments reduced the regulation of businesses in pursuit of a laissez-faire approach, allowing businesses such as railroads to operate independent of the law. More recently, J. Willard Hurst has argued that laws were adjusted to *promote* business, or, as he put it, to release the energy of individuals in their commercial endeavors from undue legal constraints. Thus the law supported the growth of business and the creation of wealth as a priority over other more traditional values such as merely protecting the value of existing property. Morton Horwitz has seen the laws changing to suit an entirely new definition of wealth, one based on the exchange value of goods and services rather than on the ownership of land or objects with a practical use. Each of these interpretations shares the observation that the law changed to favor the interests of commerce and commercial exchange, and played down the traditional property claims that might make industries and railroads liable under laws inherited from a more strictly mercantile or state-controlled economy.[5]

This revolution in the law scarcely occurred with the full consent of the participating parties. In fact it precipitated an intense legal conflict between the favored railroads and others with conflicting interests. Both before and after the states dispensed with the charter system, railroads found themselves regularly knocking at the doors of state courts as landowners, town officials, and injured individuals fought bitterly to sustain traditional protections of person and property. Public confrontation with the railroads centered on three legal issues: eminent domain, or the right of the state to take private property for public use; damages, or the duty of railroad companies or others to pay for property they had hurt; and a new legal doctrine of personal injury, emphasized by the high incidence of physical injuries and deaths caused by the machinery of industrial society, including railroads. The latter two became known as torts.

In the history of railroads, eminent domain emerged as the first problem, since it related to the rights of railroads to take land from its owners for the purpose of laying track. The legal doctrine of eminent domain was not new in the 1830s but dated to the English law inherited by early American settlers. The purpose of the doctrine was to reserve to government the right to take land from private owners for the public good, ordinarily in exchange for monetary compensation to the owner. With the onset in the United States of rapid industrial development, which state legislatures supported as essential for everyone's prosperity, the doctrine came to include the rights of state-chartered business corporations to use land for purposes deemed beneficial to the public, even though technically these businesses were in private hands. Thus the state governments came to support the land claims of some private interests, especially railroads, over others, with the justification that railroads benefited the national interest.[6]

In the case of the railroads, the state courts' use of eminent domain—also known as public use doctrine—had a major impact on the traditional protections of private property, chiefly because railroads took so much more land than was required by other industrial improvements, and because even after taking it the railroads represented a continual danger to the communities through which they passed. For these reasons the objections to the taking of lands by railroads were correspondingly great and were usually raised by the owner of the property taken.

State court records reflect a basic concern: was it legal for the state and railroads to take land belonging to a private citizen? In 1838 the

South Carolina supreme court declared in *Louisville, Cincinnati and Charleston Railroad Company vs. Reese* that eminent domain was in fact a legal and acceptable doctrine in the state of South Carolina. Rarely, if ever, did the railroads actually lose the right to take land. Once eminent domain had been established as a legal doctrine in each state, the role of the courts consisted in adjusting claims rather than modifying or reversing the doctrine. As early as the 1830s property owners frequently objected to the amount of compensation as inadequate, and it became the role of the railroad commissioners to settle these disputes. If they could not do so, the case went to court. The legal historian Harry Scheiber has noted that the courts clearly and repeatedly used the doctrine to favor the private interests of the railroads over the private interests of other individuals or groups. The justification was that commerce made possible by the railroads would benefit the public good more than ownership of the land by a small farmer or homeowner.[7]

At least as common as disagreements over compensation or the legality of eminent domain were suits for property damages caused by trains. This was an aspect of a new field known as tort law. Killing livestock and setting fire to trees, grass, and buildings, the locomotive caused damages far beyond those of simply appropriating the land for railroad use. Thus action for damages against the railroads became increasingly common once the trains started running. Such a case came to the Connecticut supreme court in 1842, when a party named Burroughs sued the Housatonic Railroad after sparks from a passing locomotive set fire to a building on his land. The court concluded that the railroad did not have to pay the owner of the building for damages from the fire. The court made this determination based on the legal principle of negligence. Historically, injured parties had received compensation for damages under the doctrine of strict liability. But because of the high incidence of harm caused by the railroads, state courts began to look more closely at the circumstances under which the damages occurred. If the railroad had exercised due care by observing all normal precautions, the courts reasoned, it could no longer be held liable for an accident of this kind. Only if the railroad was negligent in its operations could it be held liable for the cost of damages.[8]

While the doctrine of negligence provided a guideline for legal actions, it also suggested that the property of citizens would regularly be jeopardized by railroads, and that the law was limited in the protection it could offer. In fact, property near railroads was considered so vulnerable that one insurance company in Massachusetts refused to sell coverage for any building within one hundred feet of tracks.[9]

Landowners in other areas of the country faced the same dilemma in trying to win compensation for damages. A few years before the Burroughs decision, a South Carolina plantation owner named Felder sued the Louisville, Cincinnati and Charleston Railroad when one of its trains ran over his slave who was asleep on the tracks that ran across Felder's plantation. Again, as in the Connecticut case, the court ruled that the slave was not where he belonged, and that the railroad had exercised due care. Therefore the railroad owed no damages to Felder. Felder, Burroughs, and others now lived in a society with an elevated level of risk, for which there was no legal remedy.[10]

This is not to say that railroads were always excused. In cases where the railroads were found negligent, they certainly did pay. Such a case came to the Connecticut supreme court in the late 1840s. A man named Beers, owner of a herd of oxen, was shepherding them along a road that crossed a railroad track when the train arrived unexpectedly and killed a number of the animals. Because the train's schedule varied so greatly from day to day that the farmer could not have predicted its arrival, and because the train "sped" through at twenty miles per hour, allowing Beers no chance to save his stock, the court ruled that the railroad company had not exercised due care and must pay the farmer for his losses.[11]

The issue of locomotives running down livestock on the tracks plagued relations between railroads and farmers throughout the country. In addition to the doctrine of negligence, a separate legal issue arose regarding the construction of fences between railroad tracks and adjacent fields where livestock grazed. Neither the farmers nor railroads wished to absorb the substantial expense of constructing fences. Historically fencing had been a source of controversy between farmers since the seventeenth century, when property boundaries were unclear and livestock strayed through gates, along roads, and through breaks in fences. In the 1830s, state courts and legislatures were extremely reluctant to require railroad companies to fence their track, because the high cost would slow the development of commerce. But neither could they require farmers to foot the bill if they did not wish to do so. And if the track ran through the center of a meadow, the farmer had no wish to erect a barrier across the middle of his property.[12]

In Ohio the high court found the railroad liable for damages to livestock on open lands, since legally the farmer had the right to graze his herd without erecting fences. In Pennsylvania, however, the Internal Improvements Commission levied a $25 fine against any person who "shall willfully and wantonly, without the consent of the person having charge of any such railroad, lead, drive, or cause to be led or driven, any horse, mule, ox, sheep, swine or other cattle on such railroad. . . ." But in time the bias of the law shifted, and the railroad was much less likely to be found liable for hurting animals that wandered onto the track.[13]

In Pennsylvania, where the state owned the railroads for a number of years, it was the state that had to pay both compensation for lands taken and for damages stemming from rail operations. The Pennsylvania state legislature had repeatedly to appropriate tens of thousands of dollars to allow the Internal Improvements Commission to pay these damages to private property holders along railroad routes. Although the historian Harry Scheiber has found that state courts tried to minimize grants of damages from property injury caused by railroads, still the cost was substantial. It could well have been one of the expenses that in 1836 drove Pennsylvania to sell its railroads to private owners.[14]

In many of the legal cases that confronted railroad companies, the stakes were even higher than land compensation or damage to property. Damage to livelihoods caused owners of businesses other than farming to take their cases to court. In Baltimore, for example, the Maryland supreme court heard a case in which the Delaware and Maryland Railroad received state permission to build track on the shoreline and over water already in use by a fishery. The fisherman came to court, claiming that the railroad had ruined his business. The railroad won the case. In a similar case decided by the Massachusetts supreme court in 1842, the Eastern Railroad had to pay damages for

This 1839 poster warned of the dangers of the Camden and Amboy Railroad running its tracks through the main streets of Philadelphia, also implying that the new railroad connection with New York City would allow New York to dominate Philadelphia by controlling its railroads. (UNION PACIFIC MUSEUM COLLECTION)

the use of flats near a wharf used for trade. In Boston the state supreme court prevented Hale's Boston and Worcester Railroad from building track across a dam owned by the Boston Water Power Company. Those who used water or rivers to earn their living fought vigorously to curb the expansion of the railroads.[15]

The confrontations between landowners and railroad owners never resolved itself but continued to be settled case by case in the state courts. As the number of railroad companies and the population rose, the conflict came to represent a chronic issue in the legal system and a chronic weakness in the protections extended to landowners.

Town officials also faced a series of legal crises brought about by the growth of the railroads. Many companies built their tracks across or right down the middle of established town thoroughfares. This was deliberate, so that the railroads, in the tradition of stagecoaches, could stop at hotels and taverns in town to pick up or drop off passengers. Cities including New York, and towns both North and South, recognized the danger, dirt, and noise that accompanied the locomotive as a hazard to life and limb. They sought to modify the railroads' arrangements by passing ordinances requiring that steam locomotives be detached from trains before they entered town, and that the train be pulled into town by horses or other beasts of burden.[16]

The danger nonetheless plagued towns or neighborhoods where such laws were not in effect. An outcry of local citizens resulted wherever railroads caused injury or damage within town boundaries. State court records reveal extensive litigation between towns and the railroad companies operating within them. As early as 1832, for example, the inhabitants of Lowell, Massachusetts, took the Boston and Lowell Railroad to court because the railroad removed safety barriers on a road in order to build tracks across it. The court ruled that the railroad must pay for the damages that resulted from the removal of the barriers.[17]

As a general rule, however, with the exception of Southern towns and a handful of rural areas in the North, very few towns blocked the expansion of railroads within their boundaries. And when they did, most required the railroad to stop at the edge of town not for safety reasons alone but to force passengers to patronize town institutions before they proceeded on the next leg of their journey. Litchfield,

Connecticut, discouraged the construction of railroads, and as a consequence it declined as an educational and cultural center of New England. More typically, New England towns such as Lowell, Springfield, Hartford, Danbury, and New Haven courted industry, and either started railroads of their own or encouraged railroads to pass through town.[18]

Towns eager to have rail connections did not work out all the legal arrangements in advance. Frequently they had to do battle with the railroads over the years, when the ambiguities in these new relationships became difficult for the town to manage. Lowell, Massachusetts, for example, allowed the railroad into town in 1832, but the railroad then wished to expand its track dramatically within town boundaries in order to connect with most of the major industries in the city. Lowell allowed the railroad to do this but spelled out in ordinances exactly what the rights of way would be and what damages would be owed to other businesses in the city with conflicting title to the right of way.[19]

Another major growing pain in towns' relationships with the railroads was the issue of taxation. Because of differences in charter obligations and in state and city laws, there was no rule of law as to whether towns had a right to tax the railroads passing within city limits. Even when circumstances warranted a change in the tax structure, charters still in force long after the charter system had lapsed prevented towns from sharing railroad profits through taxation.

In an early tax case the inhabitants of Worcester, Massachusetts, sued the Western Railroad in 1842 for permission to tax railroad structures on land awarded to the railroad by charter. But the inhabitants lost this case. The city of Baltimore lost a similar case in the 1840s when it sought permission to tax its own creation, the Baltimore and Ohio Railroad. The court ruled that the railroad's charter specified that the city could not tax the railroad. The issue of who had the power to tax railroads became increasingly tangled during hard times, such as the Panic of 1837, and then during the Civil War when it reached a crisis. Local, state, and federal governments all sought greater wartime revenues. In taxation as in civil protection, the presence of the railroads compromised governments' legal assurances to their citizens.[20]

The third area of law that evolved to meet the needs of industrial society, and in particular the needs of railroads, was the emerging field of personal injury, another aspect of tort law. Here again the doctrine of strict liability gave way to a principle of negligence, under which it was determined whether or not injured parties would receive compensation for their losses. Approaching the problem from the standpoint of injury to railroad employees, the courts began to consider whether or not the railroad had been negligent in its duties. If so, the railroad owed compensation to an injured party. If, however, the court determined that the railroad had been operated in a responsible fashion, exercising due care, the injured party could not receive compensation. Likewise if the injured party had been negligent, not behaving in a reasonable and cautious way, the injury would not be compensated.

In this context a turning point in the development of tort law was reached in the case of *Farwell vs. Boston and Worcester Railroad,* decided in 1842 by the Massachusetts supreme court. Chief Justice Lemuel Shaw concluded that injuries brought on by the actions of railroad employees could only be compensated if the actions were outside the employees' ordinary duties. If the railroad employee was simply doing his job, the injury could not be compensated. In keeping with this decision, most state courts began using the criteria of negligence to determine in which cases railroad accidents were the fault of the railroad company. Legal authorities felt that the old doctrine of strict liability would inordinately hamper the growth of railroads and industries. The determination of negligence gave the railroads more latitude to develop without serious legal restraints.[21]

In a late 1840s case the Massachusetts supreme court applied this doctrine to passengers. Jacob Richardson sued the Boston and Lowell Railroad for injuries suffered when the axle and wheel of a passenger car broke and a corner of the car in which he was riding fell to the track. When a door of the car also flew open, Richardson tried to jump to safety but fell on frozen ground. He passed out, bleeding from ears, nose, and forehead. When the case came to court, Richardson cited hearing loss, memory loss, loss of ability to concentrate, and nervousness as additional consequences of his injury. The judge found the railroad liable for failure to keep its equipment in repair, indicating that the railroad must take the utmost care to operate safely. The passenger won $227.32 in damages.[22]

By 1858 the legal expert Isaac Redfield had published a substantial volume of railroad-related legal cases under the title *Railroad Law*. Here he defined some of the circumstances under which railroads had been found liable for damages due to personal injury. In general he found they were liable "only for negligence, proximate or remote," and were "not insurers of the safety of their passengers. . . ." He then distinguished between those who were legally passengers and could sue the railroad, and those who, though riding on the train, could not sue because of their behavior. A passenger injured while getting off because the train started up too soon was still legally a passenger. A passenger riding on a free ticket, such as a news reporter, could sue in the event of injury due to railroad negligence; passengers on a train hired for an excursion, or by state officers, could sue; and a passenger hurt while attempting to escape danger could sue. On the other hand, said Redfield, passengers guilty of misconduct or boisterous play which contributed to the injury (actions called contributory negligence) could not receive compensation for damages; neither could a passenger leaping from a moving train, even for good cause. Nor could the relatives of a passenger killed by the railroad sue. With time the number of qualifications in each category lengthened and changes occurred, such as the legal ruling that families of the deceased or injured might sue for damages. But over the next fifty years Redfield provided a substantially reliable guide to the spirit of the new and growing field of tort law as it applied to the railroads.[23]

One important qualification to the negligence rule persisted: not every court agreed on whether railroads were common carriers or private carriers. The difference between the two lay in the degree of responsibility that the railroads owed the public. A private carrier carried only such passengers as it chose to carry, only when and where it chose to carry them. A public or common carrier had a legal responsibility to carry any member of the public on legally equal terms. The fact that railroads were privately owned suggested that they were private carriers. The fact that they were chartered or incorporated by the states and had their lands and capital courtesy of eminent domain and state funding measures indicated that they should by law be common carriers.

Lemuel Shaw took the view that railroads had public duties, and that these duties could be legislated by the states. But this did not invariably translate into a decision that the railroads were common carriers. For example, in the *Richardson* case the court determined that even though the railroad owed damages, it was not a common carrier, not an "insurer of safe carriage" but a private carrier. Historically the growth of the railroads coincided with a transition between private law, expressed in charters written and enforced individually, and public law, which provided uniform state regulation over all institutions of one type. While over the long term courts came to consider railroads common carriers, like ships and other forms of public conveyance, exceptions persisted throughout the century, particularly on small roads with a very specialized business, such as those carrying coal or lumber exclusively and taking passengers only incidentally.[24]

Shaw's insistence that the railroads had public duties, including protection of the passenger, eventually became the legal norm in most states. But often the definition of these duties took a long time and had only begun by the outbreak of the Civil War. In the interval, the railroads' own definitions of their social responsibility were minimal and varied with the company, the weather, the technology of train and track, and the proclivities of the crew. Some states began using statutes before the Civil War as a new means of regulating the railroads and their most glaring failures of social responsibility—and those of passengers, too.

Massachusetts passed a statute in 1849 requiring its railroads to provide "reasonable accommodation" for passengers. New York followed with a similar law in 1850, requiring "sufficient accommodation" and asking that "cars" travel at regularly scheduled times, presumably for the convenience of passengers. Also in 1850 New Hampshire required railroads to establish depots for passengers. That the state had to require railroads to arrive and depart on schedule, to provide reasonable accommodations, and to build passenger depots implies a notably lackadaisical approach by railroad corporations to the social aspects of rail service.[25]

State statutes also provide evidence that passengers had little respect for other passengers or for the company running the railroad, and little understanding of the risks involved in railroad technology.

They frequently violated the most fundamental rule—paying for the ride. In 1850 New York gave railroad conductors legal authority to "eject passengers refusing to pay fare," then qualified the power by specifying that the train had to stop when the conductor did this, though it did not necessarily have to stop at a station. New Hampshire gave conductors the legal right to collect tickets. New York elaborated this point by requiring conductors to have an identifying badge on their caps before they could legally collect fares. In 1853 Indiana gave conductors the power to eject nonpaying passengers.[26]

Overall the social realities of train travel before the Civil War appear to have been extremely freewheeling. Not only did railroads fail to set social standards in their services, but passenger behavior ranged far from the traditional image of waiting quietly at the station, boarding the train when it stopped, and remaining seated throughout the journey. Social evidence as well as legal cases and the public press give a strong impression that passengers would sit with arms, heads, or legs dangling out the windows; rode any train they could board, including freight trains; and rode in caboose, in locomotive, or on the tender, and sat on the tops of cars as well. They jumped on and off rather than waiting for the train to stop, and since the trains had to stop frequently for wood and water, or for repairs, the passengers got off the train during the journey itself, and wandered off to explore, eat, or drink while waiting for the train to start again. In succeeding generations, more and more of this behavior was curtailed by law in order to avoid injuries.[27]

Conflicts of interest plus the patchwork nature of local legislation made it difficult to hold the railroads to a local or state legal standard. And passengers in transit also evaded traditional legal boundaries, which is why leaving town by train became a common means of avoiding prosecution. Between the bias of state legislatures and courts in favor of speedy railroad expansion, and the difficulty of enforcing the law on a train, the social aspects of train travel remained risky. Poor, unsafe, or unpredictable service became considerations secondary to building the railroads and providing whatever commercial service was possible. The principle of commercial exchange embodied in railroad service weakened the ability and resolve of governments to enforce the law according to traditional principles.

A Force for Good
or for Evil?

Not a great while ago, passing through the gate of dreams, I visited that
region of the earth in which lies the famous City of Destruction. It
interested me much to learn that by the public spirit of some of the
inhabitants, a railroad has recently been established between this populous
and flourishing town, and the Celestial City.
                    —Nathanial Hawthorne, "The Celestial City," 1843[1]

Passage to India!
I see continual trains of cars winding along the Platte carrying freight and
    passengers,
I hear the locomotives rushing and roaring, and the shrill steamwhistle,
I hear the echoes reverberate through the grandest scenery in the
    world . . .
                    —Walt Whitman, *Leaves of Grass*, 1871[2]

Before the civil war, literary figures bore witness to the transformation of towns and older ways of life in the coming of the rail-

road, and wrote about it in stinging, uncompromising terms. They characterized the locomotive as satanic and the greed of commercial interests as irreligious. But the buoyantly optimistic business and tourist trades, seconded by the nationalistic poetry of Walt Whitman, drowned out these warnings with grandiose articles that characterized the railroad as the greatest force ever known for the expansion of Christian and civilized values. For these interests the railroad represented a panacea, not only for uniting the country but for bringing peace and prosperity to all parts of the country and the world.

The opposing point of view appeared in the works of James Fenimore Cooper and Nathaniel Hawthorne, where allusions could be found to virtually all the legal, social, and economic problems that the railroads created. Cooper, writing in the late 1830s, portrayed the taking of land and the loss of an older social order as functions of widespread commercial avarice. Hawthorne, writing five years later, focused on the railroad journey itself. By comparing it satirically to a religious pilgrimage, he suggested that the coming of the railroad meant the passing of an older, religiously inspired social order. In Hawthorne's view, the effects of this transition made the new industrial pilgrimage of the United States appear more like a journey to hell than to heaven.

In *Home as Found,* a novel of 1838, Cooper excoriated the values of a society in which greed and vanity born of new wealth had replaced moral values, compassion, and loyalty. Cooper identified the emergence of a new aristocracy, especially in New York City, whose elegance and airs could be traced to new fortunes made in railroad investments. Cooper created the fictional Effingham family who became the target of many of his barbs about this new class. Travel for them was one of the social graces conferred by wealth, rather than a desperate errand into the wilderness in search of prosperity and freedom. Cooper's Effingham family, however, contained a lawyer and land agent whose remarks about railroads and the taking of land revealed the grim realities behind the family's social graces. Aristabulus Bragg, a lawyer whose first name conferred upon him an ennobling Greek heritage of learning which he did not in fact possess, and whose last name reflected the crass realities of his calling, frequently offended the sensibilities of his clients while continuing to earn money for them.[3]

Bragg embarrassed himself in several ways. As a suitor for the hand of Eve Effingham, he reached far above his social station. And as an advocate for internal improvements, he exposed himself as a greedy and unfeeling scoundrel. In conversation with Sir George Templemore, an English friend of the Effingham family, Bragg inadvertently described the most destructive aspects of railroading while trying to promote it. About his own legal profession he said that business was slow in New York since "many of the attorneys have turned their attention to other callings." Upon being asked what other callings, Bragg responded, "much the greater portion are just now dealing in western cities . . . in mill-seats, and railroad lines, and other expectations"—a reference to the many legal conflicts accompanying the construction of railroads, mills, and cities.[4]

The conversation then turned more specifically to the taking of private property for the use of railroads, an issue which at the time had begun to concern local and state courts. Mr. Effingham asked Templemore whether it was true that "in England, there are difficulties in running highways and streets through homesteads and dwellings; and that even a railroad or a canal is obliged to make a curve to avoid a churchyard or a tombstone?"[5]

"I confess to the sin, sir," Templemore answered. Mr. Effingham then challenged the American habit of removing forests and dwellings that stand in the path of the railroad interests as "all means and no end." What would the country become? Where would the building of tracks end? Bragg, defending the course of internal improvements, responded,

> I am for the end of the road at least, and must say that I rejoice in being a native of a country in which as few impediments as possible exist to onward impulses. The man who should resist an improvement in our part of the country, on account of his forefathers, would fare badly among his contemporaries.[6]

His English associate then questioned the loss of local values and humane attachments that attended this type of improvement. He asked if you [Bragg] feel no local attachments yourself? . . . if one tree is not more pleasant than another; the houses which you were born in more beautiful than a house into which you never entered; or the altar at which you have long worshipped, more sacred than another at which you have never knelt?

Bragg, echoing the outlook of commerce, responded that he loved a locality based on the profit he might derive from it.

. . . The pleasantest tree I can remember was one of my own, out of which the sawyers made a thousand feet of clear stuff, to say nothing of middlings. The house I was born in was pulled down shortly after my birth, as indeed has its successor. . . . As for altars, there are none in my persuasion.[7]

Five years later, in 1843, Nathaniel Hawthorne published a short story entitled "The Celestial Railroad," in which he too raised moral questions about railroad travel. He compared the experience of the railroad passenger to that of the religious seeker named Christian, depicted in John Bunyan's *Pilgrim's Progress,* a book known and read in almost every colonial Puritan community. Hawthorne managed to find parallels between almost all of Christian's trials of faith and the experiences of the average railroad passenger of the 1840s. Internal improvements, poor service in stations, unsafe tracks, dangerous locomotives, crowds, and even the cities protecting themselves from the hazards of the rail all had a part in the plight of this fictional railroad passenger.[8]

Accompanied by a guide named Mr. Smooth-It-Away, who promoted his railroad as a member of the company's board of directors and as a major stockholder, the railroad passenger began his journey. Even before reaching the station, the passenger and his guide found themselves traveling in a coach over an extremely rickety bridge, or "improvement," over the Slough of Despond, the first encounter on Christian's journey to salvation. The bridge's foundation, the passenger noted, consisted of granite into which all the great historical teachings of moral philosophy had been placed in order to hold up one rickety structure.[9]

At the depot the passenger received a ticket, instead of the scroll given to Christian, and his first lesson, not about morality but about poor service. He deposited his luggage with the baggageman instead of carrying his burden on his back, as Christian had to do. But the baggagemen were former employees of Prince Beelzebub, a fact which did not bother Mr. Smooth-It-Away at all.[10]

Once on the train, the passenger discovered the meaning of unsafe travel, finding that the engineer was named Apollyon, or "one who exterminates." Apollyon, who attempted to kill Christian in the original tale when they met in the Valley of Humiliation, belched fire and smoke again in the 1840s, as did the railroad engine. But Mr. Smooth-It-Away remarked that the Valley of Humiliation should not prove a serious problem anymore, since it had been filled by leveling the Hill of Difficulty, another of Christian's trials. The passenger's fears were aroused again as the train approached the Valley of the Shadow of Death and gained speed until the passenger felt certain they would not survive the journey. But once again Mr. Smooth-It- Away assured him that he would be "as safe as on any railroad in Christendom."[11]

During an encounter with the crowds of Vanity Fair, where the inhabitants come to see and be seen, the passenger discovers that the railroad does not extend all the way into Celestial City, his destination, because the city, to avoid the noise and danger, "has refused and ever will refuse, to grant an act of incorporation for this railroad."[12] The passenger must therefore ride on a steam ferryboat to make the final approach to the city. At the conclusion of *Pilgrim's Progress*, Christian awoke to find that he had dreamed his religious journey. Thus also ended the journey as retold by Hawthorne: the passenger discovers that his entire rail journey has been a dream.

Other writers of the antebellum era wrote skeptically of the railroad as a dangerous intrusion into the serenity of the natural world. Henry David Thoreau, from his retreat at Walden Pond, characterized the Fitchburg Railroad as a "devilish iron horse." Charles Dickens complained of the crowds, the lack of comforts, and the unattractive views on his American tour in the 1840s, and he pronounced the locomotive a "mad dragon."[13]

In the business press, however, attitudes epitomized by Mr. Smooth-It-Away predominated. Every bit as optimistic as their fic-

tional counterparts, business writers promoted the railroads uncriti-
cally and went a step further by claiming their invention had the potential to spread moral and Christian influences as far as the railroads
extended. Henry Varnum Poor, editor of the *American Railroad Journal,* in an article in 1851, declared that "the locomotive engine has in
twenty years become the great agent of civilization and progress, the
most powerful instrument for good the world has yet reached, and
become the most effective messenger for proclaiming peace on earth
and good will toward men."[14] In Poor's opinion, technical progress
and Christianity did not compete, they complemented each other.

As early as 1829 citizens in Baltimore, fearful of another attack like
the one they had endured in the War of 1812, saw the railroad's potential to move troops quickly, and therefore touted it as an instrument of peace. This idea ballooned into the notion that the railroad
was an agent of national peace as well as the religious peace evoked
by Henry Varnum Poor. In 1832 Poor's *American Railroad Journal*
quoted Dr. Charles Caldwell of Boston on his belief that "the certain
prevention of foreign war . . . will be one of the numerous advantages
of Railroads."[15]

Other railroad promoters echoed this theme. The Cincinnati *Daily
Chronicle* of 1843 elaborated on the connection between military
preparedness and peace: "It is of vast importance that we have main
lines of permanent railroad, extending from the principal cities to the
interior, to the frontier, to the far west, that troops, provisions and
munitions of war may be transported rapidly from place to place." Simultaneously the trains would be "dispelling prejudices and cement-
ing friendships, calculated to perpetuate the institutions under which
we have risen from a mere handful. . . ."[16] No voice rose to predict
that trains might disseminate bad behavior as well as good, or widen
the scope of war beyond imagining.

In 1848 an article in *Merchants' Magazine* argued that the spread
of railroads, connecting commerce all over the world, would overcome hostilities among regions and peoples through social intercourse and "intelligent Christianity." The railroad would extend the
Christian mission of America beyond its borders, through commerce.
The theme of universality in such articles was in fact more than
rhetorical exaggeration. As the magazine went to press, an American

railroad company had just formed to build a railroad across the Isthmus of Panama. Plans were afoot for building a railroad in Cuba, and American investors, American engineers, and American companies had begun looking for opportunities to lay track in South America. Even Asa Whitney's bid to build tracks to the Pacific reflected the historical effort to find or create a passage to India by which missionaries could travel to convert the heathen and merchants could trade.[17]

The poet Walt Whitman, fifteen years younger than Hawthorne and thirty years younger than Cooper, did not share their dark view of the railroad as an agent of greed and irreligion. Written in 1871, after both the Civil War and the completion of the transcontinental railroad, his poem "Passage to India" echoed the theme that all parts of the world would meet and unify in consequence of railroad expansion.

> Passage to India!
> Lo, soul, seest thou not God's purpose from the first?
> The earth to be spann'd, connected by network,
> The races, neighbors, to marry and be given in marriage,
> The oceans to be cross'd, the distant brought near,
> The lands to be welded together.
> A worship new I sing,
> You captains, voyagers, explorers, yours,
> You engineers, you architects, machinists, yours,
> You, not for trade or transportation only,
> But in God's name, and for thy sake O soul.[18]

The possibility that "neighbors" from different regions might meet and not unify but rather fall into conflict with each other did not occur to Whitman, even though he had witnessed the violent conflict between North and South.

7

||||||||||||

A Crowded and Uncomfortable Home Away from Home

The cars were of considerable length, with a range of windows alternating with polished mahogany panels along the sides, an ornamental ceiling, and a flooring of painted cloth. Each accommodated fifty-eight passengers, who sat, two together, in arm-chairs covered with red plush, in a row on each side, leaving a passage in the middle which communicated with a door at both ends. The passengers faced the engine, but by shifting the backs of their seats, they could look in a contrary direction. Outside, at the two ends of each car, there was a small platform, whence to descend by steps to the ground, and by stepping from platform to platform, the passengers could move from one car to another along the whole train. Each car was provided with a stove, which stood in the middle, on one side, and was heated with billets of wood.

—William Chambers, *Things as They Are in America*, 1854[1]

THE EARLIEST PROVISIONS for railroad travelers were locally diverse and idiosyncratic. Services varied according to the customs and economy of each region that supported rail travel. But by the late 1840s, as tracks extended beyond state boundaries to connect economic regions as well, the earliest signs of uniform services emerged, though still unenforced by any uniform system of law. All attempts to provide uniform services were also checked by traditional customs regarding differences between rich and poor, male and female, black and white, immigrant and native, urban and rural. The consequence, during the years before the Civil War, was not a uniform rail service but a tapestry of services, affected by great differences in wealth, population, local cultural attitudes, and even the attitudes of individuals on each train. Before the coming of the telegraph in the late 1840s, a train out on the track was completely on its own, and decisions regarding service, including speed, schedule, stops, and even the behavior of passengers were still made individually, usually by the conductor or engineer, and sometimes according to the needs or wishes of an individual traveler. Finally, railroads did not always provide the services that passengers needed. A shortage of cars or seats, failure to stop at stations, failure to build any stations at all, and failure to care for baggage were but a few of the hindrances of rail service before the Civil War.

Station house and train car became the somewhat chaotic meeting ground between traditional local and individual considerations on one hand, and the requirements of an emerging mass society on the other. Consequently early rail service was subjected to many criticisms by passengers who judged it from diverse social points of view. In making adjustments for the accommodation of men and women in different regions and social levels, train services had to accommodate the crowds they engendered and the established values of individuals in those crowds. But in general, elaborate services for the masses came to cities first; rural services tended to retain the individual, piecemeal nature of an older way of life.

As the expanding network of railroads tugged in this way at the traditional local foundations of the American social order, it created the

The interior of a passenger day coach built about 1836 shows upholstered seats but reveals a low ceiling, just over six feet, and an absence
of luggage racks. Lighting apparently consisted of a single candle at
each end of the car. Adjustable wooden shutters controlled ventilation.
(SMITHSONIAN INSTITUTION)

crude beginnings of an alternative order based on national and commercial public services. The elements of service did not fall into place quickly but tended to develop according to a particular pattern, that is, first the provision of services sufficient to individual and local needs, then the realization that services had to meet the needs of all comers over a larger and larger geographical area, and that provision had to be made for larger and larger crowds. This was essential if the railroads were ever to serve a national purpose.

The early evolution of the train car illustrates the transition from individualized attention to the service of crowds. The earliest train cars resembled stagecoaches and provided seats for only about eight to thirty people. A few more passengers might choose to sit on the roof of the coach. But this design proved too fragile and too small for the number of passengers wanting to ride the train, and gave way to an elongated car with a central aisle. Forty to sixty passengers could be accommodated in each car, and the aisle provided a means of transit for the conductor, who had to collect tickets and fares on board. While this style remained in use for the life of the railroad industry, later cars were substantially longer and heavier than those of the 1830s and 1840s.[2] All passenger cars of this period were constructed of wood.

The internal appointments of railroad cars before the Civil War differed little from those in a somewhat primitive household of the same era. Candles provided lighting, a wood- or coal-burning stove provided heat, and windows provided ventilation. As the size of the cars increased, however, and as the length of the average railroad trip grew, traditional solutions to heating and lighting came under public attack. "A solitary lamp burned at one end of the car and its sickly light fell upon the sleepers," wrote a dismayed passenger. Another commented on the "gloomy cage" of a train car after dark.[3]

Railroad companies did little to improve the lighting in their passenger coaches until the early 1850s when longer lines made regular night travel possible. Candlelight and oil lamps continued to provide illumination, however, until quite late in the century. With a number of candle or oil lamps fixed to the inside walls of the train car, the conductor or trainmen could light the car as darkness fell.[4]

Lamps, of course, carried an inherent risk of fire. If the train lurched or ran off the track, a fire might turn a minor mishap into a major disaster. The railroads put a glass chimney over each candle or oil lamp to keep the flame enclosed, but during the 1850s, accidents involving fire became a matter of intense concern.[5]

The use of one iron stove, a descendant of the Franklin stove, to heat the passenger car also illustrates the railroads' acceptance of traditional technology for passengers. Not only households but canal boats and steamboats used these stoves for passengers. The stove stood either at one end of the car or in the middle, with some seats removed to create a clear space around the stove. Before the Civil War a container of wood or coal stood by the stove; the conductor and the brakeman were responsible for keeping the container full and keeping the stove burning. On trips of more than an hour or two, the train had to stop while these men got off to forage for wood. They took wood wherever they found it, without compensating the owners of the land.[6]

The stove created even more problems for the passengers than did poor lighting, partly because in the larger train cars most passengers had to sit either too near the stove or too far from it. Public lore about train stoves described experienced passengers rushing to take seats a comfortable distance from the stove, leaving inexperienced travelers to freeze at the end of the car where heat did not reach, or roast if they were too close to the stove.[7] Scottish tourist William Chambers reported that the heating in his car was perfectly comfortable. But Charles Dickens noted that in cold weather, when the windows had to be closed, the stove fire created bad air in the car. In his *American Notes,* published in 1842, Dickens wrote:

> In the centre of the carriage there is usually a stove, fed with charcoal or anthracite coal; which is for the most part red-hot. It is insufferably close; and you see the hot air fluttering between yourself and any other object you happen to look at, like the ghost of smoke.[8]

Like the lighting arrangements, the stove also created a high risk of fire in cars made principally of wood.

While the earliest train cars had open sides without glassed-in windows, leaving the passengers exposed to the air and elements, car builders of the 1830s began using glass windows for several reasons.

Exposure to the air did not matter in good weather, but as it became clear that railroads would run in all seasons, the passengers required more protection from the weather. More important, the passengers needed protection from dust, from small rocks and debris that flew up from the rail bed, and from burning embers that, despite the spark arrester, still flew back from the locomotive. To avoid complaints and demands for payment of damages to passengers, windows were installed in the sides of the cars. They opened, however, and passengers usually wanted them open in warm weather, which meant that passengers remained vulnerable to cinders, sparks, and debris.

Some railroads adapted another traditional technology to improve ventilation in hot weather while avoiding flying debris. They installed adjustable wooden louvers, like venetian blinds, between the windows, an arrangement that admitted fresh air while keeping the windows closed. Louvers did not entirely solve the problem of ventilation, since fresh breezes blew in passengers' faces if they sat next to the louver ventilators, and in cold weather louvers allowed cold air in, negating the effects of the stove. To remedy this problem, some railroad builders installed ventilators in the roof of the car, to catch the wind.[9] While some versions of this invention appeared odd and unwieldy, ventilators succeeded to a limited extent in providing fresh air to passengers.

The quality of seating attracted a great many innovators even before the Civil War; nothing so defined the level of service as the passengers' seats. The early classification of travel into first and second class meant chiefly an upholstered seat in a car with interior decoration as opposed to a plain wooden seat in a very plain, undecorated car. The car-building firm of Betts, Pusey and Harlan advertised four classes of cars which they produced: each sixty feet long and eight feet six inches wide, and each with "crosswise" seats, meaning that the seats were positioned at right angles to the central aisle. All four types of cars also had adjustable seating, but in the quality of seating materials and decor the classes differed. The first-class car, the most lavish, had "spring seats . . . with shifting [adjustable] backs, trimmed in best style, with silk or worsted, venetian blinds to the windows. . . ." The second-class car included "seats crosswise with shifting backs, hair or cloth seating, worsted head lining, festoons, and sun curtains. . . ." The third-class car had "seats crosswise, with shifting backs, cloth or leather seating . . . canvas roof painted and sanded. . . ." Finally, the fourth-class car had "plain wooden seats, with shifting backs painted . . . canvas roof as above." The external finish of each car also reflected class distinctions: the first-class car had "gilt border and lettering" while the fourth-class car was "plainly painted on the outside."[10]

Seating for railroad passengers represented a distinct technological departure from available traditional models. Neither steamboat nor canal boat offered anything comparable for carrying large groups of passengers in relative comfort. But the railroads, aware that many passengers would not be willing or able to pay for luxury, offered a choice of accommodation.

In areas where passengers did not have enough money to pay the regular fare, the railroads introduced second-class travel, which cost less. The Western Railroad, which opened in 1842 to carry passengers from Boston to Albany, charged a first-class fare of $5.50 for the trip; second-class fare for the same trip was $3.66. Second-class fare generally was about two-thirds of the first-class rate. In 1843 the much shorter Attica and Buffalo line charged a first-class fare of 85 cents for through traffic and a second-class fare of 43 cents. In 1845 the Boston and Lowell Railroad charged a first-class fare of $1.00 to take passengers the entire distance, and a second-class fare of 75 cents.[11]

Most early railroads had only a few second-class cars, and their annual reports indicate that second-class travel did not carry as many passengers or bring in as much revenue as the first-class service. Many railroads referred to their smoking cars as second-class cars, where travelers could travel for less if they could tolerate the smoke and a somewhat rougher social environment. While some Eastern railroad lines used emigrant cars or freight cars to carry the very poorest class of paying passengers, second-class service also served those emigrants who could afford a higher level of comfort. In addition to emigrants, second-class cars apparently served early factory workers. The Boston and Lowell had a second-class service between those two cities, and it was likely used by laborers who worked in the Lowell textile mills.[12]

Class distinctions in train cars and service represented the railroads' early adaptation to social and economic differences among passengers. Other social distinctions, including those based on race and sex, also found expression in passenger service before the Civil War. But the classification of passengers varied from region to region, depending on the social and economic composition of the area and the policies of the conductor on each train.

For example, some black passengers, both slave and free, might ride in a day coach with white passengers on certain railroads but not on others. Company policy on some Southern trains forced slaves to travel in the baggage car or freight car, reflecting their status as property rather than as citizens. But this rule did not apply in all cases. According to the historian John White, "Many of the [Southern] lines contained half-fare compartments in the baggage car for Negroes, but Negroes could also ride in the coaches at full fare." White added that a diarist who described the accommodations for blacks in the North indicated that they invariably rode in separate cars. Author Charles Dickens corroborated this view in his *American Notes:* "As a black man never travels with a white one, there is . . . a negro car, which is a great blundering clumsy chest." In the West railroads had less money, fewer passengers, and fewer cars, and rich and poor, black, white, and Indian frequently rode together.[13]

Women passengers too were afforded protections in the East that seemed unessential or unwieldy in the West. But again, variations according to train and conductor made the enforcement of these provisions local or even individual. Many railroads had a ladies' car to protect the single woman traveling alone and the woman who traveled with a family, with or without the father. Many trains forbade smoking in the ladies' car, and forbade single men from entering this car. In some instances these cars were designed differently from other day coaches in that they included couches where a woman or child could nap. Conductors had a key to the doors of this car and had the option of locking it if the need arose.[14]

Charles Dickens's attention was drawn to these provisions because he had not anticipated seeing so many women traveling alone.

In the ladies' car there are a great many gentlemen who have ladies with them. There are also a great many ladies who have nobody with them; for any lady may travel alone, from one end of the United States to the other, and be certain of the most courteous and considerate treatment everywhere.[15]

Dickens's view must be qualified by the fact that he tended to generalize about the entire country from only one or two examples, as did many foreign travelers who wrote about the United States. While his observation that women could travel alone appears accurate, it is not true that women were always treated considerately.

Dickens also distinguished between the day car and the ladies' car when he wrote that "in the first, everybody smokes; in the second, nobody does." Smoking aboard trains was controversial because of its effect on air quality in the cars. In general the railroads provided some type of smoking car while the public and press debated the issue. In connection with smoking on the Georgia Railroad, one commentator wrote, "There is no use . . . in denying accommodations to smokers, on the ground of objection to the habit. . . . Too many great and good men have smoked or do smoke, to allow anyone stigmatizing the practice as vulgar or indecent."[16]

Surveying the controls put in place by American railroads for distinguishing among social classes, races, and sexes, it becomes clear that the roads felt an obligation to impose on this crowd a social order which reflected established customs of the region through which the train traveled. But the order was enforced only selectively, and frequently the poorer or shorter lines did not have the number of cars or number of passengers to justify this kind of segregation. In the long run this meant that the more elaborate services for passengers could usually be found on the longer or "through" routes. This difference held into the twentieth century.

Services for railroad passengers in the stations and towns along the route also took note of local economic and social differences. Taverns, hotels, restaurants, and waiting rooms in stations reflected no uniform plan for the treatment of railroad passengers except that, as the numbers of passengers swelled to crowd proportions, larger hotels and stations lined the route, frequently slighting the old stage and toll road routes that did not bring in the same volume of business.

The earliest stations in the antebellum era were adaptations of existing buildings to the purposes of the railroads. Modifications were made primarily to house engines and cars rather than provide services for passengers. Thus the oldest surviving records of stations show structures of many shapes and sizes, including an old six-sided building in Baltimore where tickets were first sold for the Baltimore and Ohio Railroad, and, in other towns, a number of large, rectangular sheds that marked stopping places but did not house passengers. One such station stood in Frederick, Maryland, also on the B&O. Other stations, such as the first one built in Schenectady, New York, for the Delaware and Hudson Railroad, were adapted from houses.[17]

The impetus for building a station, or adapting one, began with the railroad company, but the town had to approve the building site, and the town also had the option of selling railroad shares or bonds to townspeople to raise the money necessary for construction.[18] But with miles of open country between towns, many railroad companies saw little merit in building stations in the wilderness, wherever a few passengers might wish to board. The earliest stations constructed specifically for the purpose were usually found in the terminals at each end of the railroad line. Even at this early date, station designers distinguished unequivocally between the urban station planned to serve large crowds, and the rural station, which was little more than a bungalow with eaves extending over the walls to shelter passengers and goods from the rain.

The first urban stations of a permanent character went up in the 1830s, notably for the Boston and Lowell Railroad in Boston, and for the Norwich and Worcester in Norwich, Connecticut. From the late 1840s through the 1850s, the major Eastern cities opened railroad stations, most of which included extensive services for passengers. The terminal station of the Old Colony Railroad, in Boston, opened in 1847 and featured "a lofty gaslit smoking room equipped with inside shutters, a popular barber shop, telegraph office, newsstand, lavatory, bootblack, and check room." In the next three years, major stations opened in New Haven, Plainville, Collinsville, and Hartford,

Connecticut; Providence, Rhode Island; and Detroit, Michigan. Each of these received compliments in the press on their elegant architecture and decor as well as the civilized comforts provided for passengers. The New Haven station included

> extensive Parlors, that on the left side being for the accommodation of ladies, and is furnished with a profusion of rich and costly divans, chairs, ottomans, mirrors, etc., with convenient dressing rooms attached. Obliging servants are always in attendance. The Parlor on the right is for gentlemen's use, and is to be furnished as a Reading Room. . . . The ticket office is on the left side of the grand hall. . . .

The Hartford station included a hundred-room hotel and an enormous dining room. During the 1850s large stations went up in New York City; Troy, New York; and Baltimore.[19]

Among the large stations, a few took the name of Union Station, notably the Providence and Troy stations. This designation had more than one meaning. While it meant that more than one railroad used the station, therefore uniting the services of many railroads, it also referred to the old idea of uniting the country through a railroad network. In some towns, even if the station did not bear this designation, the building might be constructed on Union Street or Union Avenue. The name, of course, gained new popularity during and after the Civil War, when the practice of naming towns, streets, squares, and buildings "Union" identified the railroads with the Union cause.

These city depots confirmed an alliance between the railroads and the major cities of the early nineteenth century. A station only miles from these centers differed so markedly that no one could mistake an elaborate and often elegant terminal station for the small-town stations along the track, or on the branch railroads. These were extremely simple. In general, a structure resembling a large country cottage, with overhanging eaves, housed a central ticket office with a waiting room at each end, one for men and one for women. More forward-looking designs also included toilets in the main structure, while traditionalists put the toilets in an outhouse, separate from the main building.[20] This system of organization became extremely common after the Civil War as the railroads built a myriad of stations, many based on a single design.

Fire decimated many of the earliest railroad stations. While the largest city stations were usually made of stone, many other stations, composed entirely of wood, caught fire in the same way that farm buildings and fields caught fire from the locomotive's flying sparks. The Schenectady station burned down within ten years of its construction. Others burned because they functioned both as train sheds and waiting areas, and steaming locomotives were driven into the sheds.[21] But wood, being cheap and locally available for building, remained popular despite the cost in destruction by fire.

In some towns the trains did not stop at a station but proceeded up a street through the center of town to stop at hotels. Having been the traditional custom for stagecoaches, this seemed appropriate for trains as well, until the dangers and noise proved too upsetting for townspeople. Travelers who ventured farther than the major cities and their suburbs found that many passengers got on and off in any convenient spot, sometimes without waiting for the train to stop. Many country travelers had no station built for them, and they could not easily travel any distance to get to a station. So the railroads accommodated many informal flag stops along the route, where engineers stopped or at least slowed to allow passengers who flagged the train to board or alight. Charles Dickens commented acerbically about this habit, as if he thought the country stops might best be skipped: "The train calls at stations in the woods, where the wild impossibility of anybody having the smallest reason to get out is only to be equalled by the apparently desperate hopelessless of there being anybody to get in."[22]

Stations further west, apart from the river towns that developed between the Allegheny Mountains and the Mississippi River, had little formality or plan. Jumping on a moving train, to ride in a passenger car or a freight car, was a skill needed by many classes of passengers in that region of the country.

Railroad schedules were relatively formal for urban dwellers but reached rural folk haphazardly. Railroads published schedules as early as the 1830s. They appeared in weekly newspapers, and railroad companies also arranged to have them posted in major hotels and in hotels along the track routes. Curiously, passengers could not depend on finding a schedule at the station, because the railroads frequently did not post schedules there regularly. Travelers often complained about the inconvenience of arriving in town without knowing when to catch the next train.[23]

The newspaper schedule announcements resembled classified advertisements and could be found along with steamboat, stagecoach, and canal boat schedules. During the 1830s and 1840s only about two trains, headed in opposite directions, stopped at a city station each day. The number would have been higher in the union stations that served more than one railroad company. In the summer of 1841 transportation ads in the weekly *Connecticut Courant* indicated that for two dollars a passenger could go south to New York City on the steamboat *Cleopatra,* leaving Hartford at 3 p.m. every Monday, Wednesday, and Friday. Philadelphia packet boats also headed south, while the New Haven and Northampton Railroad advertised a "safe, cheap, and expeditious route" north or south. Competing with these alternatives, the New Haven and Hartford Railroad advertised trains running daily, except Sunday. The steamboat train left Hartford daily at 10:30 a.m., arriving in New Haven in time for passengers to connect with a steamboat bound for New York City. An accommodation train, so called because it made every stop, accommodating everyone along the route, also left Hartford daily at 5 p.m. for passengers going to New York City. A stagecoach company advertised a daily run starting at 8:30 a.m., or when the New Haven and Hartford train arrived from the south, and rode north to connect passengers in Springfield with the Western Railroad train to Boston.[24]

While ships, stagecoaches, and railroads gave precise times of departure and arrival, they were commonly late.[25] Passengers on all modes of transport experienced delays so often that the one train or boat leaving daily had nothing to lose by waiting, while it might well lose fares if it set out promptly, before a connecting ride had arrived. Furthermore, the schedule specified only times of arrival and departure, not times for intermediate stops, so that presumably some time could be made up along the route. Finally, the times given for departures and arrivals were local times, so it was difficult for passengers from outside the area to know precisely when a connecting train would set out. Most railroad time schedules only specified which local time they used.

Purchasing a ticket before departure entailed many of the same problems faced in determining the schedule. In a city the prospective passenger could go to a ticket office, which might be located in the station or anywhere the railroad chose to sell tickets. Hotels sold them too.[26] But if he was beyond the reach of the network of urban passenger services, the traveler often had to board the train without a ticket and purchase one from the conductor.

During the earliest years of railroading, passengers had to "book" passage by rail just as they booked boat or stagecoach passage. This meant making a reservation in advance and having one's name written down in a book, sometimes along with the passenger's point of departure and destination. According to one historian, the practice of booking survived at least until 1840, but by that time the writing of names had given way to writing "Boy," "Lady," "Stranger," "Friend," or "Whiskers" in the book. And with the dramatic increase in the numbers traveling by rail, the practice of booking gradually ceased altogether.[27]

While the earliest tickets were reusable pieces of metal, leather, or wood, their potential for reuse without repayment encouraged the railroads to switch to paper tickets. These too contained a space in which the passenger was to write his name, but as the number of passengers increased, using names went out of fashion.[28]

Despite complaints, the baggage system used on the longer American railroad lines was one of the most successful adaptations of service to the uniformity required by large numbers of people. Americans developed the system of checking luggage, i.e., giving it to baggage men at the station in exchange for a check, metal or leather, with a number stamped on it.[29] The baggage was then loaded in a baggage car, usually at the front of the train.

American railroads also had liberal policies regarding the amount of luggage that passengers could take without an additional payment. Toll takers on the early state-run railroads allowed fifty pounds of personal luggage free of charge. As railroads became exclusively private rather than state-owned, the provision for free personal luggage remained. One historian has estimated the upper weight limit for free luggage at one hundred pounds. Canal boats allowed only sixty pounds of luggage and household goods free of charge.[30]

Despite the novelty of the checking system and its relative success, complaints about loss or damage to luggage were common, even in the 1830s and 1840s. Nathaniel Hawthorne's fictional portrayal of the baggageman as a former employee of satan fit a stereotype among those who frequently grumbled about the services provided by railroad companies.

Thus the earliest services for railroad passengers in the United States emerged as a mixture of traditional technologies and local customs adapted to new circumstances, as well as new technologies and systems specific to the railroad service. Passenger services featured traditional systems for lighting, heating, and ventilating railroad cars, and adopted forms of scheduling and ticketing from stagecoaches and steamboats. But for long-distance travel by large numbers of people, railroad companies had to rethink traditional techniques, experimenting continually with heating and ventilation, and both scheduling and ticketing procedures. Their solution to seating large numbers in trains, and checking baggage, set standards that have come to be used internationally.

No description of early railroad passenger service would be complete without noting its decided urban orientation. The elegance and services provided in the urban depots were substantial evidence of this bias. Those in the country and on the frontier still depended on river traffic more than railroads, and remained outside the expanding gyre of stations, specialized train cars, and schedules that served the passenger traveling in the Northeast but not far beyond. Not until after the Civil War did the still expanding railroads bring the niceties of service to rural travelers. At the root of rail services lay a new contract: the towns had constructed their institutional services with the social contract in mind; the railroads built their services around the commercial contract, the relationship between buyer and seller.

Private and Public Unions

Last night I met him on the train
a man with lovely eyes,
and he gave me such a searching glance
of sweetly charmed surprise
I knew 'twas he a lady meant
who once my fortune told
by his jet black eyes,
his grand mustache,
and his buckskin bag of gold!

The dearest man you ever saw
how much I love him now,
and if I should live a thousand years
no other hears my vow
like Ju . . . no like Jupiter
he looks so brave and bold
with his jet black eyes,
his grand mustache,
and his buckskin bag of gold!

Sweet boy bring me the Morning Call
perchance I'll find his name
at the Grand Hotel he must have stopped

I wonder when he came
he must have charmed
those lumpkin girls
so haughty proud and cold,
with his jet black eyes,
his grand mustache,
and his buckskin bag of gold!

How can I see the name oh no
oh tell me where he went
what's this I see papa's bank is robbed
of every cent
the thief it seems
left town last night
well, well I'm nicely sold,
he had jet black eyes,
his grand mustache
and his buckskin bag of gold!
—Henry Clay Work, "The Buckskin Bag of Gold," 1869[1]

O NCE REMOVED FROM the context of home, railroad passengers had to adapt to the public world, which increasingly mixed immigrants and natives, economic groups, sexes, and races, despite efforts at segregation in train cars. The inhabitants of every region of the country also began to come into contact with one another when traveling by rail. South met North, East met West. And immigrants from Ireland, Sweden, and Germany joined New Englanders in a search for prosperity in the West. Although the railroads promoted some segregation of women, children, and blacks, they nonetheless made up part of the crowd in the stations and frequently in the cars as well. Men of very different means also crossed paths: businessmen sat with frontiersmen, Indians with immigrants. All were strangers to one another. Often their behavior, clothes, belongings, and habits seemed strange and unfamiliar too.

In their travels they sought farm land, business opportunity, or work on internal improvements projects, or commuted to factories or to schools. Others traveled to visit with friends and families, shop, vacation at a resort or hotel, pursue political interests, study the botany, biology, and geology of the land, gather at the increasingly common agricultural and industrial fairs held in every state, meet in associations, take outings, visit museums, go to the seashore or park, attend picnics, reunions, concerts, or other public diversions, or simply tour, to see the land, its new institutions, and its people. While some migrated west to escape the growing "aristocracy" of wealth that had begun to dominate the East, tourism gave people a temporary way of achieving the same end: escaping the routine demands of home and work, its responsibilities, and its hierarchy of authority.[2] Others, also seeking escape from authority, found opportunity in the anonymous crowd to defraud travelers who were too willing to trust strangers.

With each passing year between 1828 and the outbreak of Civil War in 1861, the mileage of railroad track increased, enabling passengers to venture farther and farther from the familiar surroundings of home. By the late 1830s all-day journeys were possible, and shortly thereafter those who traveled the first night trains witnessed the introduction of railroad services for night travelers—enhanced lighting, reclining chairs, and the first experimental sleeping cars.[3] Hotels and restaurants had already opened close to most city railroad stations, and others had begun serving the public at more remote locations from the city. Passengers on these long journeys required other basic services too, such as toilets and washrooms, included in most stations but only in some cars. Frequent stops en route still being the rule, passengers could adapt to circumstance.

As journeys lengthened, passengers spent more and more time in the presence of others, identifiable only by their personal habits. Privacy disappeared as passengers found themselves in a position to observe and hear the talking, smoking, reading, chatting, eating, sleeping, arguing, complaining, and even fighting of people from all walks of life. Some observers reveled in the diversity and display of the crowd, interpreting it as an example of democracy in action, the leveling of social barriers; others found the crowds in the day coach barbaric in their habits, with manners and morals that could easily decline into promiscuity.[4]

While the travel crowds of the nineteenth century were the sum of many individuals on specific missions, the crowds themselves gained an importance in the context of nineteenth-century American history. Their origins and characteristics help to understand some of the attitudes toward train travel that developed before the Civil War.

The emergence of crowds in American society had of course begun in the cities, which were invariably river ports or seaports during the colonial era. Boats and commerce brought crowds, which migrated westward as trade expanded. As steamboats spread the population along the banks of the Ohio and Mississippi rivers, frontier river ports grew, profiting from the trade with new farmers who needed every type of manufactured product. Before the Civil War, New Orleans, Vicksburg, St. Louis, Cairo, Louisville, and Cincinnati all gained from trade on the rivers. These towns drew crowds too but they did not succeed in segregating their diverse population in the fashion of the Eastern cities. Despite the idyllic portraits of these racially and socially diverse waterfront crowds in the paintings of George Caleb Bingham, the crowds of Western riverfront towns gained a reputation as more dangerous than Eastern crowds, due in part to the presence of great numbers of speculators and confidence men.[5]

Besides the many legitimate businessmen who traveled west, speculators pursued get-rich-quick schemes among the passengers on steamers and in the towns that commerce had begun to build. The new Westerners needed all sorts of things—from livestock to food to tools and cooking supplies and seed—that cities could provide.[6] But the speculators had a reputation for making quick profits without providing the needed product. Gamblers, confidence men who took customers' money and left town, and men who bought land cheaply from the government and sold it to farmers for a much higher price, all fell within the definition of speculators.

As trade lured businessmen to the West, confidence men followed, counting on anonymity in their activities. Thus the river towns developed a reputation for rough crowds that gathered along waterfronts, where financial sharks, gamblers, the homeless, and other wanderers preyed on immigrants and passengers who were without friends or family close at hand. The scene inspired Herman Melville's novel *The Confidence-Man*, in which the characters adopt changing identities as deals are made and broken in the midst of an anonymous crowd on board a Mississippi steamboat.[7]

The railroad, with even greater potential than the steamboat for speed and the transport of large numbers, eventually expanded the reach of the crowd to every part of the nation. Legitimate business-men traveled nationally from community to state to region, investing in corporations and making money without having any investment or interest in the communities at all. With the passage of time, the West-ern crowd became increasingly diversified, including more women, children, and passengers of all social and economic levels. Not just urban dwellers but all Americans gained a familiarity with the char-acteristics of crowds in the railroad stations and the day coach.

In a crowd most passengers had no way of knowing the exact mis-sions of fellow travelers, but they quickly developed a number of skills in identifying types of people by sex, age, and race as well as clothing, luggage, and, above all else, behavior. Many travelers took detailed note of the dress, weight, and idiosyncrasies of their neigh-bors on the train, and held their descriptions up to the public eye, as if to say, "See what I have had to endure?" or "How amusing!" Some went a step further and tried to deduce their neighbors' background or reasons for traveling. Even the open-minded Frederika Bremer, a popular Scandinavian writer of the 1850s, felt no compunctions in de-scribing a fellow passenger in the most devastating language she could conjure: "The amusement of the journey was furnished by a fat, jolly-looking gentleman in my own carriage, a man in a cap and gray coat, in person not unlike a mealsack, upon which the head was set, round and movable as a top. . . ."[8] Presumably she kept her thoughts to herself while in the train.

William Chambers, more restrained than Miss Bremer in his de-scriptions of people and places, nonetheless singled out a traveling companion whom he had observed in great detail, and interposed his own estimates of the man's background, based solely on his appear-ance: "My companion was a man of probably forty years of age, stout made, with sandy hair and whiskers, and, had I seen him in England, I should have said he was a working-mechanic, probably a stone-mason, dressed in his Sunday clothes, and out on a holiday."[9]

Some passengers did not need to do much guesswork before they realized that their traveling companions were worth describing in detail. The historian Eugene Alvarez described the experiences of a number of travelers during their railroad journeys through the South.

> Amelia Murray . . . lamented with good cause that her trip to Virginia would have been more enjoyable had she been with 'pleasanter companions in the car.' Miss Murray noted that in front of her was a man who called himself 'the American Dwarf.' . . . This being was 'about two feet high, with fin-like hands, and a head nearly as large as his contorted body.' Sitting to her right in the car was a Negro woman attired in a 'fancy straw bonnet, trimmed with white' and 'artificial roses.' Unfortunately, the stale interior of the car caused the Negro to become ill, and soon she was leaning across Miss Murray in order to use the window. In Charles Lanman's car the only passenger 'worthy of note' was a blind missionary. However, Lanman talked with an eccentric traveling to Savannah whose only possessions were a violin, a gold watch, a huge cane and cloak.[10]

While the railroads sometimes provided separate accommodations for women and blacks, no service attempted to sort out traveling companions with compatible manners and acceptable appearances.

Probably the most universal observation about the crowd in the station and the day coach concerned the bad manners of other passengers. In the crowd, a passenger's most intimate habits might become a matter for public attention. For example, when Charles Dickens observed during his American tour that in the day coach "everybody smokes," and in the ladies' car "nobody does," he raised an issue on which there was substantial disagreement among passengers. Smokers were confined to the day coach so as not to impose on women and children, but smoking nonetheless irritated others in the crowd who, though strangers, felt they had a right to prevent fellow passengers from smoking in the train or station. This question became a matter of public debate in the press, but the railroads never took a unified stand against smoking, and passengers continued to complain about the bad air in the cars.

Although Dickens reported that women who traveled by themselves were well treated, the status of women as passengers became an issue for public debate. As early as 1835, Samuel Beck, a traveler on the Boston and Providence Railroad, had strong words about women who could be comfortable with the manners of railroad crowds. Far from being the fault of the people around her, he suggested, it was her own fault for exposing herself to the crowd.

> . . . Talk of ladies on board a steam boat or in a railroad car. There are none! I never feel like a gentleman there, and I cannot perceive a semblance of gentility in any one who makes part of the traveling mob. When I see women whom, in their drawing rooms or elsewhere, I have been accustomed to respect and treat with every suitable deference—when I see them, I say, elbowing their way through a crowd of dirty emigrants or lowbred homespun fellows in petticoats or breeches in our country, in order to reach a table set for a hundred or more, I lose sight of their pretensions to gentility and view them as belonging to the plebeian herd. To restore herself to her caste, let a lady move in select company at 5 miles an hour, and take her meals in comfort at a good inn, where she may dine decently. . . .[11]

Comments of this kind evidently depended as much on the social level and geographical origins of the onlooker as on the behavior observed. Many travelers, particularly those of rural or frontier origins, would not use the words "gentleman" or "lady" to describe their station in life. Without parlors or dining rooms at home, they would not suggest that behavior befitting a private parlor be the standard in a railroad dining room. Comments of this kind likely found more sympathetic readers in the Northeast and in urban areas than in the farming communities of the West.

This interpretation is borne out by the observations of a foreign traveler who saw different types of people and different standards of behavior in the travel crowds of the West. Frederika Bremer was quick to learn about the notorious crowds along the Mississippi riverfront when she visited the West in 1850, traveling on both trains and steamboats. She noted how many of the crowd were outcasts.

> There are Indians; there are squatters; there are Scandinavians, with gentle manners and cheerful songs; there are Mormons, Christian in manners, but fanatics in their faith in one man . . . ; there are desperate adventurers, with neither faith nor law, excepting in Mammon and

club-law; gamblers, murderers, and thieves, who are without con-
science, and their number and their exploits increase along the banks
of the Mississippi the further we advance south.[12]

Here could be found many of the "plebeian herd" and the "lowbred
homespun fellows" that Easterner Samuel Breck decried. But Bremer's attitude was that of an excited onlooker at a new society, rather
than one who applied the older standards of ladies and gentlemen to
a new social reality.

Descriptions of Western crowds in the 1850s beg the question,
What about crowds in the South? The South had fewer crowds because it had fewer urban areas than either the Northeast or the West.
And because the trains served local rather than long-distance passengers, railroads brought fewer outsiders into the South. Still, a dispro-
portionate number of outsiders wrote about their trips to the South,
primarily to witness and comment on the Southern institution of slavery, which became a focus of national and international attention
after about 1820. Not surprisingly, the crowds of Charleston, Atlanta,
and other Southern towns reflected the predominance of the slave
population. Rather than crowds of "desperate adventurers" and other
outcasts, the visitor to the South saw crowds of black laborers and loi-
terers, carrying luggage and other valuables, working in and around
the railroad station, selling food and other goods to passengers, and
carrying out the duties of a laboring class. Frederika Bremer, one of
the later visitors to the South during her tour of 1850, wrote that in
Charleston, "Negroes swarm in the streets. Two-thirds of the people
whom one sees in town are negroes or mulattoes." Of Richmond, Virginia, traveler William Chambers wrote, "Everywhere, the number of
black faces is considerable; for in a population of 27,000, as many as
9000 are said to be slaves."[13]

Crowds differed by neighborhood, city, and region, yet all crowds
were promiscuous to some extent, in that nationalities, races, sexes,
and economic levels were mixed with few immediate controls on
their behavior. This caused concern and complaint among those accustomed to a more ordered life, such as those from the Northeast
who had pretensions to gentility. But the promiscuity had little impact on the behavior or opinions of rural, poor, and outcast travelers

who comprised a good portion of the crowds typical to the West and South. To some degree, complaints about the behavior of fellow passengers drew on the biases of class, region, sex, and race peculiar to each area of the country.

Compared with the behavior of travelers in the United States today, or even at the turn of the century, railroad passengers before the Civil War were unself-conscious, spontaneous, and even raucous. Initially railroads enforced few company rules to guide passenger behavior. Travelers routinely extended their heads and limbs out the windows in good weather, until casualties were sufficient to induce the railroad to prohibit such behavior. In 1852 the *American Railroad Journal* suggested that the safest position for any railroad traveler was entirely within the confines of the car.[14]

Frederika Bremer, usually a detached observer, condemned the casual and destructive behavior of passengers on her train trip through the state of New York. Like those railroad men who took wood and water for the locomotive from the side of the track, without regard for ownership, Miss Bremer's offenders stole fruit.

> The train had stopped just beside a large and beautiful orchard, which was separated from the railroad by a rather low wooden fence. I had just called Maria Lowell's attention to the really paradisiac beauty and perfection of some young appletrees . . . when, to my astonishment— and I must confess my grief also—I saw a number of young men, passengers of the train . . . well dressed and well looking in all respects, leap over the fence into the orchard, and in the most merciless manner fall upon and despoil those beautiful young trees . . . their branches broken. . . .[15]

The conductor had a measure of authority over passengers as long as they were on the train, and during the 1850s some railroads began requiring the conductors to wear badges or uniforms to emphasize that authority. In some instances the conductor had to maintain order by force. Drunkards, the scourge of the nineteenth-century family and the target of many temperance compaigns, could make life difficult for both conductor and passengers. Charles Lyell, the geologist, witnessed an encounter involving a drunken man who put his feet up on a seat and began singing loudly. Complaints by fellow passengers ended only when the conductor, fortified by the exhortations of other passengers, stopped the train and put the man off.[16]

Conductors also had to deal with passengers who refused to pay their fare. The conductor had no recourse but to forcibly remove the offending passenger from the train. During a trip through the South in the late 1850s, a rail passenger named George Pierce witnessed a fight between the train conductor and a passenger who would not pay his way. He described the incident in his travel diary: "The passenger having made it obvious that he would ignore the conductor's orders, the train was stopped and the scuffle began." Only with the help of several fellow passengers was the conductor able to remove his burly opponent from the train.[17] In this context, state statutes of the 1850s, giving conductors the right to carry guns, made sense.

Other questionable behavior, such as spitting tobacco juice in the aisles, cornering fellow passengers with endless talk, or making sexual overtures toward unaccompanied young women, was left to the condemnation of public disapproval rather than to any set of rules. While the railroads provided separate cars for women, stories about the promiscuous mixing of the sexes on the train became part of popular culture well before the Civil War. Popular songs told the tale of young girls led astray by the wrong sort of men, whom they had met "Ridin' in a Rail Road Keer."

> Suke Sattinet was a comely gal,
> And loved her parents dear,
> Till she met Slim Jim, the miller's son,
> A ridin' in a rail road keer.[18]

Men had cause for worry too, according to a popular song of the 1860s. In a twist on the story of the traveling salesmen, the salesman loses his heart to a woman who works for the railroad:

> I traveled for a firm in Woonsocket,
> In the cotton and woollen trade,
> And never had cause for a moment's woe
> Till meeting a fair young maid
> Who served in a first class restaurant
> On the Chicago and Alton line,

Refreshment room I ought to say,
But that mistake is mine.[19]

Henry Clay Work, one of the best-known songwriters of the 1860s ("The Grandfather's Clock" and "As We Were Marching Through Georgia" were two of his compositions), also wrote the song that appears at the beginning of this chapter, "The Buckskin Bag of Gold." The young girl, carried away with love by the appearance of a handsome man whom she does not know, tries to trace him in order to make his acquaintance, only to find out he is the man who has just robbed her father's bank!

Cultural diversity accounted for the great mix of values and behavior in the train car. The leveling of social barriers, heralded by the advocates of the common man, also caused tremendous anxiety and confusion, and fear for those accustomed to any measure of protection or privacy. Crowds were dangerous and unpredictable. The "King Mob" that elected Andrew Jackson president in 1827 repelled John Quincy Adams, representative of one of the oldest families in New England. The same division of opinions about the "mob" prevailed in the train car.

Some blamed the crowds and their attendant dangers on people who were simply too rustic and lowborn to learn manners—an objection based on class bias. Others, in the new nativist tradition of the time, blamed immigrants who would surely ruin the quality of life for all Americans. But the drive for national prosperity had more influence on train service than the objectionable habits of strangers. These strangers, after all, included frontier farmers and immigrants who created farms and built institutions both in cities and in the countryside. Those who measured the economic advantages of allowing immigrants into the country approved the presence of these "strangers in the land." The annual report of the Ohio State Board of Agriculture for 1857 laid particular emphasis on the benefit of "strangers and sojourners" as a factor in the economic growth of Cincinnati.

> We cannot estimate too highly the wealth and benefits which a city receives from the influx of strangers and sojourners. We are too much accustomed to regard mere trade and produce as the only elements of a city's prosperity. They are, of course, essential; but after all, as our

most valuable import consists in the energy and industry—and even of the mere material wealth—of the great crowd of hardy immigrants which pour into our country from the Old World, so, too, a city may find its highest policy in entertaining multitudes of visitors and strangers intent on business or pleasure.[20]

The Ohio report also recognized that many of the tourists, vacationers, and others who used the train for leisure rather than for business purposes nonetheless brought economic benefit to Cincinnati and all American cities. Caring for these crowds of strangers demanded attention.

Let a calculation be made of the sums expended and goods purchased by the ten thousand persons per day, that have rushed to our city during the past week; and it will be found to overtop the product of several of our most valuable trades. Hence, the duty and importance of increasing these attractions and giving most liberal encouragement to even the amusements, and much more to the arts, which delight and gratify the public taste and imagination. There can be no better investment of the funds of the corporation than in judicious expenditures on even the amusements of the people. Not only as an attraction for strangers, but as the means of drawing the minds of our people from ignoble and vicious gratifications, and supplying them with elevating and expanding recreation, should this policy be adopted and liberally pursued.[21]

Union Through Competition

On a chilly night, November 29, 1852, the first railroad train from the East reached Pittsburgh. It had started from Philadelphia the night before and spent most of the intervening day crossing the heavy mountain grades of the Alleghenies, the route being by the Portage Railroad connecting Hollidaysburg and Johnstown. Although the trip was not made over a through line, inclined planes being used to cross the mountains, this "long distance triumph of the iron horse" was recognized as a marvelous feat. All those interested, even the tired and hungry passengers who rode in boxlike cars without dining and other accommodations, recognized that a new epoch in inland transportation was at hand. Already they were talking about the probable exit of the steamboat, and fears of national disintegration were vanishing, the West having at last been bound to the East by a tie that was thought to be permanent and effective.
—Charles Ambler, *A History of Transportation in the Ohio Valley,* 1932[1]

THE CONFLICTING PERSONAL VALUES that emerged in travel crowds during the 1840s and 1850s had their counterpart in the nation at large. It was rapidly becoming evident that putting people together in new situations did not necessarily unify them. Conflicts of interest made crowds disorderly and dangerous. In the quest for a Union connected by railroads, public conflicts of interest emerged too, each threatening disunity. Railroads competed among themselves, sometimes viciously, to control the most track. The major economic regions of the country, North, Midwest, and South, found themselves at odds over the terms by which the three sections would unify. States and cities vied to reap the greatest economic benefit of rail transport. Farmers vied with railroad corporations to keep them from ruining farm properties. Steamboat companies tangled with railroads about the navigational hazards of railroad bridges across rivers. And townspeople vied with railroads to maintain local control as travel schedules, track gauges, and the type of service provided by each railroad started on a long road toward national standardization. The process of national unification through rail proceeded, but on a very stormy course, as corporate and political powers clashed at every level from legal wrangling to the tearing up of track and the taking up of arms against the railroad companies.

The political climate of the 1850s was equally stormy, as a national debate arose over the disposition of new Western lands. Immediately after the Mexican War, immigrants began to flood the West, arriving by wagon train and by ships sailing around South America to California. Gold, discovered in California in 1848, accelerated this migration and led to a general demand for better transportation in the West. But while the population moved rapidly west, the Congress of the United States was deadlocked over the issue of extending slavery into the West. Despite the Compromise of 1850, which provided a superficial solution by which the slavery issue would be decided state by state, the federal government's attempts to organize the West politically into territories, and unite the region with the rest of the country through a transportation system, remained stalled.

The deadlock over slavery stymied the expansion of railroads into the West. The South, under the leadership of Congressman Jefferson Davis, wanted a Southern railroad route; the North called for a railroad to connect with Chicago. The Mexican War itself, some Northern parties charged, was fought to provide the land needed for a

Southern railroad route. But Northern interests, led by Stephen Douglas and Abraham Lincoln, both of Illinois, would not relent. When the Union, despite its proliferation of railroads, steamboats, and canals, began to crack—it was precisely between the two regions least connected by railroads or any other form of transport, the North and South.

Undaunted by these tremors, indeed almost impelled by them, the railroads of the Northeast proceeded to triple their mileage of track in the 1850s, chiefly in the Northeast itself. Miles of track in the United States jumped from 9,021 in 1850 to 30,626 ten years later.[2] No longer content to connect bodies of navigable water, the railroads also fell into competition with river and canal traffic. During the 1850s laborers laid the track of the Hudson River Railroad parallel to the river from New York City to Albany, thus competing with the river that connected the Atlantic Ocean to the Erie Canal. The railroad route to Pittsburgh which opened in 1852 served passengers and shippers who had used a mix of rail, canal, and river routes. Canal digging, which had declined to about 375 new miles during the decade of the 1840s, all but stopped by the 1850s. While steamboats continued to ply the waters, their relative importance to travel and trade fell. In the West the Illinois Central Railroad extended rapidly southward from Chicago, parallel to the route of the Mississippi River. In 1857 railroads connected the cities of the East to the Mississippi for the first time, thus competing with water traffic on the Great Lakes and with canals that crisscrossed the upper Midwest.

Of these challenges to water traffic, a railroad connection with the Mississippi River was the most exciting to the states of the North, and most controversial and threatening to the South. The railroads and towns along this new through route to the West organized "the Great Railway Celebrations of 1857" to inaugurate this connection of two sections of the country.[3] That year a large party of notables from state and national government, with railroad owners and their families, were invited to travel west to the Mississippi to celebrate the opening of a through rail route from East to West. A large party of guests boarded the Baltimore and Ohio Railroad in Baltimore on June 1 and traveled westward to the Ohio River. There they transferred to steamboats that carried them west to Marietta, Ohio, where they boarded the Marietta and Cincinnati Railroad. The railroad took the guests to Cincinnati, which had organized a celebration of its own to mark the arrival of this special train. In Cincinnati the party boarded the Ohio and Mississippi Railroad, which brought them safely to St. Louis on June 4—altogether a trip of three days.

Why did Southerners resent this new through route? Ever since the settlement of the Mississippi River Valley, the towns and farms in its northern reaches had sent their products south on the river, for sale in towns from St. Louis to New Orleans, or for shipment to the East Coast. The opening of a more direct route to the East threatened the economy of the river and the Southern states and towns that bordered it. The riverboat pilots and merchants of the South foresaw their own decline if Northern railroad interests continued to expand. Even the town of Cincinnati, which welcomed the new route, quickly declined as a center of commerce because so much of its prosperity had depended on steamboat travel up and down the Ohio and Mississippi rivers.

As railroad through routes proliferated, they challenged not only water transport but the value of local railroads that met the needs of a local economy. Local railroads could not survive independent of the emerging network of long-distance lines. They had to connect if they wished to remain part of the national economy and of the nation itself. While some railroads continued to perform only local duties, others struggled for the connection that would put every town on the route in touch with the world beyond its borders.

The process of connecting thousands of railroads was fraught with practical problems, however; every political boundary that the railroads crossed raised legal questions, and every corporation that sought to connect its lines with another railroad was also, to some extent, in competition with the other line. The unification of the rail system resulted in thousands of legal cases between railroads, between railroads and steamboat lines, and between railroads and the towns or states they served.

Most of the conflicts came as a consequence of railroads expanding in such a way that they encroached on other business or legal interests. The Baltimore and Ohio, for example, faced a number of legal conflicts as it expanded beyond the boundaries of its hometown. The local canal and turnpike companies saw the railroad as a competing business that might violate the provisions of their charters. Only a few years after the opening of the B&O, the Chesapeake and Ohio Canal Company sued it to prevent the B&O from expanding and thus competing with the business interests of the canal. In 1839 the Washington and Baltimore Turnpike Company took the B&O to court for the same reason: competition. In both cases the B&O won.[4]

One of the most famous of such legal contests occurred when the Baltimore and Ohio tried to expand into the city of Pittsburgh and build a station in that city. The B&O's chief opponents in this matter were the directors of the Pennsylvania Railroad, who wanted all business in the state for their own. The Pennsylvania, however, had been so dilatory in its expansion plans that the state legislature decided to encourage competition between the two lines in hopes of pressing the Pennsylvania to build more quickly. The legislature determined that it would grant the B&O a charter to build into Pittsburgh, but only if the Pennsylvania Railroad did not build track into Pittsburgh within a certain time limit. By meeting the legislature's deadline, the Pennsylvania managed to keep the B&O out of Pittsburgh for the time being. Eventually the B&O did enter Pittsburgh, and the Pennsylvania had a station in Baltimore.[5] Other railroads, towns, and states faced similar claims of conflicting interests as railroad companies expanded far beyond their original boundaries. Service to or for hometowns and home states became less and less significant as local boundaries were overridden by competing transport companies.

Even before conflict arose over the B&O's plan to enter Pittsburgh, that railroad had obtained a charter to build within the boundaries of Pennsylvania. It therefore operated under two charters, a situation faced by all railroads that crossed state lines. Many railroads were built to the state line, at which point passengers transferred to another railroad, chartered and built in another state, also terminating at "State Line." The Housatonic Railroad of Connecticut, chartered in 1836, originated in Bridgeport and extended only seventy-four miles to the state line. In the Midwest the Terre Haute and Indianapolis Railroad, constructed during the 1840s, extended from Indianapolis to the state line of Illinois.[6]

Many interstate railroads developed when two or more state-line railroads merged, and, like the B&O, operated under two or more state charters. The Philadelphia and Baltimore Central Railroad, for example, grew from the consolidation of the Baltimore and Philadelphia Railroad, chartered in Maryland in 1852, and the Philadelphia and Baltimore Central, previously chartered only in Pennsylvania. In the Midwest the Cleveland and Pittsburgh Railroad was chartered in Ohio in March 1850, and in Pennsylvania in April of the same year.[7] Railroads operating under more than one charter made it all but impossible for any one state to control railroad operations. A change in state law might affect only part of each railroad, not the entire line. Enforcement of laws pertaining to railroads therefore became increasingly problematic as their ownership extended far beyond the bounds of any one state.

In many cases the conjoining of two railroad lines was not a cooperative effort but the culmination of fierce competition between two short lines, each trying to extend its sway by controlling the other. The history of the Old Colony Railroad, one of eight railroads serving Boston by 1860, is typical of this process that was at work in all sections of the country except the South, where consolidations were not welcome. From its opening in 1844 the Old Colony embarked on a career of empire-building, albeit on a local scale. Originally intended to connect South Boston with Plymouth, Massachusetts, the railroad received permission from the city of Boston in 1845 to bridge the Jones River and enter Boston proper, where the management of the new line arranged to build a passenger station right next door to the already established station of the Boston and Worcester, Nathan Hale's old line.[8] Without actually connecting the two roads, by the location of its station the Old Colony made the transfer of passengers between the two lines as simple as possible.

Also in 1845 the Old Colony received permission to build a branch line from Abington, a stop on its main line, southwest to Bridgewater. In the same year another short-line railroad received state permission to connect its line from Bridgewater to any point on the Old Colony Railroad, and also to connect with the Fall River Railroad, a direct line west from Bridgewater. The Fall River Railroad, in turn, had ambitions to extend northward to Boston, thus competing with the Old Colony Railroad; and the Old Colony had ambitions to extend south and west, thus entering the territory of the Fall River line.[9] They pulled at the intermediate short line connecting them like men pulling at the two ends of a rope.

The next nine years of railroad history in this region proceeded at the breakneck pace of the first two years—branches established, bridges built, rights of way extended, towns connected, depots constructed—until the fortunes of the Fall River Railroad began to flag. Soon it did not have enough money to continue expanding or to compete with the Old Colony, which had continued to prosper. In 1854 the Old Colony agreed to merge with the faltering Fall River line, and the Old Colony & Fall River Railroad came into existence. The Old Colony continued its pattern of expansion and acquisition, so that by 1892 the Old Colony & Fall River line included more than 608 miles of track plus 418 miles of steamboat service.[10]

This kind of commercial expansion took place on the national level as well. By the close of the nineteenth century, the most successful of the national railroad empires dominated the American transportation business.

The first generation of transportation moguls became public figures during the 1850s. Cornelius Vanderbilt, who had become a millionaire from the operation of steamships, began shifting his allegiance to railroads during the 1850s and invested in a number of Eastern lines, including the Erie. This road opened its full length in 1851, connecting the Hudson River with Lake Erie and competing with the many short lines built in the 1830s to parallel the Erie Canal. These lines had consolidated to form the New York Central, making two competing trunk lines to the west in the state of New York.[11]

Daniel Drew, also owner of several steamship companies, emerged as a railroad entrepreneur in the 1850s, working variously as confederate and competitor with Vanderbilt. Both men sought control of New York's two trunk lines, which competed with the Pennsylvania and the B&O for control of the Western trade. One of Drew's tactics demonstrates the way in which cutthroat competition prevented any rational system of travel connections from emerging during the 1850s. Drew manipulated travel connections between his Hudson River Steamboat line and the two trunk line railroads in

order to control the Erie Railroad. In the words of railroad historian
Peter Lyon,

> That unfortunate road could prosper only at Drew's sufferance: when
> he chose, he could link his steamboats at Albany with the New York
> Central so that passengers might travel from New York to Buffalo
> more cheaply and far more comfortably than was possible on the Erie.
> The directors of the Erie sensed their plight, but only dimly.

Vanderbilt proceeded to take control of the New York Central in 1864
in an equally unscrupulous effort.[12]

In addition to arranging passenger schedules and connections to
suit their financial interests, both Drew and Vanderbilt became
known for their high-handed manipulation of city and state governments for their own ends. The process of acquiring the rights to use
stations and routes built under the authority of city and state governments was as complex as every other aspect of railroad law at this
time. Every boundary crossed brought the railroads into a new legal
jurisdiction. What made Vanderbilt and Drew famous was their ability to simplify the process by using financial pressures to force legislatures and city councils into granting them whatever they sought.
When the city council of New York, for example, stood in the way of
his taking control of the New York and Harlem River Railroad, Vanderbilt "rigged three corners on the stock exchange, two of them simultaneously, a feat that called for all the available millions even of
the Commodore [Vanderbilt]. In one corner he squeezed the state
legislatures. . . ."[13] The first men to control the major trunk lines of
the Northeast gained their reputations thusly, by cutting—often ille-
gally—through the endless red tape that accompanied railroad expansion.

Thus the ideal of national political unity was translated practically
into a series of cutthroat schemes by which a small group of nationally known railroad directors virtually declared war on one another to
sweep away competition and control as much track mileage as possible. Only when one of these men controlled his own railroad empire,
or system, did the ideal of providing quick and dependable travel
connections become attractive to him. Even then, connections within
a single railroad system were bound to be more reliable than inter-

line services. The struggle for national unity came to equal a struggle for commercial monopoly among a small coterie of railroad magnates.

These men, and others like them, disdained the rule of government and paid scant attention to the interests of any town or section of the country outside their own. Caring little for the mechanical side of railroading that so fascinated the first generation of railroaders, they sought to maximize their profits by running more and longer trains at higher speeds. These policies took their toll in numerous dramatic and fatal accidents. Drawings and descriptions of these catastrophes filled the pages of newspapers and magazines during the 1850s.

According to one historian, 138 train wrecks occurred in the year 1853 alone. One of the first major disasters of that year took place in Norwalk, Connecticut, on the New Haven Railroad, when the engineer drove onto an open drawbridge, causing the death of forty-six people. On the same day in Secaucus, New Jersey, two trains collided head on, and another forty-six died. One of the biggest wrecks of the decade took place in July 1856 at Camp Hill, Pennsylvania, when sixty-six people lost their lives in a collision on the North Pennsylvania Railroad.[14] The rapid and often indiscriminate means used to extend and consolidate the railroads did not allow technical change to keep pace. Inadequate signaling systems, poor communications, flawed bridges, and poor mechanical maintenance of trains all contributed to the accident rate.

As the manipulations of Vanderbilt and Drew became public knowledge, as railroad service suffered accordingly, and as the accident rate soared, a public outcry arose against the unregulated expansion of railroads. Some critics voiced their disapproval, others resorted to outright resistance. These critics attacked the railroad interests for different reasons, but they shared a belief that the railroads had lost sight of the public interest and must be regulated by government.[15]

At the local level, towns and states resisted railroads that entered their boundaries without regard for local interests. In Indiana, for example, some opposed the expansion of unnecessary passenger services. An editorial writer in that state wrote in 1855:

We renew an idea which we have propounded before, but which has been lost sight of by Railroad managers and by our citizens—namely that an unnecessary number of trains are run on our railroads to accommodate travellers from distant States, and that one train daily would be all the passenger business that is now done on any of the railroads. This extravagance is wrong and ought not to be continued. I have no doubt that to change it would add 8 to 10 percent to the dividends of these railroads. They should arrange their running and time to suit the citizens of Indiana, and not those of Massachusetts or Texas. All trains should arrive in this city between 11 and 12 a.m., and leave from it at 1 or 2 o'clock p.m.[16]

The citizens of Indiana, a state on the through routes from the East Coast to Chicago, also witnessed one of the most famous railroad wars, played out by the Michigan Central Railroad and the Michigan Southern line, over which was to be first to build into Chicago. The Central failed in this battle despite the handling of its case by railroad lawyer Abraham Lincoln. It also lost the support of farmers in its home state, who placed every obstacle in the path of the railroad, including livestock, to wrest settlements from the company. By 1850 the Michigan Central had to hire detectives to break a local conspiracy against the line that included rock throwing and destruction of stations and equipment. In February 1852 the Michigan Southern's first train entered Chicago; the Michigan Central arrived in May, using the tracks of the Illinois Central Railroad. Unfortunately the two sets of tracks crossed south of Chicago, and in April 1853 a major collision at this point, involving a train of each Michigan railroad, took the lives of twenty-one people.[17]

The running of trains on Sunday was an especially sensitive local issue. In the early 1840s the text of most railroad schedules routinely concluded with the phrase, "Daily except Sunday." Over the next two decades the railroad companies gradually abandoned this policy of respecting religious tradition. In Michigan no protest accompanied the arrival of the first train into Kalamazoo on a Sunday in 1847; in fact a church service dissolved when the locomotive whistle was heard, and the church members rushed to the station to witness the event. In Galesburg, Illinois, however, when the first Sunday train pulled into the station in about 1850, the president of local Knox College protested by standing in front of the train to block its passage. He failed. Wrote a chronicler of the event, "The railroad was no longer a neighborhood enterprise, controlled by the little groups of pious men who had founded Galesburg to be a Christian town. . . ."[18]

During the 1860s the supreme court of Pennsylvania heard a case against the running of Sunday trains but decided in favor of them. The presiding judge argued that the poor needed trains to go to church. He cited the existence of church trains run on Sunday specifically for this purpose, and, he added, "Sunday trains are used in Boston, New York, Albany, Troy, and Brooklyn, Hoboken and Jersey City in New Jersey, Baltimore, Nashville, Cincinnati, Washington, St. Louis, and Chicago, and give universal satisfaction."[19] It may be concluded from these examples that the cities led the way in inaugurating Sunday railroad service, and that towns such as Galesburg were behind the times in effecting the transition. Nevertheless Sunday trains did change the nature of the Sabbath, days on which many state and local laws had prohibited travel.

Another kind of local resistance to the railroad occurred when through trains began adjusting track gauges—the measure between the pair of rails—in order to reduce the amount of time spent in transferring passengers and goods from one train to another every time the gauge changed. Locally built lines varied in gauge. As the short lines were consolidated, new owners established uniform gauges within their own railroad systems. For the smaller towns this meant a potential loss of revenue, since trains had previously stopped to let off passengers who would bring their business to local shops, restaurants, and hotels.

In Erie, Pennsylvania, tucked into the northwestern corner of the state between New York and Ohio, New York railroad interests sought to change the gauge of the track through Erie to make their through route to the West faster. The townspeople of Erie objected strenuously because a uniform track gauge would make it possible for the train to breeze through town without stopping. To prevent this calamity, which would diminish Erie's commercial importance, the Pennsylvanians proceeded to rip up the new track each time the New Yorkers laid it down.[20]

Steamboat interests, as we have seen, also rallied against the railroads, for their economic interests were clearly threatened by railroad competition. Particularly galling to steamboats were the railroad bridges built over navigable waterways. Boat pilots claimed the bridges substantially impeded navigation and therefore violated the steamboats' rights under state charters. In most instances, however, the steamboat companies fought a losing battle.

In 1849, for example, the Northern Railroad received permission from the New York state legislature to bridge Lake Champlain, at Rouse's Point, quite close to the Canadian border. Shipping interests opposed the bridge, claiming it not only would obstruct navigation but would benefit Boston's trade with the West over that of New York City, which had interests in shipping on Lake Champlain. Furthermore, argued opponents of the bridge, permission to build the bridge was a federal matter, because the bridge spanned the border between two states, Vermont and New York. Therefore, they reasoned, it should be regulated under the interstate commerce clause of the Constitution, not by the legislatures of Vermont and New York. By this reasoning, the argument continued, the New York legislature did not even have power to charter the railroad as it had four years earlier, because, like the proposed bridge, it passed between two states.[21] Despite these quite substantial arguments, the bridge was built, and the role of the federal government in regulating interstate railroad commerce remained undefined.

The most famous railroad bridge case of this type concerned the Rock Island Railroad bridge built across the Mississippi River in the 1850s. Steamboat interests raised a hew and cry. When the steamboat *Effie Afton* ran into the bridge on May 6, 1856—some said deliberately—and caused both the ship and the bridge to burn, the steamboat company sued the railroad for damages. The plaintiffs claimed that the bridge blocked navigation. Abraham Lincoln, arguing on behalf of the railroad, pointed out how farcical it would be to force all commerce with the West to stop at the Mississippi River, be loaded into boats, and then be reloaded into trains on the other side.[22] In fact, many railroads had been doing just that for twenty-five years, until they had the money and technology to bridge the rivers that crossed their routes. Southern states even intended to continue this practice at state lines. Bridges, like other links connecting rail lines, did not come easily, and often took litigants to court.

By the 1850s, the unification of the country by means of a railroad network had devolved into something close to a free-for-all. Local conflicts over railroad routes, predominant in the 1830s and 1840s, now hatched into major national political conflicts. The uprooting and transplanting of individuals and families spawned crowds in which contact with strangers was considered distasteful or even dangerous. And the railroads themselves fought over control of the national track system just beginning to connect the sections.

In crisscrossing the boundaries that defined legal jurisdictions, railroads defied simple legal control. But they also defied the systems of social and political organization that had traditionally separated society's conflicting groups into different geographical areas. In a mobile society, all those groups distinguished by nationality, race, wealth, sex, and even religious differences, and which had traditionally lived apart from one another, came together. From the personal to the social and political levels, and from the local to the national level, the movement promoted conflict.

The impetus for construction of railroads nevertheless prevailed. And with them, the other clear victors were the major cities: New York, Boston, Philadelphia, and Baltimore. The bases of wealth in these cities were similar to those of the railroads: they courted large crowds to buy and sell, they pooled large sums of money, and they benefited most from extending the railroads, which brought both increased numbers of people and increased trade. Despite aspirations to be as wealthy as these major cities, smaller towns, such as Troy, New York; Springfield and Northampton, Massachusetts; and Hartford and New Haven, Connecticut, were among the many locales that began to measure their fortunes in terms of contact with one or more of these major urban centers. Trade and money began to concentrate in the cities—in banks, in the stock exchange, in manufactures, and in capital available for investment. Consequently the largest cities also enjoyed the most extensive rail service. Boston boasted eight major railroads radiating outward from the city hub. New York City proved a center for transport to Connecticut, New Jersey, and Pennsylvania, in addition to railroad lines within the state. Even in

Chicago, a city in the midst of relative wilderness, ten railroad lines operated in and out of the city.[23]

The idea of social and commercial exchange that dominated the major cities and the major railroads also came to characterize the immense conflict that the construction of railroads had created. Two areas, however, remained off limits to this philosophy. One was the South, which refused to connect its local railroads into even a regional system, let alone a national system; the other was the trans-Mississippi West, where no railroad could penetrate until North and South settled the sectional dispute over slavery.

10

||||||||||||||||||||||||

The State of the Union

Hitherto, the two systems [slave and free labor] have existed in different States, but side by side within the American Union. This has happened because the Union is a confederation of States. But in another aspect the United States constitute only one nation. Increase of population, which is filling the States out to their very borders, together with a new and extended network of railroads and other avenues, and an internal commerce which daily becomes more intimate, is rapidly bringing the States into a higher and more perfect social unity or consolidation. Thus, these antagonistic systems are continually coming into closer contact, and collision results.

Shall I tell you what this collision means? They who think that it is acci-dental, unnecessary, the work of interested or fanatical agitators, and there-fore ephemeral, mistake the case altogether. It is an irrepressible conflict between opposing and enduring forces, and it means that the United States, must and will, sooner or later, become either a slave-holding nation, or entirely a free-labor nation. . . . The one or the other system must exclu-sively prevail.
   —Senator William Henry Seward, "The Irrepressible Conflict," 1858[1]

O NCE THE RAILROADS embarked on the effort to connect all points of the compass by track, the position of the Southern states as proponents of local trade and travel, under state control, became increasingly difficult to sustain. The Northeastern states, connected from Maine to the Mississippi River and south to Washington, D.C., and the Ohio River, yearned to continue their program of expansion into the West and South, to settle the land, and to exploit the natural resources in these rural areas. But expansionist interests in the North were hemmed in by slave interests in the South, who would not tie their railroads into the emerging railroad "system." They did not want the individual states to lose control over the railroads, and they particularly did not wish to forfeit local control to the railroad empire-builders of the Northeast.[2] Furthermore, the South continued to stanch the flow of railroad companies seeking to bridge the Mississippi and extend the tide of Northern-controlled commerce into the West. River and steamboat interests in the South claimed repeatedly that bridges over the Mississippi River would impede navigation. Many Southerners wanted to see the West developed into plantation land—large estate farms that employed slave labor.

Despite the deadlock on this issue, expansion proceeded into lands west of the Mississippi, largely without benefit of the railroads. Settlements in Iowa, Nebraska, and Kansas were followed by the development of towns such as Council Bluffs, Iowa; Omaha, Nebraska; and Independence, Missouri, into jumping-off points for immigrants bound westward. They went on foot, on horseback, and by wagon train, tracing their route on the Oregon Trail, the California Trail, and the Santa Fe Trail, three of the most traveled routes connecting the Mississippi River Valley with the far West. The migrants who followed these routes were not Southern plantation owners or Northern merchants; for the most part they came from the ranks of the poor or were farmers seeking to create family farms in the West.

Following settlers west were those who sought to make a profit by supplying basic services. Stagecoach companies, for example, were created to transport mail, passengers, and goods, because the sec-

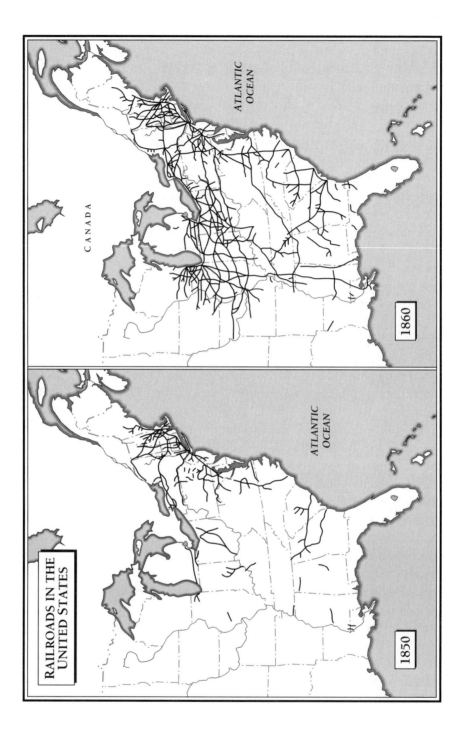

RAILROADS IN THE UNITED STATES

1850

1860

ATLANTIC OCEAN

CANADA

tional conflict between North and South effectively prevented rail-roads from doing so. One transportation historian has described this substitution of stages for railroads.

> . . . The stagecoach business came to the trans-Mississippi West at a time when portions of the eastern United States were undergoing a rapid transition from horse to steam power. In view of the fact that steamboats could not serve all settled parts of the West, and due also to the slowness with which the railroads penetrated the region west of the Missouri River, stagecoach enterprises emerged that were both local and transregional in character. Isolated western communities re-quired—in fact demanded—that some means be provided not only for carrying passengers locally, but for transporting people, mails, and express by horse-drawn coaches between eastern railroad and steam-boat connections and west coast cities.[3]

Previously the mails had been carried to the West Coast by sea, around South America to California. But Congress and the United States Post Office heeded the call for a more direct service and in 1857 awarded a mail contract to a stagecoach service that traveled twice a month from San Antonio, Texas, to San Diego, California. As agreement on the route of a transcontinental railroad continued to elude Congress, it further established what became known as the Butterfield Overland Mail, a stagecoach service that took both mail and passengers on a more regular basis.[4]

The Western stages did not provide sufficient profits to keep them solvent, however, and, with other private stagecoach companies com-peting, the Butterfield stage failed to thrive. Northerners were out-raged that part of the Butterfield stage route lay in the recently acquired lands of the Southwest rather than farther north. In 1860, therefore, the Pony Express began operations, employing men to ride relay, with their ponies at top speed, carrying mail pouches between St. Joseph, Missouri, and Sacramento, California. The Pony Express also failed to thrive financially and went out of business shortly after Kansas City and San Francisco were connected by telegraph lines in October 1861. Subsequently, many private stagecoach companies, in-cluding the well-remembered Wells Fargo Company, provided the only public land transport for passengers and goods in the far West.[5]

The settlers, the mail, express, and passenger services, and even the telegraph, which had first come into use in Eastern states in 1847, all went west, but without the railroad. This fact accounts for many of the characteristics associated with Western life even after the Civil War, such as its low population, isolation, lack of public services, relative lawlessness, and the slowness with which Western states entered the Union. After the end of the war in 1865, only two new states, Nebraska and Colorado, entered the Union before 1889.

In the absence of trains, wagon trains became a popular alternative means of reaching the Western territories. Compared both to trains and to ships, the Conestoga wagons, or prairie schooners, moved westward in slow progression, following trails marked by Indians and early explorers. For the most part their routes ran along the course of rivers, such as the Missouri and the Platte, which also served as sources of water. But the earliest pioneers also produced maps and travel guides that estimated the mileage between watering holes, judged the terrain as to safety and ease of passage, and recommended the supplies that wagon trains would need in order to survive the trek across dry open land and Indian territory.

Even the most ambitious tourists and observers of the 1840s and 1850s did not venture much farther west than the Mississippi River Valley, where most railroad and steamship services terminated. Albert Koch, for example, a paleontologist from Germany, traveled west to the Mississippi River during the years 1844–1846, in an extremely successful search for dinosaur bones and other fossils. But even near the Mississippi his tour involved many risks—relying on the kindness of strangers when stranded or lost, waiting long times for steamboat and rail connections, walking distances by himself, and being prevented from traveling by high or low water or mechanical hazards. The West lured Frederika Bremer as far as Minneapolis in 1850, and down the Mississippi by steamboat. She chose tried and true routes, however, rather than exploring, and always traveled with a crowd. In so doing she had fewer adventures in the frontier wilderness. In 1853 William Chambers, the Scotsman who wrote one of the many traveler's guides for emigrants, went north to Canada and westward only as far as Toronto.[6] Like earlier travelers, he took railroads as far as they extended, then transferred to steamboats.

East of the Mississippi, travelers enjoyed fewer services for travelers the farther west they ventured. Railroad connections became less dependable, and food, washing, and sleeping accommodations became more difficult to find. Although services improved somewhat over time, rural areas and the West offered the least reliable circumstances of travel.

Amelia Barr, a traveler who migrated from Illinois to Texas with her children in 1854, found that through travel and the need to transfer from one conveyance to another in the Mississippi River Valley region could be extremely uncomfortable.[7] Her lot was made doubly difficult because she traveled with children, for whom no special provisions existed. Nor did passengers find hotels and restaurants for sleep and food. Against the social mores of discreet Easterners, she had to rely on the kindnesses of a fellow traveler. Referring to this journey in her memoirs, she wrote:

> Travel was travail then. There were no Pullman cars, and few conveniences, and even something to eat was not always to be counted on for long distances. But I was young and full of life and spirit, and everybody was eager to help me. The first night I got the porter to bring me pillows and I laid my children on the sofa at the end of the car, and then sat down opposite to watch them. I could hardly keep my eyes open; indeed I think I was dropping alseep, when a kindly-looking man said, 'Let me watch your children. I am used to waking all night, and sleeping all day. I will take good care of them.'
>
> So I left them in his care, and slept as soundly as the children did. All the way to Cairo [Illinois] he looked after food, and fresh food, and fresh milk, and anything needed for our comfort. I do not remember how long we were in reaching Cairo. I think two days and three nights, but it might be nearly three days, for it was dark when we came to the place. At that time it was not much of a place. . . .
>
> There were plenty of negroes loafing about the little station, and he called a big black man and said, 'Uncle, give this lady your arm, and be sure to keep her on her feet.' Another negro was called to carry the trunk. Then I asked anxiously, 'The children?' 'I will take care of the children,' he said; 'now follow me.'
>
> It was the hardest feat I ever performed. The road was down a steep

hill, ankle deep in liquid mud of the stickiest description. The steamer
[Cairo is at the confluence of the Ohio and Mississippi rivers] lay at
the foot of the hill. . . . The screams of men and women fast in the
mud, and the escaping steam and ominous ringing of a bell, were but
items in the hellish confusion.[8]

In rural areas, numerous connections between boat, stage, and railroad continued to be a common need as late as the turn of the century.[9] As long as the West remained rural, with a low population, this
experience characterized the Western way of life.

The South, also largely rural, was nevertheless more accessible to
travelers than the far West. In the 1840s and 1850s, travelers made
their way into the deep South by railroad, stagecoach, and steamboat.
For the most part they saw the South from the vantage point of their
vehicles of transport and of the few cities then existing in the region.
With the exception of Albert Koch, who busied himself with fossils,
all these travelers made a point of commenting on slavery, which had
become an international issue partly because the American South was
one of the very few places left in the world where slavery was still
legal.

Whatever Southerners themselves might have believed about slavery, on the national and international stages they were portrayed in a
poor light and expected to conform with current standards of morality. The slave system in many respects depended on the relative inability of the slaves to travel; the agricultural society in which they
labored moved cotton products from place to place, but not people,
who were needed to work the land. In this context it was barely possible to justify the states' rights doctrine, since the people who lived
in each Southern state tended to stay in that state. But the mobility
made possible by railroad travel brought to the South strangers who
could see for themselves the degraded conditions of slave life. It also
made possible the travel of the slave Dred Scott and his master, which
resulted in the most famous Supreme Court decision of the 1850s on
the problem raised by travelers passing from one state jurisdiction to
another.

Travelers to the South also noted its rural poverty. Between the station at Richmond, where omnibuses met passengers and travelers

could find hotels with dining rooms, and Charleston, the landscape grew monotonous, with sandy soil, brush, and little development of any kind. Some train stations were not in town at all but were situated in isolated and empty rural landscape. There were generally fewer passengers than on the Northern trains, and the more complicated connections caused delays and inconveniences.[10]

Many travelers remarked on the poor quality of Southern railroads and their services for passengers. Mary Livermore, writing of a trip south during the 1840s, bluntly declared that

> There was no system of travel south of Philadelphia. Railway tickets were bought from point to point, and it was necessary to recheck baggage with every change of ticket. On some of the roads no baggage checks were in use, and where this was the case an employe [sic] would thrust his head inside of the car and bawl at the top of his voice, 'Passengers will please come out to the baggage car and identify their trunks!' or, further South, 'Come out to the baggage kyar and 'tend to yer plunder!' This would occasion a rush, a confused squabble, a good deal of profanity, and, one by one, the passengers returned to their seats with an air of exhaustion.[11]

Other travelers welcomed the friendly attitude and hospitality of Southerners. In some respects these perspectives complement each other. Southerners did not wish to bring crowds of strangers into their world, and therefore did not cater to them, but they still abided by the old rural ideal that required individual homeowners to make room for individual strangers passing through. In the South and the West, the hospitality of individuals and families sufficed until hotels and eating establishments were developed to serve the needs of crowds.[12]

While the diaries of travelers underscore regional differences in the antebellum United States, travel guides were compiled to help travelers anticipate and adapt to the changing circumstances of their journeys no matter where in the country they found themselves. Appearing in the 1840s and thereafter, a number of these guides attempted to put as many as possible of the country's transportation schedules together under one cover. One of the earliest of these, *Doggett's Guide,* first became available in 1847. In 1850 the

Pathfinder Railway Guide was first published, providing schedules, distances, fares, and maps for all rail services in New England. The *American Railway Guide* also appeared in 1850.[13] For these schedules to be helpful, the traveler had to know the local time by which departures and arrivals were determined. Therefore the guide also specified which local time was used. While this improved the convenience of rail travel for many, it still remained for the traveler to ascertain the local time, which could usually be done only after he arrived in each different locale.

Such aids toward a unified country and a uniform travel system were essentially weak and useless in the winds of sectional conflict. The differences that drew travelers to the South and West were the very differences at issue politically. The South had refused to adapt to Northern systems in many ways. And it stalled development of the West in order to strengthen its refusal. Northerners tended to abide by William Seward's dictum, quoted at the beginning of this chapter, that the entire country had to have the same economic system. Local and regional differences could not be allowed to stand in the way of national unity based on commerce.

Where Is This Train Going?

RAILROAD BUILDERS saw the almost limitless potential of railroads as a means of advancing trade throughout the country. While the *+ in effect - creating a nature economy.* earliest goal was to connect Eastern towns with the frontier for trading purposes, others outside the trade in goods also began to see a potential for profit. Investors were drawn to railroad construction not only on behalf of their towns but as individuals who might purchase shares of railroad stock and realize a personal financial profit in the long run. The railroad might be anywhere, but the return came back to the individual investor regardless of location. And governments at all levels shared an enthusiasm for connecting towns to larger markets. Town governments anticipated larger markets, state governments anticipated a larger share of the Western trade, and the federal government endorsed railbuilding as a means of uniting the South and West with the more populous and settled Northeast.

Experiences of the earliest passengers seemed to reinforce the promise of the railroads. Speculators and businessmen saw the potential for investment all along the routes of the railroads: in land, in mines, in services for travelers, and in the future development of underpopulated sections of the country. The poor saw the possibilities of a new beginning further west, perhaps with land of their own for a new farm. Others who felt as downtrodden as the poor also traveled to begin life again, out from under the oppressive social and economic hierarchies of the East which favored only the few. The slave saw the potential for freedom, and women sought a

place in the public world where they could see and experience life
beyond their doorsteps. And German and Irish immigrants glimpsed
a new beginning in farms, in burgeoning factories which sold goods
in an expanding marketplace, and in jobs working on the railroad
and other internal improvements.

The massive migrations encouraged by the construction of
railroads did in fact lift many of the economic, social, and legal
restraints that people and institutions faced. But in the process,
many of the structures that defined American society and its social
relationships were severely weakened. By overwhelming traditional
geographic and legal boundaries, the railroad reduced the power of
local institutions—such as churches, families, and local
governments—to control and protect their own. Instead, towns
faced an increasingly mobile population of citizens departing and
strangers arriving. Because the railroads crossed traditional
jurisdictions, the law was only partially effective for railroad
passengers. And in the taking of private lands, and in the
construction of tracks down the middle of major town roads, the
railroads created a new legal and social crisis which towns were
almost powerless to resolve. After all, permission to build had come
from the state legislatures, not the towns. Legal suits involving
railroads, towns, and harassed individuals became a common part of
the legal landscape.

This defiance of boundaries and the weakening of traditional
legal, social, and economic structures had another effect, probably as
unintentional as the weakening of town authority. People uprooted
by railroad travel did not reestablish themselves in traditional
communities like those they had left behind. They mixed in greater
numbers over broader regions. The railroad was a key factor in
creating the crowds that were one of the earliest signs of an
emerging mass society. Passengers of many racial groups, both sexes,
all ages, and all economic levels, and from all regions of the country,
came into contact with one another in trains and stations. While
some looked favorably upon this development as an aspect of
emergent democracy, others sought refuge from these "mobs" and
thought they represented a breakdown in social order. In either
event, friends, family, and business associates had to make room for

the stranger: the wayfarer whose origins, political opinions, economic level, and religious beliefs were unknown.

By the 1850s enough railroad track had been laid so that Americans could see the potential of a railroad network or system which would indeed connect and unite all sections of the country. But that lay in the future. Close contact between the newly connected North, South, and Midwest had raised a titanic regional struggle. The Southern states could not accept a system of unity imposed by corporate interests that exceeded state power and was located chiefly in Northern states and fueled by Northern money. The resistance of the South to this formula for unity moved the country as a whole toward Civil War.

PART TWO

"The Old Standards Are Destroyed"

FROM LOCAL CONTROL TO NATIONAL PURPOSE, 1861–1890

This Currier and Ives lithograph of 1868 dramatized the anticipated opening of the Western frontier through the completion of the first transcontinental railroad, which opened the following year. The abrupt end of the settlement in the foreground, and the extension of tracks through empty landscape, underscore how crucial the railroads were to the development of the West. (MUSEUM OF THE CITY OF NEW YORK)

11

||||||||||||||||

The South Leaves
But Returns

Ho! the Car Emancipation Rides majestic thro' our nation,
Bearing on its Train, the Story, Liberty! a Nation's Glory.
Roll it along, Roll it along, Roll it along, thro' the Nation Freedom's Car,
    Emancipation.
                                    —*Long Steel Rail*, 1844 Abolitionist Song[1]

THE FAILURE of the Union that followed the election of Abraham
Lincoln in 1860 split the two sections of the nation with no rail connections to each other. This split pitted the Northern states, bound by
through rail routes from the Atlantic to the Mississippi, against the
Southern states, which had only local railroads, having rejected
through routes as a threat to state control over rail travel. In the war
that followed, many issues the nation had already confronted on a
small scale were restated in more extreme form. From the transportation of large groups and their care and feeding away from home,

to the uprooting of stable populations and the creation of wanderers who had no home after the war, the function of the railroads in wartime resembled their role in peace. In place of civilian populations on the move came armies on the march. And armies, like the railroads, operated outside the bounds of law. Other than obeying orders from commanders, soldiers on the move had no obligations toward the people and property in their path.

At the outset of the war both North and South had to draw together local populations spread out over a large area without being able to call on a strong central government bureaucracy. In the North, Lincoln and his cabinet took the extraordinary measure of calling for volunteers to rendezvous in Washington. The president also took control of Northern railroads while leaving their operation largely in private hands. In the South, President Jefferson Davis faced the states' rights issue among his own ranks, so that mustering troops outside their state of origin proved difficult. Taking control of the railroads proved even more troublesome, since the tracks were not connected across state boundaries. While Robert E. Lee and others called for a Confederate government program to connect the Southern railroads, executive power and money were lacking. The outcome of the war seemed to justify the North's more consolidated railroads and more centralized government.

Lincoln's use of the railroad en route to his inauguration also seemed to justify it as an agent of union. He traveled by rail for two weeks between his native Illinois and Washington, D.C., talking to crowds about the importance of union, especially crowds that had not voted strongly in his favor. Having run the first whistle-stop election campaign in the nation's history he now stopped at towns to give short talks, sometimes no more than a few minutes in length, trying to calm the fears of Northerners who saw war on the horizon. Yet on the same journey he also made war policy, speaking with political and economic leaders in key cities and delivering more than twenty speeches. In New York he spoke at the state capital in Albany, then proceeded south along the Hudson River to New York City. Lincoln felt out of place in this Eastern city which had cast only a third of its ballots for him, and thanked its citizens for a reception "given me . . . by a people who do not by a majority agree with me."[2]

Lincoln did in fact share with New Yorkers a faith in industrial progress: he favored the national bank, internal improvements, and a high protective tariff. He championed the Union and the strategy of holding the parts together through transportation and trade.[3] His arguments in the Rock Island Bridge case—that railroads must have the bridges they needed—later found a reflection in his presidential railroad policies. In the absence of Southern congressmen, Lincoln's government established a Western railroad policy that gave hundreds of thousands of acres of Western land to railroads that would be connected to Northern cities.

But Northerners, particularly Northern business interests, had an aggressive, expansionist stance and an interest in financial profit that not only Southerners found offensive. English novelist Anthony Trollope, traveling in the United States when the war opened, suggested that sentiment in the Northern states extended beyond a wish to control the South and West. They wanted to annex Canada too, and make it part of the United States. Since Canada was part of the British Empire, ambitions of this sort did little to make the Union cause popular in England. Like the South, Trollope distrusted the interested parties of the Northeast who, like Edward Everett, grandfather of Edward Hale, had hopes "as to the one nation that is to occupy the entire continent."[4]

Secession, Trollope felt, was the natural consequence of attempting to create such a large and culturally diverse nation. Other parts of the Union, he wrote, particularly the West, would probably follow the lead of the South, with the result that North America would have many more than two nations governing it. "As population increases and trades arise peculiar to those different climates, the interests of the people will differ, and a new secession will take place beneficial to both parties."[5] Parts of the North, particularly in the Midwest and near the Confederate border, also sympathized with the South, though they stayed with the Union. Feeling against the Union was so strong in Baltimore that the president-elect's life had been threatened. When Lincoln's train passed through Baltimore he was not in it; he traveled through on a separate train, guarded by members of Pinkerton's detective agency.

This division of loyalty to the Union included strong feelings about slavery but also extended to fundamental differences over land. In the railroad many Northerners felt they had the instrument by which to control any amount of land under one union. The railroad gave them the confidence to expand and take in land far in excess of what any European nation or ancient civilization had been able successfully to control. They also saw in the railroad the ability to expand civilization beyond its historical boundaries, for the railroad seemed to promise that towns, cities, and industries could be put down anywhere as long as they were tied to the rest of the Union by rail. With steam power factories could be put down anywhere too, and cities no longer needed to be ports. Civilization could become in large measure portable.

The Confederacy understood this view and took deep exception to it. The South saw land in a more traditional light, as home and heritage, not just as a natural resource to benefit capital and state. Southerners saw Northern advances as a kind of imperialism. The willingness of the North to put down roots anywhere in order to find profit demonstrated a lack of loyalty to place, an opportunism. Thus the definition of the Union as a commercial venture, controlled by private enterprise based in Northern cities, troubled the Southerners as much as the slavery issue.

Lincoln, who had lived in both worlds, sought to mediate. With a Southern and Midwestern farming background, he sympathized with the farmers, but his education and legal career had given him an understanding of business and politics as well. In making his cabinet appointments he chose Northerners as well as a number of men who had ties in the West and South. But among his appointments were men who had strong ties to the railroads. William Seward, secretary of state, came from New York, the financial capital of the country since the opening of the New York Stock and Exchange Board, and had spent his career promoting and analyzing the interests of steamships, railways, and canals as well as the trade on which they thrived. Simon Cameron, Lincoln's first secretary of war, represented Pennsylvania, which, with its iron, coal, oil, and railroads right on the Virginia border, needed to be firmly attached to the Northern cause.[6]

On April 14, 1861, when Lincoln responded to the firing on Fort

Sumter by calling for the recruitment of 75,000 men into the army, he also took control of the railroads by requiring that trains on government business have priority over civilian passenger and freight traffic. On the 15th Secretary of War Cameron wired each of the Northern state governors to call up a state quota of soldiers and send them to Washington by train.[7] Since the Confederacy had already made plans to attack and take Washington, so near the Virginia border, the federal government, with no more specific military strategy in mind, directed all troops to assemble in the capital city.

Trollope and other witnesses noticed that the Northern mobilization had a number of local aspects, despite the plan to assemble all soldiers in Washington. Even in the North, for example, the regiments were organized by state. Those who would fight and live together for the duration of their enlistment would all be from the same state. And in many cases the regiments also determined the appearance of their own uniforms.[8]

Nevertheless the army had already begun to subordinate the spirit of localism to an intense, highly organized mobilization of troops southward. Edward Dicey, a reporter for the London *Spectator,* wrote that

> The numbers were so vast that it was hard to realize them. During one week fifty thousand men were embarked from Washington, and yet the town and neighborhood still swarmed with troops and camps, as it seemed, undiminished in number. And here, remember, I saw only one portion of the gigantic army. Along a line of two thousand miles or so, from the Potomac down to New Mexico, there were at that time Federal armies fighting their way southwards. . . . At this time the muster-roll of the Federal army numbered 672,000 men. . . . The wonder to me is, that the American people were not more intoxicated with the consciousness of their newborn strength.[9]

The speed with which Northern mobilization took place, and the numbers of men that were drawn together, were both directly attributable to the availability of railroads.

The South faced an initial mobilization characterized by even greater localism. Even under the Confederacy the states rejected a strong central authority, and each state made preparations of its own.

"State sovereignty," writes one historian, "was as rampant in military affairs as in politics, and the states were reluctant to transfer the control of their troops to the Confederacy." While Robert E. Lee, general of the army of the state of Virginia, gradually gained sufficient confidence from state governors to gather their troops under his command, the governors wished to retain the power to bring their troops home to defend state borders.[10]

The Southern railroads, initially built to expand the wealth of Southern plantations and states, remained almost entirely in the control of these local interests who put states' rights ahead of the long-distance exchange of goods and people. Consequently the complex efforts to connect numerous short lines into trunk lines had not occurred in the South, and transporting troops over long distances required many more time-consuming changes of conveyance. A number of Southwestern states, chiefly Texas, Louisiana, and Arkansas, had almost no railroads at all, making mobilization and communications extremely slow.

Only one rail line connected the Southwestern states to the Southern states along the East Coast, since most of the Southwestern rail lines had been constructed south to north. The Mobile and Ohio started on the Gulf Coast at Mobile, Alabama, and proceeded northeastward to Kentucky, where a number of shorter east-west lines carried troops to Chattanooga or Nashville, Tennessee. Both these cities had rail ties with the Atlantic coast. But even this one route involved a number of train changes; and Union armies along the Ohio River soon realized the importance of breaking this one rail route across the South.

Jefferson Davis, who had opposed the construction of the Rock Island bridge that Lincoln had successfully defended in court, and who had championed the older trade ties that brought goods down the Mississippi River to New Orleans, now faced opposition to connecting Southern railroad routes, even with one another. Authorities in Southern towns and cities did not want tracks built into their communities, where such connections could most reasonably be made. While the North had come to tolerate the disruptions and danger of the railroad passing through a settled community, even they still required that the engine stop on the outskirts of town and that horses bring the cars into town from that point. The South did not have the experience to call for this adjustment, and therefore seriously compromised whatever unity might have emerged from an efficiently connected system of railroads.[11]

Southern railroad companies nevertheless wanted to serve the Confederate cause and offered to provide their services to the government free of charge. But the length of the war, the lack of capital to maintain tracks and cars, and the lack of any facility in the South to build new engines led them eventually to charge the government for use of their lines.[12] The government paid the railroad managers in Confederate bonds, which had an inflated value and which by the end of the war were worthless. These circumstances, as much as the destruction caused by Yankee armies, brought the complete ruin of the Southern transportation system.

As the war progressed a number of key battles were fought over control of strategic railroad depots. In Virginia, where fighting raged inconclusively for years between the capitals of Washington and Richmond, the small railroad town of Manassas became a focus of struggle. A crossroads for the short Manassas Gap Railroad and the Orange and Alexandria Railroad, Manassas changed hands several times during the war. The town proved valuable as a supply depot for each army in turn, and both sides fought to seize and hold the town and its two railroads. More than once, supplies stored at Manassas were destroyed to avoid having them fall into the hands of the "other" army.[13]

In the West, key generals on both sides also tried to take control of Corinth, Mississippi, where the Mobile and Ohio Railroad crossed the Memphis and Charleston. Because the Mobile and Ohio was the only link between South and Southwest, whoever held Corinth could control most of the rail communications between the southwestern parts of the Confederacy and its capital in Richmond. Grant's army took Corinth in 1862 but later lost it. The rails into Corinth, and the depot and military supplies stored at this key crossroads, continued as a focus of conflict until very near the end of the war.

Probably the best-known railroad center of the Civil War was Chattanooga, in eastern Tennessee, adjacent to the northernmost part of Georgia. From the beginning of the war the Confederacy had

stretched a line of troops across Tennessee and continued to protect
Chattanooga from Union advances until the end of 1863. The city,
a stop on the Memphis and Charleston coming east from Corinth,
was also the western terminus of the Western and Atlantic Railroad, which extended to Atlanta, Georgia. The theft of the Confederate railroad engine "General" took place between Atlanta and
Chattanooga on the Western and Atlantic in early 1862, as part of an
early and unsuccessful attempt by the Union army to take Chattanooga.

After the Union capture of the city in 1863, two highly successful
Northern railroad strategies helped bring the war to an end. The first
involved a rapid transfer of no less then 25,000 Union soldiers from
the Army of the Potomac by railroad to Chattanooga within twelve
days. The need for this rapid mass mobilization arose when Union
General Rosencrans found himself in possession of Chattanooga but
surrounded by Confederate troops and completely cut off from any
supply line. His men would have been starved into surrendering the
city had not the War Department, under Secretary Edwin Stanton,
ordered the unprecedented movement of troops, cannon, horses, and
supplies to rescue Rosencrans's army.[14]

Following a successful campaign to break through Confederate
lines outside Chattanooga, the Union moved General William T.
Sherman's army into the area, where it made plans to march through
Georgia to the sea. Chattanooga became a supply depot for the Union
army as it marched deeper into the Confederacy. The march could
succeed only if the Union supply line, the Western and Atlantic Railroad, remained in Union control, preventing Confederate raiders
from tearing it up. Indeed, shortly after Sherman reached Atlanta, he
had to retrace his steps back toward Chattanooga to push Confederate troops back from the railroad line.[15]

Overall, Union armies could penetrate Southern territory only as
far as supply lines allowed, and in most instances the supply lines
were railroad tracks. Union troops would first destroy them to eliminate their usefulness to the Confederacy, then seize and rebuild them
as quickly as possible under Union control. The mastermind of
Northern reconstruction of Southern railroad lines was a man named
Herman Haupt, who was hired by the federal government to coordi-

nate the rebuilding of tracks and railroad bridges and to keep supply lines open. Haupt headed a group known familiarly during the Civil War as the Construction Corps, and known in later wars as the United States Military Railroad Service.[16]

A railroad construction engineer from Massachusetts, Haupt set the standard for rebuilding destroyed railroads when he made over, within one month, two bridges and much of the track on the Richmond, Fredericksburg and Potomac Railroad in Virginia. After he took charge of the Construction Corps as well as the shipping of military supplies to the Army of the Potomac, Lincoln gave him final say over everyone in the army, including generals, over matters affecting the movement of supplies by rail. The relatively greater centralization of the railroads by both private corporations and the government in the North seemed to be justified by superior results in battle.[17]

In war as in peace, however, trains en route were in control of no one but their crews, and individual choice remained a significant factor in determining the efficiency of the lines. The locomotive engineers and conductors, cut off from their civilian managers and placed in the service of the Union army, suffered the high-handed practices of officers who would order them to move a train without reference to formal plans. The historian George Edgar Turner has noted that "Constant bickering went on between field officers and railroad men over which units would have preference in transportation. . . . Despite [Haupt's] remarkable foresight and careful arrangements, best results repeatedly were prevented by failure of officers to load or unload cars as he ordered. Cars of forage and supplies were detained needlessly."[18]

Managerial problems in the South were much more difficult because the South had not enough track, engines, or cars to carry troops. When Confederate General Stonewall Jackson wanted to move his troops quickly and secretly from Gordonsville, Virginia, north toward Washington on the Virginia Central Railroad, his men endured an extremely crowded and snaillike trip north, in every type of car available, only to return the way they had come, for reasons unknown, and set out again the next morning. At that time Jackson's officers asked the crew to have the trains ready in forty-five minutes or be shot. A conductor named Charles S. Anderson, who later wrote about this experience, observed that his engineer could not get enough steam in the locomotive to start out because of the poor quality of the wood fuel. When Confederate officers began to accuse Anderson and his engineer of sabotage, the crew finally threw a coat and seat cushion into the firebox to raise the steam pressure.[19] In the field as elsewhere, local circumstance tempered the efforts of railroad management to apply nascent rules of uniformity to the train service.

The confusion of authority in the field reflected a general absence of rules of behavior in times of war. The use of any type of car available to move troops; a prevalence of drunken engineers as well as soldiers; unscheduled stops to pick up or drop off escaping slaves, wounded soldiers, and even single women traveling alone—these kinds of conditions bedeviled the railroad in wartime at least as much as in peace. They echoed the older, rural railroad service where slow trains, frequent stops, riding the locomotive or the freight trains, and traveling without means to pay the fare were the rule. Trainmen also resorted to the old habit of taking wood and fuel from local farmers, though some farmers were reimbursed by the railroad or the government.[20]

Despite this thoroughly pragmatic usage of the railroads, Union forces experimented with important new ideas about train service during the war years. The most important of these was the development of the hospital train, which evolved into an institution on wheels, complete with beds, kitchen, and toilet facilities to protect and care for the wounded while removing them from danger. After the outbreak of war, the use of trains to bring supplies to the front had included the transport of medical supplies and medical personnel, nurses hired by the federal government's new Sanitary Commission, and local volunteers to help the wounded. A short leap of the imagination resulted in the outfitting of train cars to carry the wounded from the field of battle to safety.

These trains first consisted simply of a string of passenger cars or even boxcars to carry the wounded with no special regard for their comfort, simply to get them out of harm's way. One of the earliest such trains carried Union wounded from Rolla, Missouri, to St. Louis in boxcars which had come into the field laden with supplies. Further experimentation introduced the spreading of straw or mats on the floor of the train car, and then the erection of supports on which stretchers or cots could be attached.[21]

By 1863 one railroad company, the Philadelphia, Wilmington and Baltimore, had designed and manufactured a hospital train car in which tiers of bunk beds accommodated the wounded, while seats, a stove, a locker, a water tank, and a toilet served the nurses and other medical personnel who rode with the wounded.[22] This version of the hospital car appeared similar to the few sleeping-car trains that had come into vogue since the late 1840s. While neither sleeping car nor hospital train could claim the luxury later associated with Pullman's sleeping cars, the war encouraged the planning of cars that could carry the elements of civilization into the field: food, beds, water, and toilets all on the train so that the engineer need not stop to permit the passengers to eat, sleep, or perform their toilet.

Some hospital trains also had a kitchen and dispensary car. George Edgar Turner has described the interior:

> The kitchen and dispensary car was divided into two compartments. The kitchen unit was equipped with a cooking stove, wood box, water cooler, icebox, a sink, table and pantry. Along one wall were cases of drawers and shelves, and it carried, of course, the necessary supply of cooking utensils. The dispensary unit had a heating stove in one corner with the indispensable wood box beside it. In the opposite corner was a toilet. Cases for supplies were ranged on one side, and opposite them was a couch. A table, washbasin and chairs completed the standard furnishings.

Turner also noted that wider doors at the ends of each car, adapted for the carrying of soldiers on stretchers, made it easier for medical personnel to move from car to car while the train was in motion. Previously conductors had passed from car to car to collect tickets, but had to climb over the end railings of each car to do so. Passengers had been discouraged from imitating the conductor for safety reasons.[23]

Because of the dangers of war, hospital trains depended less than earlier railroad cars on the presence of services along the road. War encouraged the impulse to make trains as self-sufficient as possible. Further, the numbers of soldiers served by these hospital trains far exceeded the capacities of stationary dispensaries or hospitals. After a major battle, the wounded might number as many as fifteen thousand to twenty thousand or more. The numbers more than justified the creation of a specialized service to meet the need.

The hospital on wheels elaborated the services of the early sleeping car and anticipated the work of George Mortimer Pullman of Chicago, who began planning the first luxury sleeping cars at precisely this time. Both developments grew out of a perception that the train could perform more efficiently when it depended as little as possible on the surrounding environment. This proved especially useful in the settlement of the West after the war.

Both types of cars also met the need to carry groups of people over longer and longer distances. Battles raged day and night, in all weather, in virtually every Southern state, but the hospital train could still meet the needs of the wounded. Pullman could see another application for this capability, where trains carried passengers beyond the settled regions and into the Mississippi Valley and the far West. There the presence of Indians and vast stretches of desert, prairie, and unsettled land proved as forbidding as the Confederate army in the South.

In a time of extreme disorder, the railroad provided the best hope for soldiers in the field to receive the food, clothing, tents, guns, and medical supplies they needed, in enormous quantities. It provided a way into battle and a means for safe retreat. In short, it offered an element of order in a chaotic environment. In these respects it anticipated the use of the railroads after the war, when those trains most immune from weather, violence, and other environmental pressures proved the most desirable for long-distance transportation.

The railroad proved invaluable for large-scale retreats as well as large-scale advances. In the South, armies and then civilian populations repeatedly evacuated cities, towns, and countryside threatened by advancing Union troops. Such populations moved as quickly as they could to the nearest railroad depot to catch any train heading further south. Few purchased tickets, and passengers overfilled the very few trains still running. Left behind was property of every description and value; taken along were the few possessions that could be carried by hand.

In 1862 Confederate troops retreated southeast across Tennessee as Grant advanced from Cairo across Kentucky. The people of Nashville realized that if this continued the Union army might march into the city without opposition. George Turner described the panic that seized the city.

> Because of wild rumors the citizens clogged the highways and rail-roads in their desperate attempts to get out of town. There were but two railroad outlets to the south. One was the Nashville & Chattanooga . . . ; the other was the Alabama & Tennessee. . . . Drenched by a cold winter rain, the people fled to the two railroad stations and jammed into and atop every available car that could be attached to a movable train.[24]

Unfortunately for the civilian population of the South, the Union army continued by fits and starts to advance across Tennessee to the city of Chattanooga, thus threatening and uprooting the population in that part of the state as well. Nimrod Bell, a conductor on the East Tennessee and Georgia Railroad during the years 1862 and 1863, found himself and his train caught between the advancing Union troops and the retreating Confederacy. On one of his last trips for the Confederacy, he carried a trainload of troops south toward Chattanooga but had to put them off at the east end of Mission Ridge tunnel when he discovered that Sherman's forces held the west end of the same tunnel. After returning to Cleveland, Tennessee, to await orders, Bell decided to head for the Western and Atlantic line with his train. But he could already see Union cavalry as he prepared to depart, and he knew they had control of the railroad heading south. So he decided to flee to the north. At the railroad station he found civilian preparations for evacuation well under way, and he had to explain to the people that it was impossible to go south by train.

> The depot was almost full of citizens' plunder, as some of them were preparing to refugee. They begged me to take this and that. I told them it would be of no use, as there was no way to get it out by rail.[25]

Bell finally did take on a number of items, including food that the civilians wished to keep away from the Yankees, and began a retreat by rail that took him north to Petersburg, Virginia, then back south to Georgia where his family lived. By that time Sherman had control of the direct route into Georgia, the Western and Atlantic Railroad.

Sherman took Mission Ridge in November 1863, and his march through Georgia to Atlanta extended from May to September of the following year. His army began its march to the sea in November and concluded this cross-country campaign in Savannah on December 22. In the face of this advance, further retreats and civilian movements occurred. Eliza Frances Andrews, daughter of a Georgia slaveholder and Unionist, lived with her sister in Albany, Georgia, about fifty miles from Florida, until Sherman's army had come and gone. In April 1865, Eliza started homeward by rail, the war officially over and her father then feeling it safe to travel. On her roundabout railroad journey home she witnessed much of the chaos associated with the end of the war but was spared its worst effects by having obtained space on a train.

> April 17, Monday, Macon, Ga.—Up early, to be ready for the train at seven. The Toombses met us at the depot. . . . When the train arrived from Eufaula it was already crowded with refugees, besides 300 volunteers from the exempts going to help fight the Yankees at Columbus. . . . Excitement on the train was intense. At Ward's Station, a dreary-looking little place, we picked up the train wrecked yesterday, with many of the passengers still on board. They had spent the night there in the cars, having nowhere else to go. . . . When we reached Fort Valley the excitement was at fever heat. Train upon train of cars was there, all the rolling stock of the Muscogee Road having been run out of Columbus to keep it from being captured, and the cars were filled with refugees and their goods.[26]

A war strategy that relied on railroads spread the effects of war over a vast area and left hundreds of thousands of uprooted wanderers looking for a place to settle or to earn a living. Citizens as well as soldiers were left without homes or property. In the border states the

occupied towns faced major disruptions and loss of property due to
the presence of troops. While towns could shield and feed an army,
they had to cope with the subordination of citizens' interests to the
military. Cairo, Illinois, became a major military depot for the Union,
and during the war years much of its local history became entwined
with the excesses of an uprooted and mobile population of soldiers
and those who hoped to profit from their presence.[27]

A town historian writing shortly after the war recalled the military
presence in Cairo. In a strategic location for trade as well as war, the
town had "avenues of trade, commerce and travel as completely
changed as could have resulted from a change of the topography of
the whole country." The entire business of the Illinois Central Railroad, which connected Cairo with Chicago and the East Coast, was
given over to the transport of war supplies rather than commerce,
with the result that business transactions declined and local citizens
lost their jobs until the soldiers got paid. Then business converted itself to meet the needs of the military.

> . . . The town was converted into a busy sutler's tent; the camp-
> followers flooded the place, the floating population came, the vile with
> the good, tent theaters, dives and hells on earth held high carnival by
> day and by night. The contractor, the soldier, the speculator, the gam-
> bler, the thief, the highway robber—the vicious of every sex, age and
> condition, jostled each other in the street throngs. . . .[28]

At the conclusion of the war, little could be done to help the millions of people displaced from homes destroyed in the conflict, or the
wounded, widowed, and orphaned who had not the means to reconstruct the lives they had led before the war. While most of the Union
armies headed toward Washington, D.C., as a point of rendezvous,
celebration, and discharge, another army of wanderers, from both
North and South, took shape. A historian of the 1880s noted: ". . . An
army of a million tramps marched over all the country, devouring the
people's substance and making no more compensation therefor [sic]
than do the devastating grasshoppers." Of course there had been railroad passengers before the war who had preferred to ride without
paying a fare, but, as a more recent historian observes, "the railroad

tramp did not become an American institution until right after the Civil War."[29]

Northern businessmen swooped down quickly to prey on the economically prostrate South. They came from Boston, New York, Chicago, and even Cairo, Illinois, to reap profits by selling the necessities of life to a destroyed civilization. The expansionist and commercial vision of Union took control of the country, and railroaders looked South and West for opportunities to invest and build.

12

|||||||||||||||||||||||

Now We Can Settle the Far West

William Seward, long committed to the Pacific Railroad, wrote of the impending labor: "When this shall have been done disunion will be rendered forever after impossible. There will be no fulcrum for the lever of treason to rest upon."

—John Hoyt Williams, *A Great and Shining Road*[1]

Jesse James was a lad that killed many a man,
He robbed the Danville train;
But that dirty little coward that shot at Mr. Howard,
Has laid Jesse James in his grave.
It was little Robert Ford, that dirty little coward;
I wonder how he does feel;
For he ate of Jesse's bread and slept in Jesse's bed,
Then laid Jesse James in his grave.

—Late-nineteenth-century Ballad[2]

THE FAR WESTERN FRONTIER still evokes images of lawlessness, disorder, and violence. In many instances these conditions grew out of the coming of the railroad and its effort to take land from the federal government and dominate or "tame" the diverse geographies and peoples of this region in the interests of promoting settlement. Indeed the railroad, aside from encouraging the mass migrations of settlers that it brought to the Great Plains, served as a messenger from the East in grafting its legal, economic, and social standards onto the open land. By the 1890s the railroads could safely pass through the hostile territories of the far West without undue risk to passengers, but the West developed slowly, with vast tracts of land left open and the entire region subordinate to the East in population and wealth.

Guidebooks to the West proliferated during the 1850s, offering maps, suggesting supplies, and even giving advice on how to deal with Indians, if encountered. Transport in the West followed rivers and springs, much as Eastern transportation had before the coming of the railroad; forts and early settlements lined the banks of rivers. But the Missouri and the Platte, both lifelines for settlers, could not support commerce to the extent that the Ohio River did. Both proved too shallow for heavy shipping, and neither passed through territory rich in raw materials. No forests lined these rivers, and little game subsisted near them. The prairies yielded so little lumber that the first settlers had to build sod huts rather than the wooden houses deemed practical in the areas east of the Mississippi River. These Western rivers played the more fundamental role of providing drinking water and all the irrigation water to be had for hundreds of miles in any direction. It did not take much imagination to see how railroads might improve travel conditions in the West and bring settlers to the land in greater numbers. But the deadlock over slavery delayed action on this matter until Southerners abandoned the Union.

After the departure of Southern congressmen in 1861, the federal government under Lincoln proceeded almost immediately to plan a policy for the far West which favored Northern interests. The set of laws passed in 1862 had more influence on the future of the American West than did the Civil War itself. While Congress studied the problem of moving troops from Baltimore to Washington, and recompensed Eastern railroads for their transport of troops and supplies, it also passed the Pacific Railroad Act, signed by Lincoln on July 1, 1862. The act chartered the Union Pacific Railroad Company to lay track from the Mississippi River to the California state line, where track would be laid from San Francisco eastward by the Central Pacific Railroad controlled by four West Coast entrepreneurs.

The path of the planned Western railroad was a central one, to commence in Nebraska rather than in the far North or South. But the location best met the needs of the city of Chicago and the lines radiating westward from Chicago across Iowa, Nebraska's neighbor to the east. The Chicago and Northwestern; the Chicago, Rock Island and Pacific; and the Chicago, Burlington and Quincy railroads had all begun constructing lines across Iowa from the Mississippi to towns on the Nebraska border: Sioux City, Council Bluffs, and Platte City. Connection with the Union Pacific would guarantee them a direct route to the Pacific. The choice of a four-foot, eight-and-a-half-inch gauge as the standard for the tracks of the Pacific Railroad also benefited the North, where most through routes, with the exception of the Erie Railroad, had the same gauge. The potential therefore existed to send one train from any of these Northern routes through to the Pacific without unloading and reloading either passengers or freight. The Southern railroads had a variety of gauges, for they were unconnected by any formal plan. Even had they not been destroyed by war, they could have used the Union Pacific line west only by moving passengers and freight from one train to another at the frontier.

The act of 1862 granted to the Union Pacific lands for the road and authorized government bonds for $60 million in loans. The company itself was to sell $100 million in stock. When investment interest in the railroad flagged, the government amended the act in 1864, granting more financial aid and more land to the Union Pacific Company. In 1864 the Northern Pacific, which was to cross the West from Minnesota, also received its first grants of land from the government. Some congressmen questioned the need for such a road, and the wisdom of constructing eighteen hundred miles of track through uninhabited country. Others fell back on arguments that had proven successful in promoting railroads for the preceding thirty-five years: "It is a military necessity; and, secondly, it is absolutely essential to our internal development."[3] Internal improvements, long considered the province of the states, once again received the financial backing of the federal government to an unprecedented degree.

But the finances of the Union Pacific project did not unfold smoothly. Within years it became entangled in one of the worst scandals in American history: the Credit Mobilier Bank of America became a part owner of the Union Pacific Company and shared the extra profits obtained from the government by overstating the price per mile of laying track.[4] Construction of the line, which commenced with a groundbreaking on December 2, 1863, proceeded by fits and starts until the end of the Civil War, when a race to completion began.

In 1862 Congress also passed the Homestead Act, a plan to give land to settlers who would farm and develop the land for five years. The Homestead Act broke the prairie into 160-acre tracts for this purpose and hastened the migration needed to make the Union Pacific a profitable enterprise. Passage of this act also hinged on the absence of Southern representation in Congress, for Southerners had earlier objected to homesteading as reflecting Northern farming; the South wanted to see large plantations on the American prairie. Both acts defined land-use policies for the immense tracts of public lands in the West. With them, the Morrill Act of 1862 also required that certain public lands be set aside for state universities, where settlers could receive training in agriculture, engineering, or the liberal arts. The settlement of the far West thus involved the cooperative efforts of the federal, state, and territorial governments as well as private initiative and investment.

With the end of the Civil War in April 1865, large numbers of soldiers on both sides, and freed slaves, migrated westward. Many sought employment helping to lay track for the Union Pacific. The Confederacy was so thoroughly destroyed that many soldiers could find no other means there of earning a living. Others came from the Irish, German, and Swedish brigades that had marched and fought as distinct groups during the war. But in 1865 they moved west as individuals, creating an ethnically diverse work force. Grenville Dodge, a former Indian fighter in the United States army and a key figure in Union railroad policy during the war, became chief engineer with the

For workers laying track on the Union Pacific, home consisted of train cars fitted out with bunks, food, water, and other supplies needed for survival in a harsh environment. Railroad towns, the next step, were made up of small clusters of buildings which were taken down and rebuilt as the train rolled slowly west. (BEINECKE RARE BOOK AND MANU-SCRIPT LIBRARY, YALE UNIVERSITY)

Union Pacific. The railroad also invited General William T. Sherman to Omaha to view the beginnings of sustained construction in July 1865 and named the first Union Pacific locomotive after him.

General John Casement and his brother Daniel were employed by Union Pacific president Thomas Durant to hire and supervise workers. To provide for the workers as they worked their way west, farther and farther from towns or white settlements, the brothers devised a work train which closely resembled the hospital trains of the Civil War. They provided kitchens, bunks, and supplies on the train itself, and moved west with the work force over the newly laid track. Here once again the train served as a center of civilized order in an environment that often did not even provide shade for the laborers. The historian Dee Brown has described the organization of this train:

To an Iron Horse they attached about a dozen cars, each one designed to serve a special purpose—a car filled with tools, one outfitted as a blacksmith shop, another with rough dining tables and kitchen and commissary, others with built-in bunks, and at the end several flatcars loaded with rails, spikes, fishplates, bolts, and other road-building supplies. It was in fact a self-sufficient small town on wheels.[5]

Unlike an army, the Union Pacific developed a society of its own on the moving frontier. This small world had several parts, corresponding to the drastically different cultures thrown together by the need to construct a railroad. The importance of this society lay in its similarity to communities that developed in many parts of the West after the coming of the railroad. Indians, consisting in Nebraska of Pawnee, came by to watch the work; laborers lived out of the work train; and Easterners and Civil War officers either controlled the road or tried and failed to control it. The groups had little in common other than the encounters with one another which created stir and comment worthy of an 1850s day car. When Colonel Silas Seymour appeared at the site of track-laying, "Even the Pawnee Indians laughed at Seymour. . . . He usually wore a black silk top hat and carried an umbrella to protect himself from the summer sun." When General Sherman visited to view the progress of the work, he and his party adapted themselves to local custom by sitting on kegs and wearing buffalo robes, but they shared a dinner of duck and champagne more suitable to the elegance of East Coast cities than to the frontier.[6]

In 1866, when the workers had completed almost 250 miles of track, the management held a party for what President Andrew Johnson had begun calling the railroad aristocracy. This group indulged in receptions and balls in Omaha, feasted on gourmet food, and then proceeded west on the new railroad to view the achievement that had brought them there. At the end of the first day's travel the group encamped in tents with mattresses, blankets, and buffalo robes. These magnates, spouses, and friends then watched a Pawnee war dance, arranged and paid for by Thomas Durant.[7] In keeping with the see-and-be-seen spirit of the occasion, Durant had hired a photographer to document the occasion. The viewist, as the photographer was called, did find time to take one picture of the workers, though he devoted most of his time to recording the activities of the partygoers.

These relationships remained prominent even after the completion of the road and the running of regular transcontinental trains. Most settlers lived at a subsistence level, much like the railroad workers, and both depended on the railroad for a substantial portion of their income, household furnishings, lumber, and other appurtenances of living. In extremely isolated surroundings, the coming of the train and the arrival of new emigrants in the crude but inexpensive emigrant cars was a central feature of social life in the West. Meanwhile the wealthier Easterners rode in Pullman Palace Cars, viewed the settlers and Indians as cultural curiosities worth the price of the trip, and then rode home again, east, west, or even back to Europe, with a fascinating tale to tell about the American West and the luxurious comforts of the train. They produced voluminous guidebooks featuring such wonders of the far West as the Grand Canyon and Yellowstone Park, sights on a par with Niagara Falls. And they dotted the West with hotels that rivaled city hotels but boasted magnificently landscaped grounds, views, and even outings on horse or donkey to see this wonderful but no longer quite virginal landscape.[8]

In Nebraska the Pawnees, the best part of the view, suffered a fate that cannot be described in brief. As they lost more and more land, they also lost their wealth and dignity. They began turning up at railroad stations to sit idly or to beg, or to ride the train. Through a car window they significantly increased the charm of a tourist's view, but on the train or at close range in the station they did not appear to be as clean as some tourists would have liked. The Indians of the West did not succumb quietly to this fate but attacked trains in an effort to make their political views known.[9]

Thus while the railroad brought the first elements of Eastern civilization to the West, the comparative comfort of a train ride was not soon translated into comfort for those living in the surrounding landscape. For those of established wealth and status, the West was a view whose dangers and curiosities must be kept at a distance. If the picturesque Indians, settlers, and even outlaws of the frontier had pretensions to equal status, conflict and even violence resulted. Such were the elements of railroad society in the West.

The lives of railroad workers during the 1860s reflected the more general experiences of those who lived or traveled in the West, and close inspection of society along the moving frontier illuminates the temporary, eclectic, and conflicted nature of early settlement. The temporary aspect of frontier life for the railroad laborer grew out of the need to keep moving west with the track. Historians have described a phenomenon called the railroad town, which was the next stage of settlement beyond the work train and consisted of houses, stores, and other buildings constructed quickly and cheaply, then literally taken down, moved westward in parts, and rebuilt further along the railroad route.[10] Railroad towns primarily served the need for shelter during the severe winter months when blizzards and subzero temperatures made track-laying all but impossible.

Built in the middle of nowhere, these towns had no legal or economic security beyond the presence of the railroad itself. A railroad town called North Platte, which housed railroad workers and provided a depot for settlers headed beyond the end of the railroad line, went up in weeks, complete with hotels, bordellos, and saloons.

The diverse and eclectic nature of society in these towns drew on the cultural confrontations between East and West, Indian and white. Like Eastern cities where immigrants from Europe had begun to flood in, Western towns attracted anyone in search of wealth. This included Indians, miners, cattle ranchers, laborers, former slaves, shopkeepers, and Europeans of diverse backgrounds. A key difference between the frontier town and the Eastern city, aside from the former's economic fragility, lay in the absence of segregation of different cultures in the West. Since the 1840s travelers had described the segregation of New York and other Eastern cities. The beauty of public areas, such as Broadway, contrasted sharply with the poverty of certain neighborhoods such as Five Points, which even then had a transatlantic reputation for crime and degradation.[11] The Western towns, more temporary and more dangerous, had no established system of organizing Indians, ranchers, and hotelkeepers into segregated neighborhoods. A source of fascination for the tourists, this

After the opening of the transcontinental railroad in 1869, Chicago became a jumping-off point for rail passengers headed west. (CHICAGO HISTORICAL SOCIETY)

eclectic society retained a high level of friction and confrontation, and diversity often led to violence.

Without doubt the long-distance trains that proliferated in the far West between 1865 and the 1880s encouraged the founding of these spontaneous young towns and the unplanned meeting of many cultural traditions. The Atchison, Topeka and Santa Fe through the Southwest; the Southern Pacific Railroad; and the route of the North Central and Northern Pacific through the Dakotas and Montana to the Pacific coast all brought much of this heterogeneous population with them.

Gradually all were subordinated in one way or another to the task of putting arable land under cultivation. The Indians, who had been given large areas of land in present-day Oklahoma and further west, found their economic hold in the West gradually dwindled as Congress repeatedly granted permission to the railroads to build across Indian reservations and then settle the land adjacent to the tracks. The cowboys lost the open spaces that made possible their cattle trails north from Texas; now ranches fenced in these spaces with barbed wire. And additional miles of track made it less necessary to herd the cattle a long distance before being shipped to the stockyards of Chicago and St. Louis. Outlaws, gamblers, hoboes, and other wanderers saw a gradual reduction in public wilderness land outside the bounds of any law, as most Western lands came into private hands before 1890. After that, less and less of the land that remained in government hands was available for development, though some homesteading activity continued into the twentieth century.

Thus the colorful diversity of the West was minimized through the growing dominance of Eastern legal, economic, and social forms. But the process was not spontaneous. As they had in the 1850s, the railroads advertised farm land for sale along the railroad track in order to encourage settlement. Even then, settlement in the West fell far short of settlement east of the Mississippi.

The Northern Pacific Railroad, which received federal grants of land in 1864, opened for service through to the Pacific in 1874. In need of a population to serve, the railroad sent recruiting agents to English markets and county fairs to enlist families willing to migrate to the American West and settle on railroad land. The railroad had already laid out town sites and even named the towns, which sat empty, waiting for inhabitants to take possession and use them. At one point the Northern Pacific had more than eight hundred agents working in Europe, some as far east as Russia.[12]

Railroad brochures described the West as a paradise, and discount tickets, which included all transportation from Europe to the West, encouraged emigrants to seek their fortunes. Americans who wished to see the land before buying could avail themselves of land-seekers tickets which allowed them to travel about by train until they found a plot suitable to their purposes. If the users of these tickets bought land from the railroad, they would receive free transportation for themselves, their families, and their worldly goods back to the desired site. Discounts and special tickets were taken advantage of by those who simply wished to sightsee, but the railroads did succeed in luring hundreds of thousands of Europeans and Americans to new homes in the West.[13] From these migrations came the Western farm communities that supplied the Eastern cities with more grain and produce than the East could consume.

A family that left Pennsylvania after the Civil War and moved to Virginia for reasons of poverty, joined the migration westward during the financial panic of 1873 after reading a book issued by the Union Pacific Railroad intended to lure prospective settlers westward. The youngest member of this family, who much later wrote about this experience, quoted the book's description of the Platte River Valley in Nebraska.

> The traveller beholds, stretching away to the distant horizon, the undulating prairie, a flowering meadow of great fertility, clothed in grasses, watered by numerous streams, the margins of which was [sic] skirted with timber. . . . During Fall and Winter, the weather is usually dry. The heat of Summer is tempered by the prairie winds, and the nights are cool and comfortable. The Winters are short, dry and invigorating, with but little snow. Cold weather seldom lasts beyond three months, with frequent intervals of mild, pleasant days. The roads in Winter are usually hard, smooth, and excellent.[14]

The father bought land in Nebraska, and the family took the train to Grand Island, "a town which had been settled in 1866 when the Union Pacific had made it a storage place for supplies while the men building the track moved on ahead." The family packed cooking utensils and bedding and prepared to move west with a six-month-old baby. They shipped their luggage ahead as freight and rode to Grand Island, arriving there to find a small railroad station with an overcrowded dining area. Since the railroad land plots had all been taken, the father had bought land sixty miles from Grand Island, and to this parcel the family began to walk, through a blizzard.[15]

After locusts, the father's drinking habit, and poverty made it seem impossible that the family could ever flourish as farmers, the mother moved into Grand Island and took a job at a corral. The father and his son went to Deadwood, South Dakota, during the gold rush, where again wealth eluded them. Thus discouraged, the entire family then moved further west, only to find more disillusionment in Carbon, Wyoming, a mining town set up by the Union Pacific to provide coal for its trains. Like LaFayette Stone in the 1840s, and like the railroad laborers of the 1860s, this family found it impossible to put down roots in the West until the children finally made it to Oregon.[16] This was a pattern that permitted few towns in the West to prosper, grow, or develop a dependable capital base. Into the twentieth century Westerners continued to depend on cities east of the Mississippi for manufactured products, and continued to sell farm produce in the East for money to buy these products.

Culturally the railroads incorporated this split by developing separate services for the poor who settled or intended to settle in the West, and for the well-to-do who could observe the loveliness of the Western landscape and the excitement of its colorfully diverse population without facing the hard realities of conflict and survival. The services provided a study in contrasts, between emigrant cars or even freight cars, roughly built to hold large crowds of emigrants, and the elegant parlor, sleeping, and dining cars that carried many fewer passengers in much greater comfort.

In an essay entitled "Across the Plains," the English novelist Robert Louis Stevenson described life aboard a crowded emigrant train which he took west in 1879. Accommodations and service were minimal and reflected a rural experience compared to travel aboard a Pullman. Stevenson boarded an emigrant car on the Union Pacific at Council Bluffs, Iowa, the easternmost point on that line. Despite the crowding, the railroads imposed elements of social order that reflected prewar notions of civility. A man whom Stevenson understood to be a railroad official divided the throng into men, women and their children, and Chinese. The women and children took the last in the line of passenger cars, deemed the safest place in the event of a head-on collision. The men took the middle passenger cars, and the Chinese, considered the least valuable travelers, somewhat on a par with American blacks, rode in the most vulnerable position, just behind the locomotive. Each passenger car had a stove for cooking, and a toilet. Behind the passenger coaches followed baggage cars, at least twelve by Stevenson's count, carrying the worldly possessions of the immigrants. Before the war, baggage cars had almost always traveled just behind the locomotive in order to protect travelers from collision and explosion, and it is not clear why they took up the rear on Stevenson's train. Among his fellow travelers he found representatives of all the Northern states mixed together, all hoping to start over economically in the West.[17]

In the course of the journey, all emigrants had to fend for themselves in cooking, cleaning, and finding a comfortable spot to rest. Some bought a board and cushions from hawkers in the station and laid them across the seats to make a bed. As the journey progressed the air grew foul and the discomfort extreme. Breathing became difficult, yet the windows had to remain closed at night against the cold. At intervals the train stopped, and the passengers could eat a restaurant meal if they could afford one. At Ogden, Utah, the passengers left Union Pacific accommodations for Central Pacific cars, which appeared much cleaner, larger, and more comfortable.[18]

The Pullman cars for sitting, dining, and sleeping, which the Union Pacific began leasing for their own use in the 1870s, reflected urban standards of service for those who wished to see the West but did not live in it. They insulated riders from distasteful realities and made it possible for the wealthy to extend their grand tour beyond the major cities to include the far West.

Frank Leslie, publisher of *Leslie's Magazine,* was host to an entourage on an extremely elegant journey across America in 1877. His magazine's highly successful coverage of the Civil War had made him wealthy, and he turned his sights to the West for a pleasure trip on which his wife and a number of friends accompanied him. He also aimed to provide a firsthand account of the wonders of the transcontinental trip for his magazine. The itinerary included the major cities of the West, more noted for their colorful and rapid growth resulting from financial speculation than their wealth or grandeur: Cheyenne, Denver, Salt Lake City, Virginia City, and San Francisco. Among the guests were two artists to provide pictorial renderings for the magazine, and a photographer.

The accommodations on this journey were as far from the immediate realities of the West as New York was from Fort Kearney. This way of viewing the West was an experience similar to viewing pictures through a stereoscope in a parlor, or to the later experience of going to a movie. Pictures of the train's kitchen featured black chefs and servants, "pots, kettles, pans, and knives . . . arranged around the apartment in perfect order, . . . [and] two large tanks suspended from the roof . . . supplied with water. . . ." These and the linen closet, the wine closet, bunk beds, bathrooms with running water, rugs, divan placed a great deal of social distance between the emigrant cars and those on the grand tour. The "characters" pictured as representative of the Western railroad station, however, bore more resemblance to the emigrants: men in boots and carrying guns, women carrying children and bundles of luggage, buying goods before setting out for the isolation of distant farms.[19]

Leslie looked for signs of commerce, and in the course of this found thriving stores for clothes and equipment catering to gold miners, hotels, newly constructed bridges, mining towns, mine elevators, railroad towns, a Chinese laundry, new snow fences, snow plows for the railroad, cattle, corrals, and other man-made wonders, all testimony to the future economic prospects of the West.[20] He paid relatively little attention to the beauty of the natural landscape.

Mrs. Leslie also wrote a number of articles in which she criticized life in the West as drab, depressing, and immoral. Omaha was the first target of her pen.

> We took a carriage and set forth to view the town. We found it big, lazy, and apathetic; the streets dirty and ill-paved; the clocks without hands to point to the useless time; the shops, whose signs mostly bore German names, deserted of customers. . . . Returning to the station, we found the platform crowded with the strangest and most motley people it has ever been our fortune to encounter. Men in alligator boots and loose overcoats made of blankets and wagon rugs, with wild unkempt hair and beards. . . . The women looked tired and sad and were queerly dressed in gowns that must have been old on their mothers. . . .[21]

Mrs. Leslie had inadvertently gotten to the heart of the cultural gap between East and West. She did not wish to mingle with these people. Many of those who went west did so to avoid the kind of attitude Mrs. Leslie had, and to enjoy a more democratic society, free of the "aristocracy" that had grown rich from industry and then the Civil War. At the conclusion of the five-month tour, Mrs. Leslie went home, and the West continued its struggle for wealth and order.

Mrs. Leslie's blunt commentaries on the West did not go unchallenged. After her return to New York she faced a rebuttal of sorts from Rollin F. Daggett, editor of Virginia City's newspaper, the *Territorial Enterprise.* Daggett called her "an adventuress, a bastard, a fornicatrix, and a snob."[22] Sniping between West and East grew as it became more obvious that little railroad money would ever enrich the people living west of Omaha and east of California.

Among those who actively resented the intrusion of the railroads and the wealth they represented were the train robbers. In the Midwest and beyond, stagecoach robbing had a long tradition on the wagon trails. While robbers took passengers' possessions, they more often sought the money carried across the plains in both directions: gold and silver mined in the West going east, and currency for banks and payrolls traveling west. In headline after headline the press described attacks on expressmen for the cash, gold, or bullion they guarded in the express car, or on stationmasters or expressmen for goods kept in locked safes.

Robberies increased after the Civil War when great numbers of wanderers crossed the country. The most notorious train robbers of the 1860s hailed from the Midwest: Sam Bass from Lawrence County, Indiana; the Reno brothers from Seymour, Indiana, less than a hundred miles away; the Younger brothers and James brothers, all from Missouri; and the Dalton brothers, from Kansas and Missouri. Beginning in 1865 or 1866, a number of robberies occurred on Midwestern railroads north of the Ohio River, and later followed the railroads as they were built to the West Coast. While most of these men were too young to have served in the Civil War, Jesse James had, and later he brought his experience to bear in raiding railroads for money.[23]

Allan Pinkerton, the detective who had helped Lincoln escape the Baltimore conspiracy on his life in 1861, also shifted his interests westward after the war when he was asked in the 1870s to apprehend members of the James and Younger gangs. His sons, William and Robert, who undertook the work, succeeded in killing one of the Younger gang and an eight-year-old brother of Jesse James, an outcome that won few friends for the agency. In 1878 the Texas and Pacific Railroad hired Pinkerton's to apprehend Sam Bass, who was finally killed by the Texas Rangers. Railroads also employed Pinkerton's after the war to infiltrate and break up the unions that organized a number of major strikes against the railroads for higher pay and safer working conditions between the 1870s and the depression of 1893–1894.[24]

The excitement of a holdup, involving the sudden appearance of armed men on horseback stopping the train, tying up or killing crew members, and making off with thousands of dollars in gold, silver, or other currency appealed to many, who composed songs and poems in honor of the thieves. Displays of wealth and corruption by the "railroad aristocracy," combined with the attitudes of families like the Leslies, created considerable resentment among struggling farmers and merchants, and among Southerners then living under the military occupation known as Radical Reconstruction. The West too, including the railroads, was "protected" by the United States army, composed of the remains of the old Union army fortified by former Confederate soldiers. Many people had no sympathy for the railroad and saw train robbers as democratic heroes rather than villains.

Hoboes, historically thought to have emerged in great numbers during the upheavals of the war, cast a mute yet destructive vote for democracy as they rode the rails free of charge and frequently broke into freight and baggage looking for food or valuables. Those who rode free generally had to conceal themselves from the conductor and other members of the crew. They rode on top of, underneath, or between cars, or in empty freight cars. Hoboes boarded the trains at night when they stood in or near a station, or as the train, still moving slowly, pulled out of town, slowly gathering speed. Despite risk of injury, men, and sometimes women, ran alongside the train as it pulled out and jumped aboard, lodging themselves wherever space could be found—anywhere but in the passenger coaches themselves.[25]

Like train robbers, hoboes enjoyed a measure of popular support, and for the same reason. The transportation historian Oscar Osburn Winther has written, ". . . Passenger sentiment favored the person who could cheat or 'beat' the 'soulless' corporation." Fare-paying passengers did not turn their ire against the poor who rode for free but against railroad chieftains who gave free passes to their friends and to legislators who might give the railroads favorable consideration at the state and national levels.[26] "Deadheads" and "fare beaters" were the names given to those who did not pay but who usually traveled in the most comfortable cars available.

Hoboes had different reasons for traveling and living as they did. Many were itinerant workers who traveled the length and breadth of the West, working to earn money and then leaving when other opportunities arose, or before they felt trapped by the rules and other demands that employers made to refine their work force. Some of these who worked took railroad jobs, knowing that railroads in most parts of the West were desperate for workers, so that they could leave one job at will with a good chance to find work further down the line. Railroad workers were asked to refrain from drinking, but for many men with no home and no security, drinking was their way of life.27 Despite the risk, railroad brakemen, engineers, firemen, and conductors went right on drinking, through the accidents of the 1850s, through the Civil War, and through the vast and lonely West, in the heat of summer and the intolerable cold of Western winters.

The railroads aimed to bring social and economic order to the West, but at first the region became a colorful meeting ground for an incredibly diverse and unsettled population. The scheduled train—a refuge from enemies, ostracism, uncertainty, and bad weather—had no capacity to spread its potential for civility and order to the poor who sought a new beginning in the West. The social order imported by the railroads consisted in providing a haven from the disorder of the surrounding lands, and in echoing the standards of established Eastern society. While rectangled towns, grain elevators, town halls, and courthouses did eventually follow the crowds of passengers west, those forms imitated an established society and culture farther east. They did not reflect a new center of capitalism in the West. Western institutions imitated those in the East, but Western towns and states still depended on the manufacturing power of the East and remained the granary of the country. In the long run, the railroad did not transplant capitalism but only extended its reach.

13

||||||||||||||||||||

Poor Relations in
the South

"The bill provides for a right of way and land grant of about two hundred thousand acres—um, mostly swamp—to the Midland railway company?"

The old man glanced up quickly. "What's that?" he said. "What railroad?"

"Well the corporation, Governor, as yet has not been completely organized."

"Um—that's mostly swamp, too, is it?"

—Opie Read and Frank Pixley, *The Carpetbagger*[1]

To an even greater extent than the far West, the South under Reconstruction exposed the limitations of the idea that the railroad could put down a civilization anywhere. With ruined cities and a much poorer and smaller population than the North, the South found it difficult to rebuild railroads. And when it did, so few people could afford to use the railroad that such services paid very little, and bankruptcies were frequent. Nevertheless, in connecting the population centers of the South, and in bringing supplies, money, and mail from the North, the railroad, for all its inadequacies, was one of the only links holding this ruined society together and tying it to the rest of the Union.

The plight of the South at the conclusion of the Civil War has often been expressed in terms of the all but complete destruction of its transportation network. Images of railroad track torn up, heated until soft, and then bent around trees to cool and harden in position, have survived to the present day.[2] Without factories or materials to produce engines or cars, the South had completely depleted its rolling stock by 1865, and such cars that still ran needed repair. After the war the South set about reconstructing what remained of its rail service.

Between 1865 and 1869 the South reopened a great many of its short lines. In some cases the name of the line and the route remained approximately what it had been before the war. For example, the Richmond and Danville became the Richmond, Danville and Piedmont. Other lines, such as the South and North Railroad of Alabama, developed out of the reconstruction of two or more railroads bankrupted during the war.

The governments of Southern states labored in difficult circumstances during the entire Reconstruction period because the former leaders of the Confederacy had no respect for the new state legislatures composed of freed blacks and Northern whites, and because many corrupt men found their way into positions of power. Furthermore the legislatures had no means to enforce order in an environment torn by economic crisis and racial division. Nevertheless they promptly addressed the rebuilding of the railroads, and several states authorized bonds to finance the restoration of rail service within the state. In five years more than seventy-five railroads began or resumed service in the states of the old Confederacy.[3]

The overwhelming majority of these roads operated locally, as they had before the war. The only lines that could honestly advertise a trunk or through route were the Louisville and Nashville, and the Mobile and Ohio, both of which followed a north-south route from the Gulf of Mexico to the Ohio River. All Southern rail service, including the tracks of these two lines, centered on Kentucky and Tennessee. Rail lines radiated from these two states to all the Atlantic coast states of the South, and through Alabama and Mississippi. The ultimate destinations for all of them were the Atlantic coast ports, including Charleston and Savannah, and, of course, New Orleans. Despite the mandate of the Civil War that Southern railroads should join the Northern "systems," this did not happen until the end of Reconstruction. Before the 1880s the South continued to follow its traditional economic pattern of connecting the interior with the sea. This long delay in uniting the two rail systems persisted despite efforts by Northern bankers and investors to rebuild the Southern railroads in such a way that they complemented the interests of the major Northern roads.

The numerous short lines of the South did not lend themselves to easy adjustment. Built in a variety of gauges, torn up by war, bankrupt, and lacking new equipment, their only hope for more extensive reconstruction lay with bankers and investors from New York and Boston who might buy large blocks of Southern state railroad bonds. But these creditors were reluctant to deal in Southern railroad bonds until they were convinced that sufficient demand existed to make the roads profitable. Thus until about 1867 the South sold bonds largely at the local and state levels to rebuild local lines.[4]

By 1869 the South had opened enough railroads to disguise the deep contrast that still existed between Northern and Southern passenger service. Each Southern state had its own lines, and their schedules appeared in the *Travelers' Guide* alongside the schedules of the burgeoning Pennsylvania Railroad and the Illinois Central. On close inspection, however, the traveler could find clues that a journey across the deep South would lack many of the comforts and conveniences taken for granted on Northern trains. Numerous Southern lines scheduled only one train a day; additional trains might carry mail and take passengers only as space permitted.[5]

Of the seventy to eighty Southern railroads listed in the *Travelers' Guide* for 1869, only about twenty scheduled a passenger train that had no mail, freight, or express duties as well. Transporting the mail took on greater importance in the Reconstruction South than did transporting passengers. Mail held the South to the North when railroads could scarcely continue running. Delays might produce angry passengers, but the government and the economy did not, for the most part, depend on passengers reaching their destination on time. The Southern rail conductor, Nimrod Bell, noted in his reminiscences that some crew members did not care to work on a mail train because it had to proceed without delay, and this proved extremely difficult for most local lines. To save money and labor, many Southern railroads scheduled a daily mixed train, which combined the services and expenses of a freight and a passenger train.[6] Express trains carried passengers but did not depend on them to make the trip profitable.

The package mail business, which developed in the 1830s, grew rapidly after the war with the introduction of mail-order businesses, such as Montgomery Ward, and farm tool companies, headquartered in Chicago, which sent catalogs and delivered goods throughout the country by way of the railroad. This so benefited Reconstruction efforts in the South that it came to the attention of Northern business writers shortly after the war.

> People who have settled in Texas have an intense liking and affection for Chicago as a trading point. . . . They say it is the only city in the world. They send there for all manner of articles, including agricultural implements, steam engines, machinery of all kinds, plows, reapers, seed corn of fine class and varieties, and everything that they require. They have been used to dealing with your merchants and are eager to continue their custom, and hence they look forward with great anxiety and hope for the railroad in Texas to be finished to New Orleans, that they may reach Chicago as quickly as possible, either in person or by orders, for the articles they require.[7]

From this perspective, the reconstruction of the railroads seemed an essential first step reinvigorating other aspects of the economy by importing necessary manufactured goods from the North.

The Southern lines also commonly scheduled accommodation trains. In theory these were slower than mail or express trains and stopped at every station and flag stop where a passenger or package waited. In reality all Southern trains, whether mail, express, or accommodation, proceeded at a similar crawl. The poor quality of

Southern track and the short distances traveled encouraged Southern passengers to board any train that showed promise of arriving at their destination.[8]

Travelers north and south of the Ohio River experienced a major difference in passenger fares. As in pre–Civil War days, a Southerner paid about six cents a mile on the railroad while a Northerner paid only half that amount, on average, for far superior service. High prices deterred many Southerners from train travel during Reconstruction, and passenger receipts ran low. The uprooting of entire communities during the war years left the South with a large population of wanderers who had almost no means. Even the Louisville and Nashville, one of the most financially sound railroads in the country, ran trains frequently for only a handful of passengers. One source reports that on a 360-mile journey between Montgomery and Mobile, Alabama, the L&N earned only thirteen dollars in passenger receipts. Conductor Nimrod Bell recalled a run on the Alabama and Chattanooga road during the early 1870s when he collected "fifty cents and very few tickets."[9]

Despite the poverty under which Southern railroaders labored during the 1860s, they tried to meet some of the minimum requirements of through passengers by establishing a system of connections among the various short lines, even though track gauges and station stops were irregular. Each railroad advertised the lines with which it connected at one station or one town, and in some cases advertised the fact that one railroad crossed another—perhaps assuming that the traveler might be willing to jump off one train and onto another at the intersection. The East Tennessee and Virginia Railroad, for example, a 130-mile line that connected Knoxville with Bristol, right at the Virginia border, advertised four connecting routes: the Tennessee and Georgia road from Knoxville; the Cincinnati, Cumberland Gap and Charleston road at Morristown; the Rogersville and Jefferson line at Rogersville; and the Virginia and Tennessee Railroad at Bristol.[10]

While this reads well, the passenger connecting with the CCG&C would find that it had only 34 miles of track in operating condition; and the passenger bound for the Rogersville line would find only 14 miles of track. Clearly the local passenger would have had more use for these connections than any through passenger. The Virginia and

Tennessee had 204 miles of track but scheduled only one train a day, so a traveler would have a lengthy wait before boarding a connecting train.[11]

A group of Southern short lines cooperated to provide through service to the U.S. mail. The "Great Southern Mail Route" advertised for passengers as well, promising they would go through as fast as the mail. This route consisted of seven short lines, from the Orange, Alexandria and Manassas in Virginia to the Western and Atlantic in Georgia. Their literature assured travelers they would experience "No Detention to Travelers by Omnibus and Ferry Transfers. PASSENGERS CHANGE CARS AT UNION DEPOTS." Passengers could buy tickets at a railway office or in any principal hotel. The trip took four to five days from New York City to Mobile, Alabama.[12]

Despite efforts to reconstruct a transportation system, traveling the Southern lines was a tedious and hazardous enterprise, more comparable to Northern railroads of the 1840s than to those after the Civil War. The Southern rail service remained beset by lack of money and maintenance, good track, cars, engines, and even paying passengers.[13]

By 1870 bankers and investors from New York and Boston, who had extended credit to railroads throughout the North and far West, began to consider Southern railroads a potential opportunity for profitable investment. The South had a word for Northerners who came south to make a profit from the South's desperation: carpetbaggers. But representatives of the Northern banking community proceeded south nevertheless, to buy up railroad stocks and state railroad bonds to sell in the Northeast and even in Europe. Firms such as Morton, Bliss and Company, the Morgan banks, and Jay Cooke of Philadelphia had expanded their reach to international markets even before the Civil War, opening offices in London to sell American railroad stocks and bonds to British investors. After the war, expanding into the South was a natural extension of their investment in the Union Pacific Railroad in the West and the further development of trunk lines throughout the Northeast. In the late 1860s and thereafter, the bankers frequently had as much to say in the planning of railroad networks as did railroad presidents and their boards of directors. The roads needed the constant cooperation of large banks to remain competitive in an emerging national transportation network. And among banks, those with national and international contacts offered more opportunities for capital than small local and state banks that could not boast such far-reaching services.

In 1869 Morton, Bliss and Company of New York City joined the ranks of bankers who, after initial skepticism about railroad bonds, followed the lead of banking houses that made a fortune selling bonds for the Union Pacific Railroad in the West, and began selling bonds for Southern railroads. Morton, Bliss took part in the financing of three major through routes connecting the South to the West—the New Orleans, Mobile and Texas, a through line paralleling the Gulf Coast; the Missouri, Kansas and Texas Railway, which later became known as the "Katy" line; and the extension of the Illinois Central from Cairo south to New Orleans.[14]

These and other bankers were key in reconstructing Southern railroads and joining them with existing through lines in the North, East, and West. In the Midwestern cities of St. Louis and especially Chicago, these new routes from the South linked with numerous established routes across Iowa and beyond to the West, and from Chicago to the East, which by 1870 included the New York Central, the Baltimore and Ohio, and the Pennsylvania.

In the short run the return on these investments did not justify the expenses of building mile after mile of new rails as well as repairing large stretches of war-damaged track. The New Orleans, Mobile and Texas went into foreclosure during the depression year of 1873, and the Katy line also lost money and defaulted on a mortgage in that year. The Illinois Central lost revenue in 1873 but managed to stay in business.[15]

The story of two Boston investors, John Stanton and his brother Daniel, is a typically grim tale of investment in a Southern railroad. The Stanton brothers came south in 1868 and chartered a new railroad which they called the Alabama and Chattanooga. It ran southwest from Tennessee across Alabama and into Mississippi. Parts of this 253-mile line consisted of the remains of prewar railroads; other sections were under construction. Conductor Nimrod Bell began working for the Stantons in 1868, first supervising a grading crew and living with them in cabins they built for themselves. Oxen and mules were used to haul track, rather than work trains such as those used to carry track in the West.[16]

Bell worked about eight years for the Stantons as a laborer, but more often as a conductor, his chosen profession. His position was frequently threatened by the Stantons' habit of recruiting railroad crew members from the Northeast, men considered to be more loyal than Southern whites and more capable than Southern blacks or Chinese. Bell also suffered from a malady common to all the Stantons' employees: he frequently was not paid. The workers, facing debts resulting from months without pay, went on strike in the early 1870s and shut down service on the Alabama and Chattanooga. Stanton went north to borrow more money and returned with enough to resume service but not enough to provide back pay. Bell, owed one hundred dollars a month, lived with friends, slept in cars, and finally began asking to take money out of his passenger receipts to buy food. The construction crews also worked without money and stopped working when food ran out. The Stantons' road, like the major railroads financed by Morton, Bliss and Company, went bankrupt in 1873.[17]

Looked at from both business and personal perspectives, the efforts of Northern investors appear not only self-interested but unsuccessful. They created railroads but lost much of their profit in the Crash of 1873. They ran trains, but the services they provided were as unpredictable as their financial backing.

The South lurched toward railroad recovery through boom and bust, but the recovery demanded an interdependence with Northern economic interests that Southerners had fought a losing war to avoid. In the western part of the South, the Illinois Central was an extensive interstate system of track. Controlled by Northern interests, it served the South from St. Louis to New Orleans and met the needs of Northern manufacturers who wished to ship products from Chicago into the deep South. Further east, in the South's midsection, the Louisville and Nashville had early adopted the policies of many Northern railroads in constructing one of the few Southern trunk lines that also crossed state lines. After the war the L&N again paralleled the efforts of Northern railroads in creating not just trunk and branch lines but a regional empire of connected lines, stretching as far east, south, and west as it could. A company historian reports that the road extended from Louisville south to Montgomery, Alabama, "through various acquisitions and some new construction."[18] This line too increased the ability of Northern shippers to reach Tennessee, Kentucky, and points in Alabama on the Gulf of Mexico.

Aside from the Illinois Central, which paralleled the Mississippi River, and the L&N, which connected the Northern states with the Gulf of Mexico, the third important rail system in the South during Reconstruction grew from a series of short lines that extended down the East Coast from Virginia, then turned west and headed into New Orleans. This set of lines, which eventually united to form the Southern Railway, initially came under the control of the Pennsylvania Railroad, which before 1870 took control of the Richmond and Danville, a key Virginia railroad during the war. But like the lines backed by Morton, Bliss and by John Stanton, financial problems plagued Southern lines to such an extent that the Pennsylvania relinquished its hold on these short lines just before the Crash of 1873.

Even Northern investment could not ensure solvency or profit for most Southern lines. Railroads could not earn the profits they needed in order to repay the elaborate state and bank financing required to build or repair them. To some extent even Northern roads shared this problem, caused in part by building more railroads than any town or state would ever need—in order to make money on financial speculation, without regard for the future usefulness of each line.

In the South the problem hinged in part on degraded social conditions which, during Reconstruction, bordered on chaos. The difference between the L&N and the Alabama and Chattanooga, however, was that the L&N ordinarily kept running whereas the Alabama line, which could not make payroll, stopped running and started again, as the flow of money permitted.

Nimrod Bell's recollections confirm an image of the L&N as financially more stable than most Southern railroads. He had been working as a conductor on the South and North Alabama Railroad when the L&N assumed control of it. While he did not care to remain with the L&N because they put him in charge of a freight train, he did record that his "wages were pretty fair for those times and promptly paid." Even on the L&N, however, "One or two bad wrecks occurred between Decatur and Birmingham with passenger-trains and several passengers killed."[19]

On the short lines for which Bell worked, hazards made the conducting of a passenger train a perilous business. The track, hastily laid, caused frequent derailments. Across creeks and swamps the track frequently stood on trestles rather than a bridge, and under the weight of his train the trestles and track sank from view below the surface of the water. Sometimes the trestles, made of rotting wood, broke under the strain and sent the train into the water below. The trains ran through a great deal of such wild country, in low, wet areas that discouraged building and into towns, including Chattanooga and Atlanta, that had been ravaged by war.[20]

In the Southern countryside a state of lawlessness similar to that in the West persisted during Reconstruction. Bell frequently carried a gun and had to resort at times to hitting contentious crew and passengers with a stick. Once a large group of black men boarded his train and insisted on being carried to Chattanooga without paying the fare. Bell locked his train and held them off with a pistol until he could wire his supervisor for instructions. A number of the violent incidents he dealt with involved race issues, among blacks, Irish immigrants, Southern whites, Northern whites, and Chinese. They vied for jobs and frequently traveled the rails in large groups to wherever work might be found. Bell reported the death of a black mail agent who was shot while on board a train, his assailant being a sniper in the woods nearby.[21]

The Southern rail service, barely surviving, lacked many of the finer points of passenger service. While hotels with dining rooms could be found near the track at some points, any hope of coordinated services for railroad passengers was a faint hope indeed. With few towns of any consequence along the line, and few passengers who could pay the fare, elaborate services had no reasonable place. A passenger might ride all day without any break for a meal, simply because the train did not pass any restaurants. Passengers might have to spend the night in a hotel if the train had broken down or was otherwise delayed. Making connections for long-distance travel had many of the characteristics of rail travel in the 1840s. Frequent delays made it all but impossible to rely on smooth connections from one rail line to another, except in major urban areas.[22]

Occasionally a Pullman sleeping car passed through the wilds of the Southern landscape, but in general they served the needs of long-distance passengers, traveling from the Gulf Coast area to the relative peace and stability of the Northeast. In the absence of coordinated through routes, Southern rail lines attached the sleeper cars to any local train traveling toward the sleepers' ultimate destination.[23] In this respect too, Southern passenger service resembled that of the West; Northerners might invest in the South, but few wanted to live there or even visit until more social stability had been achieved. In the interval, however, they gained the advantage of being able to travel by rail through the South to more prosperous regions such as the Southwest.

In the late 1870s the country began to pull out of the economic slump which had begun when the failure of Jay Cooke Bankers in Philadelphia caused widespread railroad bankruptcies. In most in-stances of bankruptcy a railroad could continue service while the company and creditors came up with a scheme to reduce debt and in-crease profits. Commonly the railroad looked for a buyer, usually an-other line that could afford to take it over. Thus the consolidation of many railroads into fewer and fewer hands characterized the period from 1873 to about 1877. The largest, longest, and wealthiest rail-roads benefited most from this situation, since they had the means to gather in financially troubled short lines. The railroad empires of the Gilded Age emerged from the chaos of financial panic.

By the early 1870s the cities of the South began to evidence signs of recovery. Birmingham, Chattanooga, and Atlanta were emerging as centers of social and economic order in the midst of widespread poverty. While the railroads connecting these cities to the North con-tributed to recovery, investment made the difference in the return of prosperity. With the withdrawal of all remaining Union troops from the South in 1877, business picked up throughout the country, and the South finally began the long-delayed process of connecting its local rail lines with the major systems of the North and West.

As in the North, the connections were achieved not through a co-

Crowds were small and stations simple in rural areas.

operative linking of track but through a power struggle by which the financially stronger railroads won control of the weaker lines. The evidence of these struggles showed up in the nation's law courts, just as the earlier railroad conflicts of the North had. In the long run, Southern poverty led directly to an extension of the financial reach of New York and Boston investors, who were the only people with the money needed to buy out numbers of small railroads and run a rail system of any kind.

Just as the railroads provided a haven and supplies for soldiers during the war, and for travelers in the West, it provided the tools of survival to another army of uprooted people, the civilian South during Reconstruction. And belatedly it provided the tools for uniting the three regions through trade. But as the South had known and the people of the West were learning, the railroad did not set down civilization in the wilderness. The price of unity for the nation was a distinctly uneven tradeoff in which the owners of the railroads took the profits which might have enriched the West and South at the local level. The South, like the West, remained predominantly rural and poor.

14

||||||||||||||||||||||

The Traveling Public and Its Servants

On one road we find the cars well-lighted, kept at a comfortable temperature, the ventilation watched by an intelligent trainman; and we find high-back seats, spaced so far apart that a long-legged man can sit in them without doubling up; and the cars are provided with continuous basket racks and glazed with double windows, so that passengers can see out in frosty weather. On the other road, which unfortunately is closer to the typical road, except in the immediate neighborhood of the great Eastern cities, we find day cars heated by cast-iron stoves made in the company's foundry, and burning wood. The cars are not ventilated except through accidental cracks; they are lighted by cheap lamps with bad oil, which are apparently never cleaned; the seats are close together; there is one small basket rack about every three seats, and the single glass in the windows keeps the car cold by rapid radiation and prevents an outlook by the condensation on the glass.

—"Comfort in Day Cars," *Railroad Gazette,* 1893[1]

P ASSENGER SERVICES available to those who traveled the railroads in the northeastern United States, from Maine to the Mississippi River, and south to the Ohio River, were the most extensive, diversified, and specialized of any in the country. By the 1890s they ran the spectrum of social and economic needs. New railroads were now built with vacationers, commuters, and excursionists in mind, not simply seekers after land or wealth. Those who spent, whether for shopping or leisure, joined the passengers on late-nineteenth-century trains in the prosperous Northeast.

During this high-water mark of diversified railroad services to the public, however, signs began to appear that passengers did not pay their way when it came to rail company profits. Passengers formed a shrinking proportion of the business done by rail. Mass migrations to the West declined toward the end of the century, and the need to supply new settlers in the West and survivors in the South encouraged growth in mail and express and freight services.

Nevertheless, from 1865 to 1900 the major rail systems, including the Boston and Maine, the New York and New Haven, the New York Central, the Baltimore and Ohio, the Pennsylvania, and the Chicago and Northwestern, expanded their stock of specialized cars, bringing ever-greater comfort, space, and speed to the routes between major Eastern cities.[2] The invention of the Pullman sleeping car, which originated in Chicago, led to a growing inventory of saloon, parlor, and dining cars that aped the elegance of the major urban hotels and protected the widening class of those with discretionary income from the raucousness, dirt, and discomfort of the day cars.

Technological changes also transformed the braking systems, ventilation, and lighting systems of the better cars designed for through travel. Still, by the turn of the century much local rail traffic continued to practice an older craft, still traveling with a much older technology, without the means or the traffic to justify the expenses of an updated technology for passenger service.

By the 1870s settlement and trade throughout the Northeast had yielded an emergent middle class, not identified so much with towns, states, or regions as with one another—a style of living with similar habits, whether in Pennsylvania, Illinois, or Massachusetts. These

people of middling means took great advantage of national travel and
developed social and economic practices that enlarged their sphere of
activity beyond the local area. While the poor had to restrict their
wandering for lack of means, the middling sort pursued business and
pleasure at ever-greater distances from home.

One group with a bird's-eye view of these travel habits was the
American Association of Passenger Traffic Officers, which established many of the special rates for groups traveling to the same destination at the same time. While the agents still provided discounts
for "colonists" and "land grant excursionists," they also served students, club and association members, theatergoers, religious groups,
businessmen, teachers, and political party members with a generally
middle-class membership.[3] These kinds of groups gave the rail system a more dependable source of income than did the migrants who
pushed west but had few contacts with national interests outside the
sale of their own crops.

Groups and organizations approached the railroads for favors in
much the same way that individuals historically had approached the
government for private legislation. Instead of legislation they asked
for reduced rates because of the amount of business they would bring
to the railroads by traveling in groups. In 1872 the traffic officers had
no firm policy on which groups should receive "consideration." In the
minutes, they recorded that

> Applications have been and will be made for reduced rates and round
> trip tickets to political, musical, and other convocations, to be held at
> competing points during the coming [summer] season; and for teach-
> ers, pleasure-seekers and other individuals. What rule shall be
> adopted as between competing lines, regarding this class of busi-
> ness?[4]

By the 1880s the number of requests had reached flood tide. They
included, for example, the Millers' International Convention held in
Cincinnati, the National Commercial Travelers of America, and the
International Cotton Exposition and World's Fair in Atlanta, all in
1881. By 1884 the groups seeking special rates included the World's
Exposition in New Orleans, a national meeting of the Phi Delta Theta
fraternity, the Women's Christian Temperance Union, the National

Laundry Association (request rejected), the National Education Association, and the national convention of the National party.[5]

In 1885 the Colored People's World's Exposition sought favors along with the Young Men's Christian Association, the Wholesale Merchants of Chicago, the Traders and Travelers Union, and the Civil War's Grand Army of the Republic, which held numerous reunions as long as aging soldiers survived. Organizing nationally was the work of the age, and ticketing records show that railroads made possible the growth of organizations with a national membership of people with middling means.[6] Ticketing records indicate that shoppers too could take advantage of special rates.

In the post–Civil War era much of the nation's political life centered on railroads. Lincoln's whistle-stop campaign had set a precedent for politicians and reformers who traveled for voters and other forms of support. The women's movement gained much of its momentum this way, through the hundreds of thousands of miles traveled in railroad cars, to all states, by suffragists such as Susan B. Anthony and Elizabeth Cady Stanton, municipal reformers such as Jane Addams and Alice Hamilton, and temperance advocates such as Frances Willard.[7] The American Federation of Labor and, of course, the American Railroad Union both brought local union chapters and brotherhoods under a national organization made possible primarily because of the railroad.

The railroads developed services specific to other social classes too. In fact, the popular view of railroads during the Gilded Age was less their service to the middling sort than their catering to the rich. Lucius Beebe, who spent a lifetime documenting the elegant private railroad cars and services that enough money could buy, created a number of photographic histories depicting the Pullman cars, the Pullman Palace Cars, and the private cars owned by individuals who would pay to have the car attached to a train and thus travel in complete privacy.[8]

While the simple fact that railroad journeys became long enough to justify a sleeping car made the Pullman successful, it was also considerably larger, cleaner, and more elegant than the numerous sleeping cars in existence before the Civil War. Even the poor and the middle classes made public complaints about the beds and bedfellows in the earliest sleeping cars; the rich disdained them entirely until Pullman, during the Civil War, introduced the Northern railroads to his sleeper, deliberately more elegant and comfortable than any earlier car. He rented these cars to railroad companies, including Pullman employees to serve the passengers, on all major through routes out of Chicago. They cost the passenger more than the day coach, carried fewer passengers in each car, and provided the services of porters, frequently black, to passengers. The porters converted the seats used in the daylight hours into beds for the night, and covered the beds behind drapes. They provided towels and other toilet articles and moved luggage to the station platform at journey's end. Even with so many amenities, some passengers still felt uncomfortable at the thought of an open sleeping car where all passengers lay in bed without intervening walls between them.

Pullman provided this alternative to the crowds and other discomforts of the day cars at a price. He followed the successful sleeper with his dining car, which provided a kitchen, cook, china dishes, tablecloths, and silver service, all with the distinctive design of the Pullman Company or the logo of the railroad on which the cars were running. The wealthy could take a through train from New York to Chicago without stopping for the night or for meals.

Other specialized cars included several types of day cars that demanded higher fares and had fewer seats and more upholstery, padding, and decor. These parlor cars resembled high Victorian living rooms, complete with interior wood paneling, mirrors, and draperies. The chairs, however, had the added advantage that they swiveled, so that the passenger could look out the window or turn to face other passengers. Saloon cars also charged more for added elegance while smoking cars might either be day cars or more elaborate cars with fewer seats, where only a few passengers could smoke comfortably. The Pullman Palace Car and the hotel car were variations and combinations of sleeping, dining, and parlor cars. Many of the cars were unique in design and carried individual names, such as the City of Aurora, the Plymouth Rock, the Western World, and the City of New York, much as day cars had been named before the Civil War.[9]

These highly specialized cars that began to characterize through trains during the 1870s and 1880s raised the issue of passengers moving safely and comfortably from one car to another. With the invention of dining cars and other specialized cars, passengers needed to walk from car to car safely. Starting in the 1880s many through trains built vestibules to enclose the platforms at each end of the car, and removed the platform railings, thus making possible a relatively safe passage between cars. The through train, especially the more elegant ones, became more than ever a self-sufficient unit where the passenger need not ever venture outdoors in the course of the journey.

At the other end of the economic spectrum, rail service for urban workers, rural residents, and the poor also had distinctive features. Like the Union Pacific and other transcontinental lines, the Eastern trunk lines also had emigrant cars. While emigrants were traveling alone or in families, the trunk lines herded them into large groups who rode the cars together without comforts or privacy. These poor received the lowest priority of any passenger business. Second-class cars were less comfortable and cost less than first class, and a step above emigrant cars. Second-class travelers had no stopover privileges, as first-class travelers did.[10] This meant that the poorer class of travelers could not get off the train for a visit and later get back on, but had to proceed directly to their destination. A small minority of poor passengers traveled second class, which could be most often found on railroad lines with large numbers of emigrant passengers, blacks, or laborers.

While some trunk lines, including the New York and New Haven Railroad and the Pennsylvania Railroad, did not report owning second-class cars during the 1870s and 1880s, others further west used a number of them. The Chicago and Northwestern Railroad owned and used a few second-class carriages throughout these two decades, but since the C&N did not report owning emigrant cars, its second-class travel probably differed very little from transport for emigrants. The Illinois Central did not report ownership of either emigrant or second-class cars but did indicate that it used a small number of "old passenger cars."[11]

Another railroad service that drew many working poor as well as middle-class customers was the commuter service, which brought laborers into cities from suburban homes. Railroads in Boston, New York, Philadelphia, and Chicago, among other cities, daily carried

passengers to industrial jobs and offered monthly commuter discounts on tickets for this service. Of these cities, New York probably
had the greatest number of commuter trains arriving daily, especially
on the Central Railroad of New Jersey, which in 1870 ran trains in
and out of the city every hour during the early morning and early
evening. In 1879 the Chicago and Northwestern began reporting its
profits from commuter traffic separately from other categories of income, and indicated that commuter revenues for that year accounted
for 2.33 percent of all income from operations.[12]

The working poor and the middle class could also be found on the
branch lines and local lines that had little or no through traffic. These
innumerable short lines carried local residents and products to local
markets and took local visitors, wanderers, and other passengers who
did not venture as far into the world as the new nationally based middle class. In many instances the local trains combined freight and passenger functions, carrying one or two products from small farms to
small towns. Here, as in the South, the mixed train saved money for
the railroads with a low operating budget. Lumber from logging
camps, chickens and other animals, granite and other stone, and ice
were a handful of the products from a myriad of small-scale industries
that sold to local markets and had no designs on national trade. The
workers in these industries, and their families and friends, traveled
the railroad, whether in a freight car or passenger car. Workers in
urban areas who lived near a train station could take the working-
man's train, the equivalent of a commuter train for the laborer.[13]

The development of specialized services in the Northeast had its
drawbacks. Just as railroads provided expensive services for the
wealthy and budget services for the poor, they also selectively
adopted new train technology, introducing safer and better equipment only on the most profitable routes. This pattern of stratification
appears in the way railroads adopted improved brakes for their cars
after the Civil War. In 1869 George Westinghouse patented the air
brake, which automatically set brakes on all cars of a train at the same
time rather than relying on brakemen who stood on top of the cars to
set brakes by hand. The increase in safety was obvious, and, as the accident rate of railroads rose during the 1880s, many roads advertised
the superior safety of their passenger trains by noting they had air

brakes. The cost, however, prevented some through railroads and many branch lines from investing in "replacement technology." They continued to use the old braking system. In 1893 a federal law required the use of air brakes on trains traveling interstate, but brakemen continued to perform their hazardous duty the old-fashioned way well into the twentieth century.[14]

A similar story can be told regarding the adaptation of electricity to railroads. A few trunk lines experimented with electrically lit trains in the early 1880s, but passengers who rode the trains after the turn of the century could later recall that the conductor still lit the gas jets in cars on local routes. Heating and ventilation equally passed through a period of trial and experimentation, and proved their worth on through routes; but they found few takers on the branch lines, which did not have the capital to invest in these improvements.[15]

Even on the profitable routes, income from passenger services was substantially less than could be earned through freight services, thus raising questions as to how much new technology any passenger service could afford. The gap between freight and passenger income that had developed on many lines before the Civil War continued to widen despite a rapid increase in population. In general, passenger profits climbed annually, except during the panic of the 1870s and the depression of the 1890s. But on through lines, profits from freight rose much faster, frequently bringing in three to four times as much money annually as did the passenger business. The Pennsylvania Railroad reported that in 1876 it earned $3,646,673 from the passenger service, and $15,924,275 from freight. The Chicago and Northwestern, a link on the transcontinental route, in its fiscal year 1874–1875 earned $3,205,059 from its passengers and $8,837,828 from freight.[16]

A small but increasing share of railroad revenue came from the mail and express businesses, which required specialized cars that were usually combined with a passenger train on intercity routes. The mail cars, complete with files for sorting, stamps for dating, and bags for delivering mail, traveled with the passenger trains called mail trains or fast mail trains; they usually traveled about thirty miles an hour, somewhat faster than other through trains. These trains did not stop at every station, and if they took on mail from a small station they did so without stopping, by catching a bag raised on a hook at the local depot.

Similarly, the passenger trains carried express packages, consigned to the railroads by American Express, Southeastern Express, and other firms that supported the growing national mail-order business. In fact, the practice of combining mail, express, and passenger business became so widespread that very few trains were exclusively for passengers. A look at the *Travelers' Official Guide of the Railways for 1869* shows that most through passenger trains were called mail or express trains, terms which became synonymous with speed, since the contracts to carry these items required haste.[17] These, plus the mixed trains, all carried a combination of passengers and goods, another sign that passenger business was to some extent propped up by the burgeoning exchange of goods in areas that had not even been settled before the Civil War. For passengers who wanted a train that stopped at all the local stations, accommodation trains ran along through routes, usually at ten to twenty miles per hour. But the designation on a train did not guarantee a given speed: mail trains could be as slow as accommodation trains, express trains as slow as mixed trains. Trains traveled at different speeds in different terrains, at different seasons of the year, and at different hours of the day.

While the railroad system in the Northeast showed a remarkable inventiveness in meeting the needs of an extremely diverse population of travelers, the roads were moving toward ever more centralized control, as the Pennsylvania, New York Central, Boston and Maine, and other trunk systems bought or leased so many lines that they eliminated much local control over branch roads during the 1880s. Much of the track mileage in the Northeast was controlled by a small group of men who sat on interlocking boards of directors. By 1906, when a joint annual statement was published of the financial status of fourteen roads, including the New York Central and the Michigan Central, certain names recur on the fourteen boards of directors. Directors of the New York Central included Chauncey Depew, William K. Vanderbilt, William Rockefeller, and J. Pierpont Morgan, all of whom also sat on the boards of the New York, Chicago and St. Louis, and the Michigan Central. On the board of the Lake Shore and Michigan Southern Railway sat Vanderbilt, Rockefeller, and Morgan.

Vanderbilt and Morgan had seats on the board of the Lake Erie and Western Railroad, and Vanderbilt alone on the Chicago, Indiana and Southern Railroad. The Cleveland, Cincinnati, Chicago and St. Louis Railway Company was under the control of a board that included Depew, Vanderbilt, and Morgan.[18]

This close control of the railroad system by a few was the logical consequence of competition. By the end of the century large numbers of local railroad promoters and investors had sold out to fewer and fewer buyers until monopoly control was achieved. This control had a profound effect on railroad passenger services in all major regions of the country. The flexibility and diversity of services, based on regional needs, began to evolve toward a philosophy of efficiency and uniformity in pursuit of profit. The railroads sought to draw all lines under the same rules of operation, regardless of passenger needs. Beginning in the 1880s the science of railroading began to displace the remarkable social diversity of passenger travel.

15

||||||||||||||||||||

The Law Tries to Catch Up

Every railroad company shall provide its passenger, baggage, mail, and express cars with suitable platforms to secure the safety of persons passing from car to car, or connecting aprons or bridges, . . . shall from the first day of May until the first day of November, annually, carry through each passenger car, once an hour, a suitable quantity of good drinking-water for the free use of the passengers, with suitable appurtenances for carrying it, and a clean glass tumbler for using it; . . . and shall conspiciously post on each passenger depot building the name of the station, and on each passenger car which leaves the *termini* of their own or any other road, a legible card, or cards, not less than three feet in length, with large letters, distinguishing way from express trains, and designating the direction in which the trains are next to move. . . .

—Thirty-Third Annual Report of the Railroad Commissioners of the State of Connecticut, 1886[1]

THE NORTHERN VICTORY in the Civil War and the completion of the transcontinental railroad in 1869 both moved the country a long way toward unification by rail. A few investors headed south to rebuild shattered rail lines; others headed west, where transcontinental lines soon paralleled the Union Pacific and Central Pacific to the north and south. The Northern Pacific, connecting Minneapolis with the West Coast, was federally chartered in 1864 and completed in 1883. The Southern Pacific, connecting New Orleans to the Pacific, and the Texas and Pacific also opened in the 1880s. In 1893 the Great Northern, competing with the Northern Pacific, opened its full route. Publicists hailed the railroads as the symbol and agent of a new national order.

But the price of unity had not yet been fully paid, even in the aftermath of the Civil War. In addition to reducing the South, the railroads dragged the political, legal, and social structures of the North in their wake. Huge, monopolistic railroad companies emerged, controlling extraordinary amounts of capital and expanses of track, and driving competitors from the business. The question of who was in control, the government or the railroads, arose in all sections of the country, restating the problem that had faced towns and states before the Civil War. Louis Brandeis, a Harvard lawyer and strong opponent of unrestrained corporate power, took the historical view. In a later Supreme Court decision, he reminded the public that until the passage of the general incorporation laws, government had recognized the potential for abuse of power. Corporations had been few in number, and they had been founded to function for two to five decades, not permanently.

"Severe limitations" had been deliberately imposed on corporations, and the lifting of these restrictions seemed to have been prompted simply by government's inability to enforce the laws. "The removal by the leading industrial states of the limitations upon the size and powers of business corporations appears to have been due," Brandeis wrote, "not to their conviction that maintenance of the restrictions was undesirable in itself, but to the conviction that it was futile to insist upon them; because local restriction would be circumvented by foreign incorporation."[2] While some have objected to Brandeis's extreme view, the government did systematically remove legal obstacles to commercial development.

Conflicts abounded between the public need for basic transporta-

tion services and the railroads' intense drive for expansion and profits at the expense of comfort and safety. Crowds engendered by railroad transport grew larger and more unruly. Finding themselves
beyond the boundaries of a defined and enforceable legal structure,
passengers discovered that the temptations of gambling, theft, drunk-
enness, and violence were easy to pursue, even in public. In the absence of any devices of law enforcement, states began to confer police
powers on conductors, many of whom carried guns. Thus even the
crowds of the settled Northeast began to resemble those in the uprooted areas of the South and West.

In addition to creating a disorderly social maze for their passengers, the railroads themselves balked at completing the process of
national unification that they had undertaken in cooperation with all
levels of government. In the interests of maximum profits, the roads
refused to set their rates publicly and frequently charged arbitrary or
discriminatory rates for both passengers and freight. In the interests
of competition, they often refused to connect their services with
those of competing lines, thus making the movement of freight and
passengers over long distances unnecessarily inefficient.

As interstate travel became more common, the absence of a system
of national laws to govern railroads or passengers left the former free
to seek maximum profits to the detriment of public welfare, and the
latter free to disrupt crowded stations and cars in any number of
ways. In addition to drinking, gambling, and boisterous behavior, passengers pursued their own plans without regard to the rules of the
railroads. Riding without tickets, jumping on and off moving cars,
traveling in the engine, caboose, or aboard a freight train, passengers
made the experience their own. The railroads too retained their self-
interested notions: competition and profit came first, service came
second.

The litany of public complaints about service was long. Train
schedules were unreliable; equipment was often unsafe; passengers
could not buy tickets when and where they needed them; stops might
have station accommodations or not; passengers might find seating or
not aboard the train; toilets, water, ventilation, and other mechanical
aspects of service might or might not be available. Passengers found
that the price of a ticket was frequently determined by the caprice of

Even after the Civil War, train breakdowns allowed passengers an opportunity to stretch and tour the landscape on foot.

a railroad company, its agent, or an employee, not by the distance traveled. And the speed of trains and their questionable equipment continued to cause severe accidents, many of which resulted in deadly fires.

Reorienting the legal system to address the problems of railroad transport and other changes brought on by industrialization took many years and never entirely resolved the conflicts of interest inherent in railroad practices. While the railroad became a key element in a newly emerging national social order after the Civil War, it still functioned in large part beyond the boundaries of existing law.

Constitutionally the federal government could provide no leadership in resolving these railroad dilemmas. Between the 1850s and 1870s it confined its interest to enormous grants of public Western land to the railroads, to further the prewar dream of extending railroad transportation to the West Coast. But a number of state governments saw that legal changes were essential if railroad service was to have any measure of order. Trains must be safe and efficient, and passengers must be orderly. Town law was no longer sufficient to protect and restrain the individual in the postwar world, for he spent much more time traveling. And only a few laws, local or state, existed to restrain and protect the railroad corporation.

First in the North and later in the West and South, states began passing statutes to control the behavior of passengers and the quality and safety of passenger service. It is clear from the nature of this legislation that railroads did not, on their own initiative, ensure basic standards of service or behavior except on their most expensive through trains. Most states also created state railroad commissions to monitor the rates charged by railroads, primarily for freight but in many cases for passenger traffic as well. These commissions also dealt with some of the immense number of legal cases against the railroads, cases about railroad mismanagement and passenger injury which were clogging the schedules of state courts.

The legal challenge to the railroads and to their failure to protect the passenger did not, however, resolve all these problems. Despite new state laws and the creation of state railroad commissions, both states and nation still lacked a coordinated legal system that would address many of the abuses of railroad service. In the South and West particularly, legal restraints of any kind were minimal during the 1860s and 1870s. The older and more prosperous states led the way in railroad legislation, with the South and West following suit during the 1880s.

In all states the fight for railroad regulation was a prolonged public struggle. Like the Grangers, who organized among the farm communities of the upper Midwest during the 1860s in order to pass laws regulating freight rates, other advocates of railroad legislation faced the zealous political opposition of the railroads. Company directors made a point of buying legislative votes at both the state and federal levels to obstruct the passage of regulations. Far from encouraging the development of standards for passenger service, the railroads struggled to keep the legal requirements of service to a minimum.

Anger and conflict continued to build through the 1870s and 1880s while state legislatures gradually mandated minimum standards for passenger service. Finally, in 1887, the federal government took its first tentative step toward a national system of legal standards for the railroads: the creation of the Interstate Commerce Commission.

In the broadest sense this struggle for regulation was regional. Farmers of the Western and Southern states blamed the high-handed policies of railroads on the arrogance of the Northeast. More highly industrialized, with greater sources of capital, the bankers and investors of the Northeast controlled more and more of the railroad mileage in other sections of the country; and they developed a reputation for caring only about profit, to the detriment of service and fares. Even in the Northeast, the press fumed about the lawless attitudes of the railroaders and the need for regulation. And regulation came to the Northern states more quickly than to the less populous and less organized West and South.

In many respects the tension between sections was recast as a tension between the railroad corporations and their customers or "public," mediated by the states. Antagonism and opposition replaced the sense of excitement and adventure that had invigorated both railroaders and their customers before the Civil War. Writers in the public eye discussed "the railroad problem" rather than the national mission of unity through commerce. Discord between the railroads and the people threatened disunity instead.

The acceptance by some state courts of the railroad as a common carrier during the 1850s made it possible for legislatures in those states to apply the laws of common carriers to protect the welfare of passengers. The states also began adding new regulations to existing law, hoping to control railroad activities. Even so, uniformity did not prevail. As late as 1889, other state courts continued to reject the notion that a railroad had the public responsibilities of a common carrier. The state laws passed during the years after the Civil War tell a tale less about the development of a national passenger service than about poor quality or absence of services, magnified by unruly passenger behavior and remedied only by piecemeal legislative adjustments.

In the 1860s both during and after the war, Northern state legislatures began creating standards of service in statute law both to protect and discipline passengers as well as to strengthen the police powers of railroad officials, particularly the conductor. But in a country where more and more railroads crossed state lines, the effectiveness of these early laws was limited. In 1863 New York passed a law granting railroad conductors police powers with the stipulation that each must wear a "railroad police badge." The following year Maryland gave railroad officials the power to arrest pickpockets and thieves in the station or on the train. In 1865 Pennsylvania approved the creation of railroad police, to be appointed upon the request of a railroad company.[3] All these laws point to the presence of unsavory types riding in the same car with more restrained citizens, and to the previous absence of a successful remedy.

Other policies addressed by legislation in the 1860s included fire safety and racial segregation, both aspects of the railroads' crowd control. A Wisconsin law ended the locking of cars to keep passengers in or out, probably because of the fire hazard, and in the same year a regulation provided for greater care in the use of kerosene lamps aboard trains. In 1867, following the Civil Rights Act a year earlier, Pennsylvania prohibited racial discrimination aboard a train. The spirit of this law was evaded in the South, where after Reconstruction many states began passing Jim Crow laws that required segregation of the races.[4]

Among Southern states in the 1860s, Tennessee appears to have had one of the only legislatures to pass laws specifically about railroad services. This is probably because other Southern states had experienced too much destruction to provide even minimal protections. In one act of 1865, Tennessee stipulated that railroad ticket offices had to be open for business at least one hour before train time; that the conductor must call out the name of each station stop; that all train cars must be provided with heat, light, and water; and that the conductor must make certain that each passenger occupied only one seat, so that as many passengers as possible might be seated.[5]

In the West, Nebraska was one of the few states to provide protection for passengers and police powers for conductors. A law passed in 1866 required that while conductors could continue to put off passengers refusing to pay their fare, the train had to be within five miles of a station when the conductor did so. The same law specified also that trains must run at "regular times," in other words, on a schedule, and provide "sufficient accommodation" for all passengers.[6]

During the 1870s certain Northern states, including New Hampshire and Indiana, also gave increased police powers to conductors, New Hampshire specifying that conductors had the power to put noisy passengers in the baggage car. Indiana gave conductors the specific power to arrest passengers and to put disorderly passengers off the train. Massachusetts required railroad conductors and other employees to wear badges and uniforms. In the West, California was one of the few states to grant similar powers to the conductor, spelling out in law some aspects of the conductor's responsibilities: to wear a badge and to eject nonpaying passengers. And in the South, North Carolina passed an extensive railroad law which included provisions similar to those of California.[7]

Other 1870s legislation addressed the responsibility of the railroads to improve basic services. Wisconsin required companies to maintain their stations while Massachusetts forbade loitering in stations and required adequate signs marking depots. California mandated that car space be furnished for all passengers, and that the railroad company be liable for refusing to carry a paying passenger.[8]

During the 1880s state railroad legislation of this type became more common and much more uniform. Many states imitated the others' language in setting standards for passenger service. This necessarily put more pressure on interstate railroads to conform to uniform legal requirements. States from the South and West as well as the North showed more initiative in the passage of these acts.

The quality of station service was the chief focus. Illinois, Connecticut, and Vermont were among Northern states that set legal requirements for services at depots. In Illinois they had to be "open, lighted, and warm"; in Vermont "suitable"; and in Connecticut every depot had to provide "suitable water closets."[9]

West of the Mississippi, Iowa reiterated the Illinois requirement that depots be "open, lighted, and warm"; Missouri asked for "waiting room or rooms sufficiently comfortable"; and Idaho's territorial legislature mandated "sufficient room and accommodation." In the South, South Carolina, Alabama, and Tennessee all passed legislation to set standards for depot service, such as "comfortable seats," "comfort and accommodation," or, more specifically, as in the case of Tennessee, a heated, lighted, clean, and ventilated waiting room with

seats for waiting passengers. Other railroad legislation of this period
included a Wyoming statute that prohibited gambling on trains; a
number of statutes to regulate passenger fares and free passes; and
many acts to regulate the way passenger cars were heated, quite
clearly because of the risk of fire.[10]

The focus on station legislation in the 1870s and 1880s is explained
in part by the number of personal injuries that took place in stations.
A glance at state supreme court records reveals the nature of the
problem. In 1873 the supreme court of Wisconsin heard a case
against the Chicago and Northwestern Railroad.

> The plaintiff, being a woman seventy-two years old, was put off, with
> her trunk, at defendant's depot between nine and ten o'clock at night.
> The depot was not upon any public highway; it was not open or
> lighted, and there was no one there to give her information. . . . In try-
> ing to reach the other end of the platform to shelter herself from the
> cold wind, she fell down a flight of three steps . . . and was injured.[11]

In 1879 the same court heard the following, against the same railroad.

> . . . The defendant had constructed a platform at Glendale, about one
> hundred and five feet long and about six feet wide, the north end of
> which was about three feet above the ground, with no rail or other
> guard, and with no stationary or other light kept thereon at night when
> the passenger train stopped . . . the only lights being those in the
> hands of the station agent, conductor, and brakeman. . . . Mrs.
> Quaife . . . in attempting to get upon the steps of . . . car, stepped off
> the end of the platform and fell the distance of three feet or more, and
> received the injuries complained of.

Two similar suits were brought against the Chicago and Northwestern in 1885 and 1887.[12]

In 1889 a passenger alighted at a Connecticut station from the
New York, New Haven and Hartford train, but was injured when he

> . . . passed by one flight of stairs, which led from where a light shone
> on the platform on which he was standing, and started to go to another
> flight, which he was accustomed to take in common with other peo-

ple, to reach the ground, but which on that night was not lighted in any manner.

Other passengers, in both Wisconsin and Pennsylvania, filed suit when they had to alight from a moving train and were injured.[13]

Bringing suit became the norm for passengers seeking redress of damages, because while statutes regulating passenger service proliferated, enforcement proved difficult. Conductors, despite their police powers, could not ensure legally required services. All state courts, without exception, and the Supreme Court of the United States began hearing more personal injury cases after the Civil War. While the ɔupreme Court appears to have heard very few such cases before the war, it heard more than two dozen between 1865 and 1890, and many more were resolved by state supreme courts.[14]

The cases sound familiar: they rephrase in legal terms the kinds of risks commonly taken by both passengers and railroads before the Civil War, and they try to determine who was legally at fault in each case where injury resulted. In an 1870 case, a passenger in Kansas asked to ride on a construction train, was allowed to, and then sustained an injury; the construction train, stated the court, was "not subject to the stringent obligations and responsibilities of carriers of passengers." On the other hand, in 1880 the Supreme Court held the railroad responsible for a passenger injury sustained when "he was injured by the falling of a berth in the sleeping car."[15] While the risks of railroad travel still held an element of adventure for travelers, a strong element of antagonism had entered into the relationship between the carrier and the passengers by the late 1860s, and it carried through the remaining decades of the century.

To address thousands of complaints about passenger and freight traffic each year, a number of states responded by updating the old commission system of regulation. Between 1869 and 1890 twenty-five additional state commissions were formed, most of them in the East or in the grain states of the Midwest and West.[16] Although their primary mission focused on rate discrimination facing freight customers, their importance for passengers must not be underestimated. By the end of the 1880s state legislatures and state railroad commissions in all parts of the country had addressed two of the most difficult problems facing all railroad customers: discriminatory rates and poor connections.

Discriminatory rates grew out of the railroads' competition for potential freight customers. Before 1890 state commissions such as those in Kentucky, Massachusetts, Missouri, and Connecticut prohibited discrimination only for freight rates. Other states, including Pennsylvania, Illinois, Iowa, Minnesota, California, Arkansas, Georgia, and Florida, protected passengers as well as freight shippers from paying unreasonable rates. And they limited the use of free passes as a gratuity for regular customers. The language of the law varied little from state to state, indicating that the states' intent was to nationalize this legal protection as uniformly as possible. The wording of the Illinois law was typical:

> If any such railroad corporation shall charge, collect, or receive for the transportation of any passenger or freight of any description upon its railroad for any distance within this State, the same, or a greater amount of toll or compensation than is at the same time charged . . . of any passenger or like quantity of freight over a greater distance of the same railroad . . . [it] shall be deemed and taken against such railroad corporation as prima facie evidence of the unjust discriminations prohibited by the provisions of this act.[17]

Most state commissions had the authority to hear complaints pertaining to this legislation, and frequently the judicial authority to render a verdict, though it could be overridden by a court. In states including Wisconsin, Mississippi, Missouri, North Dakota, Nebraska, and many others, the commissions had the responsibility to "hear and determine complaints subject to revision by the courts." A number of states also required the railroads to publish and post their rates for the benefit of the public. But as late as 1890 a number of states and territories, such as Arizona, Idaho, Utah, Delaware, Louisiana, Maryland, Montana, New Jersey, New Mexico, and Pennsylvania, had no commission at all.[18]

The second major responsibility of state commissions in the creation of a national passenger service was to require all railroads to make connections with other lines, regardless of the railroads' inclination to make or shun these connections as profits dictated. For example, the Interstate Commerce Commission reported that in Wisconsin, "Intersecting lines . . . [were] authorized and required to connect tracks by switches, etc." In Indiana,

> Among the general powers of railroad companies . . . [were]:
> Sec. 3903, clause 6. To cross, intersect, join, and unite its railroad with any other railroad before constructed, at any point on its route, and upon the grounds of such other railroad company, with the necessary turnouts. . . .

Idaho provided the same power to all railroads, and then added:

> And if the two corporations can not agree upon the amount of compensation to be made therefor, or the points or the manner of such crossings, intersections, and connections, the same must be ascertained and determined as is provided in the Code of Civil Procedure.[19]

Such connections made all long-distance travel faster, safer, and more efficient.

In creating the Interstate Commerce Commission and defining its powers in 1887, Congress followed many of the precedents set by state commissions. The ICC regulated a list of abusive practices that closely paralleled those regulated at the state level: rate discrimination, lack of adequate facilities for service involving more than one railroad. The major difference was that the ICC dealt only with railroads that served more than one state. Like the state commissions, the ICC required that rates be reasonable, public, and changed only with sufficient notice to the public. And the ICC included passenger fares as well as freight rates in these provisions. It also required that all interstate railroads "provide facilities for the receipt and delivery of passengers or property and for the interchange of traffic between different lines."[20]

With the creation of the Interstate Commerce Commission, something close to a hierarchy—albeit a weak one—came into existence to address the laws pertaining to railroads. But law did not equal enforcement, and many railroads were able to evade conformity with commission regulation. Furthermore, considering the number and

diversity of complaints about rail service, the focus on rates and connections proved to be too narrow to make much difference in the experiences of the traveling public. Both economists and historians
have concluded that the ICC did not even resolve the problems it was
created to address. Both state and federal commissions were quickly
swamped with requests for investigation and judgment of legal viola-
tions.

While the regulation of railroads continued to increase through the
end of the nineteenth century and into the twentieth, litigation
against the inordinate power of the roads also grew proportionally.
The reorientation of the law to the requirements of the emerging national transportation system did not resolve the tendency of corporate
leaders to view themselves as exempt from the law. Nor did it defin-
itively establish the rule of law over the power of the railroads. Finally, it did not turn crowds of strangers into cooperative, amicable
groups. It simply provided injured parties with the legal grounds for
seeking redress.

16

||||||||||||||||||||

Why Bigger Towns Get
Better Service

. . . Every human being along the railroad lines, irrespective of sex or age,
was tributary to the railroad corporations. Any increase of population in a
given district meant an increase of revenue to the corporation serving it of
nearly $20 per annum to each person of which that increase was made up.
Fully appreciating this fact, the various corporations had been for years in
the custom of holding out the inducement of special rates to those
proposing to settle along their roads.
                    —*History of the Old Colony Railroad,* 1893[1]

DESPITE THE DEEP CONFLICT between railroads and the people
they served, the roads and their stations emerged as the central institution in town and city life after the Civil War. The arrival of a railroad and the construction of a station marked the transformation of
towns once identified by local or regional self-sufficiency. In their
place developed towns dependent on the national economy. Also

gone were towns where all the members of the community knew one another. In their place came any number of strangers and crowds, whose numbers became one important measure of the economic vitality of the town.

Because the towns depended on trains for their prosperity, obtaining rail service and a railroad station in town became matters of consuming political importance. Here too, conflict of interest was the rule by which complex negotiations and cutthroat competition determined the nature of rail service. Such conflict considerably retarded the impulse for uniformity and connection of services. Furthermore, small towns and communities that provided the lowest revenues to railroads had the greatest difficulty in obtaining the train and station services they needed. Without doubt, the centers of highest population had the advantage in securing the best rail service. Nevertheless, every town that depended on railroads went through a similar process of reorienting town institutions to the railroad station and its services, so that crowds gathering in the station would make full use of local institutions and bring maximum revenues to the town's businesses.

From agrarian towns with a commons at the center, to market towns with small shops lining the streets, the evolution of American towns after the Civil War proceeded to make shops accessible from the railroad depot. And the trains brought crowds of people into town to take advantage of the many thriving institutions and services intended to draw them: banks, department stores, restaurants, theaters, libraries, hospitals, churches, schools, and parks as well as hotels. Workers could live in growing suburban communities and take the train into town to the mills, factories, and offices that also served the public. All these institutions drew crowds and wealth into town, and their success measured the extent to which a town had successfully become part of the national economy.

At or near the center of these numerous institutions stood the railroad station or stations, built to serve the crowds sought by local merchants. The wealthier town institutions even provided transport from the station to their front door, to encourage patronage. Department stores such as Marshall Field's in Chicago benefited from the provision of horse-drawn omnibuses from the station; horse-drawn taxis waited in line outside the depot doors; transfer companies brought passengers to the better hotels, or the hotels were constructed so close to the station that passengers could reach them on foot. Wrote a historian of hotel history, ". . . Nearly all railroads had extensive hotel buildings, either directly or by means of subsidiary companies."[2] The road frequently named Station Street or Railroad Avenue, on which the depot stood, generally connected it with the shops of Main Street.

The services connecting railroad stations to the community were of course most highly elaborated in the East and in cities, where more town institutions vied for the patronage of more people. One railroad official went so far as to define a science of railway services. From the perspective of 1894 he wrote about services that had characterized the largest urban stations for years.

> The introduction at stations of placards announcing the arrival and departure of trains, the placing of clocks in conspicuous places, the employment of men to direct passengers, the establishment of bureaus of information, the institution of lunch counters and receptacles for packages, the placing of boxes into which complaints may be dropped, and many other conveniences were unknown in the early history of railroads, but are now regarded as essential, and have become, so to speak, public rights.[3]

These services not only aided the passengers but gave them every reason to tarry, so that they might spend money in town.

With time the idea of providing services to arriving and departing railroad passengers spread to rural areas in the South and West, but such services were considerably more modest and subject to local variation. "The Golden Hotel at Promontory, Utah," wrote Lucius Beebe, "where the transcontinental trains stopped in the seventies advertised . . . that its fare was top notch, but accounts differ." Again, the provision of food was an example of how local businesses oriented their services toward the railroads and their passengers. Businesses could count on some profit from any train that stopped long enough to let off passengers. Even in Iowa, a Western traveler of 1871 reported that "On arrival at Council Bluffs, we found omnibuses waiting at the station" to take the passengers into town. And at Omaha, outfitters sold goods to migrants heading north into the Black Hills of

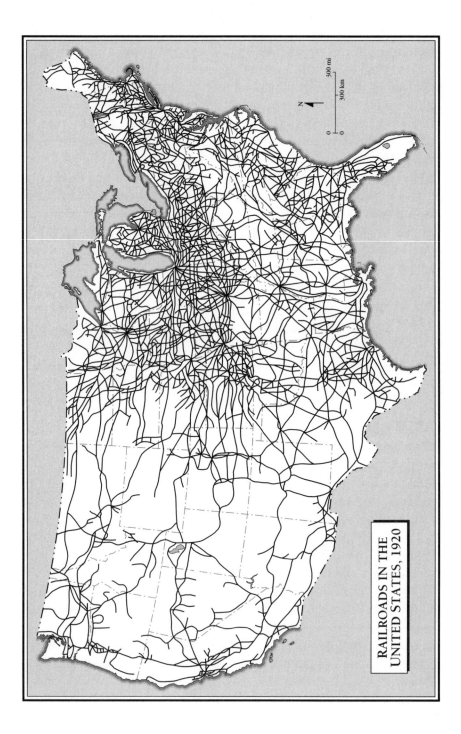

RAILROADS IN THE
UNITED STATES, 1920

the Dakotas. Other Western stations provided showers and beds for immigrants. In the South, "On the Southerners main line at Charlotte [North Carolina] in the 1890s, two horse drawn omnibuses wait (Central Hotel, Buford Hotel) for debarking passengers from the train."[4]

The trains helped business in other ways as well. They brought freight for the stores, materials for construction, mail, packages, and newspapers. The station clock usually provided the best estimate of the correct time, and, after 1882, railroad time became the correct time for almost everyone in the country except the federal government.[5] Western Union usually had its telegraph office right in the station, since the telegraph wires paralleled the railroad track throughout the country, and because the railroads and their patrons were the most frequent users of the telegraph service. The station also drew peddlers, newsboys, and others hoping to make money providing the amenities of civilization to passers through. The railroads, for all the conflicts of law and interest they created, were the most dependable form of transport and of public service to be found.

With an eye to profit, the roads scaled their services and stations to the economic and social needs of each community as well as to the types of institutions that drew crowds of passengers. In size and design, for example, the station usually signified the size of the town or city and the number of passengers expected to arrive or depart by train, without considerations for future growth. In the most general terms, the largest city stations built after the Civil War were expected to serve through passengers. Accordingly they were provided with elaborate services ranging from shoe-shining to dining and hotel accommodations. Suburban stations built at this time usually had only two waiting rooms, one for women and one for men, plus toilet rooms, a baggage area, a platform, and a ticket office.[6]

Before the introduction of standard station designs for small country railroad stops, the rural stations were diverse in style and accommodation, reflecting climate, the size of the local population, and its wealth and cultural habits. Many local stops had no station at all; others had a small shack and were flag stations—the train stopped only if flagged down by a passenger who wanted to ride. In the South at the turn of the century, "colored" waiting rooms became common to

segregate black passengers from the rest of the crowd. But west of
Texas the scant rural population and money could not justify the expense of elaborate, segregated services for any group. Passengers of
all sorts usually waited and rode together.[7]

Station services in the West were in fact so minimal that railroads
attempted to introduce a few elements of civility to small rural stations by improving appearances and services. The Union Pacific, for
example, introduced a simple, standard depot design for each station
to replace the variety of shacks and markers that characterized the
earliest rural stations in all sections of the country. Few Western stations outgrew the scale of these small, simple buildings. During the
1870s the Union Pacific also began landscaping the grounds surrounding these small stations, putting in gardens to brighten the en-
trance to otherwise rather depressing Western towns.[8]

Also in the 1870s the Atchison, Topeka and Santa Fe contracted
with Fred Harvey to open Harvey Houses along its route. These
restaurants, the first of which opened in Topeka, Kansas, in 1875,
competed with the saloons and hash houses that typically supplied
roadside services. They introduced good food, clean accommodations, and civil behavior to railroad service. Lucius Beebe described,
in colorful terms, the difference between a Harvey House and other
railroad restaurants.

> For his waitresses Harvey eschewed the Gold Tooth Tessies and Dirty
> Girties of the hash-house tradition and employed neat and respectable
> young women of unimpeachable morals, an impressive proportion of
> whom married handsomely, and the Harvey House girls became cele-
> brated in song and verse. . . . To secure prompt service for all patrons
> of his restaurants without holding up trains longer than the twenty
> minutes allowed by immemorial practice he had the train conductor
> wire ahead the number of prospective customers and the steak, eggs,
> and chops were put on the fire when the engineers whistled for the
> yard limit a mile out of town. The waitresses put on the hot plates, bis-
> cuits, and coffee as the train slowed to a stop and the manager in per-
> son, in the pleasant manner of an older tradition, passed around the
> meat platter with all the patron wished to take for the universal Har-

vey tariff of four bits. It is part of the legend that no Harvey patron ever missed his train or even had to bolt his food.[9]

From the smallest towns to the largest cities, obtaining a station and rail service was not simple. It raised a number of political questions for both townspeople and the managers of the railroads. For the largest cities, one of these questions pertained to the extent to which railroads coordinated their services so that passengers did not have to move from one station to another in order to change trains. The idea behind the term "union station" was that most or all of the incoming railroad lines would unite under the roof of one station and make the process of changing trains, known as "making connections," rapid and efficient for passengers and freight. The idea that time was money had already influenced the operations of the major seaports, and businessmen who shared this understanding wanted the railroads to save them time. Indeed, the earliest trains into a city usually went to or near the waterfront, to connect with shipping. Chicago's earliest trains did so, as did the Little Miami Railroad into Cincinnati. Minneapolis directed many of its railroads to the vicinity of the Mississippi River.[10]

In relation to one another, however, the railroads still adhered to the doctrine of competition, and usually the only circumstances under which two sets of track connected with each other came as the result of a railroad buying out a connecting road and making both roads part of one corporation. Those railroads that set aside competition and shared station space were the exception. Thus the major terminal cities after the Civil War usually had a number of railroad stations, frequently at some distance from one another. Chicago built a separate depot for the Chicago and Northwestern Railroad, as did Milwaukee. Cincinnati, in the course of shifting its focus from river to land transport, built three stations during the period 1881 to 1885.[11] Passengers were left to find their way on foot or by taxi, with their luggage, to the depots of lines that should have been connecting but instead were competing.

A few cities built union depots during the 1870s and 1880s, but most of the substantial structures inherited by twentieth-century pas-

sengers were built after 1890. The few major urban terminals providing services to more than one major railroad before 1890 included
a union station in Columbus, Ohio, opened in 1862, and the first
Grand Central Terminal of New York, completed in 1871. Union Station in Worcester, Massachusetts, opened in 1875, to serve five railroads: the Boston, Barre and Gardner; the Worcester and Nashua;
the Providence and Worcester; the Norwich and Worcester; and the
Boston and Albany. One set of waiting rooms served all five lines. The
union station in Louisville, Kentucky, served trains on the Louisville
and Nashville Railroad as well as the Pennsylvania and the Indianapolis and Louisville; and a union depot in Indianapolis, completed
in 1889, served a number of the many Midwestern railroads that
linked the cities of that region. The 1890s witnessed the construction
of massive union stations in at least five cities, and many more followed in the years before World War I.[12]

Another political problem that affected the nature of station service concerned the extent of train service to specific institutions
within towns or cities. While department stores might arrange for service from the station, factories, mills, warehouses, and the other
workplaces of industrial society frequently went a step further, seeing
that tracks and trains were routed to nearby stops to facilitate the
movement of freight and enable workers to use the train when com-
muting to and from their jobs. Creating a railroad spur or small
branch line which stopped at the doorstep of a factory came as the result of petitioning and bargaining among at least three parties—the
factory owners, the city government, and the railroad itself. Before
the Civil War the mills in Lowell, Massachusetts, negotiated with the
Boston and Lowell Railroad to provide a spur and stop, then went to
the Lowell city government to obtain a right of way for this service
through the streets of the city.[13]

After the war many cities had more than one train stop, to meet the
needs of institutions at a distance from the center of rapidly growing
urban populations. Private spurs were built to serve the freight needs
of industries near the main line. The population too began to spread
away from the center of the city, yet required stops to remain part of
the urban economy.

Small towns faced the more basic problem of obtaining any station at all, especially if the railroads had chosen to bypass them for financial or geographical reasons. During the 1870s and 1880s, with the coming of state regulation over aspects of rail service, groups could petition the state to construct a station or at least create service to their community. Such a case arose in Boston on the Old Colony line, when "an application came to the Board of Railroad Commissioners from some thirty or more inhabitants of the Dorchester district of Boston, asking its good offices to induce the Old Colony Company to put upon its road a workingmen's train similar to that on the Eastern [Railroad Company]." In 1872 Massachusetts legislated that if two hundred or more people applied for railroad service to a particular locale, the railroad had to provide inexpensive trains, morning and evening, into and out of Boston.[14] The service stipulated by this petition, however, would be discontinued after two years if there were insufficient revenue.

The right of petition was possible in consequence of the railroads' emerging legal status as a common carrier, rather than just a private business with no obligations to the general public. In 1880 the state legislature of Vermont stipulated that

> . . . railroad corporations shall establish and maintain depots or station houses with suitable accommodation at such points on their roads as the supreme court shall, on petition for that purpose, adjudge the public good to require. Such petition shall be signed by ten freeholders, resident in the town where the depot is proposed to be located. . . .

Other states, such as Tennessee, required the railroads to "provide, at or near every town containing as many as three hundred inhabitants, a waiting room for the use and accommodation of passengers." New Mexico also gave citizens the right to petition for service.[15]

Petitioning also became one of a number of ways in which small towns overlooked by the railroads could seek service or the construction of a station. The 1870s and 1880s still found many communities fighting for their local railroad service while Bostonians and Chicagoans already had multiple competing lines running in and out of their cities, and more than one station in each city. Small towns issued bonds, raised funds, petitioned, and negotiated with railroad companies to get themselves onto a rail network and to get the kind of service that community leaders believed the town needed. But they had a tiger by the tail, for local railroads were falling under the control of larger lines every year, and larger railroads looked to major urban centers for their profits.

A case illustrating this point came to the United States Supreme Court in 1885 from Iowa. A town in Iowa gave municipal aid to a railroad company, which returned the favor by promising transportation services to the town. Later, however, a new corporation leased the railroad and changed the route of the track, bypassing the town.[16] While the Supreme Court ruled that railroad service must be restored to the town, breakdowns in negotiations between towns and railroad companies over bonds, taxes, and charters were extremely common and frequently had to be resolved in a court of law.

As the public became aware that railroads favored the transport of large groups because of the potential for profit, petitions from groups for special consideration flooded both the legal authorities and the railroad companies themselves. In addition to the request for workingmen's trains mentioned earlier, some towns asked for and received a special monthly fare for workingmen, in consideration of their low income and steady patronage. Boston and Lowell were among the first towns to institute this type of service in agreement with the local railroads.[17]

Businessmen working in New York, Philadelphia, and Chicago also had the advantage of commuter trains, schedules, and commuter rates. All these were the result of businesses seeking such services from the railroad and the city, and the city making the required legal arrangements with railroad companies whose multiple lines radiated outward from the downtown area toward emerging suburban residential areas. Large groups of travelers received special consideration from the railroads because of the profits they would bring.

Petitions seeking reduced fares or special trains for groups also came from organizations, associations, and institutions in all parts of the country. Many of these special rates were granted by the railroads. Trains carrying students traveling to and from school, particularly colleges, offered reduced rates, thus assuring themselves of more business and meeting the needs of the colleges and college

Crowds pour from the railroad station on the grounds of Chicago's 1893 Columbian Exposition. The fair was one of dozens held in the late nineteenth century to display new inventions and achievements from around the world.

towns. In its college catalog of 1884–1885, the University of Nebraska published the following announcement.

> Students residing in the State are allowed half-fare in going to and from home by the railroads entering Lincoln. This privilege is also extended to those about to enter the University. Half-fare certificates may be obtained by addressing the Chancellor, and in case of new students should be applied for at least two weeks before the beginning of a term.

During the 1890s North Carolina Agricultural and Mechanical College, the University of New Mexico, and the University of Nevada all offered reduced rates for students on railroad lines to and from school.[18]

Any event that promised to draw a crowd could also justify special train service into or out of a city. In Ohio, for example, just before the Civil War, the state board of agriculture arranged to have the railroad tracks into Cincinnati stop quite close to the Ohio state fairgrounds.[19] State agricultural fairs, held throughout the second half of the century in the Midwest and South, were a major annual event for farmers, who might stay for days while contests for best foods, best stock, and best homemade goods went on. These fairs also served to educate farmers to the latest innovations in farm equipment and scientific farming. The Ohio fair brought profits to Cincinnati and to the railroads, which likely put additional trains into service for this event and offered discounted tickets.

Special rates and special trains favored those going to and from the highest population centers. The organizers of the 1876 centennial celebration in Philadelphia offered special rates for visitors, who then viewed the inventions and mechanical wonders displayed by the urban business community and patronized the hotels, restaurants, and shops near the fairgrounds. The world's fairs held in New Orleans, St. Louis, Chicago, and other cities drew throngs of railroad passengers, many of whom traveled on special trains scheduled for the fair, and paid special reduced fares.[20]

The system of petitions for service, stations, special fares, special trains, and special schedules gave the railroads a remarkable responsiveness to local needs and the changing requirements of travelers. But this responsiveness also had its dark side. Many railroads gave special favors to those in positions of power. The major trunk lines distributed free passes lavishly to legislators and to businessmen as a way of buying votes or freight shipments. Since not every group that applied for favors received them, the have-nots riled at the injustice of favors granted only to others. And since special services favored large groups, those individuals who were not attached to a larger organization—often rural folk—were among the few who still had to pay full fare.

Special fares and services came under attack for this reason and because they fell into the same category as freight rebates, which were given to those shippers who promised their business to the railroad that offered a rebate. The system of rebates was one target of late-nineteenth-century railroad commissions' reform efforts, and state statutes also attacked the favoritism of special fares. While some forms of special fares remained legal, the states cracked down on free passes and discounts that were blatantly discriminatory.

Still the sway of the railroads grew. Before the Civil War, negotiations for the placement of track within town limits centered on the taking of land from private individuals and on the dangers of railroad tracks that ran down the middle of main thoroughfares. These considerations continued to plague railroads and town dwellers after the war. The cost for railroads in restitution for damages and injuries soared. But the battle to exclude railroad traffic altogether had ended. Station and track placement in towns with growing populations and a growing number of business, manufacturing, educational, and professional institutions centered on the proximity or accessibility of the tracks to their potential sources of revenue: passengers and freight. Such decisions were determined by a series of specific agreements between local governments, local institutions, the local population, and railroad corporations. These legal agreements also specified the financial terms that would govern the presence of the railroad: for example, what taxes the railroad would owe the town, or, conversely, what financial help the town might give the railroad to construct a line through town. As in all aspects of railroad service, these "agreements" were frequently either the result or the cause of much controversy and litigation.

The tendency of railroads to concentrate their services in areas of highest population and give short shrift to smaller towns and to individuals angered many town leaders, passengers, and shippers who watched the centralization of services in urban areas. By the end of the nineteenth century, trade as well as passenger services had become concentrated in the largest cities. Small towns, whether ports, market towns, or industrial centers, generally sold their goods through Boston, New York, or Philadelphia, rather than developing the banking, investment, and management institutions that large cities could already offer. And the pattern of travel followed suit. As a priority for the railroads and as a source of revenue, through travel between major cities dominated; local travel took second place.

17

||||||||||||||||||||||

City Slicker and
Country Bumpkin

Any man could have sold those rail saws but very few men could have done the rest of the job. "Get to know the important men in every line," Charles A. Moore had told him, "find out which ones are doing the buying. . . . Make them trust you." . . . As Jim rode throughout the country the rails clicked: "Make them trust you. . . ."
> —Parker Morell, *Diamond Jim: The Life and Times of James Buchanan Brady*, 1934[1]

The mixed train hauled fifteen to twenty-five freight cars and sometimes a coach full of passengers who idled their time away as the train, stopping at every other siding to set off and pick up cars, inched its way along. . . . True, passengers often got off to pick berries or flowers or visit with farmers . . . such stories originated mostly from the mixed train that also hauled freight.
> —Victor L. Morse, *36 Miles of Trouble: The Story of the West River R.R.*, 1959[2]

I N THE FULL FLOOD of industrial society that emerged in the 1880s, the older affiliations of region, town, family, and religion gave way to the identification of people by their institutional affiliations. These ran the gamut from the monopoly business enterprises, exclusive clubs, and posh vacation homes of the very rich, to the local Grange, women's clubs, libraries, and saving societies that characterized the life of less affluent Americans. Somewhere in the middle could be found the schools, national professional societies, and resort hotels frequented by an emerging middle class. To this extent the chaos and confusion of the nineteenth-century crowds of travelers had begun to sort themselves into types, proceeding individually or in groups, most of whom could be identified by dress, habits, and purposes traceable to income, region, and to the institutions they represented. Individual identity was submerged, partly to protect the individual from the prying eyes of crowds, and partly because traveling crowds were almost invariably strangers to each other. In its place came public stereotypes, born of habit and experience, which informed strangers, in general terms, what kind of people their fellow travelers might be.

The stereotypes of railroad passengers grew from the curious and detailed character descriptions left by an earlier generation of travelers, writing about their unfamiliar neighbors in the stations, day coaches, smoking cars, and ladies' coaches of American railroads. Frederika Bremer's letters describing American passengers of the 1850s were the forerunners of public literature about travel which identified the traveling salesman, the unaccompanied young woman, the mother, the businessman, and the immigrant, alongside shady gamblers, white slavers, confidence men, and women of ill repute as types to look for—or look out for—in the American traveling crowd. All these people represented institutions and values of American society, rather than just their individual missions.

In the popular literature of travel diaries, biographies, newspaper stories, and magazine stories available to the public in the 1870s and 1880s, passenger stereotypes were informed by years of published travel accounts by individuals, many of whom had become common types in American life.[3] Readers and other observers of the American scene could not avoid knowing about the travel habits of the country's richest citizens: the capitalists who controlled not only railroads but oil, steel, and the other national businesses of the late nineteenth century. The new business elite, composed of Andrew Carnegie, Jay Gould, John D. Rockefeller, E. H. Harriman, Leland Stanford, and many others listed in the social registers of the largest cities, liked to travel in their own private train cars, either with their own locomotive and conductor, or hitched to the back of a scheduled train. The attraction of a private car lay in the absence of crowds or strangers of any kind. In an age of crowds, privacy was a prerogative of the rich.

The earliest private cars were owned by individual railroad companies and used by company executives in the course of their duties. In traveling to inspect work on the track or to meet with other executives, railroad companies used simply designed private cars even before the Civil War. Shortly after the war, however, George Pullman, who invented the best known of the sleeping cars, also produced a hotel car, which had all the amenities of a hotel, including a kitchen, dining facilities, china and silver services, upholstered lounge chairs, beds, and even wood paneling, draperies, and cut glass lamps.[4]

The hotel car became popular for leasing to parties of wealthy travelers on holiday, and for wealthy railroad executives who wished to entertain business associates. The magazine publisher Frank Leslie, for example, chartered a number of hotel cars on his well-publicized Western jaunt of 1877.[5] Within the confines of the hotel car, all the activities of daily life, from morning ablutions to evening prayer, could be pursued without ever having to associate with outsiders, except perhaps the cooks and servants hired for the journey. Not for the wealthy were the crowded services in hash houses, railroad hotels, and Harvey Houses of the 1870s.

Among those who actually purchased private cars during the decades before 1890 were any number of railroad presidents and owners, who traveled the lengths of their own lines free of charge and liberally extended the same privilege to equally wealthy colleagues. Shortly after the completion of the connection of the Central Pacific Railroad with the Union Pacific in 1869, the wife of Leland Stanford, an owner of the Central Pacific, bought him a private car for his birthday: the *Stanford,* costing $25,000. Jay Gould owned the car *Atalanta,* aboard which he carried a chef and a doctor, both needed to tend his

Many late-nineteenth-century Pullman cars were decorated in the ornate style associated with Victorian England. (SMITHSONIAN INSTITUTION)

ulcer. George Mortimer Pullman himself traveled in one of his two private cars, *Pullman* or the *Duchess*.[6]

Where did the rich go, thus protected from the anonymous crowd? Gould used his modest car primarily for business. Of his adventures, the following story survives.

> Gould was out on an inspection trip on one of his Western lines, and for some reason, on account of the stock market . . . his presence was required in the city. He was more than 100 miles from this city, and he told [his private locomotive engineer] Hadlock . . . to get back to town and get there fast. Because Gould was what he was, they literally owned the railroad. They were on a mountain division . . . they lit out. To maintain a speed of between fifty and sixty miles an hour over a mountain range is a little better than remarkable, but that's what Hadlock did. . . . Gould arrived in the city in time. . . .

Another railroad titan, James J. Hill of the Great Northern Railroad, also used his private car for business, once taking it out in a snowstorm to help laborers shovel snow off his track.[7]

When not at work, many owners of private cars rode them to one of the fashionable resorts located up and down the East Coast, and along long-distance routes west. In addition to Saratoga Springs in New York, a gathering place for fashionable society even before the Civil War, other spas such as White Sulphur Springs in West Virginia and Poland Springs in Maine drew small, select crowds of idle rich during the 1870s and 1880s. Newport, Rhode Island, and Palm Beach also drew wealthy vacationers who traveled in private cars. So common was the use of private cars to reach these destinations that private car tracks were constructed near hotels, to receive guests and to store their cars during their stay.[8]

Both at work and at play the wealthy purchased and used private cars chiefly for long-distance travel. Only on overnight trips would the kitchens, beds, and dining areas have any function. The ability to travel great distances at will was in itself a mark of privilege not shared by other, more budget-conscious travelers. While railroad companies could not boast, as they did before the Civil War, that railroads would overcome all geographic obstacles separating peoples and communities, the rich came closest to that goal, and flaunted their freedom in a gaudy splendor associated primarily with the urban wealth of the Northeast.

These habits of long-distance city and resort hopping, combined with the isolation of the rich from crowds of unwanted strangers, reflected an exclusiveness that favored cities, ignored intermediate stops, and treated the countryside as a glamorous retreat with beautiful scenery, despite the presence of a few locals who might profit from serving their wealthy guests. The more complete the services of the private car, the more irrelevant the train became to the local economies along the route. The train did not have to stop for anything except fuel and water.

The exploits of the rich did not become irrelevant to the public, however. Through splashy stories and pictures, newspapers and magazines followed the excesses of the rich at parties, exclusive resorts, vacation homes, and city mansions in all the reaches of the republic. While private cars were a preferred mode of transport, little remained private about the lives of this reclusive elite. Some, like the Leslies, who wrote stories about their own travels, sought the attention deliberately for business reasons. Others, like Jay Gould, were followed by the press despite their somewhat antisocial behavior.[9] The middling sort and the poor could only gawk at such people from a distance and aspire to the freedom that money could buy.

Partly because so many of the very rich were railroad men, the railroads on which private cars traveled tended to be the best maintained and equipped. With more capital, the long-distance roads were in a better position to update their equipment than were local lines, funded only to support local traffic. Starting after the war, the wealthier lines, such as the Pennsylvania, the Baltimore and Ohio, and the New York Central, could replace iron track with harder and more durable steel track; replace wooden bridges, which rotted or caught fire, with iron or steel bridges; buy engines of sufficient power to pull long trains up and down hills over long distances; construct numerous stations along the route; and diversify their passenger rolling stock to include the sleepers, parlor cars, and dining cars that charmed the patrons of long-distance travel.[10]

To understand how the poor traveled, the nature of these luxurious rail facilities for those who could afford them form a useful comparison with the trains and track that did not cater to the rich. If rich passengers were mainly long-distance travelers, representing major national businesses, the poor travelers of this period can be divided into two groups by the distances they traveled: first, the local travelers, whose commutes on city rail services and country branch lines were frequently the farthest geographical reaches of their experience; and second, the immigrants, transients, migrants seeking work, and hoboes, who made quite daring long-distance journeys in search of wealth or at least temporary employment.

In addition to the workingmen's trains and accommodation trains that brought laborers into and out of Boston, New York, and Philadelphia during the late nineteenth century, railroad facilities for the working poor included virtually hundreds of short lines, many of which provided the only local transportation in isolated rural regions of the West, South, and Northeast. Railroad historian Lucius Beebe distinguished between the branch lines and the short lines:

> A Short Line Is a Country Thing
> The definition of a short line is precisely what its name implies, and it is not to be confused with the branch lines of a main-line railroad. It is independently operated with motive power and rolling stock bearing its own name or insigne, even though it may in some cases be owned or controlled through stock ownership by a great railway system.[11]

Short lines were the poor relations of main lines in a number of ways. They used a small number of cars and locomotives, many of which were bought secondhand from the main lines when the larger roads updated their equipment. Thus even the appearance of a country short-line train could be anachronistic compared with the latest trends in car design among the main-line railroads. Certainly the short-line roads had little use for the sleepers, parlor cars, and dining cars that came into vogue during the 1870s and 1880s. The best that most short-line passenger services offered were a few day coaches, still heated by the wood-burning iron stoves that main-line roads began to replace during the 1880s, when state statutes proclaimed the stoves too dangerous in the event of an accident. Without the capital necessary to fund replacement technology, short-line roads fre-

A day coach in the 1880s was far more comfortable than passenger cars of forty years earlier, with higher ceilings, luggage racks, large lamps, and adjustable seats. Still, the arrangements were simple and crowded compared with the furnishings of a Pullman car.

quently kept their iron track and wooden bridges even after the turn of the century. And the locomotive, another castoff from big brother, might not have sufficient power to pull a full train of cars uphill.

Such conditions demanded improvisation in the workings of short lines. The West River Railroad in Vermont, also known as the Brattleboro and Whitehall, owned engines that had to pull longer trains uphill in two parts. Built after the Civil War, it nevertheless had a number of wooden bridges until the turn of the century. Cars ran off the track on a regular basis, and in a flood, passengers had to walk across the bridges. The Belfast and Moosehead Lake road in Maine had no equipment for putting derailed cars back on track. With the use of jacks and manpower, they lifted some derailed cars and built new track underneath them. They also used quite old passenger cars still equipped with open platforms at each end. And they still used a coal stove for heat.[12]

In the South the East Tennessee and Western North Carolina Railroad, one of the first Southern railroads constructed after the Civil War, had a track made partially of iron and partially of wooden rails with strap iron on top, a style of rail deemed unsafe and outmoded by the 1840s. And in the far West, a short line called the Walla Walla and Columbia River Railroad made itself the stuff of legend by its makeshift operations. In a twentieth-century retrospective of short lines, the Walla Walla was said to have ". . . lacked certain of the conveniences for smooth running. . . ."

> It was about twenty miles long, but it had no turntables and it had no water tanks. When the little engines needed water, the engineer stopped on a bridge or by a creek, and the fireman took a bucket tied to a rope and dipped up water, pouring it by bucketfuls into the tank until he had enough. The bucket was an old tin oil can, salvaged from the junk pile. Regular bearing oil was expensive, but hog lard, made locally, would do, and so hog lard, poured out of another tin can, lubricated the locomotives and cars.[13]

While this description may stretch the truth at points, it has survived because it typifies the plight of poor, short-line railroads throughout the country.

Against such odds, why did short-line railroads continue to run? Many of them justified their existence by hauling one or two local raw materials from their source to the main line. These loads included lumber in upstate New York, granite and marble in Vermont, iron in Michigan, iron and lumber in North Carolina and Tennessee, coal in Pennsylvania, and gold, silver, or copper in the West. The gathering and transport of these products supported local economies, until the supplies of local raw materials were exhausted. These trains also carried local fresh produce: eggs, chickens, milk, butter, and other farm items destined for a market in the closest town connected by rail.[14] Aside from that, these lines provided the only link to the outside world, and as such they had contracts to carry the United States mail. They also carried express packages, the kind of service on which mail-order businesses such as Sears, Roebuck depended.

In some instances the short lines did not even have the designation of common carriers. Running primarily for the benefit of one industry, they varied in their policy toward passengers. Some, such as the West River Railroad in Vermont, had passenger coaches. Others, such as the East Tennessee Railroad, tried in some instances to avoid carrying passengers. But the railroad was so much a community effort that passengers found their way on board, even if only to ride home after work. For this reason most rural trains were mixed trains, carrying both passengers and freight, express, and mail.[15] Country lines serving an area of low population could not afford to run trains carrying only passengers, except on the special occasions when they knew the seats would be filled.

Given such circumstances, how did the passengers fare? The rural passenger service, with its outdated inventories of equipment, resembled the pre–Civil War passenger service when trains were slow and unreliable, when passengers might or might not pay, got on and off as they chose, and could be found riding in the caboose or engine, or even on the cowcatcher, according to the availability of space, and when the passengers helped chop wood, draw water, shovel snow, and put derailed cars back on the track. Prices might depend on the whim of the conductor, and scheduling depended greatly on whether the train made it from one end of the track to the other.[16]

The passengers who rode these small rural trains tended to know the conductor, brakeman, and engineer if they rode more than once or twice, because the trains simply could not accommodate the crowds that larger lines carried. And they knew many of their fellow passengers, who came from the same small and isolated communities. These trains had distinct local identities, defined by the local people who depended on them for decades to bring mail, newspapers, and packages, to connect small local markets, and to connect the region, however tenuously, to the larger world. Lucius Beebe noted that the short line, "to achieve its ultimately proper setting . . . must be removed and essentially divorced from the contrivings of industrialization."[17]

Because of the close connection between the communities and the short-line trains, each train's operation was idiosyncratic. Beebe celebrated the diversity of these small lines, which reflected local and regional differences rather than the technological advances and elaborated services of through lines. "The short line," concluded

Beebe, "is the negation of regimented uniformity and it survives as a triumph of individualism and even eccentricity. . . ."[18]

Another major difference between the short lines and the main lines can be found in the passengers' errands. Rural passengers, still measuring the world by local geography, local resources, and the changing seasons, traveled in the interests of maintaining their farms, pursuing their labor in local mines, and responding to changes in the weather and the maturity of crops rather than the urban rhythms of financial dealings, industrial dominance, and leisure activities. They came to town for a meeting of the Odd Fellows, Sunday church services, an agricultural fair, market days, the Fourth of July. On the West River Railroad:

> Its biggest days were those of the Brattleboro Valley Fair. The entire West River Valley or as much of it as could get aboard the trains went down to the big town, and all rules were cast aside. Every piece of rolling stock was in use. Before a train pulled out of South Londonderry, all passenger cars were jammed, and passengers down the line sat on crude plank benches in box cars. At that, by the time the train reached Brattleboro, some were sitting on top of the cars, hanging on the sides, bulging out of the doors.[19]

Unlike the rich who favored elegant private cars and exclusive destinations, the rural poor, who still depended on the land for their living, also traveled closer to the land. The trains stopped frequently, and passengers got on and off to help "serve" the train. The existence of the train itself depended on wealth derived from the land: stone, lumber, coal, iron, and farm goods. Obstacles such as rainstorms, which revealed leaky roofs in the cars, or blizzards, which stopped trains for days while the passengers and crew dug out, were only variations on the theme of struggling with nature for survival.

The immigrants too traveled without the services that the rich could buy. Many of them journeyed long distances, from the East Coast to Chicago, Milwaukee, St. Paul, St. Louis, or points west. But the long immigrant trains scheduled by main lines were composed of old passenger cars, inexpensive immigrant cars with wooden seats and no decor, or old freight cars. The trains were slow, since every express or mixed train had priority for the use of the track. The stops were many; immigrants sometimes spent days on a side track waiting for the right of way. They took advantage of scheduled stops to get out onto the platform, stretch, get fresh water, and buy small items from peddlers. Without dining service or sleeping cars, immigrants performed all their activities of daily life in the car to which they had been assigned. They cooked on the heating stoves, ate on metalware available from peddlers, and slept on shelves, with their own coats or blankets for warmth. Space, specialized services, and privacy were the prerogative of the rich. The poor tolerated one another's presence and provided their own services.[20]

Blacks and former slaves, all of whom were usually poor, at times rode in segregated circumstances. The Black Codes imposed in most Southern states following the Civil War required segregation of blacks. Mississippi, Florida, and Texas required segregation in first-class passenger cars but not in second-class cars, which tended to be older and less comfortable, and not in smoking cars.[21] In these instances blacks could not buy the comforts of travel even if they could afford them.

After the repeal of the Black Codes in the late 1860s, some blacks who had the means to buy first-class tickets found themselves riding unchallenged in first-class cars, and only occasionally challenged by conductors when they entered dining cars. The historian C. Vann Woodward recounts the experience of a black man traveling from Boston to South Carolina in 1885.

> "On leaving Washington, D.C.," he reported, . . . "I put a chip on my shoulder, and inwardly dared any man to knock it off." He found a seat in a car which became so crowded that several white passengers had to sit on their baggage. "I fairly foamed at the mouth," he wrote, "imagining that the conductor would order me into a seat occupied by a colored lady so as to make room for a white passenger." Nothing of the sort happened, however. . . . At a stop twenty-one miles below Petersburg [Virginia] he entered a station dining room, "bold as a lion," he wrote, took a seat at a table with white people, and was courteously served.[22]

This gentleman was not the only black passenger confused by the inconsistency of segregation policies on Southern trains. In a case that went to the supreme court of Kentucky in the 1890s, a black couple complained that even though they had taken seats in the compartment reserved for "colored passengers," the conductor forced them to leave these seats and sit in the tool car. The Louisville and Nashville Railroad, against whom suit was brought, won this case, claiming it was not responsible for the actions of the conductor.[23]

Segregation policies were not hard and fast during the 1880s or the 1890s, and no individual, black or white, could know with certainty what the policy on services for black people would be in any given part of the country. So far as blacks were deemed poor, they might expect to travel second class. But blacks with money appear to have had the option of challenging unspoken assumptions about their right to purchase services and accommodations. In either instance, the issue for black passengers concerned not their choice of service but their acceptance by crowds of passengers.

Most passengers who rode suburban trains, through trains with sleepers and dining cars, and day coaches were people of middling means or middle-class aspirations. They represented, in great part, the emerging urban middle class who identified themselves not so much with local or rural institutions, as did the rural population, or with monopoly capital, as did the very rich, but with emerging institutions of national influence or membership.

And they endured the crowds that their own national institutions encouraged. In their struggle to maintain respectability, they developed the most elaborate systems for identifying themselves in the crowd and for distinguishing different types of strangers. They dressed well when traveling, emulated the rich when possible, and developed a code of public behavior that stressed polite reticence and detachment from the common herd.

Whether in the day car or the sleeper, the tension of maintaining private standards in a compromising public setting characterized middle-class travel behavior as well as writings about it. After all, those of dubious reputation might maintain a place alongside those of unimpeachable morals partly because class identification aboard a train could be purchased with the right suit of clothes, the right luggage, and the right sort of accommodation. Books of etiquette therefore advised the vulnerable, especially women, how to avoid the dangers to be found in a crowded train car or station house. With the right attitude and behavior, passengers could maintain a moral standard that was threatened in the promiscuous crowd.

Beginning in the 1840s and increasingly through the later years of the century, etiquette books devoted chapters to travel advice and rules for behavior in such public places as hotels, restaurants, ships, and trains. These books attempted to define standards for behavior that were not new but that needed restatement in the new, public environment. They addressed themselves to those who wished to maintain appearances in the crowd and avoid risky encounters with strangers.

"Traveling is one of the severest tests of good-breeding. Gentlefolk worthy of the name will behave as well abroad as at home," advised one author. "A lady rises in a public conveyance and gives her seat cheerfully to any woman carrying a baby, or to an elderly man or woman," wrote another. "Be wary of conversation on personal matters in the railway train," and "Avoid any personal indulgence which might offend strangers." The most extended advice concerned relations between the sexes. Florence Hartley's *The Ladies' Book of Etiquette and Manual of Politeness* explained the details.

> There are many little civilities which a true gentleman will offer a lady while traveling alone, which she may accept, even from an entire stranger, with perfect propriety; but while careful to thank him courteously, whether you accept or decline his attentions, avoid any advance towards acquaintanceship. If he sits near you and seems disposed to be impertinent, lower your veil and turn from him. . . . If you find yourself, during your journey, in any awkward or embarrassing situation, you may, without impropriety, request the assistance of a gentleman, even a stranger, and he will, probably, perform the service requested, receive your thanks, and then relieve you of his presence.

The woman who did not "lower her veil" might compromise herself to the point of social and moral ruin. Another etiquette book elaborated on a case in which the man and woman allowed themselves to become too familiar. "If they had announced their engagement . . . no one would have been really surprised."[24]

The traveler seeking safety from the perils of the road was usually the one who did not travel regularly and who needed guidance. The public press warned these innocents to avoid people who traveled so much that they had no fixed abode and no loyalties. Of these, traveling salesmen were the most notorious. The day coach was home for these perennials, identifiable by their brash behavior and their ability to gain the confidence of would-be customers. Their reputation did nothing to enhance the attractiveness of the trains in which they rode. While they extended the reach of the marketplace by taking orders in all parts of the country, they strained the credulity of the traveling public—and could leave town by train whenever the local populace discovered their tricks of the trade.

Some took to the press in order to chastise or satirize the type of salesmen who would try to sell anything from insurance to soap for more than its true value. The fictional character J. P. Johnston did exactly this in a book entitled *Twenty Years of Hus'ling,* published in 1887. He abandoned the soap market, he wrote, when "letters began pouring in from our customers, condemning us and our soap. . . . The general complaint was that it had all dried or shriveled up, and as some claimed, evaporated." The outcome? ". . . I paid my board bill and bought a ticket for home." As for insurance, it galled him to have to share his profits with the insurance company: "I can't afford to go out and rob my neighbors and acquaintances, and give you any part of it."[25] On the basis of this outburst the insurance company promoted him and sent him on the road.

For the respectable traveler, extricating oneself from the company of such people was important and marked journey's end. A reunion with family and friends, fellow workers, or fellow students meant the return of personal identity, understanding, and comparative safety. For the rich, the private car had originated in the need for a private place to meet with friends and business acquaintances on the road. Rural riders seldom traveled far beyond the bounds of their acquaintance. But in an urban setting many stories persisted, especially regarding the railroads between New York and Chicago, that white slavers and other criminals might kidnap women and children, preventing them from ever reaching their destination. For this reason, such services as the Travelers Aid Society, founded in 1888, and later the Immigrants' Protective League, were formed to help new Americans find their way safely. A Travelers Aid pamphlet described the Society's work:

> Volunteer workers were stationed in railroad terminals to meet and assist newly arrived women seeking employment in Chicago. With the city's rapid formation into a busy urban center and a railroad terminal point, it became a destination or stopping-off point for immigrants, the unemployed and traveling servicemen.[26]

Children and immigrants sometimes wore tags to identify themselves to those waiting for them at the station.

Middle-class passengers found their way among the station crowds with more aplomb than the poor, being accustomed to railroad travel and to crowds. For these passengers, breasting the crowd and finding one's own party was adventure without undue risk. Frances Willard, president of the Women's Christian Temperance Union, traveled the length and breadth of the country by train in her campaign against alcoholic beverages. At each stop someone, usually a sympathetic member of her own organization, met her. The president of the Prohibition Home Protection party greeted her and a friend "with the utmost cordiality, coming with his daughter to meet us at the early morning train." On the occasion of her father's death, "A committee sent for the purpose met us on the train some hours before we reached Chicago. . . ." Lucretia Hale, a member of the Hale family of Boston and author of *The Peterkin Papers* and other children's books, traveled constantly to see friends and family and to pursue her interest in children's education. To her brother Edward she wrote,

> If you have leisure to talk kindergarten, I could meet you at Worcester R.R. after arrival of A.M. train at 11—in Boston, or at any place you will support . . . or can meet you at Albany station Ladies' Room (outward) after 11 AM—time of arrival of Worcester train. . . ."[27]

The successful transition of local communities to a place in the national pattern of commerce and culture occurred because each community developed its own institutions and then connected them to others via the railroad. This pattern was most pronounced for the rich and the middle class. The poor, who had no means to travel nationally in order to sustain influence in national institutions, followed a more conservative route—on local trains, using outworn cars and even secondhand track to transport the produce of their farms, mills, and mines, and other natural resources. When these resources played themselves out, through soil erosion or the depletion of minerals, the communities lost their contact with the national economy and fell back into poverty.

18

||||||||||||||||||||||

Private Property in
Public Places

A writer in the Peoria *Review* describes as follows a lady traveler whom most conductors will recognize:

"She comes down to the depot in an express wagon three hours before train time. She insists on sitting on her trunk out on the platform to keep it from being stolen. She picks up her reticule, fan, parasol, lunch basket, small pot with a house plant in it, shawl, paper of candy, bouquet (she never travels without one), small tumbler and extra veil, and chases hysterically after every switch-engine that goes by, under the impression that it is her train.

"Her voice trembles as she presents herself at the restaurant and tries to buy a ticket, and she knocks with the handle of her parasol at the door of the old disused tool house, in vain hopes that the baggage man will come out and check her trunk. She asks everybody in the depot and on the platform when her train will start. . . . She sees, with terror, the baggageman shy her trunk into a car. . . . She sits to the end of her journey in an agony of apprehension that she has got on the wrong train, and will be landed at some strange station, put in a close carriage drugged and murdered. . . .

"She finally recognizes her waiting friends on the platform, leaves the car in a burst of gratitude, and the train is ten miles away before she re-

members that her reticule, fan, lunch basket, verbena, shawl, candy, tumbler, veil, and bouquet are on the seat where she left them."
—"How She Takes the Train," *Railroad Gazette*, October 4, 1873[1]

In a commercial society, what railroad passengers of every social level took with them could be almost as important as the journey itself. Luggage and clothing defined all that remained of home and traditional identity during a long journey. They also characterized the connections between passengers and their business, and reflected old and new economics. If luggage was lost, mislaid, or stolen, the link that connected the passenger to the larger society was lost. And at the conclusion of a journey, all that remained of home far away were the few portable toiletries and other small effects packed in the luggage; all that remained of the journey were the small souvenirs and remembrances purchased en route. Thus portable property, once considered only in the context of a home or business, in the late nineteenth century came to be regarded more and more in the context of the weight, strength, and design needed for convenience while traveling or moving.

Before the building of the railroad, domestic containers for personal property took the form of large, well-built cabinets, shelves, and chests which stood within the walls of a house and provided storage for clothes, blankets, linens, dishes, and the other paraphernalia of daily life. Travel equipment consisted of small trunks and bandboxes that could fit into stagecoaches or wagons, or cloth bags, small leather pouches, and circular containers that fit comfortably on the back of a horse. Those who packed for a long journey, or for trading purposes, arranged their wares in larger wooden and leather boxes that fit on the backs of pack animals or into the backs of wagons; they contained a variety of gear for sale on the road, or for cooking, dressing, and sleeping away from home.

One of the most obvious differences between colonial-era luggage and that carried by railroad passengers lay in the number and size of the trunks and bags. Larger and more powerful locomotives enabled trains to carry more and heavier luggage as well as more passengers.

Many of the small trunks of the antebellum period, designed to carry freight but also used as luggage, gave way after the Civil War to much larger trunks specifically made for passenger travel.[2] Often these measured as much as three feet in length by two feet in height and width. For those traveling without a trunk, the carpetbag provided quite a bit of room, if the traveler did not mind having all his personal effects jumbled together, without the protection provided by the rigid walls of a trunk. This problem, plus the blight of moth holes, led the carpetbag to a gradual loss of favor among travelers who could afford new luggage.

After the power of the locomotive, the most important factor in the design of luggage after the war was the increasing length of railroad journeys. Having one trunk or bag sufficed for a day's travel, but overnight trips, which became possible for the first time in the 1850s, required a type of luggage that could be taken on board the train, even if it contained only a shawl, blanket, or small pillow to make the journey more comfortable. After the Civil War, the success of the Pullman Company encouraged luggage designers to provide for the necessities for sleeping on the train.

A notable influence in changing luggage design was the erratic availability of public services equal in comfort to those at home. The wealthy could afford luxury hotels and restaurants, and they rode in private cars and parlor cars that included desks, cabinets, toilets, bathing areas, and other furnishings considered essential to comfort. Hotels and vacation homes also provided these furnishings. Those of middling means or less had to carry along the tools for bathing, eating, taking medicine, and meeting other homely and personal needs.

The middling sort and the poor frequently carried out their eating, work, and ablutions right in the day coach or emigrant car, without any special furnishings. While the Pullman cars provided some relief from this public display, the absence of household conveniences was a distinct handicap for most travelers. According to the many anecdotes about Pullman cars, display was sometimes even more of a problem there than in the day cars. The *Railroad Gazette* reported the story of an old couple who went to bed shortly after 6 p.m. in the only berth made up for them. After changing in the ladies' dressing room, they became a phenomenon in the national press when they emerged.

> ... A slam of the door and a snort of laughter from some innocent youth attracted the attention of all the occupants of the car to a grand triumphal march executed by the old couple from the dressing-room to their berth. ... The old lady had apparently nothing on but her "robe de nuit" and a nightcap, and the old gentleman brought up the rear with his clothes and those belonging to his wife in his arms. ... [3]

Clearly these older people were committing the same errors as did the woman who came to the station too early with too much luggage. They had not learned the ways of public life, and proceeded in public much as they did at home.

The largest and heaviest luggage accompanied the rich, who wished to look and feel their best at a distance from home. They usually did not carry the luggage themselves but hired porters or personal servants for the task. They brought changes of clothing, nightwear, bath articles, towels, toiletries, and other items that would have been considered impossible luxuries to even the most comfortable travelers of the early nineteenth century.[4] This extended inventory fit into the cabinets, desks, and other furnishings provided by railroads, steamboats, and hotels. Others who carried this much luggage were those who visited or vacationed for an extended length of time. They too unpacked and set their personal goods about them at their destination. Both these types of passengers had the money to buy privacy, personal service, and luxury in an otherwise increasingly public world.

The middle class and the poor suffered most from a lack of comfortable spaces and furnishings while traveling. Like the anxious woman described at the opening of this chapter, and the couple in the Pullman, they carried their home goods with them and juggled the odd assortment from hand to seat to rack, as the situation warranted. Not only were they often poorly organized, but they brought along personal items that were ill-suited for use in the public environment of a day coach. This mistake reflected one of the most important cultural tensions that railroading created. Those who brought their accompanying luggage directly from the home inventory of houseplants and lunch baskets into a day coach, which had no provision for them, failed to recognize the fundamental change from a private, land-based society to a public, exchange-based society. They were old-fashioned and out of step. Many women could be found in this group, as well as the poor, particularly the migrating poor, who carried their farming and household inventory "on their backs," to be laid down when they reached their new home on American land.

The cognoscenti among travelers, including the rich and those who traveled routinely, carried a set of trunks, bags, straps, and carriers designed specifically for a train journey. Their luggage was crafted in size and strength for the day coach, Pullman, or baggage car, and was fitted internally to organize the contents more precisely so as to be re-trievable *during* the journey, not just at the end. (This internal orga-nization grew more sophisticated with each passing decade.) But migrants, as well as women who stayed at home more than men, car-ried their household items and made do despite the awkwardness and jumble this created en route.

These two types of travelers can be seen as representatives of two different economies and the social realities of each: the old agricul-tural and land-based economy which still held the fortunes of many migrants, blacks, and housewives; and the new business economy which put the exchange value of every item ahead of its usefulness in the context of a household. For the immigrant farmer, the ex-change, or journey, was a means to the end of settling the land; for businessmen, traveling salesmen, and professionals, the exchange of passengers and their luggage was integral to the creation of wealth.

With the routine of travel sufficiently frequent to warrant the cre-ation of a whole new inventory of portable items for the traveler, many people looked for solutions through invention. Starting before the Civil War, and more frequently afterward, inventors took out patents on "new and useful improvements" in luggage, hoping to profit by solving the dilemma of carrying a home inventory on an extended trip. One of the charms of these patents lies in the efforts of inventors to reproduce not just the conveniences of an orderly home but the furnishings themselves, so frequently lacking in a crowd environment—portable desks, bathtubs, toilets, medicine cab-inets, and sinks.[5] In retrospect many of the solutions seem impractical or amusing because of the incongruity between the local, home-centered life, complete with furniture, and the life of the road, with few furnishings beyond the car and its seats. But the attention to this dilemma also indicates discontent with the lack of public services for travelers.

In the effort to make the comforts of home accessible to travelers, innovators conjured plans to recreate many home furnishings designed to fold up and double as hand-held luggage. Tavern owners of the eighteenth century would have been quite surprised to see some of these items cross their thresholds. In 1871 a woman named Esther Hoare, a resident of Massachusetts, patented a child's toilet for "use at home or while traveling"; it "attached to the bottom of a carpet or travelling-bag. . . ." The ingenuity of Ethelbert Watts, resident of Pennsylvania, resulted in a patent for "convertible portmanteau and bath-tub," granted in 1876. Watts notes in justifying his patent the lack of services for passengers while traveling.

> The object of my invention is to provide a portmanteau, valise, traveling-bag, or other equivalent article used for the transportation of clothing, which shall be convertible into a bath-tub, so as to afford travelers in places where such conveniences are wanting the luxury or comfort of bodily ablution.

In 1884 a Benjamin Kiam of Texas patented an inflatable pillow designed to be attached to a satchel.[6]

During the 1890s and into the twentieth century, fewer patents were issued for these kinds of portable home furnishings, though portable desks and medicine cabinets were patented after the turn of the century. Instead inventors focused on hand-held luggage that took up as little space as possible but contained a maximum of pockets, compartments, and organizers.[7] This shift likely developed in part from the wider use of the Pullman cars, which put home furnishings, including beds, lounge chairs, tables, and food, within reach of the general public.

Among 1890s patents that most reflected this change was one for a traveling bag with a hatbox nested inside it, invented by Ashley Bancroft of Oregon. Another, patented by Thaddeus Young of North Carolina, combined two common baggage types, one the well-known valise and another called a "cabinet bag," "whereby a broad box base is provided having hinged to the sides thereof the ordinary valise sections having packing compartments." Compartments corresponding to the drawers or shelves of a cabinet became increasingly common toward the end of the century with the ever-expanding inventory of small portable properties. Pockets or envelopes made of cardboard were attached to the insides of the case to house small items easily lost or crushed.[8]

The retail market in luggage also reflected the change from simple cases to complex organizers, as the need for handbags extended to all economic classes and regions. During the 1870s cheap luggage became available to a national market through the mail-order firm of Montgomery Ward. In 1878 the company advertised twelve different styles of hand-held traveling bags, each available in two to eight different sizes. The cheapest, called a Railroad Traveling Bag, cost from 85 cents to $1.20, depending on size and materials. The most expensive, the Grained Leather Pelissier, with one outside pocket, cost $5.00.[9] All were quite similar in appearance and imitated the Gladstone bag, named for the English statesman, which opened flat into two halves.

By the 1890s both Montgomery Ward and Sears, Roebuck offered a far more diverse collection of handbags, all emphasizing space-saving or expandable features and internal organizers. Even the simple Gladstone had within it straps to hold clothes in place, internal pockets, portfolios (which also held clothes in place), and shirt pockets. Ladies' satchels, known as club satchels, were sold for daytime use, the equivalent of a large purse for longer trips. And the telescope bag made its appearance. This bag, while lacking internal compartments, came in graduated sizes, each capable of fitting within the next larger bag. The bags themselves were composed of two separate halves, the sides of which completely overlapped when empty but which could expand outward, the sides overlapping less and less, until six to eight inches of additional space were available.[10]

By 1901 Sears, Roebuck sold a similar line of inexpensive bags, plus leather suitcases, luggage tags, trunk straps that wrapped luggage and buckled like a belt to increase holding strength, and shawl straps, which were handles with attached straps which could be buckled around a loose assortment of clothes. Within a few more years Sears carried a wide assortment of ladies' handbags and change purses.[11]

As might be expected, makers of more expensive luggage offered more types of organizers and specialized travel containers than either Sears or Wards. In its 1892 catalog the J. J. Warren Luggage Company of Worcester, Massachusetts, described an enviable array of small travel gadgets in leather cases, each with all intriguing charm of a doll's house complete with miniature furnishings. In this catalog the inventory of travel was detailed and extensive, ranging from novelty items such as leather change purses and match cases complete with the name of the customer's own business stamped into the leather, to leather cases for most of the musical instruments of a marching band.[12]

For the well-dressed and well-groomed traveler, Warren sold round leather boxes to hold extra collars and cuffs, in dozens of sizes; dressing cases supplied with tooth and nail brushes, hair brushes, combs, tweezers, button hooks, soap boxes, and shaving equipment, in hundreds of combinations; picnic kits; and drinking cups bound in a leather case. For the salesman Warren offered sample cases fitted with bottles; for the doctor, medical bags; for the courier, mail and specie bags; for the student, book bags; for the sport, gun cases, tennis racket cases, and bicycle bags; and for all travelers, suitcases, telescope bags, shawl straps, and suit valises, scarcely distinguishable from suitcases.[13]

Business and professional travelers eagerly adopted the use of portable, specialized luggage that could be managed by one person. These were known variously as valises, grips, bags, pullmans, and suitcases. Family travelers and those of middling means, on the other hand, continued to use trunks, the reliable standard for long-distance travel since the eighteenth century. A trunk could hold the property of more than one person, the bulky clothes of a traveler who intended to stay away for weeks or months at a time or the extended household inventory of a woman who wanted some of the comforts of home with her on the journey. Commercial mail-order firms lured travelers to purchase trunks by giving each style of trunk a name that evoked the most romantic connotations of travel. Before the Civil War, the

The large trunks carried in baggage cars were useful for the extensive layered clothing typical of nineteenth-century travelers, but they were inadequate for overnight Pullman travel. Suitcases and organizers were more suitable for the train journey.

Charles T. Wilt luggage makers of Chicago produced the first "Jenny Lind" trunk, named for the Swedish singer who toured the United States during the 1850s. This style was extensively imitated for decades by manufacturers of lower-priced luggage. After the war the Gladstone bag also became a popular style, imitated in cheaply priced, mass-produced bags of the 1870s and 1880s.[14]

After the war both Sears and Montgomery Ward named their trunks after fashionable public figures, stylish resorts, national landmarks, or places in the American West made accessible to the public through railroad travel. The "Patent Eugenie," "Empress," and "Crown Prince" trunks suggested that railroads and steamships put American travelers on the same footing as royalty. The "Saratoga," "Glen Cove Belle," "Rye Beach," and "Manhattan Beach" trunks somehow connected the owner with the more fashionable resorts on the Eastern seaboard. The "Yosemite," "Western Belle," "Union Pacific," and "Texas Siftings" evoked the possibility that the owner of one of these trunks might someday see the wonders of the great American West.[15]

All these trunks were quite low-priced and were available through mail order, not from an exclusive luggage dealer. Because trunks were difficult to carry and had to be entrusted to the care of baggagemen, beneath the catalog's suggestions of romance were specifications that made quite clear the first duty of a good trunk: to survive the bumps and crashes of baggage room and baggage car. Even inexpensive trunks, such as Montgomery Ward's "Eugenie," were valuable chiefly for their strength rather than their romance.

Eugenie
Imitation Leather—Lady's Trunk
Barrel stave top, iron bound, slats the whole length of trunk with bumpers on top, iron hinges, rollers, handles with caps, hasp lock with best patent bolt lock on each side, patent iron stay. . . .[16]

If there was romance to be found here, it consisted in an interior lining decorated with abstract patterns and pictures of faraway places; a bonnet box; and a few specialized compartments of the kind that were built into virtually all commercially produced trunks of the 1870s and 1880s.

Trunks, of limited usefulness to business or professional travelers, served the family traveler who planned to stay at a hotel, resort, vacation home, or with friends for an extended period. Like the trunk itself, these habits reflected an older style of travel. During an extended visit away from home, travelers packed a number of trunks to store the very bulky clothes of the period. The infamous immigrant trunks, larger and heavier than commercially made American trunks, weighed so much that some baggagemen refused to handle them. They contained almost all of an immigrant family's worldly goods. In their weight and construction they were indistinguishable from household furniture.

Emigrant Chests

How the men who handle baggage at the Union depot succeed in transferring some of the curious-looking emigrant boxes or chests from one train to another without the aid of a derrick is a mystery to a great many people. Some of the boxes are so large that they can scarcely be thrust through the doors of baggage cars, and they are so heavy that they might be made to serve in an emergency as anchors for steamships.

So wrote an editor of the *Railroad Gazette* in 1883, the same year that railroad companies acted in concert to forbid the carriage of any accompanied luggage weighing more than 250 pounds.[17]

Women, who wore the bulkiest clothing in the 1880s, who also took responsibility for children, and who carried on the tradition of extended visits longer than men did, had a special identification with trunks even as the suitcase or pullman bag became common for other travelers. The woman described at the opening of this chapter was not one of a kind but a stereotype of middle-class women travelers everywhere. Women were more likely to bring household items along on the journey than to adopt the specialized portable travel equipment used by business and professional travelers. Despite the presence of ladies' waiting rooms and lounges in the larger railroad stations, poor and middle-class women found no facilities available while traveling to help them care for children. Even without children, trunks were vital.

Today is our wedding day [wrote a Smith graduate from the class of 1888]. The queer little wedding, so far away from friends—strangers everywhere, a strange place; a wedding in old clothes, the nuptial finery having gone astray in a lost trunk.

As for Lucretia Hale, a hearty and inveterate single traveler and granddaughter of the founding president of the Boston and Worcester, she found that her female relations had so much luggage that they needed help in packing. In a brief note to a relative, she wrote of yet another relative: "She leaves tomorrow, has just now gone to the depths of her trunk. . . ." She continued, "Here I left and made some progress in Lucy's trunks which she was getting on with."[18]

For both sexes, some space had to be left for purchases made en route. Any traveler could find a great many guidebooks describing sights, local hotels and restaurants, and price ranges. Many also included a map and a pocket train schedule. In 1871 a publisher in Buffalo, New York, produced a minute book entitled *The Travelers' Guide: Containing Distance Tables, Population of the United States, Stamp Duties, Telegraph Rates, U.S. Postal Laws, &c.*[19] This paperback guide, costing only ten cents and measuring just four by three inches, fit easily into a pocket or purse and contained information for traveling on all the major through routes in the United States.

Other tempting items could be acquired in the course of a journey from the newsboys who peddled their wares both in railroad stations and on trains. In addition to newspapers they hawked guidebooks, food, candy, tobacco products, and even small conveniences such as drinking cups. The opportunities for such purchases were so numerous, and the boys so insistent, that cartoons in the public press depicted the passenger loaded down with purchases he did not want but which were thrown into his lap during the course of the journey.[20]

Lucius Beebe summed up a dominant cultural attitude toward railroad luggage during this period:

> With the upsurge of travel after the Civil War the baggagemaster entered the demonology of the American people. . . . Too much luggage when traveling became a national vice, and travel guides and handbooks took to publishing pictured warnings . . . [of people with too much baggage].[21]

Portable property was popular after the war. It suited the tastes and needs of a highly mobile population, satisfied their curiosity for new goods, and permitted them remembrances of the familiar at hand while far from home. Portable property, especially small objects that were easy to carry, came to have special significance as souvenirs of places visited and left behind. For migrants this often took the form of a teapot, bedcovers, chair, quilt, or other small reminders of the home and most of its furnishings that were left behind.[22] It helped ease the homesickness associated with settlement in a new country or state, far from relatives and friends.

For other travelers, particularly tourists, a new industry produced souvenirs of all parts of the country and the world. Flatware, notably spoons, were a popular souvenir after the Civil War. Spoons with reminders of each state, each president, major monuments, or natural wonders emblazoned on them were sold as remembrances. Ashtrays, knives, matchboxes, bags, scarves, blankets, and other items were specially made for tourists and served to chronicle their travels. In the 1890s the first picture postcards were distributed at the Columbian Exposition in Chicago and became an instant success. Railroads soon began offering postcards as gifts or souvenirs and as a way of attracting business. Around the turn of the century, Kodak's introduction of the Brownie camera put good photographs within reach of ordinary travelers.[23]

Books containing pictures and descriptions of such wonders as Niagara Falls and Yellowstone Park provided an education for armchair travelers. And, like advertising, they encouraged readers to travel. The emergence of book publishing for mass distribution gave writers an unprecedented opportunity to communicate the details of travel experiences to virtually any reader. Thus Americans need not even ride the train themselves in order to see the cultural changes that accompanied the revolution in transportation after the Civil War. Despite the fact that they romanticized regional experiences, writers such as Bret Harte, Willa Cather, and Thomas Nelson Page, drew together the strands of local color into a national vision.[24]

In this way material property contributed to the cultural unification of the country. Just as the distribution of property by through trade brought products from all parts of the country together in one marketplace, the travels of passengers made them familiar with the land and culture of an extraordinarily large and diverse country. The cultural distance among the nation's regions became less significant, at least in the marketplace, as local products were sold at ever-greater distances from home. Passengers, in discovering the country's different regions and cultures, had a hand in carrying home the goods particular to each. They were reminders that the unity of the country and the power of every American extended far beyond the visible horizon.

19

|||||||||||||||||||||||||

From Union to Uniformity

Up to this time the railway system is an accident. The mass of railway men are so by accident. . . . [In] the next half-century . . . the system itself [will no longer be] accidental. . . . Exact science must supersede guess-work.
—*Proceedings,* American Association of Passenger Traffic Officers, 1876[1]

The General Time Convention of October 11, 1883, at the Grand Pacific Hotel in Chicago, definitely adopted Standard Time. Having voted overwhelmingly for the plan, the convention issued a notice, directing that all railway clocks be set to the new standard at exactly 12 o'clock noon, Sunday, November 18, 1883.
—B. A. Botkin and Alvin F. Harlow, *A Treasury of Railroad Folklore*[2]

A s mass-produced goods became available nationally, and the railroad itself provided the means to distribute them, the railroad industry began to look beyond the goal of union to a goal of uniformity in its own equipment and delivery of services. From ticketing procedures and baggage handling to the welter of local times and schedules by which railroads ran, railroad companies sought savings and efficiency by reducing a chaotic diversity of systems to one national standard.

Beginning as early as the 1850s, railroad companies had sponsored efforts to create uniform standards by which the railroad service could transform itself from a tangled skein of competing railroads under local control into a national transportation system. While by the late 1880s both federal and state government had begun to legislate better and more predictable rail service, the corporations themselves, particularly the long-distance railroads, sought uniform standards in order to eliminate some of the worst effects of competition on the delivery of services.

The road from national union to national uniformity was tedious and difficult. In each effort, from uniform ticketing to the installation of a uniform system of train signals, conflicts of interest among rival railroads and their passengers dogged the attempts to introduce standardization. Even within the railroad industry itself, talks proceeded inconclusively for years before the adoption of practical solutions. And even after the agreement on national standards within the industry, many railroads retained their own standards and practices, either because they had no through traffic on their lines or too little money to improve their facilities and services.

The search for uniform standards had little impact on the running of trains before the Civil War. After the war, pressure from the new state railroad commissions and the courts revived the effort. But only in the 1880s, when the push for a federal regulatory commission began, did the discussions begin to produce substantial practical changes.

Many of the talks on these matters took place within the railroad industry itself. A large number of railroad associations had formed before 1880, within which representatives from the major companies met to discuss mutual concerns. The American Association of Passenger Traffic Officers (AAPTO), for example, composed of ticket agents from all member railroads, met for the first time at Pittsburgh in 1855 to set winter and summer passenger fares for through passengers.[3] Without agreement on this matter, railroads could not sell travelers through tickets covering passage on the tracks of more than one railroad company. The group also considered requests for special fares and worked on a standard contract for railroad tickets that would spell out the rights and responsibilities of member railroads and all passengers.

The General Time Convention, composed of representatives from a number of railroad corporations, first convened in 1872 "for the Arrangement of a Summer Time Schedule" applicable to all member railroads.[4] Thereafter the group continued to meet until it had agreed upon a plan to run all lines according to one standard of time. In light of the ever-increasing volume of passengers and freight traveling long distance, this decision was considered essential to the creation of railroad schedules that applied to passengers and shippers from all parts of the country.

During the postwar period the railroads also cooperated to begin converting major through routes to one track gauge—four feet eight and one-half inches between rails—so that train cars from one railroad could pass over the tracks of another. This eliminated the enormously time-consuming and expensive process of transferring passengers and freight to a new train at each junction between two railroad companies. It also represented a necessary first step in connecting competing lines, a step mandated by many state railroad commissions during the 1870s and 1880s. Primarily, however, this change affected through routes; many short lines retained another gauge for their tracks.

Railroad baggage agents took up the issue of setting limits on the size, weight, and contents of accompanied baggage, and insisted that many large or bulky items be reclassified as freight in order to ease the lot of the baggagemaster. Such standards discouraged immigrant passengers from carrying their home goods with them, and commercial passengers from carrying their samples and products as personal property. The new standards encouraged a uniformity in luggage that favored lightweight and portable personal effects.

During the 1880s many aspects of railroad technology came under scrutiny, chiefly because of a great many disastrous train wrecks and increasing numbers of accidents that disabled or killed railroad employees. Safety issues were discussed in the public press as well as in the conferences of railroad officials. Signals, brakes, and couplings used by many railroad companies differed little from those adopted by railroads before the Civil War. Yet the size and weight of train cars had continued to grow, and the length and speed of trains had also increased as the advancing technology of steam power enabled the railroads to purchase faster and more powerful locomotives. Fearful fires resulted from many train wrecks because the old iron stoves used to heat wooden railroad cars were still in use, despite available technology for steam heating.

As the record of railroad fatalities lengthened, the press focused on a number of railroad groups that were experimenting with improved railroad technology. Railroad signalmen met during the postwar decades to introduce uniform train signals to avoid accidents. And the Master Car-Builders, founded in the first decade after the war, received a great deal of publicity as they developed safer standardized train car parts.[5]

Finally, in 1893, the federal government passed the Railroad Safety Appliance Act which mandated uniform systems for brakes and couplings on trains.[6] While this law reduced the number of employee accidents, it affected passenger service only marginally, and many railroads continued to use old systems of coupling and braking well into the twentieth century.

Also in the spirit of setting national standards, the public, the railroads, and their regulatory agencies began to consider rules for the behavior of passengers as well as the operation of trains. The miscellaneous statutes passed during the seventies and eighties became a deluge during the 1890s, drawing a new line between acceptable and unacceptable behavior. More than ever, conductors were asked to crack down on such customary excesses as drinking, jumping on and off moving trains, and otherwise indulging personal preferences at the expense of other passengers. Even the emerging giant of modern medical practice had its say about the lives of railroad passengers: doctors concluded that travelers were carrying diseases from town to town. Thus the behavior of the individual was reinterpreted in light of its effect on crowds of passengers.

Uniform standards were considered by the ticket agents association in 1855 when it first met to deal with a number of bookkeeping problems. It found a recurrent difficulty in returning the profits from long-distance fares to each railroad along the route, when the entire

ticket had been sold by only one of those roads. And it sought to design a single ticket that would be accepted by all railroads traveled by
a through passenger. This was to take the form of a coupon or card
ticket, because only one small stub or coupon was removed by each
railroad, rather than the conductor taking the entire ticket or rendering it void. The ticket agents also sought to curtail the widespread
fraud associated with ticket scalping, the counterfeiting of tickets, and
passengers avoiding payment by one ruse or another.[7]

In 1856 a report advised the association of the need for a uniform system of coupon tickets on all railroads. Twenty-five years
later the association continued to have a committee that dealt
with coupon tickets and their abuses. By 1887 this committee had its
counterpart in a committee on mileage tickets, another system developed for through travelers. Despite various attempts at a common
nomenclature of tickets over the next several years, a definitive solution to the problem of uniform ticketing procedures failed to materialize.[8]

In 1894 the ticket agents association became concerned that much
of its authority was being usurped by local and regional associations
coming to their own agreements on the same issues. It seems probable that rival organizations formed in part because the national association could not resolve the accounting problems connected with
through travel. Indeed, in 1899 the association itself rejected the
idea that it could reasonably design one national interchangeable
mileage ticket.[9] Thus while railroads agreed on the general need for
uniformity in ticketing, in practice it eluded them, and fraud in the
purchase and use of tickets continued to flourish.

After its initial meeting in 1872, the General Time Convention re-
convened in 1874 and thereafter met twice annually to establish summer and winter train schedules for member railroads. The number of
railroads participating varied from year to year, from about twenty-
one to forty-seven lines, until 1881 when plans to standardize the
time of day began to take shape. After receiving advice from various
experts supporting a standard time, including the Committee on
Standard Time of the American Association for the Advancement of
Science, and a similar committee of the American Meteorological So-

The search for uniformity in ticketing practices reduced the chaos but failed to eliminate the need for a diversity of tickets corresponding to passenger needs. (HANS HALBERSTADT)

ciety, the convention concluded its debate by planning to reopen the issue at its April 1882 meeting.[10]

At the April meeting more professional groups appeared in order to recommend the adoption of standard time. The list of these groups suggests how many people were adversely affected by the adherence to local standards of time around the country: the War Department, the International Congress of Meteorologists in Rome, the International Geographical Congress, the International Association for Codification of the Laws of Nations, the Academy of Sciences of St. Petersburg, the chief signal officer of the United States army, the superintendent of the Railway Mail Service, the directors of astronomical observatories in Leipzig and Berlin, and a representative of the Canadian government.[11]

Letters from still other organizations highlighted the difficulty of having some fifty different time standards (down from seventy in the 1860s) throughout the country. John Rodgers, a rear admiral in the United States navy, wrote:

> I can speak of my own experience as a traveler. I have been annoyed and perplexed by the changes in the time schedules of connecting railroads. My watch could give me no information as to the arrival and departure of trains, nor of the time for meals, nor of the time allowed by the schedule for them. Continuous timetables would have obviated this difficulty. . . .

A professor of mathematics who worked for the navy wrote:

> . . . People do not complain because trains are run by a standard time differing twenty, forty, or sixty minutes from the local time, but because they cannot travel far by rail before the schedule time is changed to conform to a new standard differing from the first by an unknown quantity. . . .

The October meeting received word that "three kinds of time [are] now in use at New London by the railroads entering there, and two kinds in like manner, at Norwich and Willimantic. . . ."[12]

A year later, in October 1883, a General Time Convention representing thirty-six lines sponsored a nationwide vote among railroad companies on the adoption of standard time. One hundred and seventy-three roads voted to adopt standard time, to take effect the following month. It was a sweeping change that met with resistance, conflict, and apathy. First, not every railroad voted in favor of standard time. In 1883 *Poor's Manual of Railroads* counted 121,422 miles of railroad track in operation; the collective mileage of railroads favoring standard time came to only 78,158 miles. Second, many localities saw only the arrogance of the railroads in their substitution of "railroad time" for "God's time," as determined by sun, stars, seasons, and local custom. One who equated local custom with God's custom was an elderly man who denounced the new national standard:

> Damn old Vanderbilt's time! We want God's time! The Vanderbilts cannot run me if they run the rest of the country, by Jehosaphat!

The mayor of Bangor, Maine, vetoed a city council plan to adopt standard time because he considered it unconstitutional and contrary to the laws of God. Even the federal government refused to allow its departments to adopt standard time and refused officially to recognize standard time until 1918. Regardless, standard time prevailed and spread, making the work of scheduling through train service infinitely easier than it had been under the old system of timekeeping.[13]

The movement to adopt a standard gauge of track also gathered support in the 1880s. As major Northern railroad systems such as the Pennsylvania, the Baltimore and Ohio, the New York Central, and the Erie Railroad had grown, more and more track was adjusted to conform to the gauge chosen for use within that system. For example, most lines consolidated under the ownership of the Baltimore and Ohio had a gauge of four feet eight and one-half inches, known today as standard gauge. The New York Central also operated on tracks of standard gauge. But the Erie Railroad still had a six-foot gauge through the 1870s. In the Midwest and South many of the major railroad systems also had five-foot gauges, including the Louisville and Nashville, a major link between North and South.

While consolidation of railroad systems worked toward a standard gauge, the time still required to switch passengers and freight wherever two railroad systems of different gauge met cost too much money. And the state commissions had begun to require that railroad lines connect with one another. During the 1880s a number of major Southern railroad systems adjusted their gauge to match the standard gauge shared by many Northern trunk lines as well as the Union Pacific and other railroads of the far West. In 1881 the Illinois Central adjusted 547 miles of its Southern track from a five-foot gauge to the standard gauge. In 1885 the Mobile and Ohio Railroad followed suit. In 1886 a group of railroad officials met in Atlanta and decided to follow the example of these lines and shift all major Southern railroad routes, including the Louisville and Nashville, to standard gauge. This was accomplished in two days, May 31 and June 1, 1886, by workers strung out over the entire Southern rail system to make the change in coordinated fashion. This change brought most of the through routes of the country into conformity with the standard gauge.[14]

As with ticketing and time, however, some chose not to conform. Stewart Holbrook summarized the efforts of these "mavericks" who continued to build and operate narrow-gauge railroads until the mid-twentieth century. Most were short lines serving rural areas and had no need to connect their services to the through routes of the country.

> During the same two decades that witnessed the standardization of the gauge of most American railroads, the mavericks were at work building some 5,000 miles of narrow-gauge rails set 3 feet 6 inches apart, or 3 feet, and a few as narrow as 2 feet. In 1876 there were 81 narrow-gauge roads in operation in 26 states. Pennsylvania had 11, California 8, Utah 6, Ohio 5; 4 each in Colorado, Massachusetts, New York, Iowa, Nevada, and Illinois; 3 in Mississippi, 3 in Texas, and the others scattered over 15 other states. . . .
>
> The last two-footer was assuredly the Bridgton & Harrison, in Maine, which went out of business in 1941.

Among the narrow-gauge roads were logging roads in the White Mountains, such as the John's River Railroad, and mining railroads in Pennsylvania and the Western states.[15]

Other efforts at standardization included the size, weight, and contents of passengers' baggage. Before the war passengers had been able to "check" almost any item as accompanied baggage. During the 1840s the German geologist Albert Koch had taken all his crates of fossils from the Atlantic to the Mississippi River as accompanied luggage, despite a few complaints from baggage handlers. Salesmen's samples, even bags of gold and silver, were checked as accompanied baggage, only to cause a furor in the courts when the items were lost, damaged, or stolen.[16] Although some railroads adhered to a rule that up to eighty pounds of baggage could be carried free of additional charge, diversity was the rule nationally until the late 1860s. And no national consensus existed to regulate the contents of baggage.

Even during the 1850s, railroads objected to paying liability on lost or damaged baggage of inordinate value. From that time on, the courts were called upon to help determine the limits of railroad liability for personal luggage. Many baggage agents also wanted to see a maximum limit on the amount of luggage that any passenger could carry as accompanied baggage.

In 1866 the ticket agents association sponsored a survey to determine what a "reasonable" amount of accompanied baggage would be. Some respondents reiterated the eighty-pound maximum, and added that $250 was also reasonable maximum value. One respondent, however, more attuned to the complexities of the issue, wrote that a "reasonable" value or weight would depend on "the length and object of the journey, the habits, tastes and condition in life of the passenger, whether he travels alone or with his family, what it is necessary for a person in his situation to have along with him in his journey, and such like circumstances. . . ."[17] Clearly the difference between these two responses lay in the dissimilar perspectives of baggagemaster and passenger. Over the next thirty years the railroads placed increasing limits on the weight of accompanied luggage and the value of its contents, in order to limit their liability. In so doing they lost much of their responsiveness to the individual needs of passengers.

Also in 1866 three major trunk routes, the Louisville and Nashville, the Chicago and Northwestern, and the Pennsylvania, announced a new baggage policy: they would now charge the public to carry any accompanied luggage that exceeded $100 in value. Nationally the standards continued to waver however, until in 1883 railroad companies placed a 250-pound limit on the size of trunks carried as accompanied luggage, regardless of content. In January that year the *Railroad Gazette* blamed the coming changes on "the enormous trunks of commercial travelers, a few of whom, it is said, carry goods for delivery as well as samples." The *Gazette* went on to say that "With several of the . . . drummers on a train, little room was left in the baggage car for baggage of other passengers."[18]

In May 1883 another *Gazette* editorial noted "the anguish which is in store for the fashionable belle who is obliged to pack her finery in a paltry 250 pound trunk" when the new weight regulations took effect on June 1. Enormous emigrant trunks were also a target of this new regulation.[19]

In the same year the Boston and Albany was brought before the Massachusetts Railroad Commission because one of its baggagemen refused to check a package of clothes that he did not construe as containing personal effects. The commission decided for the passenger. Ten years later the debate resurfaced in the press over the question, "Is a bicycle baggage?"[20] The idea that accompanied baggage should consist only of lightweight personal effects became one standard by which baggagemen could make their judgments. But of course this screened out the more substantial types of property that many people, particularly women, customarily carried on their travels. It also allowed baggagemen to ignore the personal circumstances of travelers.

Beyond this concern for uniform services, railroads confronted material problems, none more important than the need for technological standards. With the advent of faster trains—up from about fifteen miles per hour to thirty-five or forty miles per hour—accident rates had steadily increased since the end of the war. The *Railroad Gazette* reported that in the year 1875 alone, 104 head-on collisions occurred. The numbers continued to rise, in many instances made worse by fires. In addition to greater speeds, manual signal and switching errors contributed to confusion that caused accidents. Employee injury rates also mounted as more accidents occurred in the course of making up trains or while braking them.[21]

The Master Car-Builders' Association, composed of representatives from train car construction companies and from railroads that built their own cars, set out in the 1870s to improve the technology of railroad travel. The association recommended the best type of brake, seat, coupling, heating apparatus, ventilating system, and other equipment, then sought to standardize their use in the construction of all new railroad cars. This would not only increase safety but make railroad cars interchangeable, able to be run on any track and with any other train cars in the country. Like the ticket agents association, the Car-Builders sent out numerous questionnaires to find out what types of technology were commonly used in the construction of cars throughout the country. And, like the Association of American Railway Accounting Officers, they considered uniform terminology a necessary first step in creating uniformity in car parts. In 1879 they published *The Car Builder's Dictionary*, compiled by a mechanical engineer named Matthias Forney with the assistance of Leander Garey, superintendent of the car department of the New York Central and Hudson River Railroad, and Calvin Smith, secretary of the Car-Builders' Association. From its first entry, "Adjustable-globe Lamp," to its last, "Yoke," the dictionary provided definitions and technical drawings of the best equipment available to train car builders.[22]

The influence of the Master Car-Builders made itself felt over the next two decades as public debate grew over the safest and best types of railroad equipment. Despite this new and more scientific approach to railroad technology, several problems stood in the way of complete uniformity of cars and car appliances. One involved the investment necessary to make the change from outmoded heating, lighting, and ventilating systems to safer and generally more expensive replacements. While the larger and wealthier railroad systems, such as the Pennsylvania, the Louisville and Nashville, and the New York Central could afford to upgrade their equipment, many other railroads could not. They operated on a much lower budget and often acquired the used equipment of wealthier railroads. The branch lines that served poorer areas of the country, notably the rural areas, were at least a generation behind in the cars and car appliances they used. As costs continued to rise, especially after World War I, the upgrading of railroad equipment became significantly more expensive for all railroads. Other railroad organizations, such as the association of signal-

men, faced a similar dilemma. They could experiment and make rec-
ommendations, but no law forced safer or more effective railroad
appliances onto all individual lines.[23]

By 1890 several national movements were afoot to increase efficiency and uniformity in all areas of industry, not just the railroads.
Motion study and efficiency experts advised factory personnel on
laborsaving techniques and on ways to reduce waste in time and
money.[24] 1890 is also a traditional starting date for the progressive
politics that urged government regulation of businesses that abused
the public trust. A coordinated fight to force business to accept responsibility for the public welfare extended to railroads as well. But
this reform effort was a two-way street. Passengers too had to accept
more responsibility for the welfare of other passengers on the train.
A call for conformity to public standards of behavior marked an end
to freewheeling individualism among passengers and the beginnings
of regulated public behavior: conformity not just in one town or one
state, but a new national standard of reasonable behavior.

The roots of this regulation may be found in the state laws of the
1870s and 1880s that gave conductors police powers to eject undesir-
ables, including drunks and those who refused to pay their fare. Such
laws multiplied during the 1890s and the first decades of the twentieth century. The press became a public forum for the discussion of
passenger behavior as it affected public standards of safety.

Like many other standards for the railroad service, the need for
standards of passenger behavior was seen early, but reform was late
and incomplete. In 1873 the *Railroad Gazette* ran a number of short
articles depicting those aspects of passenger behavior that were least
safe or desirable. One of these, jumping on and off moving trains,
seemed harmless as long as trains ran at slow speeds. But with trains
running at over thirty miles per hour, accidents occurred regularly.
The article traced this habit not to its historical precedents but to passengers imitating the habits of trainmen. If the railroads sought to
curtail the habit among passengers, they must forbid their own trainmen from setting a bad example. In the same year the *Gazette* published an article about the death of a passenger at the hands of a
drunken man who had been allowed to ride despite his condition.[25]

Again, the writer chided the railroad conductor for not enforcing the public standard of behavior, already being written into many state statute books, that drunks must be ejected from the train.

The press also inquired into the failure of railroad companies to control the behavior of vendors who rode the trains selling goods to passengers. On a positive note, the Pennsylvania Railroad

> issued a circular to passenger conductors which says, "It having been alleged that news agents have offered for sale in the cars of this company, without the knowledge of their employees, immoral and obscene publications, passenger conductors are directed to see that such publications are not sold, or offered for sale on their trains. . . . They should see that [newsboys] are not allowed to offer their commodities in such a manner, or with such frequency, as to discommode or annoy the passenger, and they should not permit any article to be sold which might soil or injure the upholstery or the cars or the clothing of the passengers. The sale of prize portfolios, gifts, confections, or similar devices partaking of the nature of lotteries, is forbidden on the cars of this company.[26]

By the 1880s the trains were issuing lists of rules for the behavior of their own employees. Conductors, under ever-increasing pressure both to abide by the rules and to enforce them among passengers, were charged with providing all passengers with seats, not allowing anyone to ride in the baggage, mail, or express cars, being polite to all passengers, and avoiding "Boisterous, profane or vulgar language." Conductors also had to enforce seating arrangements and were frequently found wanting in allowing blacks to sit with white passengers, or letting second-class passengers ride in first-class coaches. Emigrants of both sexes might be allowed to smoke, but a strict separation among wealthier travelers remained; these women did not smoke.[27]

Trains issued rules for the behavior of newsboys as well, and once again conductors had the responsibility of enforcing these rules. Rules for news agents riding on the Chicago and Alton line included restricting the number of agents to one per train, restricting the number of trunks he could carry his goods in, regulating the prices he

charged, preventing him from selling immoral literature, and restricting his right to advertise other businesses while engaged in selling goods.[28]

This behavior now regulated by law or by the railroad companies
had not suddenly appeared after the Civil War. Drinking, profanity,
boisterous behavior, and jumping on and off moving trains had been
the practice of many travelers, particularly rural travelers who be-
haved according to their own standards and shied away from the social standards common in Eastern cities. The standards that forbade
these practices were new and reflected the emergence of an edu-
cated class who sought to make public behavior compatible with
urban technology and with the needs of crowds rather than the needs
of the individual.

One of the most important changes in this regard grew out of several revolutionary discoveries in medicine and subsequent efforts to
reorder social behavior to conform with the requirements of good
health. The discovery that contagious diseases were spread by germs
passing from one person to another heightened concerns about the
dangers of crowds. Through breathing, sneezing, or defecating from
a railroad car toilet directly onto the railroad tracks, passengers in
crowds spread diseases.

It had long been observed that diseases sometimes spread along
the course of rivers or of railroad tracks. Quarantine, the isolation of
a contagious population, had sometimes included preventing any ship
or railroad from stopping where an outbreak of disease had occurred,
or the complete isolation of a healthy population, fearing contagion
from the arrival of a ship or train. In 1878, during an outbreak of yel-
low fever in Mississippi, rumors passed among the citizenry that the
fever had spread from a lady's dress sent in a trunk from New Orleans, or that it had arrived in a letter. One observer noted, however,
that during this particular epidemic the panic seemed unwarranted,
for people who lived in the areas around railroad tracks and stations
were healthy. Nevertheless, an observer in Natchez, Mississippi,
noted that "our city and county is quarantined. Not a boat of any kind
is permitted to land."[29]

At precisely this time period, doctors in the major hospitals in
Chicago, Baltimore, Philadelphia, and New York were learning from

European visitors about the germ theory of contagious disease: that germs invisible to the naked eye lived in and on human bodies, causing diseases; and that breathing, sneezing, spitting, defecating, bodily contact, or prolonged failure to bathe all contributed to the spreading of germs from one person to another. Thus the people who noticed that disease followed transportation routes had some scientific basis for thinking so. Disease followed crowds.

Even before 1878, many passengers had complained about the close, stale air in train cars, due to "exhalations from human lungs, human bodies, and human clothing, all more or less in need of purification." In 1873 a concerned citizen wrote to the Pittsburgh press,

> Among the many causes of ill-health among the American people, none is more potent than breathing foul air. . . . On Tuesday, the 12th, I took the morning mail train at Swissvale to come to Indiana. . . . There were but few people in the car, and the frequent stoppages and openings of the doors . . . had kept the air in the car good, although ventilation was closed. But soon the seats began to fill up with passengers, the stops were at longer intervals, and the air became loaded with exhalations from human lungs, human bodies and human clothing, all more or less in need of purification.

Later, sleeping cars and of course smoking cars also offended passengers by their close, malodorous air. The emergence of scientific information indicating that large crowds in a closed area did indeed encourage disease prompted the search for a better system of train car ventilation.[30]

By the 1890s attention focused on the fact that railroad passengers who flushed the toilet sent the contents out onto the track and, at certain junctions, into the water supply. In 1893 the New York Board of Health seized a railroad station at College Point because of its dirty toilets.[31] Sanitary measures were soon standardized in local and state law to reduce the risk of disease.

Especially between 1870 and 1900, railroads leaned in the direction of national standards in ticketing, time, track gauges, baggage, the structure of train cars, and in the behavior of passengers. These standards developed to promote the efficient and safe transfer of passengers in all parts of the country. The effort to unite the country through railroad transportation could not be completed until the many parts of the system were connected in a rational, uniform manner. But, as ever, conflicts of interest, squabbling, and lack of sufficient capital prevented many railroads from becoming part of a new, uniform transportation. Especially on the short lines and in rural areas, the old regional idiosyncrasies of travel remained intact well into the new century.

Thomas Cooley and the
Ghost of William Seward

THE EXPANSION OF railroads after the Civil War proceeded hand in hand with the settlement of the West, the reconstruction of the South, and the development of massive industrial zones in the North. While the railroads succeeded in drawing all regions and economies of the country under one system of transport, they also engendered one of the most conflicted and complex periods in American history. If the ghost of William Seward were resurrected to comment on the state of American society thirty years after the conclusion of the war, he might justifiably have remarked on the number of systems that fought with one another in the legal, economic, and social spheres of American life. He certainly could have identified more irrepressible conflicts than the one great one that tore the country apart in 1861.

From a legal point of view, the states had constructed a system of laws meant to contain the lack of regard with which railroads treated their customers—shippers as well as passengers. After 1887 the federal government had begun to follow the lead of the states in containing the dominant conflict of interest between railroads and their customers: discriminatory rates. Despite these extensive efforts to nudge the railroads toward an appreciation of their role as public servants, the roads never embraced this philosophy if they could avoid it. It cost money to obey the law. Spending money to provide safe and convenient services clashed with the search for maximum profits. Thus the practices of railroads remained in fundamental conflict with the needs of the public.

Another legal conflict grew out of the fact that the country's traditional legal structure was intended to apply to people and businesses that stayed put. The movement of trains made the enforcement of laws extremely difficult and at times impossible. Thomas Cooley, head of the Interstate Commerce Commission, defined this dilemma, which applied equally to all who attempted to pass laws affecting railroads and their passengers.

> Contracts which are of legal force in one state are held of less valid- ity in another on the same line of road. Neither the passenger nor the railway official is able at all times to tell precisely the rights of each. Each attempts to carry out his own views, and collisions, eject- ments and law-suits are the consequence. Further, the police regula- tions of our trains are of the crudest sort, and but for that general common sense and native chivalry of the American man, our passen- ger trains moving rapidly from one criminal jurisdiction to another, would be safer places for malefactors than even the shady woods.[1]

Despite the attempt to create uniform legal requirements for trains in all states, the enforcement of any law on a train remained prob- lematic. The conflict between traditional means of law enforcement and the free movement of trains remained unsolvable.

Economically the construction of a national system in trade provided perhaps the most obvious justification of railroading. The train could take resources from any part of the country and put them at the disposal of anyone who could afford to buy. But train service began to focus on those areas with large population, because they represented greater profits to the railroads, and to provide minimal services to those rural areas that needed most to grow. Thus a conflict between rural and urban interests developed, with particular reference to the railroad services each received.

Another economic conflict that created instability was the continuing competition among railroad companies for dominance. While government at all levels sought the connections between railroads that would make them truly a network and a system, the railroads themselves found more reasons to compete than to connect. Their failure to coordinate the use of tracks and stations left passengers with a patchwork service until the turn of the century.

Recorded history has few precedents for the number of cultures that came into contact with one another as the result of the uprooting of populations and their resettlement near means of production. European immigrants spread out across the West, hoping to win economic security. There they found others like themselves as well as Indians, blacks, and wanderers from both South and North seeking a stable life in the highly unstable West. In the aftermath of slavery, the South became a cauldron of racial conflict devastating to blacks and to the region in general, which remained too discordant to be a good investment for many Northern businessmen. The North itself absorbed more diverse cultures than any other region of the country, as immigrants and beleaguered farmers sought a new start in industrial employment. The flowering of dozens of cultures in each city also resulted in the unfamiliar juxtaposition of cultures and languages, and thus new prejudices and misunderstandings.

Finally, the rich and the poor, ancestral enemies, restated their conflict in terms of train travel. The rich sought privacy, comfort, and escape from the crowds of immigrants. The poor took the day coach, the emigrant car, or the slow-moving local train while the rich sped by in a fast train that protected its passengers from confrontations with land and people. The middle class selected what comforts and seclusion it could afford.

Confronted with this legal, economic, and cultural mélange of unprecedented complexity, some businessmen and legislators sought a solution in standardizing aspects of the railroad service and the society at large. Standardized time, track gauge, car parts, and safety requirements provided some of the only common denominators to the "unity" that railroads had brought to American society.

PART THREE

"We Have Broken Away into a New Scale for Life"

AN URBAN AND COMMERCIAL UNION, 1890–1929

In this 1930 painting by Charles Sheeler, *American Landscape*, the railroad is only a cog in the industrial machine rather than a triumphant conqueror. (MUSEUM OF MODERN ART, NEW YORK)

20

|||||||||||||||||||||||||

Cities First and Foremost

Everywhere in America I have seen the same note sound, the note of a fatal, gigantic economic development, of large prevision, and enormous pressures.

I heard it clear above the roar of Niagara—for, after all, I stopped off at Niagara.

As a water-fall, Niagara's claim to distinction is now mainly quantitative; its spectacular effect, its magnificent and humbling size and splendor, were long since destroyed beyond recovery by the hotels, the factories, the power-houses, the bridges and tramways and hoardings that arose about it. . . .

—H. G. Wells, *The Future in America*, 1906[1]

THE FORTY-YEAR PERIOD following 1890 saw a high-water mark in urban wealth and the submerging of rural and local interests in America. Farmers cried for reform and for a seat at the table of economic and political power. But during this period the United States became the richest nation in the world by virtue of its urban industry and the world markets it found for its products. Farmers, producing prodigal amounts of wheat, beef, and milk, kept America fed but could not command the prices needed to enrich themselves as their city cousins did.

Even the enormous steam locomotives produced at the turn of the century began to seem small when seen against the backdrop of the immense factories, warehouses, and growing skyscrapers that transformed city skylines within a few decades after 1890. All cities wanted their skyscrapers to match those going up in New York and Chicago. But none could match the wealth of those two cities. All cities watched the miracle of electric light transform the look of the night city, and the telephone make communications faster and more efficient than they had ever been. But Chicago and New York rode the crest of technological change and economic advantage.

The great cities were the ultimate beneficiaries of the wealth generated by the railroad system. Railroads carried daily crowds of immigrants in and out of New York, in and out of Chicago. They carried the wealth of every region in the nation to urban marketplaces. The banks in these cities exchanged currency from almost every country in the world. And stocks and bonds, representing all parts of the nation, from silver mines to Southern factories, could be found in the relatively small radii of these cities' business districts. The process of investment in railroads and industries, which jumped the track of geographic location well before the Civil War, reached a resting place in the chaotic and rapidly changing markets of New York and Chicago, as even Philadelphia and Boston began to fall behind.

This centralization, which had its counterpart in all aspects of business, also promoted the rise of a new managerial class. As ownership of the railroads fell into fewer hands, and companies distributed products nationally, managers were hired to handle day-to-day affairs in other areas of the country on behalf of owners who lived at a distance. Alfred D. Chandler, Jr., has chronicled this development in *The Visible Hand*.[2]

Chicago and New York, with ten other major American ports, also controlled more of the import and export trade than in the past, as well as the industrial wealth of the country. Local or regional products, such as fish from Maine, coal from Pennsylvania, or iron ore from Michigan, passed more often through the major ports of Boston,

Philadelphia, and the Great Lakes ports than through the small local ports of each state. During the year 1920, for example, of approximately $13.5 billion in trade that passed through America's port cities, almost $12 billion went through the twelve largest ports.[3]

Smaller ports that drew their income from local or regional products and markets began to stagnate. The fate of New England ports is probably the best-known example of this trend. Maine, the cradle of wooden shipbuilding in New England, gradually lost this market to steel companies and urban shipbuilders located nearer to iron mines, coal deposits, and steel factories. Maine's nine major ports therefore lost a major source of income between the Civil War and World War I, when all major defense contracts called for steel vessels. Of Maine's ports, Frenchman's Bay, Castine, and Bath lost almost all their import and export trade before 1892. Other Maine ports stopped growing. Portland, Falmouth, and Bangor lost substantial shares of their import and export business during the same period. Only Passamaquoddy, Maine, exported more in 1892 than it had in 1875.[4]

Other small ports suffered similarly. Connecticut's three ports failed to thrive. Their import and export trade remained at a standstill between the 1870s and the 1890s while New York and Boston showed vast increases. Some of Massachusetts's oldest ports, including Newburyport, Marblehead, and Fall River, showed no significant growth during the very period that brought the United States to world leadership in trade.[5]

The centralization of exports also represented difficulties for railroads serving smaller ports. Without growth in freight traffic, population and the level of wealth also stagnated, meaning that railroads to these locations experienced no growth in their financial investment. The economic baton had clearly been passed to the largest corporations and the most urbanized parts of the country.

In burgeoning cities could not only be found products from all parts of the country and the world but people and strands of culture from almost everywhere. Joining the genteel white middle class who promenaded the streets and Central Park came new races and economic groups. They converged on the city and settled into neighborhoods developed by others of their own kind. From Chinatowns and

Jewish neighborhoods to Polish, Greek, and Italian, many individuals still wore traditional clothing, spoke their native languages, practiced their religions, and ate their favorite foods. All developed institutions to protect their own people, from churches and schools to hospitals, orphanages, and charities. After the turn of the century, trains from the South added a new population of blacks to cities where industry promised more wealth than sharecropping in the Southern countryside. But rural areas and small towns experienced no such revolution in racial diversity. They were much more likely to retain the racial mix they had during their earlier history.

The many cultures that had first met in train cars and commented on one another, disapproved of one another, and in some cases had been segregated by sex, race, and economic level, also populated the cities. There they took hold of new ways, but they did not abandon their cultural backgrounds, and many of their neighborhoods survive to this day, in Boston and Philadelphia as well as New York and Chicago, and in Southern towns such as Memphis, Nashville, and New Orleans, where Jews, Indians, and blacks joined the urban crowds.

After 1900 many observers saw a growing dark side to this massive urban growth. Streets that had seemed beautiful in the past became ugly as crowds grew too large and too diverse. Some who felt threatened adopted a racist stance, saying the new foreigners had ruined the cities. But other aspects of the city had also lost their charm. Skyscrapers were too high and dwarfed the individual. And the industrial side of the city tailed out for miles in every direction, especially along the routes of the railroads. For the cities needed railroads to do business.

Childe Hassam, a painter of this period, portrayed the older, genteel city early in his career. In snow, rain, and by dark of night, the city retained its charm on his canvases. But after 1900 the buildings become too big and the crowds too congested to suggest beauty. Hassam's later paintings reflect the claustrophobia of life in a city apartment, high off the ground, and the tremendous rift between individual experience and the uncontrollable life of the city.[6]

H. G. Wells, who toured the United States in 1905, reported on the pulsating energy of American economic life. But as his train pulled out of Chicago, he described the price America had paid for its industrial might.

> I sat in the observation-car at the end of the Pennsylvania Limited Express, and watched the long defile of industrialism from the Union Station in the heart of things to out beyond Chicago, a dozen miles away. . . . I saw for the first time the enormous expanse and intricacy of railroads that net this great industrial desolation, and something of the going and coming of the myriads of polyglot workers. . . . Right and left of the line rise vast chimneys, huge blackened grain-elevators, flame-crowned furnaces and gauntly ugly and filthy factory buildings, monstrous mounds of refuse, desolate, empty lots littered with rusty cans, old iron, and indescribable rubbish. Interspersed with these are groups of dirty, disreputable, insanitary-looking wooden houses.[7]

Further along the line, Wells found another aspect of the price paid for industrial might in the death of an Italian immigrant hit by Wells's train.

> "Progress," "progress," murmured the wheels. . . . "It goes on," I said, "invincibly," and even as the thought was in my head, the brakes set up a droning, a vibration ran through the train and we slowed and stopped. . . .
>
> I got up, looked from the window, and then went to the platform at the end of the train. I found two men, a passenger and a colored parlor-car attendant. The former was on the bottom step of the car, the latter was supplying him with information.
>
> "His head's still in the water," he remarked.
>
> "Whose head?" said I.
>
> "A man we've killed," said he. . . .
>
> I descended a step, craned over my fellow-passenger, [and saw] the derelict thing that had been a living man three minutes before. It was now a crumpled, dark-stained blue blouse, a limply broken arm with hand askew, trousered legs that sprawled quaintly. . . .
>
> "Who was he?" said I.
>
> "One of tese Eyetalians on the line," he said, and turned away.[8]

Wells saw that the individual was dwarfed by the incredible scale of American industrial development. So too by the crowds that engulfed the city after 1900. So large were the throngs to be found in America's public places at the turn of the century that they swamped and overworked the main lines of the railroad system, threatening the individual with feelings of powerlessness and loss of social identity. Industrial America seemed to run itself, without further need for the participation of ordinary men and women. To a recently arrived immigrant, Edward Steiner, his first day in the city offered trepidation more than hope.

> Chicago held out no illusions; she promised nothing but toil, grime, sore feet and a ceaseless struggle for just shelter and a mouthful of food. To me, accustomed to the beauties of large cities in the Old World, she seemed forbidding, hopelessly ugly and pitiless.[9]

The population of the urban North increased far more rapidly than the population of the countryside in North, South, or West. Following the migration of wealth to the rapidly expanding cities of the East and Midwest, miners who had not struck it rich and farmers who had not prospered sought work in the nation's industrial centers. The census reflected this shift. In 1890 it reported that, for the first time, more of the nation's population lived in the cities than in rural areas. Despite the fact that the settled areas of the West were growing, about the same percentage of the population lived in the sixteen states of the Northeast in 1920 than had lived there in 1870. Half the population of the country was still crowded into the Northeast.[10]

As rail passenger service became increasingly centralized, many locales that had once heralded the coming of the railroad as an assurance of future prosperity took their place as secondary to the controlling interests of the urban Northeast. Small towns in the rural countryside of Wisconsin or Missouri still tried to attract investors, but they were now painfully aware that their hometowns would never achieve the financial preeminence of Chicago or St. Louis, let alone New York. Likewise, rural culture and customs also became secondary as the culture of technology was exported from the cities to the countryside. Telephones, electric lighting, indoor plumbing, and phonographs all appeared in the marketplace. But many rural areas of the country had no electrical power stations and therefore could not adopt the new technologies for their own use. There was no profit in setting up expensive electrical power stations for areas low in population and income. Rural families fell farther behind economically, and their culture, without a vital economic center, lost its following. Although economically healthy small towns created chambers of commerce to attract capital investment, the distribution of wealth tipped toward the cities. There the emphasis was on international trade and the capture of foreign markets to sell an overabundance of American-made goods and American-grown food.[11]

Centralization of the railroad system underscored the importance of through routes between major cities as vital to the economic welfare of the country. The Boston-to-Washington route, the New York-to-Chicago route, and the Chicago-to–New Orleans route carried food and freight to feed and clothe the nation's largest concentrations of population. They also carried the mail, the express packages, and the passengers essential to the daily functioning of business and institutions.

Many of the trains that traveled between these major economic centers were the fastest trains then running; the "express" trains, which carried packages overnight, traveled at sixty miles per hour.[12] Passengers in a hurry took these express or "limited" trains, which limited the number of stops between major urban centers. A new emphasis on speed was the death knell for local stops on a through route, and the train called the "local" earned a reputation as the slowest and therefore the least desirable from a business point of view. Likewise the milk train, which stopped to pick up fresh milk at the country stations and deliver it to the populations of the city, was slow but tolerated because of the urban demand for fresh milk.

The demand for fast trains paralleled the rise of a national movement to promote efficiency in industry. According to the leaders of this movement, which included men such as Frederick Taylor and Frank Gilbreth, increases in the speed and efficiency of manufacturing would result in a decrease in the overall cost of production, which in turn would produce greater profits. The same philosophy applied to the transport of goods and people. The faster they could be transported, the lower the cost of transport, and the sooner freight, busi-

nessmen, and customers would arrive at their destination and create
the profits they were intended to produce.

The port of New York had in fact operated according to this philosophy since the earliest years of the nineteenth century. Ware-
housemen and shippers there worked on a strict schedule, loading
and unloading ships as quickly as possible. But close to a hundred
years passed before this approach was generally accepted. Many
Southern towns had held the opposite view, that the longer it took to
make a transfer of goods and services within the boundaries of the
town, the more the town would profit from the transaction because
passengers and railroad men would have to spend money in the town
on room and board.[13]

By 1900 speed and efficiency were an accepted rule of good business in the emerging science of economics. But Southerners were
also unfortunately vindicated in their beliefs because, in the name of
speed and efficiency, many small towns found themselves bypassed in
the rush to connect major metropolitan centers by rail. Thus the business ideals of speed and efficiency worked against the smaller, poorer,
less wealthy sectors of the country. Goods and passengers were hur-
ried to the largest markets, i.e., the major cities. The word *rural* came
to connote a slower-moving society and therefore a poorer society,
clinging to its old ways, with little contact by rail or by other means
with the mainstream of American life.

The control of the nation's money supply also became more centralized in the urban areas of the Northeast. Bankers such as J. P.
Morgan of New York, who made a bold attempt to "corner" the
money market during the 1890s, also came to control a large portion
of the country's railroads during and after the depression of 1893.
Even before this time, large railroad systems under fewer and fewer
owners helped push the nation's rail service toward centralization. In
1890 twenty-five major railroad systems each controlled more than
two thousand miles of track. They continued to increase their holdings as if they were part of a stock portfolio. By 1929 there were
thirty-one systems with that much track, including enormous new
Western routes: the Atchison, Topeka and Santa Fe, with more than
twelve thousand miles of track; the Great Northern, with more than
eight thousand miles; the Northern Pacific, with almost seven thou-

and; the Union Pacific, with almost ten thousand; and the Southern Pacific, with almost fourteen thousand.[14]

These major through routes, rather than the locals, continued to benefit from most new railroad technology while the locals stayed comfortably the same. Even the Master Car-Builders, who had tried to set standards for the design of trains, could not see far enough into the future to comprehend how the through trains of 1929 would differ from the trains of 1890. Some of the changes responded to practical needs while others came as the result of technological invention.

The most obvious changes to train cars between 1890 and 1929 took place during the first two decades of the new century, when car builders began making metal cars rather than continuing to make wooden ones. This change resulted in part from a public outcry against the dangers of fire in passenger cars that crashed or derailed, especially those with a heating stove in a wooden car. Higher speeds also demanded cars made from a tougher material than wood. Metal cars, both heavier and larger than wooden cars, provided more protection to the passengers. And the technological means for making metal cars were now at hand: steel, the metal of choice, was more plentiful and reasonably priced than ever before.

This change only increased the gap between urban and rural rail service because the metal cars were put to use on the high-speed through routes between cities. The poorer, shorter train lines continued to use wooden cars equipped with heating stoves. The through routes also replaced heating stoves with heating systems that forced warm air into the cars through ducts; replaced old brake systems with vacuum brakes of a type invented by George Westinghouse during the Civil War; and improved ventilation systems so that clean air refreshed the stuffy atmosphere of the older cars.[15]

Two revolutions in motive power found application in the design of locomotives. After Edison's demonstrations of controlled electricity, a number of the trolley lines that served America's cities adopted electrical power instead of continuing to use horses or steam power to pull their cars. In the 1890s both New York and Chicago began digging tunnels under the city streets in order to run subways powered by electricity. Elevated tracks also made city train service available but safer, suspended as they were above the pedestrians at street level. This new dependency on mass transit within the cities gave rise to a new power in transportation politics as well. The cities' traction companies, as these new services were known, wielded enormous clout in city and state politics, just as the "robber barons" did at the national level.[16]

Some intercity train lines also experimented with electric power, seeing it as another way to reduce the risk of fire. Some of these lines, using lighter-weight cars that were cheaper to operate than those on major through routes, became known as interurbans. Locomotive and cars were lighted by electricity as well. Investment in these lines was another sign of reduced interest in the needs of rural America. The Baldwin Locomotive Works produced its first electric engine in 1895, and in the same year an electric cable car was in use for tourists ascending the Sierras in southern California.[17]

Why did railroaders look for an alternative to steam? In addition to the periodic stops needed to take on coal and water, the steam locomotive was inefficient and slow to operate in other ways as well. One railroad historian explains:

> From the time its boiler is lit, a steam locomotive needs three to five hours to build up sufficient steam power to be put to work. At the end of its trip, if it has been of any length, it must go into a depot to have its fire raked clear of ash and clinker and the smoke-box cleaned of soot. It will probably have to stop to be refuelled. At the end of the day the fire will be dropped, the engine allowed to cool and more maintenance work done. Then, at regular intervals, the engine's boiler has to be washed out.[18]

While the Pennsylvania Railroad, the New York, New Haven and Hartford, and later the Chicago, Milwaukee and St. Paul Railroad, along with some short lines and many overseas railroads, adopted electricity on sections of their rail systems, electricity also proved costly. In 1910 Baldwin produced the first of many internal combustion engines which worked on the same principle as the automobile engine. Substantial numbers of these locomotives were built during World War I because they emitted no steam or smoke, and therefore could travel near the battlefront without revealing their location.[19]

These internal combustion engines gained in popularity after the war because they were much cleaner and safer than steam engines.

The adaptation of the latest technology was, as always, uneven. The steam engine never went completely out of production, and both old and new steam engines continued in service through the first half of the twentieth century. Massive inflation brought on by World War I prevented many railroads from properly maintaining their routes, let alone updating their technology.[20] By a process of selection that was not natural but economic, fewer and fewer railroads remained current in their technology after the turn of the century. From 1917 to 1920 the federal government took over the railroads for military reasons and used them extensively without providing needed maintenance. When the roads were returned to private hands in 1920, the trains needed more maintenance than ever before, but at costs that were prohibitive.

This constellation of circumstances led the railroads to seek cost-saving measures in the 1920s rather than to embark on the kind of expansion that had brought them profits in the past. Not surprisingly, they began to curtail service on less profitable lines, those serving poorer and less populous areas. Thus began a great reversal of service. Many of the small towns that had struggled to win rail service now saw fewer and fewer trains coming through town. In many cases tracks and stations were abandoned altogether. Centralization of railroad service continued even as railroads struggled financially.

On the profitable lines that kept commerce moving at top speed between major cities, investments in maintenance and service kept pace. The running of high-speed overnight trains for passengers reached a peak during the period 1890 to 1929. More than any before them, these trains offered an epitome of service for the passenger in a hurry. They provided sleeping and dining accommodations and lounges, along with many of the services needed by businessmen: desks and chairs, barbershops, mail service, telegraph service, and in some cases even telephones and stock tickers.[21] Between Boston and Washington, New York and Chicago, Chicago and San Francisco or New Orleans, these trains kept the wealthier strata of society in touch with business. Conquering time and space became as important to American commercial interests as did investment.

The imposing centralization of wealth and population in major cities, and the consolidation of the railroads into only a few dozen companies, made it increasingly difficult for state legislatures, state courts, and state regulatory commissions to effectively regulate the railroads. The public, led by reform politicians battling the railroads, urged the federal government to take the lead in regulation. After the creation of the Interstate Commerce Commission in 1887, the federal government made several attempts to strengthen the ICC and break the concentrated power of the interstate railroads over the American economy. The ICC suffered from limited power to control railroad rates; public revelations of corrupt practices in rate setting made the federal regulation of railroads a political issue. In 1890, during the presidential term of Grover Cleveland, the only Democratic president between 1860 and 1912, Congress passed the Sherman Anti-Trust Act, designed to enable the government to prosecute the nation's largest companies for driving competitors out of business in order to monopolize the marketplace. Railroads that served small Western communities were particularly vulnerable in this regard, for only one line served each town and monopolized its transportation.

With the election of Benjamin Harrison and then William McKinley, two Republican presidents who championed laissez-faire economic policies, the Sherman Anti-Trust Act remained on the books but was rarely enforced. Only after the assassination of McKinley in 1901 and the succession of Vice-President Theodore Roosevelt did the Sherman Act become an important tool in federal policy. Roosevelt overturned the Republican tradition of laissez-faire at the federal level by bringing a number of corporations—the Northern Pacific Railroad among them—to court in order to break the enormous centralization of wealth and power that the railroads, along with the oil, steel, copper, and related industries, had amassed since the Civil War.

In addition to these legal initiatives, Roosevelt championed the passage of the Hepburn Act in 1906. The law increased the power of the Interstate Commerce Commission not only to regulate but actually to set the rates and fares charged by railroads engaged in interstate commerce. The Hepburn Act was a turning point in the history of federal authority over the railroads. According to William Z. Ripley, a noted authority on the railroad rates of Roosevelt's generation, "The most fundamental principle of governmental control over the most powerful corporations in the country had been fully affirmed."[22] It would be more accurate to specify *federal* control; between 1827 and 1906 state governments had never stopped trying to regulate the railroads.

In 1910, during the presidency of Republican William Howard Taft, Congress passed the Mann-Elkins Act which augmented ICC control over railroad rates. In 1914 the Clayton Act strengthened antitrust legislation, and in 1916 Democratic President Woodrow Wilson signed the Adamson Act, which gave railroad employees on interstate railroads the eight-hour work day.

The most important advance in federal authority over the railroads came in 1917, when Wilson brought all railroads under federal control in the name of military preparedness. According to the terms of the Railroad Control Act of March 1918, the government would reimburse railroads for their costs, set up a government commission to run the roads, and return the trains to private hands within twenty-one months of the war's end. Most of the railroads' managers and crews remained in their jobs while taking orders from the government. Government control lasted two years, and trains reverted to private hands with the passage of the Transportation Act of 1920.[23]

With the expansion of federal authority over interstate railroad travel, one might think that local and state legislatures, courts, and commissions rested easily, now backed by the highest legal authority in the country. But centralization of authority did nothing to resolve the tortured relationship between the railroads and the law. Complaints against the railroads continued to besiege commissioners and judges. Disputes over rates and dependable service persisted as the railroad slipped out of one jurisdiction and into another, at a distance from most means of law enforcement.

While the journey of the American railroads toward a national transportation network was all but complete, other trends were shifting. Total track mileage was still expanding at the turn of the century, but by the 1920s the smaller systems were static or losing track. Only the thirty-one largest systems continued to expand. This decline in track mileage among small railroad lines began in 1917 and continued after the war. Corporate failures and track loss during the twenties were no longer offset by new construction.[24]

The popularity of the automobile after World War I also affected the fortunes of the railroad. It encouraged an interest in building roads rather than building more track, and opened the possibility of new investments in oil and gasoline and ultimately in suburban housing that did not have to be near a railroad station. Perhaps the most telling contrast between the railroad and the automobile lay in the possibilities of travel that each provided. As railroads centralized their services, focusing on major routes between cities, the automobile provided transport that could potentially go anywhere. As railroads standardized their services with fewer and fewer accommodations to individual circumstances, the automobile met the needs of all those fairgoers, picnickers, politicians, and others who found it more difficult to arrange for special fares and excursion trains. The train required more conformity of behavior than ever before. Sitting quietly with arms and legs inside the car, no stopping en route, no rowdiness, no drinking, for many added up to no fun and precious little individuality. The car, if nothing else, held out a promise of adventure that the railroad had offered about a hundred years earlier.

21
||||||||||||||||||||||

It's Too Crowded Here

After leaving the State Department, John W. Foster joined the boards of several rich and powerful Wall Street corporations. He had built himself a lodge and several simple guest cottages at Henderson, New York, on Lake Ontario, and important guests—senators, big banking magnates, statesmen, like William Howard Taft, John W. Davis, Andrew Carnegie, and Bernard Baruch—came to stay with him for the fishing.

—Leonard Mosley, *Dulles*, 1978[1]

As soon as the immigrants could break free of the crush of the tenements, they fled. . . . In the years when they had no choice but to remain in the slums, they tried each summer to squeeze out a week or two away from the city, at least for wives and children.

—Irving Howe, *World of Our Fathers*, 1976[2]

As THE UNITED STATES became progressively more developed and settled, the urban skyline displaced much of the rural landscape, much in the way that business interests transformed Niagara Falls from an entirely natural scene to one characterized by hotels, power stations, and shops. Of course the endless miles of railroad track, the stations, the intersections of roads and track, the signal towers, water towers, coal shutes, and electric generators, the enormous freight yards, and the private track where businesses loaded their own products onto freight cars were all aspects of this new urban life.

In social terms, most of the urban environment represented public space. Despite its control in private hands, it provided no safe haven from the public eye or the company of strangers. Crowds, in fact, had become the dominant social form of industrial society. In offices, factories, shops, and streets, in theaters, concert halls, museums, libraries, hospitals, and schools, success depended on the crowd. Even parks, playgrounds, and beaches, despite their rural nature, had to provide for crowds. Skyscrapers too were created to meet the need for organizing large numbers of strangers into orderly space. Large offices housed rows and rows of workers at desks, much as factories had put hundreds of workers under one roof during the first half of the century.

Railroads, of course, had made this possible. They brought crowds from all parts of the nation and delivered them to the station doors of every large town or city. From there the business interests of the cities organized the social aspects of crowded urban living. Railroads extended the dominance of the crowd throughout the country and encouraged the development of ways to house, feed, and otherwise serve large numbers of people. It is probably safe to say that without these crowds, public services would have lost their primary function.

The growth of the public, man-made environment designed for "mass society" radically altered the social experience of individuals. Aside from the dangers of associating with strangers, crowds substantially diminished the privacy traditionally associated with the family and with private property. For urban dwellers of every economic level, expectations of how much space each family might have to itself declined. The major cities had already become notorious for crowded tenement neighborhoods in which entire families of immigrant poor had to live in one room, or even on the street. Business was also transacted in the streets and in stores or hotels rather than in private offices. The two-story middle-class dwellings that had been private suburban homes in the 1880s now accommodated two or more families as cities such as Boston, New York, and Chicago overran their own suburbs. Middle-class families made do with less or moved again to create new suburbs even farther from the center of the city. Even the spacious private mansions of the wealthy proved to be too expensive. On the eve of World War I these families, who had maintained large estates with the help of servants, and landscaped grounds with the help of gardeners, began to dismiss their staffs and sell off parcels of their property on which smaller houses could be built. Some sold their large houses, which were turned into museums, hospitals, group homes, or professional offices. In some cases the land went to the city government for conversion to parks or playing fields. The rich then accepted smaller accommodations in town houses or built more modest homes in the farthest reaches of the suburbs.[3]

Thus the public world began to crowd out the private, and the city pushed right to the front door of even the most elegant homes. The artist Childe Hassam painted pictures of cities in which the individual was either a small, undefined dab of paint in a much larger canvas of buildings and streets, or a clearly defined individual looking out a window at enormously confining skyscrapers. Artists of the Ashcan School painted equally undefined individuals, surviving in a dark world of crowds, railroad tracks, and large, impersonal buildings. George Bellows, William Glackens, and others depicted the world of poor city dwellers, much to the dismay of an audience more accustomed to spacious lighted boulevards or country scenes. In the 1920s the painter Edward Hopper favored urban landscapes inhabited by only one or two people, each encased in a world of personal isolation, around whom there was nothing of their own. Such was the mute criticism of urban life during the era.[4]

The transportation system, which had enabled the urban world to grow so far beyond the human level, also provided one of the only means of escape. Just as every economic level found itself hemmed in by buildings and crowds, every economic level found some means to get away. During the early years of the twentieth century, even the poor and laboring classes could make their way to local beaches and seaside resorts, usually by train. In New York, train riders could escape to Coney Island. Passengers could reach this beach and its amusements via the Prospect and Coney Island Railroad for a round-trip fare of thirty-five cents. New York vacationers could also ride the Brighton Beach and Brooklyn Railroad to Brighton Beach for the same price. Philadelphians needing a day trip out of the city could ride to Atlantic City in New Jersey. The Reading Railroad charged one dollar for the ride; the Camden and Atlantic charged the same. From Boston, a ride on the Boston and Maine, plus a tram connection, took bathers to Revere Beach, described in *Baedeker's Guide* for 1893 as "a popular holiday resort for Boston's lower classes." Nantasket Beach could be reached on a branch of the Old Colony Railroad. The company advertised the popularity of Nantasket:

> This is the second station along the branch, and is justly styled the "Coney Island of Boston." A fine stretch of beach runs along almost the entire sea front of the promontory, affording a most excellent drive and unsurpassed facilities for bathing. The scenes on the beach during "the season" are of the most animated character, 50,000 visitors in a single day being a not unusual number in warm weather.[5]

The city of Chicago, on Lake Michigan, offered beaches right in the city, and by taking the Illinois Central Railroad bathers could alight only minutes from the Indiana shores. While bathers did not necessarily escape the crowds, they escaped the heat, humidity, noise, and dirt that were the common lot of crowds in the city.

The middle classes with sufficient income could look to the waterfront towns for a summer home—perhaps smaller than their city dwelling, and easier to maintain. Towns along the railroad and at a sufficient remove from the city advertised their benefits for summer people. Of Scituate, on the water about twenty-five miles from Boston: "This fine old shore town is becoming famous as a resort for high-class professional people, several of whom have elegant summer homes here." And nearby stood North Scituate:

> This is a shore village of great attractiveness, located within the town of Scituate. It has good accommodations for summer sojourners, who largely augment its population each year. It is a growing locality, and

being near the bay shore, affords every facility for entertainment and pleasure.

Either location could be reached on the Old Colony Railroad within one hour for less than a dollar.[6] In New York, summer people made their way to Long Island, the Jersey shore, and northward into the Catskill Mountains to escape the oppressive aspects of city life. In Chicago, professionals could escape northward along the shore of the lake, south into Indiana, or even inland to such resorts as Fox Lake or Lake Geneva, where private homes and hotels afforded accommodations for vacationers. In general, the middle class could afford more privacy and respite from the crowds than the poor could.

Most of the summer sanctuaries for the poor were only a day trip away, while the middle class could afford to leave town for an extended stay in the country. But the escape of the wealthy could be at almost any distance from the city as long as transportation routes could carry them there. The rich had the most developed opportunities for escape, for they had been able to travel since the early days of the century. During the 1850s trains had made possible the resorts of Saratoga Springs and, after the war, Newport. They had also carried the well-to-do to Southern climes in winter.

After the war, with the incredible profits that the war brought, the rich began to return to the countryside in a more systematic way—for example, opening the Adirondack Mountain area, entirely wild, for private dwellings. Known as an area of much natural bounty, inhabited by loggers and hunters who lived in tent and log villages called camps, the Adirondacks became a summer resort for some of the wealthiest families in the country after the Civil War. By the 1890s it had reached the height of its popularity, and remained fashionable thereafter, though the price of upkeep for the enormous homes of the rich continued to rise, and the ability to maintain a staff of servants became more and more unusual.[7]

The first passenger railroads entered the Adirondacks during the late 1860s. Tracks were gradually extended further north, thus opening more land for the construction of what the owners came to call "camps"—enormous log homes with boat houses and a series of outbuildings for guests, extended family, and servants, as well as sheds, pump houses, and even a separate kitchen or dining area. Thomas C. Durant, president of the Union Pacific Railroad, was one of the prime movers in expanding rail service to the Adirondacks during the 1860s. His efforts were later complemented by the work of a railroader named W. Seward Webb, who provided private service to the owners of homes along the route, and barred the public from riding his trains.[8]

During the 1870s vacationers came north in hunting parties and "roughed it" in the old hunting camps. Or they stayed at one of the many hotels, such as Prospect House, built during the late 1870s and early 1880s. At the same time the earliest of the "Great Camps" of the Adirondacks were built: Pine Knot, Uncas, Sagamore, and Kamp Kill Kare, all designed by William Durant, son of Thomas. J. P. Morgan bought Sagamore, and after his death the Vanderbilt family bought the camp. Other owners of Great Camps during the early twentieth century included the Carnegie family and a number of Jewish families—Seligman, Loeb, Schiff, Guggenheim, Bache, and Kahn—who, according to one historian of the region, "were not readily welcome in resorts established by Gentiles."[9]

During the same period the wealthy could escape the confines of the city by taking the "Grand Tour" to the cities of Europe, complete with a large assortment of trunks and valises. They had the benefit of steamships, which were not common on the Atlantic until after the Civil War, and of the better-remembered ocean liners, which provided all the services of a small city for the select few who could afford them. The *Queen Mary* from England, the *Normandie* from France, the *Bremen* from Germany, and other famous ships such as the *Berengeria*, the *Mauritania*, and the ill-fated *Lusitania* took Americans to Europe where they could board equally famous trains such as the Orient Express or the Trans-Siberian Railroad. Pullman had penetrated the European train market, and the European firm of Wagon-Lits also provided elegance in train service.[10]

In an age of crowds, isolation and escape were the prerogative of those who could purchase it. Railroads and hotels, which had served crowds long before the explosive growth of the twentieth century, developed many of the social systems for providing privacy and order in the crowd. From public bathrooms and waiting areas to provisions for personal effects and personal attendants, the railroad and hotel had heralded modern social order. Above all, they provided ways by which money could buy quiet, cleanliness, and privacy.

Diamond Jim Brady, a gaudy man about town in turn-of-the-century New York, transacted much of his business in hotels. As a salesman of railroad supplies, he traveled throughout the country, meeting clients in hotels, entertaining them in his private rooms, and doing business in private. It was not the privacy of a home, where his own land and possessions surrounded him; it was modern privacy, purchased for the sake of selecting one's company.[11]

While the day coach shuffled crowds to work, to the beach, to parks, schools, and libraries, and home again, those with sufficient means could travel farther, and in elegant surroundings. The vestibuled train, which allowed passengers to walk safely from car to car, had given rise to through trains composed almost entirely of cars given over to specialized service: a dining car, a sleeping car with toilet facilities, and drawing room, saloon, parlor, or observation cars. These trains echoed the elegance of hotels and catered to the same clientele: business travelers who needed to conduct business en route, upper- and upper-middle-class professionals, and tourists who did not wish to sit in a day car while traveling between major cities. Contemporaries often referred to Pullman, the man who designed these cars and dominated the market for them, as the world's largest hotelkeeper.[12]

Between the late 1880s and the depression years of the 1930s, Pullman sleepers and dining cars reached the height of their usefulness and popularity. No major railroad was without its through trains comprised primarily of Pullman cars, providing dinner, drinks, toilet facilities for washing, and double-deck bunk beds that lined the walls of the Pullman sleepers, separated from one another by curtains. Passengers slept on fresh sheets and used fresh towels and washcloths, fresh soap, and fresh cups for water. The ranks of Pullman porters, a profession dominated by black men, provided personalized services, including waking up passengers in the morning, polishing shoes at night, and making certain Pullman passengers alighted safely with all their luggage. In Pullman dining cars, passengers ate off china or crockery laid on fresh linen tablecloths, with flatware and linen napkins. Many railroads, from the New York Central to the Atchison, Topeka and Sante Fe, had china and silverware designed especially for their dining service.

Fares on through railroad journeys of the 1890s ran high, more than the cost of a week's stay at a good hotel. For example, the Pennsylvania Railroad charged $21.50 for the trip of a little more than a day from New York City to Cincinnati, and charged an additional $5 for a Pullman berth. A Union Pacific journey from Kansas City to San Francisco, which took three and a half days, cost $60, plus $13 for the sleeping car. A five- to six-hour trip from New York City to Boston on the New York, New Haven and Hartford Railroad and the Boston and Albany cost $5, and $1.50 for a berth. A seat in the drawing-room car cost another $1.[13]

Despite its high cost for the passenger, rail lines adopted Pullman service in response to requests. Widespread demand led to widespread use—by businessmen, tourists, and the burgeoning middle class whose education, politics, work, and institutional affiliations made some train travel a necessity. Railroads scheduled a certain number of daily through Pullman trains, the fastest passenger trains then running. They stopped only at major stations and carried mail as well. The New York Central's Twentieth Century Limited sped between New York and Chicago, competing in speed and services with the Pennsylvania Railroad's Broadway Limited. The Pennsylvania also sent a set of fast trains to points south: the Orange Blossom Special, the Miamian, the Gulf Coast Limited, the Havana Special, the Seaboard Florida Limited, the Crescent Limited, and the Everglades. Of the Twentieth Century Limited, one historian has written:

> Each train required a crew of nearly 70 persons, which meant on the average fewer than two passengers for each crew member. In addition to the liberal staffing of sleeper and dining car attendants, the train carried maids, barbers, manicurists, and valets, as well as male secretaries who, for east bound runs, were sent ahead to Elkhart, Ind. where they transcribed closing stock prices, then boarded the Century to convey the market news they had gathered. Men and women

prominent in theater, sports, banking, formal society, and so forth, could avail themselves of functionaries who arranged meetings. . . .[14]

The railroads also scheduled Pullman trains for seasonal events and vacation travel that could be counted on to draw large groups of passengers every year. The New York Central took Pullman travelers on the first leg of their trip north for their summer in the Adirondacks, and west to Niagara Falls. The Pennsylvania took vacationers to fashionable Mt. Desert, Maine, on the Bar Harbor Express from Philadelphia. The Night Cape Codder, run by the New York, New Haven and Hartford Railroad, carried urban vacationers to that seaside community.[15]

Because of the adoption of standard gauge track, Pullmans could be shuttled from one line to another, with three or four railroads often cooperating to get them to their final destination. For example, the Bar Harbor Express was taken on the tracks of the New York, New Haven and Hartford, the Boston and Maine, and the Maine Central railroads, even though it was considered a Pennsylvania Railroad train and started its journey on the Pennsylvania's tracks.[16]

Passengers could observe the scenery, but the Pullman train maintained a self-sufficiency that separated its passengers from all local considerations. Like the private cars of the very wealthy, and the elegant hotels to be found in each major city, Pullman through trains carried the high standards of an urban culture, but without the crowds. The railroad journey was so completely planned and scheduled that any unexpected event could be considered a sign that the transportation "system" had failed to provide the best service. Gone were spontaneous stops for food or a view; unplanned stops for fuel and water; passengers who might jump on and off in the middle of the journey, or ride in the engine or caboose or on top of the train. Gone were engineers and conductors who could decide for themselves when to start or stop the train, and how fast to travel. These informalities survived on rural short lines, but the through trains ran to the beat of national commercial interests.

At the turn of the century, urban culture generally, not just railroad journeys, was subjected to much more planning than in the past. The spontaneous growth of industry and urban population had proven too chaotic to thrive without attention to the overall design of the country's cities. Urban planning had begun with designs for public buildings and parks, and then moved on to vital matters of sanitation, safety, comfort, and transportation, all in the context of mass society rather than the needs of individuals.

Historically, rural culture had depended on nature and the local needs of its inhabitants. But at the turn of the century even rural culture was falling under the dominion of urban life. The most obvious example of this was the use of rural life as a vacation retreat from the cities. Vacationers and tourists who fled to the countryside surely did not share the values of the old local culture. They redefined the country in terms of their own need to escape to a more peaceful and natural environment. They brought with them their urban values, urban technology, urban servants, urban education, and urban penchant for planning and organizing their vacations for maximum comfort. The Great Camps of the Adirondacks boasted all the comforts of home. And in time the owners installed the electric lighting, telephone connections, and indoor bath facilities they were accustomed to having in the city. They lived cheek by jowl with the locals but did not share their way of life.

This trend started in the East but spread throughout the nation. City dwellers made the picturesque states of the "Old West" and "Old South" part of their itinerary as tourists. But more and more, contact with these cultures was planned rather than spontaneous. Visits took in "local color." In this way, not only did urban development make inroads into country life, but urban culture, with its hotels, restaurants, entertainment, and technology, subordinated the rural culture of an earlier generation.

Whether one traveled to work in the city, escape its oppressive environment, or reach another city, American cities of this period depended heavily on mass transportation. Unlike the self-sufficient New England towns, plantations, and farms of a hundred years earlier, a city without constant comings and goings was a contradiction in terms. The city itself had become a depot for cultural exchange as well as trade and commerce. And outside the offices and hotels, in the streets, were the millions of emigrants and country people who came to the city in hopes of sharing the wealth. They represented the dozens of cultures that shaped the American urban experience into one of the most energetic and cosmopolitan in the world. Could there be any order to it at all?

Plans, Power, and Population

Since the construction of the through passenger terminals under consideration, Chicago has greatly increased in area and more than doubled in population and industrial importance.

In view of the extraordinary growth of Chicago, the application of the controlling factors which governed the location of through passenger terminals twenty-five to forty-five years ago, would obviously, if fairly applied at the present time, result in an entirely different location.

—Chicago City Council Commission on Railway Terminals, *The Railway Passenger Terminal Problem at Chicago, 1933*[1]

$B_{\text{Y THE MID-}1880\text{S}}$ the cities had assumed a pivotal role in the American economy. They connected trade and travel from all points of the compass, nationally and internationally, and the value of their industrial production had begun to dwarf that of other nations as well as many areas of the United States itself. But it was also clear that the social revolution that accompanied this vast achievement threatened the stability of urban life. The cities became home to dozens of nationalities, each with its own social customs, and headquarters to most major businesses, banks, and railroad companies which, like the different nationalities, put their own plans before those of the community in which they lived. Just as the railroads had been reluctant to connect, other institutions in the cities worked at cross-purposes and with conflicting interests. The city itself thus became a hodgepodge of competition and conflict, with no rational plan tying together the neighborhoods that had, like the railroads, grown like Topsy.

Even city governments represented private interests rather than those of all its citizens. The governments of Boston, New York, Cleveland, Cincinnati, and Chicago, among others, fell into the hands of corrupt politicians who held sway by making deals rather than by legislative means. The chaos of machine politics reflected the entrepreneurial spirit of business interests which sought to function entirely outside the bounds of the law. Railroad executives were chief among such renegades.

Late in the 1880s an urban reform movement began to take shape. Its leaders sought to restore social and political order by passing remedial legislation and prosecuting corrupt politicians. Social legislation echoed concerns about safety and service that prompted railroad legislation of the same period. The fire hazards created by tall buildings resulted in building codes that required fire escapes, exit signs, and laws setting maximum numbers of occupants for public rooms. Concerns for comfort and sanitation prompted laws requiring indoor running water, sufficient toilets, and indoor heat. Sewers, garbage collection, street sanitation, and other public services became the focus of attention for new city commissions, which functioned very much like the railroad commissions in enforcing the law. And utilities, including electric lighting, telephones, and water supplies, were overseen by public utility commissions. In many cases the old state railroad commissions doubled as public utilities commissions, setting rates for telephone, electricity, and water as well as rail traffic. The Interstate Commerce Commission began to set rail rates in 1910 with the passage of the Mann-Elkins Act.

In a similar spirit of reform, city planners tackled some of the long-standing problems associated with mass transportation into and within city boundaries: the danger associated with track running along city streets, and the need for different railroads to connect in a rational and efficient manner. Already generations old, these two problems continued to plague cities even into the 1920s. In addition, the problem of congestion, especially near the center of the city, had become acute. Traffic congestion posed one hazard: the streets that in 1900 were clogged with trolleys and carriages were by 1920 choked with cars as well. Of even greater concern was the need for more space to build. New city plans took into account the enormous population growth and physical expansion of the cities, which spread outward into suburb after suburb, creating an ever-greater need for internal transit and communication systems.

While general agreement could be reached on the need for change, vested interests in government, business, and city real estate made planning a slow and tedious business. For example, the need for union stations, which would organize all entering and departing trains under one roof, had long been recognized as a logical necessity. While a great number of union stations were constructed in both major and secondary cities between 1885 and 1929, no major city in the country ever put all its train operations under one roof. New York City had two major terminals. Pennsylvania Station, serving only the Pennsylvania Railroad, opened in 1906, and Grand Central Station, serving the New York Central and nine other lines, opened in 1913.

Other cities remained less centralized than New York. Boston's North Station, serving the Boston and Maine, opened in 1893, and South Station, serving only the Boston and Albany, and the New York, New Haven and Hartford, opened in 1899. The city had to build yet another major terminal in the 1920s. Cincinnati had no union station until 1933. In 1910 six stations served the city's nine incoming lines. In the same year Chicago had six railroad stations. Chicago's Union Station served only four of more than twenty railroads in and out of the city.[2]

Even the relative success of Grand Central Station and Chicago's Union Station in gaining cooperation among several lines must be taken with a grain of salt. All the lines running into Grand Central were controlled by interlocking boards of directors, and the four railroads using Chicago's Union Station included the Pennsylvania Railroad and three lines it controlled. Not all union stations were based on such cozy alliances, however. In Washington, D.C.'s Union Station, which opened in 1907, the Pennsylvania shared the building with the Baltimore and Ohio, one of its major competitors. And the St. Louis Union Station, opened in 1894, served twenty-seven railroads. Cooperative arrangements of this kind frequently involved the creation of a new corporation composed of representatives from each participating railroad. In St. Louis the Terminal Railroad Association controlled the station; the Cincinnati Union Terminal Company built and controlled the Union Station in that city; and the Washington Terminal Company, owned jointly by the Pennsylvania Railroad and the Baltimore and Ohio, built and controlled the Union Station in the District of Columbia.[3]

The cities themselves, of course, also had a stake in the location and functioning of a union station, but despite reform efforts, cities were seriously disadvantaged when it came to making major changes. Chicago, for example, failed to unify railroad services or resolve the problems created by outdated railroad facilities when it tried to reorganize railroad depots in the early twentieth century. Chicago's six stations formed a rough arc around the eastern, southern, and western boundaries of the downtown area. This ring of stations had grown up because each railroad wanted easy access to the central business district. But by the 1900s the city had expanded outward from the center, causing several transportation problems. The neighborhoods around the old center had changed, so that the stations were no longer on the outskirts of the downtown area but in it. Extensive railroad yards abutted the downtown directly to the south, and businesses lined the tracks extending southward toward Indiana.[4]

This situation, echoed to a lesser extent at each of the encircling stations, hemmed in Chicago's commercial development. Roads in and out of the downtown district were blocked by massive train yards, making for difficult transportation from neighborhoods south of the railroad yards. The construction of elevated train tracks in a "Loop" around the center of the city created a virtual second story to a number of streets and eased traffic within the area. But the elevated's support structure permanently slowed traffic on streets where the trains ran. City planners recommended that the railroad tracks be consolidated and relocated by the lake to ease congestion, but to no avail.[5] All but one of the ring of stations encircling the downtown remained in operation well past the middle of the twentieth century.

As competing institutions grew cheek by jowl in an overcrowded city, neither they nor the city government could reconcile their different interests in order to rationalize and unify public services. Using transportation and commerce to unite the country worked well as long as there was sufficient space and revenue for each competitor. But competitors frequently refused to cooperate with any plan that might sacrifice profits. And in the congested environment of the modern city, space ran out.

Cincinnatians witnessed a similar situation in trying to update their depot services and reorganize them in a way useful to passengers and residents of the city. Clustered in two groups near the Ohio River stood no less than eight railroad stations. They served the city for the first third of the new century while assorted railroad, political, and business interests failed to agree on a unified plan for a new union station. Finally, during the period when the federal government controlled the national rail network, it impressed upon the city the inefficiency of its terminal system and urged construction of a new central depot. As the historian Carl Condit writes,

> By 1920 the municipal and financial establishment had come to see the obvious fact, namely, that the passenger as well as the freight stations were inconvenient in their multiplicity and immediate environments, dirty, worn, in one case jerry-built . . . , and in another its equivalent in deteriorating fabric. . . .

Planning began for Cincinnati Union Terminal—but it did not open for use until 1933. While these terminal stations were monuments in their proportions and architecture, they were monuments only to a very partial unity of urban and railroad interests.[6]

Other conflicts developed over grade crossings—places where the railroad tracks crossed roads. Even in the earliest days of railroading, statutes in settled areas required warning signs at the intersections of roads and track. Some states required the train to sound a bell or whistle before it passed across a road. But the low population density of the surrounding countryside prevented the issue from reaching a crisis, and some communities, considering the noise of whistles and bells to be a nuisance that upset the sick and frightened livestock, asked the state to disallow them. With the creation of state regulatory commissions after the Civil War, complaints of unsafe grade crossings became more general. During the 1880s, with the size, length, and speed of trains increasing, and with considerable growth in population, grade-crossing accidents became more frequent and more severe. Requests to eliminate grade crossings were considered by commissions and legislatures; despite the expense, work began to route roads over railroad tracks by means of a bridge, or under by putting the tracks below ground level.[7]

In cities, the grade-crossing problem was taken extremely seriously, for town and city dwellers had objected to tracks in the streets ever since the 1830s. With a steady increase in traffic congestion after the turn of the century, some cities determined to put the railroad tracks underground. New York City, despite the solid rock that underlay Manhattan Island, put the railroads coming into both Grand Central and the Pennsylvania Station underground, a major engineering achievement. It also engineered the Holland Tunnel to route traffic crossing onto Manhattan Island under the Hudson River. Trains approaching Union Station in Washington, D.C., were also routed underground. Baltimore followed suit. Chicago tracks coming into the Loop went underground but otherwise stayed where they had been built in the nineteenth century. Cincinnati was among the cities that maintained most of their track at ground level, thus using valuable city real estate for an aspect of urban life that became progressively less attractive and less valuable over time.[8]

In general, the need to separate street traffic from mass transit was taken more seriously than most other aspects of city planning. While the building of track for steam railroads between cities slowed appreciably after about 1910, the building of short track for mass transit within the bounds of cities became very popular among both investors and city planners. The city of New York, inspired by the construction of an underground railway in London, determined to do the same.[9]

When New York formed a corporation to begin digging for a subway, its members had in mind many of the hard-learned lessons of
the railroads regarding the legal problems the subway would face. In
particular, the elevated railroad constructed over the streets of Manhattan before the Civil War had faced severe legal challenges. Comparing the two endeavors, a judge of the New York State Supreme
Court observed:

> Just what are the rights of the owners of property abutting upon a
> street or avenue, the fee in and to the soil underneath the surface of
> which had been acquired by the city of New York, so far as the same
> is not required for the ordinary city uses of gas or water pipes, or oth-
> ers of a like character, has never been fully determined. We have now
> the example of the elevated railroad, constructed and operated in the
> city of New York under legislative and municipal authority . . . which
> has been compelled to pay many millions of dollars to abutting prop-
> erty owners for the easement in the public streets appropriated by the
> construction and maintenance of the road. . . . What liabilities will be
> imposed upon the city under this [subway] contract . . . it is impossi-
> ble now to ascertain.

Despite the legal challenges that had become part of the grain of
American life, the subway project proceeded. By 1904 underground
transit tunnels had been dug virtually the entire length of Manhattan.[10]

How did the law accommodate this project with so many vested
interests standing in the way? The supreme court of New York overrode the protests of property owners who did not want a subway
under their private property; other interests were reconciled by the
creation of a number of new corporations and commissions, much in
the way that union stations were being built during the same years.
New York's Rapid Transit Act of 1891 created a rapid transit commission to obtain all the necessary permissions and consents to build the
road. Another Rapid Transit Act of 1900 amended the earlier act by
creating a rapid transit board, composed of city and financial officials,
who would determine a route for the subway. Bonds were then issued
and funds raised according to the long-standing practice of railroad
builders and municipal governments.[11]

Why did backers of the subway project persevere despite the incredible complexity involved in making changes to an overbuilt city controlled by private interests? The need was acute. More and more people needed rapid transit to get to work in the downtown area. As the New York Interborough Rapid Transit Company declared, "The main object of the road was to carry to and from their homes in the upper portions of Manhattan Island the great army of workers who spend the business day in the offices, shops, and warehouses of the lower portions. . . ."[12] In other words, business required it.

Other cities followed New York's example in creating rapid transit to connect the inner core of the city with newer and more prosperous outlying neighborhoods. In other words, rapid transit was needed by those who sought refuge from the excesses of crowded urban life but still depended upon it for their living. In keeping with the example of New York City, a quick glance at other cities in the state show that they too moved quickly to connect the neighborhoods developing on the edges of the city with its hub. By 1906 Rochester, Syracuse, Schenectady, Rome, Utica, and Oneida all had rapid rail service systems radiating outward from the downtown areas to bring passengers into the central city.[13]

Most of these new city rail systems used electric power. The closeness of the trains to a central power source made this possible, but the dire effects of steam locomotives in any confined area, such as an underground tunnel, made the alternative of electric power important for intercity railroads, too. By the first decade of the twentieth century, the use of electrical power in cities had become quite common. Electric street lights replaced gas lights, telephones required electricity, factories could remain active through the night with electric lighting, and electricity also carried heating into buildings. Because municipalities depended so heavily on electricity, it became classified as a public utility, operated in private hands but subject to regulation by a commission which might also regulate telephone services.

Thus the regulation of rapid transit and electricity became entangled with each other. And beneath the rational surface of commission regulation, the competition for control of city electric companies and city rapid transit became just as cutthroat as competition among rail-

road trunk lines. And, like the railroads, competition for rapid transit
moved rapidly toward monopoly. Commissioners could monitor and
guide such competition but could not stop it or fundamentally alter
its course. In Chicago, Samuel Insull controlled a small empire which
supplied both electricity and electrically run rapid transit to the city.
In New York, Interborough Rapid Transit was controlled by a board
of wealthy first citizens including Cornelius Vanderbilt, brother of
William K. Vanderbilt. But cutthroat competition resulting in monopolistic control was not limited to one city. Some companies had interests in the rapid transit systems of a number of cities. The Mohawk
Valley Company, which seems to have been little more than a board
of directors and a few shares of stock, had interests in the electric railway systems of the six upstate New York cities previously mentioned.
And on the board of this obscure corporation sat William K. Vanderbilt, Jr., a son of William K. Vanderbilt.[14]

An urban landscape of conflicting interests and abutting properties
recreated some of the legal hazards of early railroading, but this time
in the context of rapid transit. Conflicts over property use and property damages kept the courts busy but ultimately made way for new
urban transit companies to build subways and electric railroads connecting the suburbs with the center city.

Transportation engineers and investors concentrated on municipal
rapid transit after about 1895, slowly abandoning their interest in railroads. Unification of the country was all but complete. By 1907 the
United States had the maximum number of railroad companies that
ever would operate: 1,564. By 1930 it had the most miles of track in
operation that it ever would have: 429,883. After these dates, the
numbers began a slow but inexorable decline.[15]

Unifying the city now became a new goal for both city planners and
investors. After all, railroads had thrived on moving large groups of
people. And large groups of people were no longer heading west but
to the cities. It had become evident that few people became wealthy
in the West. The railroad might transplant populations, but it could
not transplant much capital. That remained in the urban areas. Instead of making a living as farmers, more immigrants opted to remain
in the city, and more rural poor followed the elusive track of wealth
back to the cities. As industrial workers they headed for work each

weekday and on many weekends aboard a mass transit system. The country's population, which had been dispersing rapidly across the land for more than three hundred years in a search for prosperity, natural resources, and freedom from laws, taxes, and government hierarchy, began to centralize again in the urban areas of the country.

As for the through trains, fewer and fewer people found reasons to travel long distances for reasons other than business travel between urban areas, or vacation travel. While Pullman travel burgeoned, providers of long-distance day coach services began to notice that more and more of their cars left the station with only a handful of passengers.[16] A complete transportation system was finally in place, but many of the historical circumstances that had called for a railroad service had begun to change. Founding new towns, building institutions, starting local factories or mines, promoting the town businesses, and attracting the railroad to town were all part of the nation's rapid growth and settlement. But the great migrations to the Western frontier had slowed, and after 1920 so did the immigration of Europeans as a consequence of severe quotas imposed by the federal government. In many respects, urban mass transit was the last frontier of the railroad system. But when the automobile became available to the middle class, and even to the laboring class, urban populations dispersed farther than ever from the center of cities and now commuted to work by car rather than by train or subway. The railroad system began to fail.

23

Touring the West and the South

If I could travel over the West for three years, I might write of it with authority; but when my time is limited to three months, I can only give impressions from a car-window point of view, and cannot dare draw conclusions.
　　—Richard Harding Davis, *The West from a Car Window*, 1892[1]

With the elasticity of the Old Dominion I was, also, going into Elsie Dinsmore's country, going to that region of broad avenues and darkies singing happily and the gleaming "great house." I was going to experience at last what was as common to Elsie as verses in the Bible. . . . I resolved that I should find on my trip a great house, a flower garden, yes, even a black mammy better than had ever come into Elsie's exemplary life.
　　—Louise Closser Hale, *We Discover the Old Dominion*, 1916[2]

THE FIRST SYMPTOMS of railroad failure were reflected in rural areas. By the end of the nineteenth century, as the West failed to develop industrially, as mining towns dwindled to ghost towns, as family farms lost money and children to the city, and as Indian tribes struggled with a culture of poverty on reservations, the railroads faced the danger of following the trend of economic failure in these vast, barely tamed expanses of land. But they retained a foothold, at least through the 1920s, through promotion of a tourist industry. This can be explained partly by the beauty of the land and partly by its rich though short history, but also by the fact that the East had become so crowded and industrialized. The West represented a temporary but much welcome escape from the pressures of urban life. The city slicker and the tenderfoot from the East could enjoy his saddle sores while pretending to be an adventurous Westerner. Cowboys in boots and spurs led tours instead of herding cattle. Indians wove blankets and baskets especially for sale at Harvey Houses, and performed native dances for scheduled tour groups. And the Western railroads, since they could no longer advertise inexpensive Western land to attract population, encouraged the tourist trade by setting up itineraries, booking hotel accommodations, and offering package tours at bargain prices. Western travel became a staple for American tourists, especially during World War I when overseas travel was risky.[3]

The South, though quite distinct as a cultural and economic region of the country, had in common with its Western neighbors large stretches of rural land and a rich history, both attractive to tourists. It remained largely rural and largely poor despite the rise of new and prosperous cities including Memphis, Atlanta, Birmingham, New Orleans, and other towns once left in ruins by Union armies. And while pockets of European immigrants settled in the South, including Jews, Italians, Swedes, Danes, and Germans, the Southern population remained essentially polarized between the two races whose presence and relations dated back to the seventeenth century: Anglo-Saxons and blacks. Into this world came the railroads, rebuilt since the early 1880s, and reorganized under Northern financial control after the depression of 1893. The railroad played a vital role in the South in two ways: by connecting the new urban and industrial centers to Northern railroads, and by encouraging Northerners to go South for vacation tours.[4]

In both South and West, the economy of railroad tourism in large measure detached itself from the indigenous economy. Its schedules, passengers, and profits were determined in the Northeast. And its success did not depend at all on the future development of the South and West but on having these areas remain relatively rural, peaceful, and unpopulated. Both culturally and socially, both areas developed only slowly, and many inhabitants lived in the poorest conditions. In adopting tourism as an alternative to settlement, the railroads made the best of a bad situation.

Personal accounts of life in the West before the 1890s portray the uphill struggle against Indians, extremes of weather, lack of electricity or communication, and illness or starvation without assistance. These conditions were at the basis of the decision many made to sell their farms and move to cities or suburbs.[5] But the railroads had an investment as well, and one that could not so easily be relocated. The thousands of miles of track in the West needed passengers to prevent bankruptcy.

Railroad efforts to promote tourism in the West had begun as early as the 1870s, when agents of the Northern Pacific Railroad successfully lobbied in Washington to have a large tract of Western land designated as a park: Yellowstone National Park. With Yellowstone accessible from the route of the Northern Pacific, the company could then promote to Easterners this scenic and historic tract of land for its desirability as a vacation spot. The Western railroads also built hotels in the West, frequently in remote locations, such as the site of an Indian battle. But the conditions in these hotels were far from primitive. They catered to the wealthy and featured the latest indoor services complete with the most up-to-date luxury bedrooms, dining rooms, lounges appointed with elegant furniture, indoor plumbing, and sometimes even electric lights.[6]

While tourists had braved the West even in the 1860s, after the completion of the transcontinental railroads they became an integral part of railroad business. Railroad poster advertisements featuring beautiful paintings of Western scenery lured would-be vacationers into tourist agencies. In 1881 Raymond's Vacation Excursions of Boston, one of the best-known tourist agencies in the East, began conducting annual tours to California by train. Each year the agency took advantage of increasing track mileage in the far West to book

On a Western railroad tour around 1908, well-dressed tourists survey the scene from the rear platform of an observation car in Yosemite National Park. (YOSEMITE PARK RESEARCH LIBRARY)

tours along the Southern Pacific Railroad, the Atchison, Topeka and Santa Fe, and the Union Pacific. Raymond's reserved excursion trains proceeded independently of the railroads' published schedules.[7]

The all-expenses-paid tours to California departed from Boston during the winter months to give excursionists an opportunity to escape the Northeastern winter. In 1889 a typical Raymond's tour offered luxurious Pullman service through to California and back at a cost from $400 to $630. Passengers also received hotel coupons good for three nights in designated California hotels—such as the Raymond, the Palace, and the Hotel de Monte, owned either by Raymond's or the railroads.[8]

Even before the end of the Indian Wars, tourists were escorted to the battlefields and then to the new towns that sprang up after the area had become safe from attack. A tour on the Northern Pacific Railroad in 1889 took visitors to the site of the Battle of the Little Bighorn, the guidebook stating, "The Sioux, and Cheyennes, under Sitting Bull and Crazy Horse, fought desperately to prevent the white from obtaining a foothold in this part of the territory." In the thirteen years since the battle, the railroads had come through, national parks had been established in the area, and the Little Bighorn had become a vacation spot.[9]

Even in 1889 the struggle over Western land had not ended. The first Oklahoma Land Rush of 1889 allowed speculators to buy up property in what had been the Indian Territory, the largest remaining parcel of Western land belonging to the Indians. And the Wounded Knee massacre, usually considered the last major Indian conflict in the West, did not occur until the following year. Rather than expressing a sense of relief that the West had become safe, many tourists soon were disappointed that the West had become too tame, or too much like the East. On the self-indulgence of a twentieth-century trip West, satirist Irving Cobb wrote: ". . . We were going west to see the country and rough it—rough it on overland trains better equipped and more luxurious than any to be found in the East; rough it at ten-dollars-a-day hotels. . . ."[10] Another early-twentieth-century tourist noted that "Such Indians as one may meet in Kansas City are civilized and citified to a sad degree."[11]

But vacations by rail in the great West continued to provide busi-

Navajos, observing the new artifacts that white settlement brought to the West, wove images of railroad trains into the blankets they made for sale to tourists. This one dates from the late nineteenth century. (SAN DIEGO MUSEUM OF MAN)

ness for the railroads into the 1920s. With encouragement from the railroads the government added more land to the public domain in the West, setting aside parks for conservation and tourism. In the 1890s President Grover Cleveland added twenty-one million acres to the government's national forest preserves, much of it in the West. During the early years of the twentieth century Theodore Roosevelt put still more Western land in trust.

And Westerners, with encouragement and publicity from the railroads and tour guides, found ways of compensating for the "tameness" of the American West. Indians were recruited to relive the fascinating spectacles of dress, lifestyle, and dance. They dressed up in feathers, buckskin, and ceremonial paint, they danced, and they made items of traditional Indian design for sale to the public. *Baedeker's Guide* alerted tourists to reservations where "Indians may be seen at the rail-way stations, selling fine Navajo blankets, silver-work, and other souvenirs."[12]

During World War I, when foreign travel and investment were severely restricted, the U.S. government published detailed railroad guides to the American West to encourage a safe alternative to overseas travel. One of these, published in 1915, promoted sights along the route of the Atchison, Topeka and Santa Fe Railroad, advising tourists that the "Hopi villages are the objective of many tourists, especially on the occasion of the far-famed snake dance, which occurs in August."[13]

As railroads and businesses staked out parts of the West for the tourist trade, Indian-made souvenirs began to show signs of adaptation to new circumstances. As early as the 1880s Indians began weaving pictures of trains, advertisements, and business logos into the blankets for sale at train stations, Harvey Houses, and other tourist rendezvous. A later rug had "Fred Harvey" woven across the middle of it.[14]

Guidebooks and Indian crafts were only some of the souvenirs that tourists could carry with them back home, to show others what they had seen. Anyone who has looked closely at the smaller, more portable items in an antique store knows that souvenirs also included clothes, boots, scarves, spoons, plates, ashtrays, cups, teapots, posters, lampshades, stereoscopic views, glass slides, photographs, and any number of other items that carried the images of the old West. Hats, headdresses, and clothes were also popular. Picture postcards carried images of the West after their successful introduction at the 1893 Columbian Exposition in Chicago. Railroads circulated pictures of their trains, stations, bridges, and the interior of train cars to attract business. In the 1920s the Sante Fe Railroad hired well-known painters, including artists of the Taos colony, to depict the splendors of the West to be seen through the window of a train car.[15]

Railroads through the South were also becoming detached from the local economy. Like the Western railroads, Southern lines catered to vacationers; and they also promoted industrial growth in the South, growth supported and needed by the Northern industrial economy. Beyond this "window" of railroad development in the South, the region remained poor and divided. The white population subordinated the black under a deluge of Jim Crow legislation, which provided two public areas for every public service: one for whites, one for blacks. Of course this included railroad station waiting rooms and railroad cars. Anger at Northern ways lingered, and devotees of the Old South hated Yankee ways, which included public education and industrial development. Industry in the South was looked at by some as Yankee inspired, with its attendant crowds, dirt, and poor living conditions.[16]

J. P. Morgan, the architect of Northern dominance over Southern railroading, did not allow these regional attitudes to stand in his way. In the wake of economic depression in the 1890s, Morgan dealt a financial hand intended to help the four Southern through lines survive—under his dominance. By the turn of the century he controlled the Southern Railroad, the Seaboard Air Line, the Louisville and Nashville, and the Atlantic Coast Line. With them he forged a system of railroads that met the needs primarily of the new industrial South: the coal, iron, steel, lumber, cotton, and tobacco industries. All these products came north on his trains.[17]

Just before and after the depression that gave Morgan his opportunity, other capitalists, railroad owners among them, began to build elegant winter homes and hotels in Southern states, accessible by railroad, as resorts for themselves and other well-to-do families. During the winter months Pullman trains headed south, just as they headed north to Bar Harbor and the Adirondacks in the summer.

In 1889 George Vanderbilt began constructing his well-known Biltmore estate in North Carolina. This encouraged other fashionable and wealthy families to follow suit. Asheville became a resort area for the wealthy, and private cars continued south to Florida, where much of the state's eastern coast was developed into popular resorts for the well-to-do.[18] In Florida Henry Flagler began expanding railroad track during the 1880s with an eye to developing large tracts of the coast into resort towns. And John D. Rockefeller promptly took advantage of expanded railroad service in Florida by building a winter home there. But in Palm Beach Flagler built hotels, a sign that he courted the business of people less affluent than himself.[19]

The peculiarities of the Southern economy left it stunted, with people at the lower end of the economic scale having little opportunity for advancement. Railroads, hotels, and vacation homes did little to promote the welfare of the local population. For this reason, and because of developing factory opportunities in the North, a northward railroad migration of blacks and poor whites began early in the new century. As tourists sought rustic culture in the South, the black population made black music a part of the national culture by bringing it north.

Roughly between 1900 and 1920, several styles of black music rode the rails from New Orleans north to St. Louis and Chicago. All these styles were informed by the experience of riding the train, leavetakings, and the rhythm of the rails. W. C. Handy, one of those who made this music, noted that his fellow travelers were usually destitute. "Some came sauntering down the railroad tracks, while others caught rides on the big road and entered town on the top of cotton bales." The rhythm of ragtime music, the busy and complex music of jazz bands, the boogie-woogie beat, and the blues all traveled along the same route, and migrated also to Detroit and to Harlem, which became the informal capital of jazz music before and during the 1920s.[20]

The railroad was as central to the music these wandering musicians played as it was to their movements up and down the Mississippi Valley. The rolling bass passages of guitar and piano in blues, ragtime, and boogie-woogie recalled the rumble and rhythm of a train. In the high long wails of voices and instruments, the musicians mimicked the long wail of the train whistle, which could be heard for miles. Jelly Roll Morton and Buddy Bolden brought this sound to piano music. Huddy Ledbetter sang and played it on blues guitar.[21]

Poor whites also brought their music north, singing and playing tunes that had lived in the South for two hundred years. With fiddle, banjo, and guitar, the Carter Family gained a national audience, as did Jimmy Rodgers, known for his wailing railroad tunes. Modern country music grew from this root, as did the urban gospel tradition. Recording studios brought this music into homes at a far reach from the hills of the South. But to record, or even to find a paying audience, these singers had to reach a major city and make contacts with other musicians. Not unlike LaFayette Stone in the 1840s, these people had their lives strung out along the railroad line and stopped in a different town each night. They quite literally must have passed in the night the Pullman passengers heading south to enjoy a rural retreat and vacation in the Florida sun. What was economic failure to the Southerner was picturesque local color to the well-heeled Northerner on holiday.

24

Hometowns and Nostalgia

Oh! the old swimmin'-hole! When I last saw the place,
The scenes was all changed, like the change in my face;
The bridge of the railroad now crosses the spot
Whare the old divin'-log lays sunk and fergot.
And I stray down the banks whare the trees ust to be—
But never again will theyr shade shelter me!
And I wish in my sorrow I could strip to the soul,
And dive off in my grave like the old swimmin'-hole.
                    —James Whitcomb Riley, "The Old Swimmin'-Hole," 1882[1]

T HOSE WHO GREW UP with the railroad and those who encountered
it for the first time at the turn of the century shared one important
awareness: they knew that while urban economies flourished, the
economically self-sufficient small town was disappearing. They also
knew that the railroad, which was supposed to have tied small towns
into a prosperous national economy, deferred this failure but did not
prevent it. For many people, childhood memories centered on the
town and the train, and entailed a sense of loss that took many forms.

Edward Everett Hale, whose autobiography *A New England Boyhood* was written in 1893, recounted the changes he experienced during the 1820s and 1830s as Boston grew from a small community into a major commercial city.[2] Even though his own father was at the forefront of the movement to bring internal improvements to Boston and enlarge its sphere of trade, Hale looked back wistfully on the school, church, and family experiences that were as lost to him as his childhood was. So closely were his personal memories allied to the fate of the town that it sometimes appeared he and Boston had grown to adulthood together. Boston too had lost its innocence as it grew from a familiar hometown into a mass society. Hale identified railroads as the key instrument of this change. By the 1890s they carried travelers in and out of town by the thousands. The products they transported made Boston into an enormous marketplace for the world.

Hale wrote another memoir in 1902, entitled *Memories of a Hundred Years*. In it he expanded on some of the changes that railroads, along with the telegraph and telephone, had brought to America. His commentary began right where Hamilton and Madison had left off. It was impossible, wrote Hale, for twentieth-century readers to understand "how far apart the states were from each other, and how little people knew each other" in Madison and Hamilton's day. Hale thought that "George Washington, if in writing he had said 'my country' in any of the last years of his life, would have meant Virginia."[3] Inhabitants of separate cities also knew little of one another.

Politically, Hale observed, the railroads and other improvements in communications had strengthened the Union by diminishing the importance of long distances. Before the railroads, "the people at large knew little or nothing of the leading characters in distant States. People had to vote as they were directed by the handful of men who knew the political public characters at Washington." Presidential candidates had been chosen by Congress, not by convention. But by 1840 improved transportation by both railroad and steamboat made possible the mass conventions which have chosen presidential candidates ever since.[4]

While no one could deny that the railroads had brought the nation together physically with incredible speed, Hale and many others argued against the loss of propriety and the unconstitutional practices that this change brought to the political system through conventions of "irresponsible delegates."[5] Others, notably Andrew Jackson and his followers of the 1830s, equated mass political conventions with democracy and saw elitism in charges to the contrary.

Another Bostonian who looked askance at the enormous growth of the cities and the emergence of mass society was Henry Adams. Like Edward Everett Hale, he traced his ancestors back to the American Revolution and before. John Adams, John Quincy Adams, and Charles Adams were, respectively, his great-grandfather, grandfather, and father. With Federalist leanings, they had all shied away from the democratic mob and toward virtues of gentility and individualism. Henry Adams's nostalgia for this lost world was so acute that he raised it to the level of historical theory—that the emergence of business capitalism marked the decline of the social order.

Later in life, Adams used the vehicle of autobiography to question the changes in American society wrought by railroads and industry. So profound was this transformation, he claimed, that his classical education was of no use to him. In *The Education of Henry Adams*, published in 1905, Adams looked in vain for a key to the social order. The order of landed wealth, family, state, and church which, he felt, had reached its pinnacle during the Middle Ages, had come apart, deteriorating in a scramble for wealth by any means. He blamed the industrialists who, he wrote, "used, without qualm, whatever instruments they found at hand." Having turned from their task to fight the Civil War, they then devoted all the resources of society on one task—

> its roads . . . and society dropped every thought of dealing with anything more than the single fraction called a railway system. This relatively small part of its task was still so big as to need the energies of a generation, for it required all new machinery to be created—capital, banks, mines, furnaces, shops, power-houses, technical knowledge. . . .[6]

This massive project, Adams added, also brought about "a steady remodelling of social and political habits, ideas and institutions to fit the new scale and suit the new conditions." While he found the consequent wealth to the nation "deeply exciting to a historian," and observed that "the system seemed on the whole to satisfy the wants of society better than any other part of the social machine," Adams predicted the demise of the railroad at a time when most people were still "satisfied" with it. From the perspective of the early twentieth century he wrote that "the railway system interested one less than in 1868, since it offered less chance for future profit."[7] Whether or not Adams knew how many railroads were struggling to recoup from financial losses at the time, he certainly understood that other investments had begun to look more attractive.

To some extent the memories of these two Bostonians mesh quite well with the perspectives of small-town natives at the turn of the century who had to leave their hometowns to make a living, or watch as most of their friends and relatives sought prosperity elsewhere. They too felt acute nostalgia for the simpler life of home left behind, despite an awareness that home had lost its economic base and was losing touch with the national economy altogether. But on the benefits of railroads, they differed. In Williamstown, New Hampshire, and Hartford, Michigan, the train was the most dependable element of daily life at the turn of the century. It took its place alongside the homestead and the country store in mists of memory.

According to R. L. Duffus, who wrote about his childhood in *Williamstown Branch* (named for the branch railroad), the automobile and not the railroad put small towns once and for all out of business. Or perhaps it was that combined with the loss of the granite mines.

> What stabbed it [Williamstown] harder—some quirk in the granite industry that shifted the movement of stone to Barre and Montpelier; or the weapon that struck at all the small towns from ocean to ocean, from border to border, the gasoline-driven Thing, the smooth highway, the consequent shrinking of the map, so that a market town every thirty miles could take the place of a market town every ten miles or so?[8]

At the close of his memoir, Duffus recalled where each building in town stood, until at last he reached the railroad station where he said his goodbye for the last time. After recalling the names of the engineer and conductor, and their familiar preparations for a train leaving town, the engine headed out for the last time.

We are moving, gathering speed, down the grade to Barre and points
north, south, east, and west. We are also headed toward the twentieth
century. I look back with homesickness and forward with eagerness.
Soon we are out of sight of Williamstown and the year 1898.[9]

When Duffus actually left Williamstown, he rode a Model T, not a
train.

Hartford, Michigan, a somewhat larger and more prosperous town
to begin with, did not "die" with the coming of the automobile. Hartford still provided a market for area farmers, attracted new industries,
and achieved the status of a small city. But even in Hartford, the automobile doomed the railroad. The automobile brought with it new
transitions in the patterns of small-town society, just as the railroad
had almost a hundred years earlier. Soon, beginning perhaps around
1910, a former Hartford resident wrote that "The depot had ceased
to be what it once was—the focus of the town's connection with the
outside world." During the 1920s the railroads through Hartford
began to discontinue service.[10]

Despite Hartford's survival, many of its young people nonetheless
had to leave in order to receive an education and pursue a career.
With deep nostalgia Willis Dunbar, who grew up in Hartford, described what one lost when he exchanged small-town life for city life.

There is still space. The air is clear; the streets are not thronged with
people. Youngsters can still go fishing and swimming in nearby lakes
and streams. There is quiet, peace, and serenity in the town.[11]

Still others who wished to preserve the memory of a vanishing way
of life wrote personal accounts of the rural rail service, sometimes
with as much endearment as Hale and Adams had devoted to life before the transportation revolution. Those who saw the railroads fail-
ing after World War II recalled train life at the turn of the century:
the rural train and station, and the familiar small crowds of passengers who made train travel a local institution and a way of life. When
Heman Chase of New Hampshire reconstructed his youthful memories of train travel in Vermont, he, like so many others, wrote of the
exciting "rubble, screech, and clatter of brakes, as the train ground to
a hasty and very brief stop" at Cold River station, starting point of his

This depression-era photograph by Arthur Rothstein of the depot
area in Winslow, Arkansas, shows a rural crossroads typical of many
towns that had once eagerly sought railroad connections, anticipating prosperity. By 1930 this prosperity consisted of little more than
a trade in agricultural products and the transport of local passengers. (LIBRARY OF CONGRESS)

family's journeys to Boston. On their return to Bellows Falls, Vermont, "We could glimpse some of the dim lights in 'the Falls' and
sometimes their reflections in the Connecticut River just below." Finally, "We always got a loving welcome on the station platform before
being escorted among the milling passengers, baggage carts, stage
drivers, and mailmen. . . ."[12]

Despite these sentimentalized memories, Chase reserved a harsh
judgment for the powers responsible for the "death" of the railroad.

> Its "death" is generally attributed to the improvement of highways and
> increased convenience of private cars for short trips and the growth of
> air travel for long. In large measure this is based on valid reasoning.

But, he goes on, "there are other factors."

Land monopoly and speculation have negated the concept of equality and have steadily narrowed the field of opportunity and economic choice for both LABOR and CAPITAL.[13]

The way of life in small towns had not simply vanished, it had been taken away by the changing demands of an increasingly centralized marketplace which no longer needed so many small towns or so many small railroads serving them.

Instead of sentimentalizing his experience of riding the rails, or denouncing the economics that took them away, a railroad memorialist who wrote *36 Miles of Trouble: The Story of the West River R.R.* concealed his nostalgia behind a caustic realism and unsparing wit. In Victor Morse's book, old equipment and frequent breakdowns were the stuff of memory.

> Cars became as rickety as the engines. Two women who boarded the train at Williamsville in the middle of a rainstorm found water several inches deep on the car floor and had to sit with their feet up. The roof leaked so badly they also had to sit under their umbrellas and at that were soaked when they reached Brattleboro. . . .
>
> A weary old man who boarded the mixed train was jolted awake with the car on its side at the bottom of a bank.
>
> "What station is this?" he cried.
>
> "It's an accident," yelled the brakeman from under a seat.
>
> "Oh, I thought that was the way you always stopped."[14]

But Morse also had a serious message. He pointed out that this rural line, like so many others, never made much money. "It was money wasted," he wrote. Its account books had always shown a deficit, from 1883 to 1938. And the railroad did not "contribute to the prosperity of the towns it served."

> It added nothing to their little industries and gave them no new ones. It made their farms no more profitable. In short it brought the valley no extra business at all, except for transient lumbering which may or may not have been facilitated. There is no more eloquent testimony on this than the census figures. All the towns lost population just as steadily after the railroad was built as in the decades before.[15]

Immigrants too found the transition from European homes to
American cities difficult. Irving Howe quotes one immigrant's reaction to train travel in New York, which reflects pain for the loss of
peace and quiet. An elevated train trip taken to Bronx Park on a Sunday "was a super tenement on wheels," filled with "excited screaming
mothers, fathers sagging under enormous lunch baskets, children
yelling, puking and running under everyone's legs, a gang of tough
Irish kids in baseball suits who persisted in swinging from the straps."
But the young passenger's mother took them on this trip as a way of
returning to the natural environment—the woods of Bronx Park,
which were the closest thing she knew to the forests of Hungary.[16]

Another immigrant who stayed in New York City before taking the
train to Chicago found the elevated trains a problem even for
passersby. The city was "relentless. . . . It is brought home . . . by the
rush of the overhead railway in Sixth Avenue, by the hurry of the
crowds in Broadway, by the grinding clamor of the subway trains."[17]

Arrivals in Chicago in the late nineteenth century reflected similar
misgivings about the ugly, crowded, and dirty city. The same young
immigrant who walked a good part of the distance from New York to
Chicago still found the railroads central to his first memories of the
city.

> An entanglement of railroad tracks, miles of hot sand dunes, a stretch
> of inland sea; the sky line assaulted by gigantic elevators and smoke-
> stacks, a block or two crowded by houses dropped into an empty
> prairie—that is the beginning of Chicago. . . . Even now, after having
> discovered the soul and the heart of her—I have a distinct feeling of
> fear when I arrive there, although I step from a Pullman car and feel
> safe, at least from want.[18]

Even in the city, the memory of trains seemed more appealing as
they began to disappear from the urban landscape. Just as small-town
residents waxed nostalgic when their trains failed, city dwellers
recorded their early struggles with the city and its trains when it became apparent that those times would not come again. Interestingly,
one of the most evocative memories of city transportation came from

Nancy Hale, daughter of Edward Everett Hale. To extend her father's legacy, in 1958 she published a collection of essays under the title *A New England Girlhood*. In it she recounted her childhood and family life, including travels from the outskirts into the center of Boston. Already the long, slow deterioration of Boston had begun, as this young descendant of Nathan Hale noticed.

> I am still haunted by that street corner where we waited [for the streetcar]. It was in a tough section of Roxbury. Saloons lined the street, with swinging doors; pieces of newspaper blew down the pavement in the freezing wind; and one day while we stood there a man came shuffling along *with no shoes*, with his feet wrapped in rags. I could not take my eyes away; and after we had boarded the nice, warm, smelly streetcar, the memory of the man joined, in a special compartment in my mind, a small but growing company: the man with no legs, with leather-covered stumps, trying to sell pencils on a street corner . . . and old Mr. Harvey, who drove the last forlorn livery hack in our town.

As yet not all parts of Boston suffered from this decay. As the streetcar approached the center of the city, "The aspects of the parts of Boston through which the streetcar passed changed gradually, from ghastly to sordid to merely dingy to smug. . . ."[19] Surely here is the first chapter of a book on urban transportation, chronicling its passage through increasingly poor and perhaps unsafe neighborhoods that many passengers would not tolerate.

From these biographical perspectives on the changes brought about by the railroads which ultimately put many of them out of business, a few strands of historical meaning emerge. Without doubt the transformation of life between 1890 and 1920 and even after left many Americans with deep feelings of loss. Whether they had to leave Europe or a small American town in order to prosper, they looked back with a longing for familiar ways, even though few could still afford to live life on the local level. Those who committed themselves to the city felt the excitement of the industrial world but also bore witness to its physical ugliness and impersonal nature.

As for the train, rather than bringing prosperity to small towns it more often adopted the characteristics of the economy through which it ran. For small-town residents the train took on the character of another institution, as familiar as the church or the general store. Its passengers were largely known to one another. It did not render the local population cosmopolitan simply by providing an avenue to the outside world. City dwellers, on the other hand, saw the railroad, elevated train, and subway as further examples of the noise and relentless pressure of city life. Most of its passengers were strangers.

Many people were moved to record their memories of a world they saw vanishing with the end of local attachments. In the new world, transportation promoted a national community organized around an urban economy and urban institutions. Bostonians and New Yorkers experienced this transition in the 1900s, but small-town America did not feel its finality until the turn of the century. A yearning for the past combined with an appreciation of the enormous prosperity that urban America promised as the twentieth century opened.

25

‖‖‖‖‖‖‖‖‖‖‖‖‖‖‖‖‖‖‖‖

Lost Hometowns,
Lost Lives

He suddenly felt the devastating impermanence of the nation. Only the
earth endured—the gigantic American earth, bearing upon its awful breast
a world of flimsy rickets. . . . We have been an exile in another land and a
stranger in our own. . . . And the old hunger returned—the terrible and
obscure hunger that haunts and hurts Americans, and that makes us exiles
at home and strangers wherever we go.
                    —Thomas Wolfe, *Look Homeward, Angel,* 1929[1]

D ESPITE THE TRIUMPH of power that the railroads brought to the
United States, the accompanying centralization of wealth left vast
areas of the country with profound feelings of loss. The rural Northeast as well as the South and West faced precipitous economic decline and loss of population. This loss was translated into cultural
terms by a number of authors who depicted the melancholy fate both
of those who remained in the country and those who picked up and

left. Thus the centralization of railroad control had cultural consequences which eddied out to every region of the country.

Author Sarah Orne Jewett was one of a number of novelists who
depicted both the loveliness and the loss of Northeastern local culture. In her *Country of the Pointed Firs,* published in 1897, the older
inhabitants of a small Maine town recall the days when their community sent oceangoing vessels to "a hundred ports." For Jewett's townspeople, the decline of local shipping is a social loss as well as an
economic one. The sea captains and sailors brought back information
about the world beyond the horizon; but in the town's present
predicament it has almost no contact with the outside world, and its
chief concerns are narrow. It "grows dreadful ignorant when it is shut
up to its own affairs, and gets no knowledge of the outside world except from a cheap, unprincipled newspaper."[2]

Jewett's themes were echoed as late as 1957 by novelist Mary Ellen
Chase, who was born in 1887 and raised in the Maine coastal town of
Blue Hill. In her 1950s book *The Edge of Darkness,* the death of a
ninety-year-old woman triggers memories of the life she had lived
during the heyday of shipping.

> "In those days when she was born," the doctor said, "this coast was
> closer to India and China than it was to the Middle West, and it kept
> on being so for thirty years longer. Even the wretched town I live in
> built ships, ten to twenty every year, and sent men all over the world
> in them. People thought of other things than just packing herring and
> canning blueberries."[3]

Willa Cather, a contemporary of Jewett's, grew up in Nebraska
where her family lived in an area just beginning to be populated by
immigrants. In books such as *The Song of the Lark* (1915), *My Ántonia* (1918), and *O Pioneers!* (1922), Cather's evocations of lovely quiet
land and enormous skies gave the countryside an almost spiritual
quality which glorified and justified the struggles of the settlers. Yet
many of her characters had to leave the land in order to seek an education or to find work, when town work looked more promising than
farming. In *Song of the Lark* the settlers have lived long enough to
have grown sons, who leave their hometown of Moonstone to work

for the railroad. But Moonstone itself retains its peaceful and contented air, especially in warm weather.

> It was in the summer that one really lived. Then all the overcrowded houses were opened wide, and the wind blew through them with sweet, earthy smells of garden-planting. The town looked as if it had been washed. People were out painting their fences. The cottonwood trees were a-flicker with sticky, yellow little leaves, and the feathery tamarisks were in pink bud.[4]

A young woman named Thea, who leaves home to pursue her career in singing, finds Chicago far less attractive or humane.

> When Thea emerged from the concert hall . . . a furious gale was beating over the city from Lake Michigan. The streets were full of cold, hurrying, angry people, running for street-cars and barking at each other.

While Thea enjoys a successful career, she fleetingly recognizes the price. Living in hotels in strange cities gives little comfort.

> She brought out an armful of muslin things, knelt down, and began laying them in the trays. Suddenly she stopped, dropped forward and leaned against the open trunk, her head on her arms. The tears fell down on the dark old carpet. It came over her how many people must have said good-bye and been unhappy in that room. . . . Strange rooms and strange faces, how sick at heart they made one![5]

My Ántonia and *O Pioneers!* also express the tension between remaining in a small Midwestern town and looking for something in the larger world, leaving loved ones behind, sometimes forever. In each case the train is the go-between, taking loved ones away or bringing them back from a world where few know or appreciate them. Toward the end of *My Ántonia,* this departure takes place:

> After dinner the next day, I said good-bye and drove back to Hastings to take the train for Black Hawk. Ántonia and her children gathered round my buggy before I started, and even the little ones looked up at me with friendly faces. When I reached the bottom of the hill, I

glanced back. The group was still there by the windmill. Ántonia was waving her apron.

In *O Pioneers!* another immigrant woman dresses up to become part of the urban world of Lincoln, Nebraska, if only for a short time. "Late in the afternoon of a brilliant October day, Alexandra Bergson, dressed in a black suit and traveling-hat, alighted at the Burlington Depot in Lincoln."[6]

In later works, Cather's depiction of the small communities that emerged from the struggles of immigrants conveyed a deep sense of disappointment at their narrowness and provincial concerns. In *Obscure Destinies* (1930), a book of three short stories, the accomplishments of aging immigrants are lost on their children and grandchildren.[7] Shut up in small rooms in the house of a grown child, or left behind on the farms by children seeking more money in town, these once proud settlers live unappreciated while their children seek a more comfortable but also more prosaic life in town. For both generations, their relationship with nature is incidental and their lives devoid of purpose. They pass the time attending church socials or in strained visiting with neighbors. While Sarah Orne Jewett found much to go back to in Maine, even after the collapse of its maritime economy, Willa Cather could find little merit in the petty lives of second-generation inhabitants of small Midwestern towns.

In the South the passing of the rural economy came much earlier: the Civil War left the region with no choice but to rebuild. Still, a number of authors gave voice to a rising nostalgia for the plantation way of life. One author who rewrote the history of the South in fictional terms was Thomas Nelson Page. In *Gordon Keith* (1903), Page described the hero's father as a relic of the past.

He knew the Past and lived in it; the Present he did not understand, and the Future he did not know. In his latter days, when his son was growing up, after war had swept like a vast inundation over the land, burying almost everything it had not borne away, General Keith still survived, unchanged, unmoved, unmarred, an antique memorial of the life of which he was a relic. His one standard was that of a gentleman.

As for strangers, the general had seen very few of them in the days before the war. But, the reader is assured, had any of those few asked for shelter, "he would have received, whatever his condition, a hospitality as gracious as if he had been the highest in the land."[8]

In addition to writers who glorified America's rural past were those who portrayed the plight of innocent country people who left home only to find themselves at the mercy of strangers. In this literature the fate of the moral individual in a crowd of unsavory strangers evoked many of the same feelings of loss that Jewett, Cather, and others described, as the country's culture migrated toward cities along with its economy and population. Theodore Dreiser's *Sister Carrie* depicts just such a transition. First published in 1900, it opens with a description of Caroline Meeber leaving her family in the rural town of Columbia City, Wisconsin, to seek work in Chicago. The opening scene is a distillation of the experience of millions of Americans boarding a train for the city.

> When Caroline Meeber boarded the afternoon train for Chicago, her total outfit consisted of a small trunk, a cheap imitation alligator-skin satchel, a small lunch in a paper box, and a yellow leather snap purse, containing her ticket, a scrap of paper with her sister's address in Van Buren Street, and four dollars in money. It was August, 1889. She was eighteen years of age, bright, timid, and full of the illusions of ignorance and youth. Whatever touch of regret at parting characterized her thoughts, it was certainly not for advantages now being given up. A gush of tears at her mother's farewell kiss, a touch in her throat when the cars clacked by the flour mill where her father worked by the day, a pathetic sigh as the familiar green environs of the village passed in review, and the threads which bound her so lightly to girlhood and home were irretrievably broken.[9]

Dreiser's view of the damage done by this parting is not withheld from the reader. His moral stance concerns the fate of such innocents who lose their contact with home: "When a girl leaves her home at eighteen, she does one of two things. Either she falls into saving hands and becomes better, or she rapidly assumes the cosmopolitan standard of virtue and becomes worse." Sister Carrie becomes worse.

While still on the train she comes under the influence of a traveling salesman, whose appearance, in the idiom of 1889, would have given him away to a more sophisticated passenger. His dress and manners, wrote Dreiser, "are calculated to elicit the admiration of susceptible young women. . . ."

> His suit was of a striped and crossed pattern of brown wool, new at that time, but since become familiar as a business suit. The low crotch of the vest revealed a stiff shirt bosom of white and pink stripes. From his coat sleeves protruded a pair of linen cuffs of the same pattern, fastened with large, gold plate buttons, set with the common yellow agates known as "cat's-eyes." His fingers bore several rings—one, the ever enduring heavy seal—and from his vest dangled a neat gold watch chain, from which was suspended the insignia of the Order of Elks.[10]

Carrie, unable to judge the man's motives, trusts him as if he were a member of her family or a resident of the small town of Columbia City. Her trust leads her into a lurid and scandalous relationship with a married man and, even worse in the eyes of many, to a career on the stage.

Crowds of travelers figured in a new genre of writing which became popular at the turn of the century—the murder mystery. A casual and popular style compared with Dreiser's detailed formality, these novels took the mysteries of identity in the crowd as their point of departure. The evil that might lurk in the hearts of other passengers on a train was the uncertainty that popular novelist Mary Roberts Rinehart used to create suspense in her relatively early and highly successful book, *The Man in Lower Ten*.[11] Published in 1909, its sense of evil was far more pervasive than *Sister Carrie's*. When a man is murdered while sleeping in a Pullman berth, all other passengers are under suspicion, and the fact that all are unknown to one another creates an atmosphere of distrust and fear. The only individuals who can resolve this tension are those who investigate all the suspects until their motives and identities are as public as the Pullman car itself. In this context, privacy became secrecy, and the integrity of an individual is meaningless if no one else knows with certainty that it is authentic. Going through luggage, pockets, toiletries, and other personal property becomes an honorable activity rather than a puerile descent into invasion of privacy.

Despite a general recognition of moral peril in the train and in crowded cities, leaving home and making one's way in the city became a central theme of early-twentieth-century literature. It was a coming of age to board the train and leave home alone for the first time; but it was a melancholy moment, tinged with uncertainty. And it was a particularly lonely and uprooted rite of passage, where visits home were brief and inconclusive, and the future held no assurance that a young person might not go astray. Of all the uses of the train in literature, the motif of leaving home had the greatest impact on the American imagination. Some found their way through school to employment, marriage, and identification with a particular economic class. Others did not. They found occasional employment, lived in boardinghouses or on the streets, had few family contacts, and remained outsiders even in a nation of outsiders. These were the tramps, hoboes, and criminals who after the Civil War never ceased to be part of the American scene. Their particular individualism was closely connected with the workings of the railroad network, and their culture at least as closely identified with railroading as the culture of the rich had been during the Gilded Age.

Hoboes represented the most extreme example of every American's fate. Known for their ability to jump a slow-moving train and ride it without paying a fare, they had become almost an institution by the early years of the twentieth century. In the shadow of railroad stations, switching yards, and other locales where trains slowed or stopped, hoboes hid until nightfall, or until it appeared that no one was looking, then ran for the trains as they pulled slowly out of the station. They clambered aboard and sought hiding places inside freight cars, on top of cars, under them, between them, or even sometimes in a passenger coach until the approach of a conductor forced them to move elsewhere. Railroad authorities might find dozens of hoboes on board a single train.[12]

Arrayed against the hoboes were a wide variety of railroad workers and law-enforcement officials who chased them off railroad property with varying degrees of enthusiasm. Brakemen were known to turn

Hoboes were the natural enemies of trainmen, who from time to time tried to flush them from the roofs, undercarriages, and interiors of the cars. Hoboes had the choice of fleeing, fighting, or facing a possible jail sentence.

their backs without giving chase particularly if they received a payoff from their prey. The dicks, a hobo term for railroad police or railroad detectives, could be dogged and vindictive, giving chase and bludgeoning the hoboes with blackjacks, sticks, or rubber tubing. If caught, a hobo might go to jail or do hard labor on the work crews that had become a favored form of punishment for vagrants.[13]

Experienced hoboes traveled widely, knew the best places to board a moving train, and frequently knew the dicks and railroad workers individually, distinguishing those who would turn a blind eye to hobo passengers from those who had to be avoided at all costs. These elder statesmen of tramps also carried a map of the railroad network in their minds—not of tourist attractions and resort spas, but of safe cities and unsafe ones, towns where free food could be obtained, and towns where a hungry soul might have to break into a freight shipment to find milk, fruit, or delicacies. They could also hunt up a shower or washroom in the train yard, spot a saloon giving away beer, and know where to find their compatriots.[14]

The inexperienced hobo ran a good many risks as he grabbed onto a moving boxcar for the first time, closed a boxcar door without realizing that the dicks would know why the door had been closed, or got off in a switchyard without knowing who guarded it. He also needed to know the right kind of story to tell at the back door of a home in order to obtain free food. He had to know what to do about lice and how to find other hoboes and get help.[15]

The fact that hoboes maintained a hierarchy almost as complex as that of a small corporation, and a language as specialized as the language of a profession, began to fascinate scholars and intellectuals, who went among them to record the meaning of such terms as "gay cat" (beginner) or "dunker" (bread and coffee), and observe their habits.[16] The University of Chicago in particular derived its reputation as a foremost center of sociology by sending students into the streets of Chicago to study hoboes, gangs, prostitutes, and other underworld groups that developed their own set of rules in the shadows of major cities.

Despite this effort to draw them into the circle of formal social relationships, hoboes deliberately defied these relationships and maintained their hierarchy partly as a parody of polite society. They respected no formal law or economic system, and no social institutions. They begged, borrowed, and stole what they needed to survive. One would-be hobo of the 1920s wrote that hopping a train "symbolized revolt from an established and disciplined order."[17] Yet he and others wrote about their experiences, just as tourists and travelers had for generations.

The question of whether hoboes really wanted to live on the margin of society, or had to, seems to have depended a great deal on the individual. Many of those who lived like hoboes were in fact itinerant laborers who traveled certain routes where they knew work could be found. Track layers, brakemen, and other railroad workers traveled this way when they could not afford the cost of a day coach. Called "boomers," these men worked only a short time for any one boss, and left when they had enough money or when the job proved burdensome. Some did not like being told they could not drink on the job, so they left to avoid this and other infringements on their freedom. Some miners were also itinerant, as were lumbermen, fruit pickers, farm laborers and other outdoor workers for whom the economy slowed in winter. Most traveled in search of money, whether it took the form of a handout or a temporary job.

Other men hoboed around the country simply to hang on to a measure of personal freedom in a time when efficiency, uniformity, and mechanization seemed to wring all the spontaneity out of life. For them the country had become just a little too unified and far too standardized in its rules and expectations. Despite the freedom of working part time or not at all, however, the pleasures of the tramping life were few. Sleeping in cold and wet conditions, smoking the remains of other people's discarded cigars and cigarettes, eating handouts, and avoiding the railroad police were scarcely enviable experiences.[18] Nevertheless there were enough indignant people in the country to attach a large measure of personal meaning to this freedom, especially to the freedom of leaving town by train. For prisoners, poor blacks, poor Southern farmers, and others trapped by circumstance, the train leaving town held the last faint hope for change.

While books about the experiences of the poor were few, songs about hopping the train to a better (or worse) place became quite popular after the turn of the century, working their way into American culture by way of recordings. Among the best known of these was "The Big Rock Candy Mountain," in which the search for something better at the other end of the line turns into a hobo's dream for a promised land where "the box cars all are empty/ and the cops have wooden legs."[19] But other hobo songs depicted the hobo dying alone on the road, or the melancholy fate of having no roots and no home.

Blacks who took to the road also composed songs about the railroad taking them to something better. But frequently that something better was all but impossible to obtain, or for some was the freedom

to be found only in death. "The Midnight Special," a song that became popular in the early 1920s, concerned a Southern train that
passed a Texas prison en route from Houston to El Paso. The head-
light of the locomotive shone through the prison bars and evoked a
melancholy memory of freedom for prisoners. The song's refrain,
"Let the Midnight Special shine her light on me," suggested the hope
that freedom might come to those trapped on the inside.[20]

"Freight Train," another Southern song, told of a woman on the
run, and asked others not to tell her pursuers where she went. Written by Elizabeth Cotton, a black woman raised in North Carolina
during the 1890s, the refrain is another plea for freedom, this time by
someone who would like to be buried near the train track rather than
returning to the place she had left.

> Freight Train, freight train, run so fast,
> Freight Train, freight train, run so fast;
> Please don't tell what train I'm on,
> An' they won't know what route I'm goin' . . . .
>
> When I die, Lord, bury me deep,
> Way down on old Chestnut Street,
> So I can hear old Number Nine
> As she comes rollin' by.[21]

While the singer in "Freight Train" found her freedom, others
found loneliness rather than opportunity at the other end of the rail
line. Having roamed hundreds of miles away from home in search of
a better life, the singer in "Five Hundred Miles" realized he would
have to travel that far back again to be with anyone who cared for
him. On the other hand, a song entitled "Blow Yo' Whistle Freight
Train" depicted a man who missed the roaming life he once enjoyed.

> That old freight train movin' along to Nashville,
> Holds a charm that is a charm for me;
> Makes me think of good old boomer days gone by,
> Makes me feel so lonely, don't you see.

In other blues songs, the message was equally sad. Girl friends and
boy friends left by train and didn't come back. The only peace might

be found by lying down on the track and letting the train do its damage.[22]

Songs of religious faith nevertheless redeemed the railroad journey and likened it to the journey to heaven. Songs like "Life's Railway to Heaven" and "This Train" optimistically asserted that passengers were bound for glory. But even this did not deter songwriters from writing songs like "Hell-Bound Express Train" and "Death's Black Train Is Coming."[23] In the well-known ballad of Casey Jones, the "promised land" became a bitter phrase for his death in a 1900 train wreck.

It is a curious irony that after a hundred years of winding its way through thousands of American crossroads, towns, and cities, and bringing crowds to markets and social institutions throughout the country, one of the best-known cultural legacies of train travel might be loneliness or a feeling of loss. This stands in stark contrast to limitless opportunity that for so many years was associated with the development of America. But it is not an irrational legacy. In a country where local economic, legal, and social controls and protections were subordinated in a rapid drive for national unity and national interest, many persons lost the local world familiar to them. Instead they were plunged into a world of strangers, a society fraught with economic, legal, and social risk. While many turned this risk to their advantage, many others did not. For them, the poor and excluded in a supposedly unified country, the promised land of American history did not exist. These people, like hoboes, were caught between old and new economic and social values at the end of the national railroad journey. By 1929 this journey to national unity was ending, and an international journey of trade and travel, requiring ships and airplanes, was under way. Yet the cultural memories of the railroad journey still resonate with all of us, whether our ancestors were New England Puritans, slaves, Indians, Southerners, later immigrants, or poor farmers. It is in the nature of the American story that we have all been uprooted, that we have all lost our traditional homes, whether we stayed behind or migrated elsewhere, and that we all live in a nation of strangers.

No Service Without Profit

Of the total number of applications filed . . . 40 were for permission to abandon lines of road. The authorization issued during the year covered about 405 miles of new construction and 702 miles of abandonment.
—*Report of the Interstate Commerce Commission,* 1921[1]

THE TREMENDOUS POPULATION IMBALANCE that remained in the United States despite the settlement of rural areas had a direct impact on the nature and quality of railroad service. Despite the fact that railroad entrepreneurs had consciously worked to spread population along their Western routes in order to create towns and business for the railroads, the South and West remained predominantly rural well past the turn of the century. With few cities and low population, the South and West failed to yield the return on railroad investments that city travel did. Even in the North, the small towns, many of which had initiated railroad development in order to enrich themselves, remained small. Investors turned to brighter options as rural railroads ran up annual deficits. Beginning during World War I, small and inefficient railroads were scrapped rather than updated.

After a long period of optimism about future wealth, the citizens of small towns in 1900 had begun to realize that while they might expect local prosperity, they would never grow into national industrial giants like New York or Chicago. The industrial world had brushed against them as it went by. Many small towns had little more contact with the outside world in 1900 than Martha Elvira Stone had had in the 1840s, or Edward Everett Hale in the 1830s. Small-town life attracted one or two trains a day, consisting of a steam locomotive and a passenger car that could easily have been of Civil War vintage. Instead of a passenger car, some trains had one combination car that accommodated passengers, freight, and mail under one roof. Some railroads, which existed primarily to bring ore, coal, or stone out of the mines, had no passenger car but carried passengers just the same, and made a substantial income doing so.

But in small towns the passengers remained chiefly local people on local errands; strangers who came to town most frequently were still the traveling salesmen who drank at the local tavern and stayed at the local hotel. Gypsies and traveling circuses also brought images of the outside world to small communities, the latter coming by train, the former still in their wagons drawn by horses. In the hiatus before movie theaters and Model Ts brought new diversions, vaudeville troupes, which came either by wagon or by train, continued to bring singers, dancers, musicians, and actors to town. Travel for pleasure, desirable as it might be, was for those who could afford it. And for a poor family, the new vehicle purchased in the first decade of the twentieth century might well still be a horse and wagon.[2]

Trains, few and old as they were, served the needs of local people. But without much potential for growth, these towns did not serve the needs of the railroads. Profits were insufficient to purchase the desperately needed new engines; the expensive and large new passenger cars with vacuum brakes, vestibuled ends, and built-in heating and ventilating; the new, heavier steel rails; or the automatic signals now becoming mandatory on interstate railroads. Rather than bring small rural lines into conformity with legal requirements, owners simply wore them out. Some collapsed at the turn of the century, some did not finally break down until the 1930s or 1940s. But the pattern was clear from 1917 onward: small and inefficient operations with low ridership began to go out of business.

The consequences of losing rural railroad service varied from town to town. Long considered the indispensable element of a successful economy, the railroads did not, in fact, determine the fate of small-town economies. The national economy passed them by despite railroad service. Towns died when their local economies died. Towns thrived when the citizens had the means to sustain themselves, by means either archaic or modern.

In the far West, railroad service stopped simply because the towns along the route had stopped growing or were actually losing population. For more than a half-century miners, farmers, ranchers, and other speculators had optimistically worked to create the institutions that Easterners had created in the 1830s and Midwesterners had built in the 1840s and 1850s. Schools, churches, newspapers, and stores went up in short order wherever the land promised wealth. Even mills and small industries opened, indicating a bright future. Alongside them sprouted saloons, hotels, taverns, and brothels, all marks of a highly transient population that would need goods and services. But Western development began to reverse itself at the end of the nineteenth century.

Many of those who had gone west did so in hopes of striking it rich and then moving on. Even before the railroaders who built the Union Pacific put up their railroad towns, which were then dismantled and moved farther down the line, miners had planted small towns throughout Nevada, California, and in the other mountain states where gold, silver, copper, lead, or even coal might be hidden in the ground or sitting in the bed of a mountain stream. Mining towns with names like Gold Hill, Goldfield, Gold Point, and Eureka promised the beginnings of a great future for the West. These towns sat in the middle of the Nevada desert while the residents competed to find the gold or silver that would make them rich.[3]

Some did get rich, but many others did not. In either case, the fortunes of the town followed the fortunes of the mine, not of a few rich residents. When the wealth of the mine seemed exhausted, the residents grew impatient. Too poor to wait for new finds, they left to try their luck elsewhere. And the mining town with no mine died. Gold Hill, Goldfield, and Gold Point all became ghost towns, as did hundreds of other Western towns founded from the 1850s to the 1870s. By 1903 the few residents who tried to make Gold Hill a permanent home were left alone with their possessions. Goldfield experienced a gold strike as late as 1906, but by 1912 the mine began to play itself out. Gold Point, never highly populated, lost its citizenry to constant squabbling over legal issues.[4]

While many of these mining towns enjoyed railroad connections, train service did not by itself determine the success of the town. The Virginia and Truckee line, for example, served Gold Hill and Eureka as well as Virginia City, site of one of the largest silver mines in the country. This small railroad carried silver and gold out of the high mountains of Nevada and down to the main line of the Southern Pacific. But by 1910 both Virginia City and Gold Hill were virtually ghost towns; the mines had been played out. The Virginia and Truckee, which continued to operate until after World War II, brought oil down out of the mountains and express packages and mail to the last remaining citizens, and finally brought tourists up into the mountains to see a bit of Americana.[5]

In other mining towns the end of local railroad service tipped the balance fatally, taking the last source of revenue away from the town. But again, the disappearance of the railroad did not by itself spell the end of the town. Austin, Nevada, for example, founded in the 1860s, had become the county seat, complete with courthouse, lumber mill, and more than four hundred houses. Having obtained a railroad connection, the townspeople anticipated success. But with the end of the mine, the town began to die. In 1938 the railroad stopped serving Austin, marking the final blow to an already dying town.[6]

Sometimes the death of a Western town could be traced directly to discontinued railroad service, but railroads were not in fact the key to wealth that many had hoped. Many mining towns had no railroad connection at all and had sent their "finds" east to market by stagecoach or on horseback.[7] If mines or farms did not prosper, the rail-

road could not create wealth or civilization. Instead the railroads enriched their owners, who so often were Easterners with no stake in
continuing local service at a financial loss.

While the West became home for hundreds of ghost towns, thousands of other small towns in other regions of the country had
stopped growing by the turn of the century. While town populations
still rose gradually, towns no longer created new institutions and new
factories, and no longer attracted new investment capital.

In 1904, for example, Missouri published a profile of its cities and
towns which summarized their progress. St. Louis and St. Joseph had
achieved the status of industrial cities and were distinguishable as the
most populous cities in the state, with the most institutions, the most
industry, and the greatest success in finding national markets for their
products. But the smaller towns, which also boasted schools, newspapers, churches, factories, and transportation routes, still had very low
populations, many well under twenty thousand, and still derived most
of their wealth from farming. Despite numerous small industries that
produced ice, cutlery, wool, wagon wheel spokes, flour, lumber, har-
nesses, saddles, pumps, cigars, and baking powder, only the railroads
and the occasional typewriter or adding machine or canned goods
factory distinguished the Missouri economy of 1904 from a booming
eighteenth-century economy. Some towns also advertised their services, which included electric lights, waterworks, and sewers. But
many townspeople, in southern Missouri and elsewhere, continued to
live without electricity and sewer systems, or even indoor plumbing,
at least into the 1930s.[8]

While the railroads brought manufactures from the North and food
from the West, and helped Missourians sell their products in a national market, few still held any hope that Missouri would some day
equal New York or Massachusetts in prosperity—a hope that had inspired many townspeople as recently as twenty years earlier.

At the turn of the century even New England towns felt the pull of
populations and wealth away from home and toward the major urban
areas. New Englanders, especially the young, still left home to seek
greater opportunity, just as LaFayette Stone had left in the 1840s. But
they were more likely to go to school than to go west, and to seek jobs
in the professions or in the cities rather than on the railroad. Spring-

field and Northampton, founders of the Connecticut River Railroad, saw it taken over by the Boston and Maine Railroad in 1892. Numerous other small New England lines, founded by local interests, came under the control of the Boston and Maine's chief rival, the New York, New Haven and Hartford Railroad.

In northern New England, beyond the suburbs of New York and Boston, patterns of life remained predominantly local and, aside from the mill towns such as Manchester and Lowell, not at all wealthy. In Williamstown, Vermont, on a "rickety branch line" of the Vermont Central, the economy depended heavily on the granite mines of Barre to the north. The railroad connected these two towns and provided Williamstown its living. Granite came out of Barre partly by rail and partly by horse and wagon. Yet for one family of Scottish immigrants, the cost of a train trip to Barre, less than ten miles away, was prohibitive. When the mines shut down, the father traveled to Manchester, site of the Amoskeag Mills, to find work. As for the amenities back home, he wrote, "nobody had hot and cold running water then, except President McKinley, Queen Victoria, and J. P. Morgan, and I wasn't sure even about them. . . . We didn't see many automobiles, and the few we did see were foolish and transitory models, whereas the Central Vermont Railroad operated with a good deal of certainty." Of the two locomotives that operated the railroad, one burned wood and dated from the mid-nineteenth century; the other, somewhat newer, burned coal. In 1919 the Barre Quarries shut down permanently, and the Williamstown branch line closed shortly thereafter.[9]

Even in Michigan, on a main route from New York and Detroit to Chicago, time seemed to run out on the small towns after the turn of the century, and the railroads followed them down. Hartford, Michigan, had a more substantial economy then Williamstown, Vermont; still, the economy of the town centered on two canning factories and the two or three trains that passed daily in each direction, and stopped on request. Typically, travelers did not venture far out of town, and seldom out of state. In either event they boarded trains that proceeded at a rate of about fifteen miles per hour, and they changed trains frequently on longer trips. A memoir written about travel out of Hartford at the turn of the century echoed Edward Everett Hale's memoir of Boston in the 1830s: "I do not think my father had ever been outside the State of Michigan, except for one trip to Chicago."[10]

The son's description of a trip within the state of Michigan made a joke of the legal effort to provide continuous travel without train changes. It offers insight into the reasons why passengers came to prefer cars to trains.

> The first time we went by train. We left Hartford about 9 A.M. on the Fruit Belt Railroad, which bore us to Kalamazoo. There we changed depots and took the Michigan Central to Albion. Then we changed to another railroad that took us to Homer, where we made the final change to the Air Line Railroad that landed us at our destination, Union City, some sixty miles from home, at 8 P.M.

While the car journey taken later had its mishaps, it was mercifully short and easy compared to the train.

> The second time we went to visit . . . we traveled in our new Model T Ford. My father was determined that we should get to Union City before nightfall, so all preparations were made the day before, and we got started before dawn the next morning. The road to Paw Paw was known to my father, but beyond there he had to inquire what the best route was. We got lost between Lawton and Schoolcraft, and my folks got into an argument about where the farm was, along the road where they had spent the night when they had driven the distance in the horse and buggy. Between Schoolcraft and Vicksburg we got mired in the black prairie mud and a farmer had to be persuaded to pull us out. We made frequent stops to put water in the radiator; and in Vicksburg, my father, to ease the tension, resorted to a saloon and had a glass of beer. Even with all these stops we arrived at Union City before noon.[11]

The Fruit Belt Railroad, which came through Hartford, used steam engines and "coaches which I think had been bought from other railroads secondhand, [and] were of great antiquity." Various speculators tried to update it or turn it into an electric interurban train, which would be lighter and cheaper to run, but nothing came out of these efforts. A town development association tried and failed to attract new industry, and eventually one of the canning factories went bank-

THE RISE AND DECLINE OF RAILROAD MILEAGE IN THE
UNITED STATES, 1890–1929

Year	No. of Operating Railroads	Miles of Track Constructed	Abandoned	Total Railroad Mileage
1890	1,013	–	–	163,597
1891	991	–	–	168,403
1892	1,002	–	–	171,564
1893	1,034	–	–	176,461
1894	1,043	–	–	178,709
1895	1,104	–	–	180,657
1896	1,111	–	–	182,777
1897	1,158	–	–	184,428
1898	1,192	–	–	186,396
1899	1,206	–	–	189,295
1900	1,224	–	–	193,346
1901	1,213	–	–	197,237
1902	1,219	–	–	202,472
1903	1,281	–	–	207,977
1904	1,314	–	–	213,904
1905	1,380	–	–	218,101
1906	1,491	–	–	224,363
1907	1,564	–	–	229,951
1908	1,323	–	–	233,468
1909	1,316	–	–	236,834
1910	1,306	–	–	240,293
1911	1,312	–	–	243,979
1912	1,298	–	–	246,777
1913	1,296	–	–	249,777
1914	1,297	–	–	252,105
1915	1,260	–	–	253,789
1916	1,216	–	–	254,251
1917	1,168	–	–	253,626
1918	1,131	–	–	253,529
1919	1,111	–	–	253,152
1920	1,085	–	–	252,845
1921	1,058	331	687	251,176
1922	1,041	318	1,188	250,413
1923	1,023	441	537	250,222
1924	995	635	617	250,156
1925	947	595	753	249,398
1926	929	881	892	249,138
1927	880	819	797	249,131
1928	849	946	710	249,309
1929	809	671	782	249,433

rupt. It became evident that little could be done about the fact that "the community was dead on its feet."[12]

Surrounding small towns did little better, similarly unable to attract new investors or new industry.

> Watervliet had its paper mill, but even that was shut down for many years. Hartford's canning factories and the leaf factory, like the small plants in other villages, were small-scale processors of locally produced raw materials and provided only seasonal employment. I think it may be said that small towns like Hartford reached the nadir of their fortunes in the years just before World War I. Back in the earlier times they had been bustling places. Stores, elevators, grist mills, sawmills, and other facilities were being established to serve the growing community. The coming of the railroads had brought new excitement and had spelled greater progress. Social and cultural organizations were being formed. In the surrounding area, there was a good deal of timber still to be cut, providing the raw materials for sawmills, a stave factory, and a plant to make sashes, doors, and blinds. But by 1910, this era of growth had become history. There was little timber left. The town had grown to a size adequate to meet the commercial and other needs of the rural community, and there it had stopped.[13]

What had happened to America's small towns? Why had they stopped growing and competing with each other, and instead accepted a minute share of national markets? The answer may be found by drawing together the strands of their experience over a hundred years. Step by step, towns that had founded railroads lost control of them, as railroads consolidated in trunk lines and then into enormous national systems. This took the profits derived from transportation itself out of the hands of the townspeople served by the railroads. Purchases of railroad stock by individuals returned very little of the dividend money to the body politic. While railroad magnates gave money away in a spirit of philanthropy, they chose their charities nationwide, not just from among the towns lining their railroads. They founded institutions such as colleges and libraries—but again, when and where they chose to found them. In other words, railroad magnates, in company with such business millionaires as Rockefeller and

Carnegie, took control of the founding of institutions and of the pattern of national growth. Small towns, lacking the profits they anticipated from the coming of the railroad, could not fund the continued growth of institutions or markets that could compete on the national level. As the control of wealth became increasingly centralized, so did the power to control the railroad service, and so did the power to profit from national trade. Population followed wealth to the cities, and small towns stagnated as they lost control over their own investments. The tourist trade was one of the few avenues to wealth for rural areas. The major cities largely invested and manipulated the wealth of the nation.

This apparently permanent imbalance of population and wealth had a direct impact on railroad services. Designed to move groups en masse, the passenger train became something of an anachronism in the vast stretches of unpopulated land in the West and South. The two-car train that took one or two daily trips down a fifty- or hundred-mile track seemed a sad counterpoint to the Pullmans and limiteds that dashed at fifty miles per hour from city to city without stopping in the small towns at all. Railroads began to lose money on small rural routes. Faced with this reversal in their long-term plan to settle the country and create prosperous new communities wherever they laid track, the railroads began to abandon the least profitable rural routes.

Abandoning service was not new to railroads. Some states had sought to regulate this phenomenon early on; eventually it became a concern of all state railroad commissions. For example, the Connecticut state legislature passed a law which stated that

> No railroad company shall abandon any station on its road, in the State, after the same has been established for twelve months, except by the approval of the Railroad Commissioners, given after a public hearing held at such station notice of which shall be posted conspicuously in said station, for one month previous to the hearing.

Connecticut law also gave townspeople the option of petitioning to reopen stations. Upon petition of thirty town property owners to the railroad commission, and the holding of a hearing in the station house, service could be restored. After the creation of the Interstate

Commerce Commission in 1887, railroads engaging in interstate commerce had to seek the approval of that commission before eliminating train service.[14]

The financial quagmire of the railroads which led to extensive abandonment developed over a long period of time. Since 1837, business panics had pushed the poorer railroad lines into bankruptcy or into the control of larger and more prosperous lines. This pattern repeated itself in the 1850s, the 1870s, and the 1890s, encouraging the process of railroad consolidation that characterized the entire service. But before the twentieth century the demand for expansion had more than balanced such losses so that from a purely statistical point of view, the track mileage of the entire country continued to increase. While construction of new lines continued into the 1920s, the miles of abandoned track for the first time exceeded the miles constructed.[15]

Other changes set the experience of the 1920s apart from nineteenth-century track abandonments. By 1920 the Interstate Commerce Commission had taken sufficient notice of the increasing number of abandoned lines that they began to keep a public record of the name and location of each line abandoned as well as the exact number of miles going out of service. And this time the abandoned stretches of track were not returned to service. The railroad companies, which in the past had repeatedly reorganized and reopened bankrupt lines, succeeded less and less often in the 1920s and thereafter.[16] It appears that the financial backing needed to restart bankrupt railroads was not there.

Virtually all the railroads that went out of business in the 1920s were small rural roads or branch lines. In the countryside it appears that the financial crisis of 1893 never entirely resolved itself; small, antiquated lines struggled on for another twenty years or so, and then collapsed. Even rural routes that had been taken over by major railroad systems began to fold during this period. The Atchison, Topeka and Sante Fe, one of the largest systems in the country, abandoned service on more than twenty-five miles of rural line in Arizona, California, and Oklahoma as early as 1921. The Boston and Maine, which had so recently taken over the Connecticut River Railroad and many other small New England lines, the same year dropped about thirteen miles of service in New Hampshire, in 1924 about four miles of service in Maine, and in 1925 about twenty miles of service in New Hampshire and Massachusetts. The Baltimore and Ohio abandoned mileage in Ohio and Indiana between 1921 and 1925. In 1926 the Atchison, Topeka and Santa Fe dropped another thirteen miles of service in Arizona, and the Boston and Maine dropped more than fifty miles of service in Massachusetts, New Hampshire, and Maine. Michigan lost more than four hundred miles of railroad through ICC certificates of abandonment from 1921 to 1929. New Hampshire lost only thirty-four miles this way. In general the Northeast lost the least mileage; the rural Midwest, South, and West lost the most.[17]

Of the many rural short lines that were abandoned during the same decade, many were losing money or had already gone into bankruptcy. Quite a few had tried to reorganize at least once before seeking permission to abandon their track. Of the seventeen railroads granted a certificate of abandonment by the ICC in 1923, seven operated with a deficit or were in receivership. Nine had been incorporated since 1893, usually to take over the operations of a defunct line.[18]

The pattern of operations on these country lines reflects the personal testimony of contemporary residents in small towns along the track. They operated with very little rolling stock. The Central West Virginia and Southern Railroad, for example, abandoned in 1929, had only five passenger cars. The Madison Southern Railway, operating in Florida, had only one passenger car, and its passenger revenues for 1919 totaled $438. The Kentwood and Eastern Railway in Louisiana had no passenger car but made a substantial amount of money each year from passenger revenues.[19]

Like the trains in Williamstown and Hartford, only two or so trains passed each way daily. The Central West Virginia and Southern went up and back the length of its track twice each day. The Denison, Bonham and New Orleans of Texas had one mixed train scheduled each day. The Fairchild and North-Eastern Railway Company in Wisconsin sent one train the length of the road each day. Substantial portions of each line were abandoned in 1929.[20]

While the railroads had settled the West, patterns of investment had succeeded in centralizing the economy. When the new towns throughout the Midwest, West, and South could no longer attract capital or industry, the towns stopped growing. The railroads, finding their profits drying up in direct consequence, frequently continued their rural services and tried to attract new capital to improve them. But in the end abandonment was the only means left to avoid further losses, and rural rail services throughout the country, but particularly in the West and South, dwindled.

Clearly the power of railroads to generate wealth proved to have distinct limits. Railroads might create towns, but the ultimate prosperity of towns still depended in great part on geography, weather, and the type of wealth that supported the town. The American people had made parts of the desert bloom, but the sources of wealth in Western towns, frequently in mines, were too short term and unreliable to support a substantial population over time. More towns survived in the North and South, partly because they were near major cities where residents could find work. But no one could doubt that when the trains no longer led to a possible job or source of wealth, the population had followed wealth first, the trains only secondarily. What finally brought them back to rural America was its great beauty, its absence of crowds, and its associations with American history, intertwined with a million strands of personal biography. Many Americans could not afford to live in the country, but they could not turn their backs on it.

Looking Backward

The grave was dug through solid marble, but the marble stone came from Vermont. It was in a pine wilderness, but the pine coffin came from Cincinnati. An iron mountain overshadowed it, but the coffin nails and the screws and the shovel came from Pittsburgh. With hard wood and metal abounding, the corpse was hauled on a wagon from South Bend, Indiana. A hickory grove grew nearby, but the pick and shovel handles came from New York. The cotton shirt on the dead man came from Cincinnati, the coat and breeches from Chicago, the shoes from Boston. . . . And as the poor fellow was lowered to his rest, on coffin bands from Lowell, he carried nothing into the next world as a remainder of his home in this, save the halted blood in his veins, the chilled marrow in his bones, and the echo of the dull clods that fell on his coffin lid.

> —Henry W. Grady in the *Atlanta Constitution*, 1889[1]

BY 1900 the social order that had emerged in the United States was overwhelmingly based on the principle of national commercial exchange. Older social forms, reflecting the social contract of an agricultural society, still existed but were crowded out by commercial considerations. Exchange of goods and people, ideas and cultures all took place in the context of railroad transport, though by 1929 automobiles and trucks had begun to displace trains. Exchange meant geographical mobility for most people engaged in the industrial nation: laborers and businessmen commuted and

347

traveled in search of economic opportunity; professionals maintained
affiliations in national societies through meetings and exchanges of
information. Politicians and other leaders relied on the trains to
carry on a national dialogue with the public. Minorities and the poor,
especially those in rural areas, saw the railroad culturally and literally
as their last best chance to exchange defeat for a better life
elsewhere. In song, story, and even in popular religion, the idea of
taking the railroad to a better life became entwined with the
American dream of self-betterment.

With exchange as the society's guiding principle, the railroads held
a prominent position in defining the social order, a position
threatened only by the introduction of an even better system of
transportation. Therefore as time passed the products of industry
and the experiences of the society at large became increasingly
eclectic. Fewer people lived in the states where they had been born;
fewer ate food or wore clothes produced locally. And fewer lived
without exposure to the diversity of knowledge and culture that
railroads and ships were offering even the poorest and most
immobile Americans. Over time, however, these exchanges proved
unequal in nature. While the West proved wealthy in gold, and the
South recovered some of its potential in agriculture and
manufacturing, Northern urban interests clearly dominated not only
the terms of exchange but the railroads themselves.

Centralized control of the economy and the railroads by Northern
urban interests had a number of implications for the new social
order. The original diversity of railroad services based on local
economic and social interests was all but lost to an overall theory
that centralized control, efficiency, and speed would characterize a
healthy national economy. In the industrial lexicon, *local* became the
equivalent of *backward.* And as the wealth of small towns and rural
America withered, railroads furthered the process by eliminating
service on rural short lines which produced the lowest ridership and
therefore the least profit.

With the shrinking of local railroad services, beginning in the
1920s, the local legal structure that had been developed to define
relations between railroad companies, other institutions, and
passengers affected ever fewer people. The domination of interstate

trade and interstate finances dictated the need for federal regulation. But such regulation was weak and slow in coming. The principle of exchange overrode even the federal government's concerns that the social contract was abrogated by the commercial practices of railroads.

With an eye to profit, the railroads calculated their earnings in terms of mass populations rather than local needs, a decision that had a profound effect on the social structure of the nation. Indeed, the major railroad companies themselves began to view with alarm the decline in ridership over large sections of rural America. They determined to sell rural America once more, not as a place to live this time, but as a place to vacation and recapture the beauties of the countryside and the glories of history. But for those who made their home in rural America, images of the railroad evoked not an engine of prosperity but a lonesome whistle.

Notes

1. E PLURIBUS UNUM

1. Henry Adams, *The United States in 1800* (Ithaca, N.Y., reprinted 1974), p. 2.

2. Francis J. Grund, *The Americans in Their Moral, Social, and Political Relations* (Boston, 1837), p. 303.

3. See John F. Kasson, *Civilizing the Machine: Technology and Republican Values in America, 1776–1900* (New York, 1986), pp. 33–36; Arthur T. Hadley, *Railroad Transportation: Its History and Its Laws* (New York, 1890), pp. 26–27.

4. A description of the early history of steamboating on the Mississippi River may be found in Mary Helen Dohan, *Mr. Roosevelt's Steamboat: The First Steamboat to Travel the Mississippi* (New York, 1981). A firsthand account of an immigrant family ascending the river by steamboat in 1831 may be found in Rebecca and Edward Burlend, *A True Picture of Emigration,* edited by Milo M. Quaife (New York, 1968).

5. Richard B. Morris, ed., *Encyclopedia of American History* (New York, 1965), p. 442.

6. CIS Congressional Masterfile 1789–1969. Descriptions of both the Quincy Granite Railroad and the Mauch Chunk Railroad may be found in Charles Frederick Carter, *When Railroads Were New* (New York, 1926), pp. 13–14. Another, more recent book which thoroughly discusses the Mauch Chunk Railroad from the standpoint of social history is John F. Sears, *Sacred Places: American Tourist Attractions in the Nineteenth Century* (New York, 1989).

7. Specific information on the interaction between state governments and private railroad companies may be found in a number of sources. For the state of New York, see *Hunt's Merchants' Magazine* 10 (1844), 476–477; 12 (1845), 381, 387; 13 (1845), 385; 15 (1846), 546–551; 16 (1847), 324; 20 (1849), 651–655; 21 (1849),

163–180. For the state of Massachusetts, see *Merchants' Magazine* 8 (1843), 187; 11 (1844), 184; 14 (1846), 34–35; 15 (1846), 234–236; 16 (1847), 324. For the state of Michigan, see Willis Dunbar, *Kalamazoo and How it Grew . . . and Grew . . .* (Kalamazoo, Mich.,1969), pp. 36–37, 46–47; and *Merchants' Magazine* 10 (1844), 478; 12 (1845), 386–387. For Pennsylvania, see *Merchants' Magazine* 7 (1842), 363; 14 (1845), 129; and *Compilation of the Laws of Pennsylvania, Relative to the Internal Improvements: Together with the Canal and Railway Regulations as Established by the Board of Canal Commissioners* (Harrisburg, Pa., 1840). For material on the South Carolina railroads, see Carter, *When Railroads Were New*. See also Private Acts for all these states as well as Connecticut and Rhode Island. The full text of most railroad charters appears in these volumes.

8. Accounts of the internal improvements movement include Benjamin Horace Hibbard, *A History of the Public Land Policies* (Madison, Wisc., 1965), pp. 136–143; see also John F. Stover, *American Railroads* (Chicago, 1976), pp. 1–10, for the connection between internal improvements and the coming of the railroads. Much information on charter limitations for railroads may be found in *Merchants' Magazine* 12 (1845), 387, 481; 14 (1846), 34–35; 15 (1846), 236, 546–551; 18 (1848), 63, 547; 20 (1849), 551, 651–655; 21 (1849), 163–180.

9. See John A. Garraty, ed., *Quarrels That Shaped the Constitution* (New York, 1975), for brief and lucid accounts of the most significant legal cases that freed private enterprise from state control: *Gibbons vs. Ogden*, the *Charles River Bridge* case, and the *Dartmouth College* case. See note 3 above for information regarding the general acts of incorporation; see Alfred D. Chandler, *The Visible Hand: The Managerial Revolution in American Business* (Cambridge, Mass., 1977), p. 28, for his estimate of when Adam Smith's "invisible hand" of the marketplace closely paralleled the American experience; and see Lewis H. Haney, *A Congressional History of Railways in the United States*, 2 vols. (Madison, Wisc., 1908), for a comprehensive account of federal railroad laws and regulations.

10. See notes 7 and 8 above.

11. *Ibid.*

12. See Garraty, *Quarrels That Shaped the Constitution*, pp. 15–29.

13. See *Laws of Pennsylvania*, also notes 7 and 8 above.

14. 1840, *Laws of Pennsylvania*, pp. 115–116; *Canal and Railway Regulations*, p. 8. *Laws of Pennsylvania*, pp. 119, 212, 246–247; *Canal and Railway Regulations*, pp. 34, 41, 49–52, 55–60.

15. *Canal and Railway Regulations*, pp. 40–41, 49–51.

16. *Ibid.*, p. 42.

17. *Ibid.*, pp. 57–58.

18. *Ibid.*, pp. 55–60.

19. *Merchants' Magazine* 20 (1849), 551, 651–655; 21 (1849), 163–180.

20. *Merchants' Magazine* 10 (1844), 476–477.

21. See note 3 above. See also Carter, *When Railroads Were New*, pp. 1–110.

22. Carter, *When Railroads Were New*, pp. 75–110.

23. See the *Charles River Bridge* case in Garraty, *Quarrels That Shaped the Constitution*, and *Merchants' Magazine*, 21 (1849), 166, and following. *Merchants' Mag-*

azine, 15 (1846), 236. See note 10, above; and see *Merchants' Magazine* 21 (1849), 164.

24. See note 8 above.

25. Massachusetts, *Resolves*, c. 59 (1827).

26. Dunbar, *Kalamazoo*, p. 47.

27. Robert J. Casey and W. A. S. Douglas, *Pioneer Railroad: The Story of the Chicago and North Western System* (New York, 1948), pp. 31–32, 72–75. Note that while the Galena was chartered in 1836, much of it was not built until the 1850s due to financial difficulties.

28. *Merchants' Magazine* 5 (1841), 469–470, indicates that the Utica and Schenectady Railroad maintained accident statistics at least as early as 1836. This article was part of a public dialogue over railroad safety which emerged in the 1840s.

29. Connecticut, *Private Acts* (1789–1836), 993. Connecticut, *Public Acts* (1836–1850), 32–40, 66.

30. *Ibid.*, pp. 59, 17–18.

2. THE LAY OF THE LAND

1. Norm Cohen, *Long Steel Rail: The Railroad in American Folksong* (Urbana, Ill., 1981), p. 43.

2. On rendering geography and seasons irrelevant by using railroads, see *Merchants' Magazine* 12 (1845), 387; 13 (1845), 181; 15 (1846), 456; Carter, *When Railroads Were New*, pp. 126–136; James A. Ward, *Railroads and the Character of America, 1820–1887* (Knoxville, Tenn., 1986), pp. 37–38, 96–97.

3. An account of early steamboat service may be found in Seymour Dunbar, *A History of Travel in America* (New York, 1937), pp. 392–414. A good account of steamboat service during the 1840s may be found in Albert C. Koch, *Journey Through a Part of the United States in the Years 1884–1846* (Carbondale, Ill., 1972), pp. 61–66, 77–85. An account of steamboating published in 1937 and recently republished is William J. Peterson, *Steamboating on the Upper Mississippi* (New York, 1995).

4. *Ibid.*

5. On the speed and cost of canal boat travel, see Dunbar, *History of Travel*, pp. 847–871, 1109–1124; and Slason Thompson, *A Short History of American Railways: Covering Ten Decades* (New York, 1925), p. 14. According to Thompson, the price of a trip the length of the 352-mile Erie Canal was about $2.50, or 1.4 cents per mile. But Harold U. Faulkner, in *American Economic History*, 6th ed. (New York, 1949), p. 279, writes that the canal was 363 miles long, and Koch, *Journey*, p. 33, writes that the canal trip cost $7.75 in 1844. Reports on steamboat fares vary. Dunbar writes that the cost of the steamboat from Wilmington, North Carolina, to Charleston, South Carolina, was $6 for a 175-mile trip. But he also indicates that the cost to a migrant of a steamboat trip up the Hudson from New York City to Albany was only 50 cents. In general, steamboat fares were higher than that. The railroad also cost considerably more than the poorest travelers could afford. Wrote Koch of the trip from Albany to Lake Erie: ". . . the train with subsistence cost about $13.50. . . ." In general, railroad

journeys of the 1840s cost between two and four cents a mile in the Northeast and closer to six cents a mile in the South. See *Merchants' Magazine* 4 (1841), 284; and 19 (1848), 332–337. See also Carter, *When Railroads Were New,* pp. 126–136.

6. Carter, *When Railroads Were New,* pp. 33–74.

7. On Baltimore and Ohio motive power, see *ibid.,* pp. 33–74. On the Baltimore and Ohio's expansion into a trunk line, see *Poor's Manual of Railroads, 1876,* p. 430. A good basic history of the line is John F. Stover, *History of the Baltimore and Ohio Railroad* (West Lafayette, Ind., 1995, first published in 1987).

8. Carter, *When Railroads Were New,* p. 22; and *Poor's Manual, 1876,* p. 430.

9. Carter, *When Railroads Were New,* pp. 19–22.

10. *Ibid.,* pp. 24–25, 44–45; and B. A. Botkin and Alvin F. Harlow, eds., *A Treasury of Railroad Folklore: The Stories, Tall Tales, Traditions, Ballads and Songs of the American Railroad Man* (New York, 1953), pp. 72–74. John H. White, Jr., *The American Railroad Passenger Car* (Baltimore, 1978), p. 540.

11. On the dangers of railroad engines, see Dunbar, *History of Travel,* pp. 1008–1035; and Carter, *When Railroads Were New,* pp. 1–32. On brakes, see White, *Railroad Passenger Car,* p. 7.

12. On logistical problems associated with early railroading, see Carter, *When Railroads Were New,* pp. 2–110; and Dunbar, *History of Travel,* pp. 872–975.

13. Accounts of bridge disasters may be found in Robert C. Reed, *Train Wrecks: A Pictorial History of Accidents on the Main Line* (New York, 1968), pp. 85–102. Accounts of railroad travel in heavy snow may be found in Botkin and Harlow, *Treasury of Railroad Folklore,* pp. 254–255, 267–269. Other weather-related problems may be found in Eugene Alvarez, "Travel on Antebellum Southern Railroads" (Ph.D. dissertation, University of Georgia, 1966), pp. 85–89. On the interest in railroads among town merchants, see Sarah Gordon, "The Connecticut River Railroad: Its Evolution in the Connecticut Valley" (unpublished manuscript, 1970). For a more extensive account, see Edward Chase Kirkland, *Men, Cities and Transportation: A Study in New England History, 1820–1900,* 2 vols. (Cambridge, Mass., 1948), I, 92–266. For a passenger's account of the railroad ride and the view in the most positive terms, see "Narrative of an Excursion on the Baltimore & Ohio Railroad," in H. Roger Grant, ed., *We Took the Train* (DeKalb, Ill., 1990), pp. 6–31. Passenger traffic on American railroads increased dramatically during the 1830s and 1840s; see, for example, *Merchants' Magazine* 2 (1840), 347–348; 4 (1841), 567; 6 (1842), 94.

14. On the use of stone ballast, see Dunbar, *History of Travel,* pp. 927, 946.

15. On changes in the locomotive, see John H. White, Jr., *A History of the American Locomotive: Its Development, 1830–1880* (New York, 1979, first published in 1968). See also Dunbar, *History of Travel,* pp. 872–1035. On the evolution of the passenger car, see White, *Railroad Passenger Car,* pp. xiii, 3–21; a diagram in the introduction to this book illustrates the size of railroad cars in each decade from the 1830s to 1940. Carter, *When Railroads Were New,* pp. 52–53, 163, 170–171.

16. Carter, *When Railroads Were New,* p. 164, describes the circumstances under which conductors had to collect tickets before the center aisle car was developed. So does Edward Everett Hale in *A New England Boyhood* (Boston, 1898), pp. 194–195.

Conductors clung to the outside of the cars and reached through the window or door to take tickets. They then clambered along the side of the train on steps and handles to the next car. English conductors collected tickets in the station as passengers entered or left the train. This system is mentioned in American Association of Passenger Traffic Officers, *Proceedings*, April 16–17, 1856, p. 13. For the very limited available information on railroad stations in antebellum America, see Carroll L. V. Meeks, *The Railroad Station: An Architectural History* (New Haven, Conn., 1956), pp. 26–27, 48–55, 69–76; Lawrence Grow, comp., *Waiting for the 5:05: Terminal, Station and Depot in America* (New York, 1977), pp. 10–15, 22–35, 38–41, 44–48; Edwin P. Alexander, *Down at the Depot: American Railroad Stations from 1831 to 1920* (New York, 1970), pp. 9–10. Alexander's book also has information on this early period scattered throughout the text. Jumping on and off the train was a common practice in the country and continued later in the century when trains moved faster and the practice was more dangerous. On early mention of this practice, see Eugene Alvarez, *Travel on Antebellum Southern Railroads* (Ph.D. dissertation, University of Georgia, 1966), pp. 111, 176. The author has not had access to the published edition of this book. See also Isaac F. Redfield, *A Practical Treatise Upon the Law of Railways* (Boston, 1858), for the legal status of those jumping on and off moving cars.

17. White, *Railroad Passenger Car,* pp. 16, 50–72.

18. On mechanical improvements in cars during the 1830s, see Carter, *When Railroads Were New,* pp. 2–110; and White, *Railroad Passenger Car,* pp. 3–115. For a detailed description of the link-and-pin design, see *ibid.,* p. 560.

19. See Carter, *When Railroads Were New,* pp. 127–128. Sears, *Sacred Places,* pp. 192–195.

20. On English trials, see E. L. Cornwell, *History of Railways* (Secaucus, N.J., 1976), p. 23. On American trials with uphill rails, see Carter, *When Railroads Were New,* pp. 127–128. On railroads in the Rockies, see, for example, Bill Fisher, *30 Years Over Donner: Railroading "Family-style" Over Southern Pacific's Donner Pass, Through the Eyes of a Company Signal Maintainer* (Glendale, Calif., 1990), pp. 65–69.

21. On early bridges, see, for example, *Laws of Pennsylvania, Canal and Railway Regulation,* p. 51. On accidents, see, for example, Reed, *Train Wrecks,* pp. 85–102.

22. In connection with fire and other hazards to bridges, it is instructive to look at the safety precautions required by law. See, for example, *Canals and Railway Regulations,* pp. 49–51.

23. In *Canal and Railway Regulations,* p. 53, Section 102 reads, "Every person who shall carry, put or kindle, or cause to be carried, put or kindled, any fire under or upon a wooden bridge or viaduct, forming part of the railway, or within one hundred feet of the same, shall, for every such offence, forfeit and pay the sum of twenty-five dollars."

24. On the Howe Truss bridge at Springfield, see *Connecticut Courant,* July 9, 1841, p. 2. On bridge accidents, see Reed, *Train Wrecks,* pp. 85–102.

25. On stopping for fuel and water, see, for example, Alvarez, *Travel on Antebellum Southern Railroads,* p. 44. See also Dunbar, *History of Travel,* pp. 1030–1031.

Stories of railroad crews struggling with storms, mountains, and bridges abound, but a good small selection about railroads versus the elements may be found in Botkin and Harlow, *Treasury of Railroad Folklore,* pp. 19–63.

26. On evolving train technology, see, for example, White, *Railroad Passenger Car,* pp. 69–79.

27. *Ibid.,* p. 540.

28. Beginning in the 1830s, every Northern state and many Southern states chartered railroads. This dramatic process was chronicled by *Poor's Manual of Railroads, 1876,* which frequently traces the history of charters, incorporations, mergers, and bankruptcies back to the beginnings of each railroad company.

29. The pre–Civil War careers of Jefferson Davis, Stephen A. Douglas, and Abraham Lincoln are relevant to this conflict. For Jefferson Davis's opposition to the railroads, see George E. Turner, *Victory Rode the Rails: The Strategic Place of the Railroads in the Civil War* (Lincoln, Nebr., 1992), pp. 17, 70, 71; for Douglas's and Lincoln's promotion of railroad expansion into the West, see, in particular, Carl Sandburg, *Abraham Lincoln: The Prairie Years and the War Years,* one-volume ed. (New York, 1954), pp. 50–52, 114, 116–117, 122–125.

30. In 1850 the United States had 9,021 miles of railroad track; by 1860 the number was 30,626 miles. These figures may be found in U.S. Bureau of the Census, *Historical Statistics of the United States, Colonial Times to 1957* (Washington, D.C., 1960), p. 427.

3. LEAVING HOME FOR THE WEST

1. Stephe Smith, "Fogeyville and the Branch," in *Romance and Humor of the Rail* (New York, 1873), pp. 11–12.

2. See note 13, Chapter 2.

3. Hale, *New England Boyhood,* pp. 171–195, discusses the local nature of even Boston life in the 1830s; Thomas Cochran, *Frontiers of Change* (New York, 1983), pp. 17–22, describes the local nature of most trade within the United States during the same period. For a description of the development of middlemen in American business before the Civil War, see *ibid.,* pp. 116–117; and Chandler, *Visible Hand,* pp. 25–27. These men had to travel continually between the sources of their products and their markets.

4. This point of view is articulated clearly in Joseph LaFayette Stone to Martha Elvira Stone, June 17, 1844; September 2, 1844; October 21, 1844. (Hereafter JLS and MES.) Cochran, *Frontiers of Change,* p. 87, is one of many sources that describe the erosion of New England soil as a cause of farming failures.

5. Dunbar, *History of Travel,* pp. 341–414.

6. Koch, *Journey,* pp. 59, 62.

7. Good descriptions of Cincinnati's booming economy before the Civil War may be found in Charles H. Ambler, *A History of Transportation in the Ohio Valley* (Glendale, Calif., 1932), and in William Chambers, *Things as They Are in America*

(London and Edinburgh, 1857), pp. 142–184. See also *Merchants' Magazine* 14 (1846), 384.

8. For Ohio, see Chambers, *Things as They Are*, pp. 142–170; for Michigan, see Dunbar, *Kalamazoo*, pp. 36–37; for Illinois, see Casey and Douglas, *Pioneer Railroad*, pp. 27–37; and for Kentucky and Tennessee, see John Leeds Kerr, *The Louisville & Nashville: An Outline History* (New York, 1933), pp. 2–17. See Ambler, *Transportation in the Ohio Valley*, pp. 185–205; and Eugene Holloway Roseboom and Francis Phelps Weisenburger, *A History of Ohio* (New York, 1934), pp. 320–328.

9. See Dunbar, *Kalamazoo*, pp. 36–37.

10. *Ibid.*, p. 47. See Casey and Douglas, *Pioneer Railroad*, pp. 57–67.

11. Kerr, *Louisville & Nashville*, pp. 1–12.

12. See Dunbar, *Kalamazoo*, pp. 36–37, 45–47, 87.

13. On the effort to keep railroads from crossing state lines, see Kerr, *Louisville & Nashville*, p. 3. On plans to connect Northern and Southern towns, see *Merchants' Magazine* 13 (1845), 459; 19 (1848), 579–585.

14. JLS to MES, May 3, 1840: January 1, 1844; September 2, 1844. JLS to MES, June 17, 1844. JLS to MES, January 30, 1847.

15. MES to JLS, April 22, 1844; August 4, 1845; October 28, 1855. MES to JLS, November 15, 1863; February 21, 1864; JLS to MES, July 13, 1846. JLS to MES, October 27, 1863. See also Anthony Trollope, *North America* (London, reprinted 1992), p. 86.

16. JLS to MES, April 2, 1844.

17. Stewart H. Holbrook, *The Story of American Railroads* (New York, 1957), pp. 101–107.

18. *Ibid.*, pp. 104–107.

19. *Ibid.*, p. 109.

20. MES to JLS, April 9, 1854.

21. Marilyn I. Holt, *The Orphan Trains* (Lincoln, Nebr.), pp. 41–48.

4. THE HOMETOWNS LEFT BEHIND

1. MES to JLS, October 25, 1863.

2. Hale, *New England Boyhood*, pp. 2–3.

3. *Ibid.*, p. 181. Stover, *American Railroads*, p. 9, balances this personal perspective somewhat. He writes that in 1826 more than two hundred stagecoaches traveled in and out of Boston each day. Hale may be saying that the local people were not the ones who were traveling in and out of town. Hale, *New England Boyhood*, pp. 115–124, 175–176, 181–182, 193.

4. Hale, *New England Boyhood*, pp. 8–10, 176–177. See also *History of the Old Colony Railroad* (Boston, 1893), p. 29.

5. Hale, *New England Boyhood*, pp. 173, 186.

6. On the local nature of Boston life, see *ibid.*, pp. 11–54.

7. See, for example, MES to JLS, April 22, 1844; July 7, 1844; March 1, 1845.

See also MES to JLS, November 12, 1846; March 19, 1848; October 27, 1850; January 1, 1851.

8. MES to JLS, September 26, 1844; May 29, 1845; December 7, 1845; April 16, 1847. MES to JLS, December 8, 1844; July 12, 1846; June 18, 1848.

9. Hale, *New England Boyhood,* pp. 86–87.

10. *Ibid.,* pp. 3–4, 76–77, 86–87; *Old Colony,* pp. 10, 29.

11. Hale, *New England Boyhood,* p. 194.

12. *Ibid.,* pp. 174–175, 186. *Old Colony,* p. 30. Alden Hatch, *American Express: A Century of Service* (Garden City, N.Y., 1950), pp. 27–29; and Oscar Osburn Winther, *The Transportation Frontier: The Trans-Mississippi West, 1865–1890* (New York, 1964), pp. 55–56.

13. MES to JLS, May 29, 1845.

14. MES to JLS, December 24, 1854. MES to JLS, May 29, 1845.

15. MES to JLS, March 1, 1845; March 6, 1845; October 26, 1845.

16. MES to JLS, July 9, 1851. MES to JLS, July 11, 1851.

17. *Ibid.* MES to JLS, October 28, 1855.

18. MES to JLS, February 10, 1847; March 19, 1848; January 24, 1850. MES to JLS, December 24, 1854. MES to JLS, March 19, 1854.

19. MES to JLS, November 25, 1855; February 10, 1856; March 17, 1856; January 12, 1857; December 23, 1855. Luther Clemence to MES, April 6, 1857. MES to JLS, July 9, 1858; January 26, 1859.

20. MES to JLS, January 1, 1851; December 12, 1851; March 17, 1856; October 27, 1857.

21. *Some Industries of New England: Their Origin, Development, and Accomplishments* (Boston, 1923), pp. 5, 1–11.

22. Quoted in Gordon, "Connecticut River Railroad," p. i.

23. *Ibid.,* pp. ii, 5, 9.

24. *Ibid.,* p. 5.

25. *Merchants' Magazine* 18 (1848), 381. Without knowing the exact banking capital of Massachusetts during this period, it is still possible to make approximate comparisons between the finances of towns and states on the one hand, and railroads on the other. For example, the budget of Massachusetts for 1839 was approximately $487,350 according to figures in 1842, Massachusetts, *Acts and Resolves,* c. 147 (1839). Passenger receipts alone for Massachusetts railroads equaled approximately $708,812 in 1840, according to figures in *Merchants' Magazine* 2 (1840), 347–348. The city budget for Baltimore for the year 1846 included expenditures of approximately $687,972, according to J. H. Hollander, The *Financial History of Baltimore* (Baltimore, 1899), p. 381. According to figures in *Merchants' Magazine* 13 (1845), 581, passenger receipts alone for the Baltimore and Ohio Railroad the preceding year were $369,882. With freight revenues added, the figure is $738,603.

26. Gordon, "Connecticut River Railroad," pp. 3–4, 9–12.

27. *Ibid.,* p. 9.

5. THE LEGAL CONFLICT BETWEEN RAILROAD AND GOVERNMENT

1. Chambers, *Things as They Are*, p. 28.

2. *Merchants' Magazine* 21 (1849), 163–164. J. Willard Hurst, "The Release of Energy" in Lawrence M. Friedman and Harry N. Scheiber, eds., *American Law and Constitutional Order: Historical Perspectives* (Cambridge, Mass., 1988), p. 118, attributes the abandonment of the charter system to the need to "provide a [legal] framework within which many may venture, rather then a favored few. . . ." See also Hurst, *Legitimacy of Business in the Law of the United States, 1780–1970* (Charlottesville, Va., 1970), pp. 13–57.

3. 1789–1836, Connecticut, *Private Laws*, vols. 1–2, 992–1032. *Merchants' Magazine* 14 (1846), 34–35; 15 (1846), 546–554; 20 (1849), 651. For an analysis of the *Charles River Bridge* case, see Garraty, *Quarrels That Shaped the Constitution*, pp. 62–76.

4. *Merchants' Magazine* 20 (1849), 651–655. 1789–1836, Connecticut, *Private Laws*, vols. 1–2, 992–1032.

5. See Haney, *Congressional History of Railways;* Hurst, "Release of Energy," pp. 109–120; and Morton J. Horwitz, *The Transformation of American Law, 1780–1860* (Cambridge, Mass., 1981), pp. 31–62.

6. Scheiber discusses the bias in favor of eminent domain for railroads in "Property Law, Expropriation, and Resource Allocation by Government, 1789–1910," in *American Law and Constitutional Order*, pp. 132–141.

7. *Louisville, Cincinnati and Charleston Railroad Company vs. Reese*, 1 Rice SC 383 (1838). See also Scheiber, "Property Law, Expropriation and Resource Allocation by Government," pp. 132–141; and Horwitz, *Transformation*, pp. 63–108.

8. *Burroughs, et al. vs. Housatonic Railroad Company*, 15 CT 124 (1842). Horwitz, *Transformation*, pp. 98–99. Scheiber, in "Property Law," writes that courts favored the railroads and other similar corporations to such an extent that "Indirect or consequential damages were not deemed compensable." There are, however, so many exceptions to this statement that it is questionable, especially for the decade of the 1830s.

9. See Scheiber and Horwitz, as above. On insurance near tracks, see *Webber vs. Eastern Railroad Company*, 1–2 Metcalf Mass 147 (1840).

10. *Felder vs. Railroad Company*, 2 McMullen SC 403 (1842).

11. *Beers vs. Housatonic Railroad Company*, 19 CT 566 (1849).

12. In the relatively undeveloped state of Ohio, for example, a strong bias against fencing among ranchers and farmers led to a number of Ohio supreme court cases in which the railroads were sued for killing stock. See *Cleveland, Columbus and Cincinnati Railroad ads. Kerwhacher,* 20 Lawrence Ohio 172 (1853); *Cincinnati, Hamilton and Dayton Railroad Company vs. Waterson and Kirk,* 4 Warden Ohio 424 (1854); and *Cleveland, Columbus and Cincinnati Railroad Company vs. Elliott,* 4 Warden Ohio 474 (1855).

13. *Cleveland, Columbus, and Cincinnati Railroad Company ads. Kerwhacher,* 3 Warden and Smith Ohio 172 (1854). 1840, *Laws of Pennsylvania*, p. 212 (1838).

14. 1840, *Laws of Pennsylvania*, pp. vi–viii. Scheiber, "Property Law," pp. 134–135.

15. *Delaware and Maryland Railroad vs. Stump*, 8 Gill and Johnson Md 479 (1837). *Ashby vs. Eastern Railroad*, 5 Metcalf Mass 368 (1842). *Boston Water Power Company vs. Boston and Worcester Railroad*, 16 Pickering Mass 512 (1834).

16. An example of the type of law forbidding steam engines from entering the city limits may be found in 1863, Lowell, *Charter and Ordinances*, 77–79 (1847).

17. *Inhabitants of Lowell vs. Boston and Lowell Railroad*, 23 Pickering Mass 24 (1839).

18. See Kirkland, *Men, Cities and Transportation*, vol. 1; and Gregg M. Turner, *Connecticut Railroads: An Illustrated History* (Hartford, Conn., 1989).

19. 1863, Lowell, *Charter and Ordinances*, 76–79 (1847).

20. *Inhabitants of Worcester vs. Western Railroad Corporation*, 14 Metcalf Mass 564 (1842). *Baltimore and Ohio vs. Mayor and City of Baltimore*, 6 Gill Md 288 (1847).

21. See *Farwell vs. Boston and Worcester Railroad*, 14 Metcalf Mass 49 (1842); and see Leonard W. Levy, "The Law of the Commonwealth and Chief Justice Shaw" in *American Law and the Constitutional Order*, pp. 151–164.

22. See *Merchants' Magazine* 18 (1848), 525.

23. Redfield, *Practical Treatise*, pp. 323, 327–339.

24. See, for example, *Merchants' Magazine* 21 (1849), 163–180. On common-carrier status, see *ibid.*, 18 (1848), 525.

25. 1902, Massachusetts, *Revised Laws*, vol. 2, c. 191 (1849). 1909, New York, *Consolidated Laws*, vol. 4, c. 140 (1850). 1901, New Hampshire, *Revised Statutes*, 518 (1850).

26. 1909, New York, *Consolidated Laws*, vol. 4, c. 140 (1850). 1901, New Hampshire, *Revised Statutes*, 522 (1852). 1909, New York, *Consolidated Laws*, vol. 4, c. 140 (1850).

27. On curtailing this type of behavior, see, for example, Byron K. Elliot and William F. Elliot, *A Treatise on the Law of Railroads, Containing a Consideration of the Organization, Status and Powers of Railroad Corporations, and the Rights and Liabilities Incident to the Location, Construction and Operation of Railroads; Together with Their Duties, Rights and Liabilities as Carriers* (Indianapolis, Ind., 1907), pp. 362–392.

6. A FORCE FOR GOOD OR FOR EVIL?

1. Nathaniel Hawthorne, "The Celestial Railroad," in *The Celestial Railroad and Other Stories* (New York, reprinted 1980), p. 185.

2. Walt Whitman, *Leaves of Grass*, in *Complete Poetry and Selected Prose*, edited by James E. Miller, Jr. (Boston, 1959), p. 289.

3. James Fenimore Cooper, *Home as Found: A Novel of Social Criticism and Observation* (New York, reprinted 1961), pp. 17–26.

4. *Ibid.*, pp. 8–16, 21.

5. *Ibid.*, p. 24.

6. *Ibid.*

7. *Ibid.,* pp. 24–25.

8. Hawthorne, "Celestial Railroad," pp. 185–202.

9. *Ibid.,* pp. 185–186.

10. *Ibid.,* p. 187.

11. *Webster's Seventh New Collegiate Dictionary* (Springfield, Mass., 1967). Hawthorne, "Celestial Railroad," pp. 190–191.

12. *Ibid.,* pp. 194–199.

13. Quoted in Ward, *Railroads and the Character of America,* pp. 29–31.

14. *Ibid.*

15. *Ibid.,* pp. 42–43.

16. *Ibid.,* pp. 48–49.

17. *Merchants' Magazine* 18 (1848), 98. Joseph L. Schott, *Rails Across Panama: The Story of the Building of the Panama Railroad, 1849–1855* (New York, 1967), p. 20. *Merchants' Magazine* 22 (1850), 357. See also Adolph B. Benson, ed., *America of the Fifties: Letters of Frederika Bremer* (New York, 1924), p. 281. Rupert Sargent Holland, *Historic Railroads* (New York, 1927), pp. 271–283. The "Passage to India" was an idea of European origin which pertained to the efforts of explorers, including Christopher Columbus, Henry Hudson, and Núñez de Balboa, to find a western route to India and China for trading purposes. In the United States it was revised by explorers such as Lewis and Clark to a "Northwest Passage" to India, sought to the northwest of the Missouri River. With the accession of Western lands to the Pacific Ocean in the 1840s, the idea of the Passage to India was revived in the United States, and plans for a transcontinental railroad route were discussed in terms of a route to China and the Far East.

18. Walt Whitman, *Leaves of Grass,* in *Complete Poetry,* pp. 288–289.

7. A CROWDED AND UNCOMFORTABLE HOME AWAY FROM HOME

1. Chambers, *Things as They Are,* pp. 48–49.

2. Hale, *New England Boyhood,* pp. 194–195. White, *Railroad Passenger Car,* pp. 50–115.

3. White, *Railroad Passenger Car,* pp. 379–432.

4. *Ibid.,* pp. 417–418.

5. See, for example, Reed, *Train Wrecks,* p. 119.

6. See, for example, Koch, *Journey,* p. 34. Alvarez, *Southern Railroads,* pp. 43–44.

7. White, *Railroad Passenger Car,* p. 379.

8. Quoted in Grant, *We Took the Train,* p. 22.

9. White, *Railroad Passenger Car,* p. 400.

10. *Ibid.,* p. 16.

11. *Merchants' Magazine* 6 (1842), 92; 9 (1843), 483; 12 (1845), 291.

12. Emigrants might travel in emigrant cars, which had wooden seats and no internal upholstery, in a freight car, or in a second-class car, the last being the most finished and comfortable accommodation. The Boston and Lowell Railroad extended

twenty-six miles from Boston to Lowell, Massachusetts. Source, *Merchants' Magazine* 12 (1845), 291.

13. White, *Railroad Passenger Car*, pp. 14–15. Charles Dickens, *American Notes*, quoted in Grant, *We Took the Train*, p. 21. Many travel diarists who went west before the Civil War noticed the deterioration of travel services and the increasingly heterogeneous nature of the crowd as they approached the frontier of settlement. A good example is Bremer, *America of the Fifties*, pp. 201–289.

14. The ladies' train car is discussed in Sarah Gordon, "Ladies' Train Travel: The Problem of Appearing in Public" (unpublished manuscript, 1973). White, *Railroad Passenger Car*, pp. 203, 208. Gordon, "Ladies' Train Travel," pp. 13–14. On locks for ladies' cars, see, for example, *Bass vs. The Chicago and Northwestern Railway Company*, 36 Wisc. 450 (1874).

15. Dickens, *American Notes*, quoted in Grant, *We Took the Train*, p. 22.

16. *Ibid.*, p. 21. *Merchants' Magazine* 15 (1846), 510.

17. See Meeks, *Railroad Station*, pp. 49–53, 70–71, 208–209; and Grow, *Waiting for the 5:05*, pp. 26–29. Alexander, *Down at the Depot*, pp. 252, 282, 300. *Old Colony*, pp. 43–45. *Merchants' Magazine* 14 (1845), 169–170. *Merchants' Magazine* 20 (1849), 342; Alexander, *Down at the Depot*, pp. 252, 282; Meeks, *Railroad Station*, pp. 52, 70.

18. See, for example, *Old Colony*, pp. 43–45.

19. *Merchants' Magazine* 14 (1845), 169–170. Meeks, *Railroad Station*, p. 51. *Merchants' Magazine* 20 (1849), 342; Alexander, *Down at the Depot*, pp. 252, 282; Meeks, *Railroad Station*, pp. 52, 70, 53, 71–73, 208–209.

20. Walter Berg, *Buildings and Structures of American Railroads* (New York, 1900), pp. 249–446.

21. Meeks, *Railroad Station*, p. 50.

22. Quoted in Grant, *We Took the Train*, p. 23.

23. *Connecticut Courant*, January 26, 1839, p. 4. See, for example, Trollope, *North America*, p. 78. The posting of schedules became a legal issue later in the century, especially in the West, because of the railroads' failure to provide this service. See, for example, Colorado, *Revised Statutes*, p. 1282, *1908*; Minnesota, *General Statutes, 1913*, p. 4401; and Montana, *Revised Code*, p. 4348, *1907*.

24. See, for example, *Merchants' Magazine* 10 (1844), 474; *Connecticut Courant*, July 8, 1841, p. 4; June 19, 1841, p. 4.

25. See, for example, *Merchants' Magazine* 5 (1841), 469–470, where the Utica and Schenectady boasts that its delays exceeded six hours only once in the course of a year.

26. See, for example, Alexander, *Down at the Depot*, pp. 12–13.

27. See, for example, Dunbar, *History of Travel*, pp. 1036–1041.

28. *Ibid.*, pp. 1036–1037. Thompson, *American Railways*, p. 66.

29. *Merchants' Magazine* 13 (1845), 581–582. *Merchants' Magazine* 18 (1848), 33.

30. See, for example, *Canal and Railway Regulations*, p. 58. White, *Railroad Passenger Car*, p. 453. *Canal and Railway Regulations*, p. 30. The Illinois and Michigan

Canal allowed sixty pounds of baggage free of charge. See *Merchants' Magazine* 19 (1848), 432.

8. PRIVATE AND PUBLIC UNIONS

1. Henry Clay Work, "The Buckskin Bag of Gold," 1849. This is the entire text of the song.

2. JLS to MES, June 17, 1844; September 2, 1844; October 21, 1844. Sears, *Sacred Places,* p. 6.

3. White, *Railroad Passenger Car,* pp. 203, 415, 373.

4. The theme of railroads encouraging democratic interaction appears in Alvarez, *Southern Railroads,* pp. ii, 182, 195; and in Ward, *Railroads and the Character of America,* pp. 69–80. On railroads encouraging crowds with barbaric habits, see Alvarez, *Southern Railroads,* pp. 200–201. See also Samuel Breck, "A Ride from Boston to Providence in 1835," quoted in Grant, *We Took the Train,* pp. 19–31.

5. See Michael E. Shapiro, et al., eds., *George Caleb Bingham* (New York, 1990).

6. See, for example, Chambers, *Things as They Are,* pp. 150–157.

7. On crowds in river towns, see Bremer, *America of the Fifties,* p. 239. On Melville's view of the river crowds, see Herman Melville, *The Confidence-Man: His Masquerade* (New York, 1967, first published in 1857).

8. Bremer, *America of the Fifties,* p. 123.

9. Chambers, *Things as They Are,* p. 270.

10. Alvarez, *Southern Railroads,* p. 154.

11. Breck, "Ride from Boston to Providence," pp. 20–22. *Merchants' Magazine* 15 (1846), 510.

12. Bremer, *America of the Fifties,* p. 239.

13. On crowds in Charleston, see *ibid.,* p. 96. On crowds in Richmond, see Chambers, *Things as They Are,* p. 271.

14. *American Railroad Journal* quoted in Alvarez, *Southern Railroads,* p. 99. See also suggested safety rules for passengers in *Scientific American,* quoted in *Merchants' Magazine* 30 (1854), 258–259. Maria Lowell was a poet and the wife of James Russell Lowell.

15. Bremer, *America of the Fifties,* pp. 202–203.

16. Alvarez, *Southern Railroads,* p. 175.

17. Alvarez, *Southern Railroads,* p. 176. Good accounts of this type of behavior may be found in August Mencken, *The Railroad Passenger Car: An Illustrated History of the First Hundred Years with Accounts by Contemporary Passengers* (Baltimore, 1957).

18. Cohen, *Long Steel Rail,* p. 46.

19. *Ibid.,* p. 44.

20. *Twelfth Annual Report of the Ohio State Board of Agriculture: With An Abstract of the Proceedings of the Country Agricultural Societies, to the General Assembly of Ohio; For the Year 1857* (Columbus, Ohio, 1858), p. 171.

21. *Ibid.,* pp. 171–172.

9. UNION THROUGH COMPETITION

1. Ambler, *Transportation in the Ohio Valley*, p. 185.

2. U.S. Department of Commerce, *Historical Statistics of the United States, 1789–1945* (Washington, D.C., 1949), p. 200.

3. See Carter, *When Railroads Were New*, pp. 68–74.

4. *Baltimore and Ohio ads. Chesapeake and Ohio Canal*, 4 Gill and Johnson Md 1 (1832). *Baltimore and Ohio vs. Washington and Baltimore Turnpike Road*, 100 Gill and Johnson Md 392 (1839).

5. See Carter, *When Railroads Were New*, pp. 143–144. *Poor's Manual, 1876*, p. 195.

6. See *Poor's Manual, 1876*, pp. 110, 148, 692.

7. *Ibid.*, pp. 736, 560.

8. *Old Colony*, p. 43.

9. *Ibid.*, pp. 45–47.

10. *Ibid.*, pp. 61, 67–69, 101.

11. Carter, *When Railroads Were New*, pp. 150–185.

12. Peter Lyon, *To Hell in a Day Coach* (Philadelphia, 1968), pp. 18–21.

13. *Ibid.*, p. 20.

14. Reed, *Train Wrecks*, pp. 9–34, 56. See also *Merchants' Magazine* 54 (1866), 183.

15. For a brief introduction to the railroad accident rate in the 1850s, see Reed, *Train Wrecks*, pp. 25–34. For a more extensive description of the social implications of these wrecks, see Kirkland, *Men, Cities and Transportation*, I, 263–264, 317–318. See also *Merchants' Magazine* 29 (1853), 245; 32 (1855), 380; 33 (1855), 247; 34 (1856), 373; 37 (1857), 629.

16. Botkin and Harlow, *Treasury of Railroad Folklore*, p. 80.

17. Holbrook, *American Railroads*, pp. 88–89, 101. See also Reed, *Train Wrecks*, p. 156.

18. See, for example, *Connecticut Courant*, July 8, 1841, p. 4. Dunbar, *Kalamazoo*, pp. 46–47. Quoted in Botkin and Harlow, *Treasury of Railroad Folklore*, pp. 78–79.

19. John M. Read, *Opinion of Hon. John M. Read of the Supreme Court of Pennsylvania in Favor of the Passenger Cars Running Every Day in the Week, Including Sunday* (Philadelphia, 1867), p. 24.

20. Chambers, *Things as They Are in America*, p. 162.

21. *Merchants' Magazine* 21 (1849), 171–178.

22. Sandburg, *Lincoln*, pp. 124–125.

23. *Ibid.*, p. 51. *Poor's Manual, 1876*, pp. 70, 94, 207. *Merchants' Magazine* 40 (1859), 624. The railroads were the Chicago and Milwaukee; the Chicago, St. Paul and Fond du Lac; the Chicago and Galena; the Chicago, Burlington and Quincy; the Chicago, Alton and St. Louis; the Illinois Central; the Pittsburg [sic], Fort Wayne and Chicago; the Michigan Southern; and the Michigan Central.

10. THE STATE OF THE UNION

1. William Henry Seward, "The Irrepressible Conflict," quoted in Albert Bushnell Hart, ed., *American History Told by Contemporaries*, vol. 4, *Welding of the Nation, 1845–1900* (New York, 1917), pp. 138–141.

2. Kerr, *Louisville & Nashville*, pp. 1–17.

3. Winther, *Transportation Frontier*, p. 47.

4. *Ibid.*

5. *Ibid.*, pp. 50–57.

6. For information on Western conditions, see, for example, Koch, *Journey*, pp. 44–70. On Chambers's journey, see Chambers, *Things as They Are in America*, pp. 113–127. On Bremer's journey, see Bremer, *America of the Fifties*, pp. 239–281.

7. Amelia Barr, *All the Days of My Life: An Autobiography; The Red Leaves of a Human Heart* (New York, 1913), pp. 166–167.

8. *Ibid.*

9. On stage connections in the later nineteenth-century West, see, for example, *Travelers' Guide*, 1881, p. 214. On boat connections in the East, see, for example, *Old Colony*, p. 124.

10. On the lack of development in the South, see Mary A. Livermore, *The Story of My Life: Or, The Sunshine and Shadow of Seventy Years* (Hartford, Conn., 1897), pp. 146–153; and Chambers, *Things as They Are*, p. 269.

11. Livermore, *Story of My Life*, p. 147.

12. See, for example, Alvarez, *Southern Railroads*, pp. 187–188.

13. *Merchants' Magazine* 18 (1848); 22 (1850), 244, 467, 569, 682.

11. THE SOUTH LEAVES BUT RETURNS

1. Quoted in Cohen, *Long Steel Rail*, p. 46.

2. Sandburg, *Lincoln*, p. 201.

3. *Ibid.*, pp. 88, 175, 383.

4. Trollope, *North America*, p. 51.

5. *Ibid.*, pp. 20–23, 52.

6. Sandburg, *Lincoln*, pp. 216–220.

7. Turner, *Victory Rode the Rails*, pp. 46, 52–53.

8. Trollope, *North America*, pp. 83–84; and Allan Nevins, ed., *American Social History as Recorded by British Travellers* (New York, 1928), p. 388.

9. Nevins, *British Travellers*, p. 389.

10. Turner, *Victory Rode the Rails*, pp. 29, 33, 62–63.

11. *Ibid.*, pp. 29–38; and Kerr, *Louisville & Nashville*, p. 3.

12. Turner, *Victory Rode the Rails*, p. 104.

13. *Ibid.*, pp. 15–17, 129–132, 136–138, 158–159, 217–221.

14. *Ibid.*, pp. 285–296.

15. *Ibid.*, pp. 353–364.

16. For a full account of the work, see Carl R. Gray, *In Eighteen Countries: The*

Story of the American Railroad Men Serving in the Military Railroad Services from 1862–1953 (New York, 1955).

17. Turner, *Victory Rode the Rails,* pp. 148–165, 205–207, 215–222, 275–281.

18. *Ibid.,* pp. 201–202.

19. *Ibid.,* p. 145.

20. *Ibid.,* p. 297.

21. *Ibid.,* pp. 297–299.

22. *Ibid.,* p. 302.

23. *Ibid.,* p. 304.

24. *Ibid.,* p. 118.

25. James A. Ward, *Southern Railroad Man: Conductor N. J. Bell's Recollections of the Civil War Era* (DeKalb, Ill., 1994), pp. 21–22.

26. Culley, *Day at a Time,* pp. 128, 131–132.

27. Nina Brown Baker, *Cyclone in Calico: The Story of Mary Ann Bickerdyke* (Boston, 1952), pp. 37–60.

28. W. H. Perrin, *History of Alexander, Union, and Pulaski Counties, Illinois* (Chicago, 1883), p. 162.

29. *Ibid.,* p. 163. Holbrook, *American Railroads,* p. 389.

12. NOW WE CAN SETTLE THE FAR WEST

1. John Hoyt Williams, *A Great and Shining Road: The Epic Story of the Transcontinental Railroad* (New York, 1988), p. 72.

2. Cohen, *Long Steel Rail,* p. 104.

3. Hibbard, *History of the Public Land Policies,* p. 248. Arthur M. Johnson and Barry E. Supple, *Boston Capitalists and Western Railroads* (Cambridge, Mass., 1967), p. 197.

4. A good account of this may be found in Lyon, *To Hell in a Day Coach,* pp. 29–48.

5. Dee Brown, *Hear That Lonesome Whistle Blow: Railroads in the West* (New York, 1977), p. 64.

6. *Ibid.,* pp. 60–61.

7. *Ibid.,* pp. 66–70.

8. A large literature of early Western guides provided tourist information. Among these, many were commissioned by the railroads themselves, to increase ridership. See, for example, Charles Nordhoff, *California for Health, Pleasure, and Residence: A Book for Travellers and Settlers* (New York, 1872), written to encourage people to ride the new Union Pacific route to California. A multitude of other guides sponsored by the Western railroads may be found in the Newberry Library, Chicago, and in the Western Americana Collection of the Beinecke Rare Book Library at Yale University in New Haven, Connecticut.

9. Accounts of Indian attacks on track layers and trains may be found in many sources, including Brown, *Lonesome Whistle,* pp. 85–87, 93, and Cy Warman, *The Story of the Railroad* (New York, 1898), pp. 46–51.

10. Brown, *Lonesome Whistle,* pp. 95–97.

11. For a description of New York's segregated neighborhoods, see Chambers, *Things as They Are,* pp. 171–209, and Bremer, *America in the Fifties,* pp. 325–334.

12. Brown, *Lonesome Whistle,* pp. 245–246.

13. *Ibid.,* pp. 235–255. American Association of Passenger Traffic Officers (hereafter AAPTO), *Proceedings,* March 30, 1870, p. 235; September 21, 1880, p. 8. Brown, *Lonesome Whistle,* pp. 235–255.

14. Martha Ferguson McKeown, *Them Was the Days* (Lincoln, Nebr., 1961), pp. 77–78.

15. *Ibid.,* pp. 79, 90–92.

16. *Ibid.,* pp. 163–203, 241–265, 266–282.

17. Robert Louis Stevenson, "Across the Plains," in *Across the Plains with other Memories and Essays* (New York, 1905), p. 156.

18. *Ibid.,* pp. 116–119.

19. Frank Leslie and Richard Reinhart, *Out West on the Overland Train: Across-the-Continent Excursion with Leslie's Magazine in 1877 and the Overland Trip in 1967* (Palo Alto, Calif., 1967), pp. 29, 31–32, 38–39.

20. *Ibid.,* pp. 33, 40–41, 66–67, 79, 84–87, 112–113.

21. *Ibid.,* p. 37.

22. *Ibid.,* pp. 137, 8.

23. Howard Lamar, ed., *The Reader's Encyclopedia of the American West* (New York, 1977), pp. 80, 285, 590, 1302; Winther, *Transportation Frontier,* pp. 143–144. Lamar, *Encyclopedia of the American West,* p. 590.

24. *Ibid.,* p. 80. See also Charles L. Martin, *A Sketch of Sam Bass, The Bandit* (Norman, Okla., 1956), pp. 153–159. Lamar, *Encyclopedia of the American West,* pp. 939–940.

25. Holbrook, *American Railroads,* pp. 389–390. *Ibid.,* pp. 387–398; Winther, *Transportation Frontier,* p. 125.

26. Winther, *Transportation Frontier,* p. 125. For an account of this problem, first published in 1905, see George W. Berge, *The Free Pass Bribery System* (New York, 1974).

27. Licht, *Workin' for the Railroad* (Princeton, 1983), pp. 31–78, 73–78, 79–124.

13. POOR RELATIONS IN THE SOUTH

1. Opie Read and Frank Pixley, *The Carpetbagger* (Chicago, 1899), p. 35.

2. McKeown, *Them Were the Days,* p. 21.

3. *Travelers' Official Railway Guide for the United States and Canada,* 1869.

4. Dolores Greenberg, *Financiers and Railroads, 1869–1889: A Study of Morton, Bliss & Company* (Newark, Del., 1980), pp. 38–39, 73. C. Vann Woodward, *Origins of the New South* (Baton Rouge, La., 1980), pp. 30–31.

5. *Travelers' Guide,* 1869, nos. 210–277.

6. *Ibid.* In Ward, *Southern Railroad Man,* p. 96, the owner of the railroad put mail on a train to force striking workers back on the job. *Ibid.*

7. *Railroad Gazette* 2 (1870), quoted in Greenberg, *Financiers,* p. 100.

8. *Travelers' Guide,* 1869, nos. 210–277. Speeds were calculated from *Travelers'*

Guide timetables and compared to timetables for Northern railroads in the same publication. See, for example, Ward, *Southern Railroad Man*, pp. 141–142.

9. This is a pervasive practice in Ward, *Southern Railroad Man. Ibid.*, p. 93.

10. *Travelers' Guide*, 1869, nos. 210–277.

11. *Ibid.*

12. *Ibid.*, nos. 217–227.

13. Ward, *Southern Railroad Man*, pp. 36–105.

14. Greenberg, *Financiers*, pp. 26, 32, 40, 61–70.

15. *Ibid.*, pp. 62–72.

16. Ward, *Southern Railroad Man*, pp. 9–105. *Ibid.*, pp. xvii–xviii, 47–50, 74–75.

17. *Ibid.*, pp. 50, 55, 74–75, 99, 94–101.

18. Kerr, *Louisville & Nashville*, p. 36.

19. Ward, *Southern Railroad Man*, p. 86.

20. On trestles, see, for example, *ibid.*, pp. 92–94. On conditions in postwar Chattanooga and Atlanta, see *ibid.*, pp. 38–40.

21. On black men going to Chattanooga, see *ibid.*, p. 58; on hitting a man, see *ibid.*, p. 90. On race issues, see *ibid.*, pp. 50–57; on the death of a mail agent, see *ibid.*, p. 100.

22. A good description of these conditions may be found in *ibid.*, pp. 88–105.

23. See, for example, *ibid.*, p. 81.

14. THE TRAVELING PUBLIC AND ITS SERVANTS

1. *Railroad Gazette* 25 (1893), 129.

2. See, for example, Chicago and North Western Railway Company, *Annual Report, 1875* (New York, 1875), p. 37; (1876), p. 43; (1879), p. 42; (1881), p. 34; (1885), p. 34. New York, New Haven and Hartford Railroad, *Annual Report, 1875* (New York, 1876), p. 9; (1888), p. 11. Pennsylvania Railroad, *Annual Report, 1866* (Philadelphia, 1866), p. 33; (1885), p. 112. Union Pacific Railway, *Annual Report, 1881* (New York, 1882), p. 15; *ibid.*, p. 124.

3. AAPTO, *Proceedings,* March 30, 1870, p. 268; September 20, 1881, pp. 18, 20; September 19, 1882, pp. 9–10, 14; March 13, 1883, pp. 9–13; September 16, 1884, pp. 10–16; March 18, 1884, pp. 9–10; March 17, 1885, pp. 10–11; September 15, 1885, pp. 9–14; March 15, 1887, pp. 8–11.

4. *Ibid.*, March 26, 1872, p. 268.

5. *Ibid.*, March 26, 1872, p. 268; September 20, 1881, pp. 18–20; September 19, 1882, pp. 9–10; September 16, 1884, pp. 10–16; March 18, 1884, pp. 9–10; March 17, 1885, pp. 9–11; September 15, 1885, pp. 9–14; March 15, 1887, pp. 8–12.

6. *Ibid.*

7. Jane Addams to Sarah Alice Addams Haldeman, August 8, 1883, is one of many letters on railroad travel in the Jane Addams Memorial Collection, Hull House, University of Illinois, Chicago. Alice Hamilton to Agnes Hamilton, N.D./1894?, may also be found at Hull House. See also Frances E. Willard, *Glimpses of Fifty Years: The Autobiography of an American Woman* (Chicago, 1889), pp. 619–632. On Elizabeth

Cady Stanton and Susan B. Anthony, see Elizabeth Cady Stanton, *Eighty Years and More: Reminiscences, 1815–1897* (Boston, 1993), pp. 261, 298–302.

8. See, for example, Lucius Beebe, *Mr. Pullman's Elegant Palace Car* (Garden City, N.Y., 1961), and *Mansions on Rails: The Folklore of the Private Railway Car* (Berkeley, Calif., 1957).

9. Beebe, *Palace Car*, p. 142.

10. See, for example, *Travelers' Guide*, 1881, pp. 93, 193, 209.

11. See New York, New Haven and Hartford Railroad, *Annual Report*, 1874–1889; Pennsylvania Railroad, *Annual Report*, 1870–1889. The Pennsylvania classified its cars as first class and emigrant class. Chicago and North Western, *Annual Report*, 1872–1889. Illinois Central Railroad Company, *Annual Report*, 1874, p. 8.

12. *Travelers' Guide*, 1869. Chicago and North Western, *Annual Report*, 1879, p. 30.

13. Botkin and Harlow, *Treasury of Railroad Folklore*, pp. 241–290. *Old Colony*, p. 87.

14. On advertisements for air brakes, see "Advertisements" in Matthias N. Forney, *The Car Builder's Dictionary: An Illustrated Vocabulary of Terms Which Designate American Railroad Cars, Their Parts and Attachments* (New York, 1888), pp. 3–4. Botkin and Harlow, *Treasury of Railroad Folklore*, pp. 241–290. 27 United States Statutes, 531–532 (1893). See, for example, H. Roger Grant, *Brownie the Boomer: The Life of Charles P. Brown, An American Railroader* (DeKalb, Ill., 1991), p. 215; Botkin and Harlow, *Treasury of Railroad Folklore*, pp. 163, 327.

15. White, *Railroad Passenger Car*, p. 422. Heman Chase, *Railroad Passenger Travel* (Springfield, Vt., 1967), p. 5. See, for example, *Railroad Gazette*, 1873, vol. 5, pp. 6–7, 54, 267, 278–279, 412, 485, 502–504; 1883, vol. 15, pp. 25, 85, 528, 858; 1893, vol. 25, pp. 8, 139, 241, 299–300, 375, 410–411, 565, 663, 704, 854, 876; 1903, vol. 35, pp. 170, 474, 475; *American Engineering Journal*, 1901, vol. 75, pp. 177–181. See Chapter 23.

16. U.S., *Historical Statistics: Colonial Times to 1957*, p. 428. *Poor's Manual of Railroads, 1876*, p. 518. *Ibid.*, p. 10.

17. See, for example, *Travelers' Guide*, 1869, nos. 39, 65–70, 73, 86, 112, 141, 152–153, 171, 175.

18. Grand Central, *Annual Report*, 1906. The names appear throughout the volume in the list of directors at the beginning of each railroad's annual report.

15. THE LAW TRIES TO CATCH UP

1. *Thirty-Third Annual Report of the Railroad Commissioners of the State of Connecticut, 1886* (Hartford, Conn., 1885), p. xxxiv.

2. *Louis K. Liggett Co. vs. Lee*, 288 U.S. Supreme Court 517 (1933).

3. 1909, New York, *Consolidated Laws*, vol. 4, c. 346 (1863). 1904, Maryland, *Laws*, 892 (1864). 1865, Pennsylvania, *Laws*, vol. 4, no. 228.

4. 1911, Wisconsin, *Statutes,* s. 1806 (1868). *Ibid.* 1910, Pennsylvania, *Statutes,* vol. 4, c. (1867). Woodward, *Origins of the New South,* pp. 211–212.

5. 1932, Tennessee, *Code,* c. 15.1-5 (1865–1866).

6. 1911, Nebraska, *Annotated Statutes,* c. 25 (1866).

7. 1901, New Hampshire, *Revised Statutes,* 522, (1874); 1910, Indiana, *Statutes,* 624–635 (1875); 1902, Massachusetts, *Revised Laws,* vol. 2., c. 372 (1874); 1909, California, *Civil Code,* c. 487, 488 (1872); 1905, North Carolina, *Revised Statutes,* c. 2604, 2608, 2629 (1871–1872).

8. 1911, Wisconsin, *Statutes,* c. 227 (1874); 1902, Massachusetts, *Revised Laws,* vol. 2, c. 372 (1874); c. 106 (1879). 1909, California, *Civil Code,* c. 482, 483 (1872).

9. 1883, Illinois, *Laws,* 125–126; 1884, Vermont, *Acts and Resolves,* 51–52; 1882, Connecticut, *Public Acts,* c. 47.

10. 1884, Iowa, *Acts and Resolves,* 31; 1881, Missouri, *Laws,* 77–78; 1887, Idaho, *Revised Statutes,* vol. 2, 69; 1881–1882, South Carolina, *Acts and Joint Resolutions,* 791–843; 1886–1887, Alabama, *Laws,* 74–76; 1932, Tennessee, *Code,* c. 225 (1887); 1910, Wyoming, *Compiled Statutes,* c. 6008 (1887).

11. *Patten vs. Chicago and Northwestern Railway Company,* 32 WI 524 (1873).

12. *Quaife and Wife vs. Chicago and Northwestern Railway Company,* 48 WI 513 (1879); *Griswold vs. Chicago and Northwestern Railway Company,* 64 WI 652 (1885); *Bishop vs.Chicago and Northwestern Railway Company,* 67 WI 610 (1887).

13. *Bennett vs. New York, New Haven and Hartford Railroad Company,* 57 CT 422 (1889); *Pennsylvania Railroad Company vs. Lyons,* 129 PA 113 (1889); *Kelly vs. Chicago and Northwestern Railway Company,* 70 WI 335 (1887).

14. One railroad case, *Philadelphia and Reading Railroad vs. Derby,* 55 U.S. 468 (1852), established the principle that railroads must exercise "the greatest possible care and diligence"; other cases of this kind in the pre–Civil War era applied to other means of conveyance, such as *Boyce vs. Anderson,* 27 U.S. 150 (1829), and *Stokes vs. Saltonstall,* 38 U.S. 181 (1839). For the post–Civil War period, see "Carriers," in West's *Supreme Court Digest,* sections 280–282 at 160–163.

15. *Shoemaker vs. Kingsbury,* 79 U.S. 369 (1870); *Pennsylvania Railroad Company vs. Roy,* 102 U.S. 451 (1880).

16. U.S., Interstate Commerce Commission, *Annual Report,* pp. 243–285 (hereafter ICC).

17. For further information on freight discrimination before 1890, see *ibid.,* pp. 245, 250–251, 253–254. For information on freight rate regulation in other states, see *ibid.,* pp. 244–249, 252–253. Quotation from *ibid.,* pp. 248–249.

18. On state commissions with court powers, see *ibid.,* pp. 253–255. On states that regulated posting of rates, see *ibid.,* p. 284; for states with no railroad commission, see *ibid.,* pp. 243–285.

19. On intersecting lines, see *ibid.,* p. 266. On regulatory powers in Indiana, see *ibid.,* p. 270. On regulatory powers in Idaho, see *ibid.,* p. 271.

20. On the contents of the Act to Regulate Commerce see Truman C. Bigham, *Transportation: Principles and Problems* (New York, 1947), pp. 151–154.

16. WHY BIGGER TOWNS GET BETTER SERVICE

1. *Old Colony,* pp. 102–103.

2. The arrangements for meeting passengers at the station receive only cursory treatment in most railroad histories. The well-known Parmalee Transfer Company of Chicago is discussed briefly in Holbrook, *American Railroads,* pp. 137–139; the standard pictorial histories of stations record in photographs and captions the rows of omnibuses, taxis, and other carriages waiting to take passengers into town. See, for example, Alexander, *Down at the Depot,* especially pp. 21, 30, 44–45, 55, 76–77, 131, 159, 179, 194, 196–197, 202, 213, 226, 238, 243. Baedeker, *United States, 1893,* lists the chief means of transit from the railroad stations in major cities. Quoted material may be found in Jefferson Williamson, *The American Hotel* (New York, 1930), pp. 121–122.

3. Marshall Kirkland, *Passenger Business,* in Science of Railways Series, 12 vols. (Chicago, 1894), vol. 4, p. 47.

4. Lucius Beebe and Charles Clegg, *Hear the Train Blow* (New York, 1952), p. 372. William Fraser Rae, *West by Rail: The New Route to the East* (New York, 1974, first published in 1871), p. 66. Beebe, *Hear the Train Blow,* p. 170. Edwin P. Alexander, *Out on the Main Line* (New York, 1971), p. 238.

5. Botkin and Harlow, *Treasury of Railroad Folklore,* pp. 514–518.

6. The author's compilation of railroad station floor plans has been drawn from Berg, *Buildings and Structures of American Railroads;* the *Railroad Gazette* 5 (1873), 31, 215; 7 (1875), 522; 9 (1877), 139; and many other sources.

7. On local stations see *ibid.* On racial segregation in stations see *ibid.* and Woodward, *Strange Career of Jim Crow,* p. 97. Remarks on segregation in Western stations are based on an examination of station blueprints for Western stations as well as photographs of the many stations that were no more than a shack or marker.

8. John R. Stilgoe, *Metropolitan Corridor: Railroads and the American Scene* (New Haven, 1983), p. 235.

9. See Alexander, *Down at the Depot,* p. 197, and Beebe, *Hear the Train Blow,* pp. 379, 386.

10. See Baedeker, *United States, 1893,* between pp. 276 and 277, for a map showing the route of the Illinois Central up the shoreline of Chicago and terminating at docks near the Chicago River. See *ibid.,* between pp. 308 and 309, for a map of Cincinnati showing all the railroads terminating near the shores of the Ohio River. See *ibid.,* between pp. 292 and 293, for a map of Minneapolis showing the proximity of the railroads and some of the stations to the Mississippi River.

11. For a complete listing of depots in Chicago and Cincinnati see Baedeker, *United States, 1893,* between pp. 279 and 280, and between pp. 308 and 309. For Milwaukee's main stations, see Alexander, *Down at the Depot,* pp. 242–245. Carl Condit, *The Railroad and the City* (Columbus, Ohio, 1977), p. 77.

12. *Railroad Gazette* 7 (1875), 522.

13. 1863, Lowell, *Charter and Ordinances,* 76–79 (1847); *ibid.,* 101–103 (1856).

14. See, for example, Connecticut, Railroad Commissioners, *Annual Report, 1886,* pp. xxix–xxxi. *Old Colony,* p. 102. 1902, Massachusetts, *Revised Laws,* 348 (1872).

15. 1880, Vermont, *Acts and Resolves,* 50–51. 1887, Tennessee, *Legislative Acts,* 385–386. 1897, New Mexico, *Compiled Laws,* 969.

16. *Chicago Northwestern vs. Crane,* 5 U.S. Supreme Court 578 (1885).

17. AAPTO, February 9, 1876, pp. 412–414; September 16, 1884. pp. 10, 16; March 18, 1884, pp. 9–10; September 15, 1885, pp. 9–10; September, 20, 1892, pp. 120–121. *Merchants' Magazine* 12 (1845), 291.

18. University of Nebraska, *Catalog, 1884–1885,* p. 43. North Carolina Agricultural and Mechanical, *Catalog, 1897–1898,* p. 71; University of New Mexico, *Catalog, 1892,* p. 14; University of Nevada, *Catalog, 1898–1899,* p. 16.

19. Ohio, State Board of Agriculture, *Annual Report* (Columbus, Ohio, 1858), pp. 109–175.

20. AAPTO, February 9, 1876, pp. 412–414; September 16, 1884. pp. 10, 16; March 18, 1884, pp. 9–10; September 15, 1885, pp. 9–10; September 20, 1892, pp. 120–121.

17. CITY SLICKER AND COUNTRY BUMPKIN

1. Parker Morell, *Diamond Jim: The Life and Times of James Buchanan Brady* (Garden City, N.Y., 1934), p. 25.

2. Victor L. Morse, *36 Miles of Trouble: The Story of the West River R.R.* (Brattleboro, Vt., 1959), pp. 9, 11.

3. These stereotypes show up in popular literature, including satire. They get full play in a satire of railroad law set against the backdrop of the social realities of the day: R. Vashon Rogers, *Legal Recreations: The Laws of the Road, or, Wrongs and Rights of a Traveller* (San Francisco, 1876). See also J. P. Johnston, *Twenty Years of Hus'ling* (Chicago, 1908, first published in 1887).

4. On private and hotel cars, see Beebe, *Mansions on Rails* and *Mr. Pullman's Elegant Palace Car;* and Leslie and Reinhart, *Out West on the Overland Train.*

5. *Ibid.*

6. Lucius Beebe, *The Big Spenders,* quoted in Ludovic Kennedy, *A Book of Railway Journeys* (New York, 1980), pp. 130–131.

7. On Gould, see A. W. Somerville, "Comin' Down the Rail," quoted in Botkin and Harlow, *Treasury of Railroad Folklore,* pp. 17–18; on Hill, see Holbrook, *Story of American Railroads,* quoted in Botkin and Harlow, *Treasury of Railroad Folklore,* pp. 149–151.

8. Beebe, *Mansions on Rails,* p. 269.

9. Holbrook, *Story of American Railroads,* quoted in Botkin and Harlow, *Treasury of Railroad Folklore,* pp. 149–151.

10. John F. Stover, *American Railroads* (Chicago, 1976), pp. 143, 156–157, 169, 171–178.

11. Lucius Beebe, *Mixed Train Daily* (Berkeley, Calif., 1969), quoted in Botkin and Harlow, *Treasury of Railroad Folklore,* p. 241.

12. Victor L. Morse, *The West River R.R.,* quoted in Botkin and Harlow, *Treasury of Railroad Folklore,* pp. 249–255; and Harry Henderson and Sam Shaw, "Cracker

Barrel Railroaders," quoted in Botkin and Harlow, *Treasury of Railroad Folklore*, pp. 255–256.

13. George Estes, "The Rawhide Railroad," quoted in Botkin and Harlow, *Treasury of Railroad Folklore*, p. 270.

14. Beebe, *Mixed Train Daily*, quoted in Botkin and Harlow, *Treasury of Railroad Folklore*, pp. 242–243; Morse, *West River R.R.*, quoted in Botkin and Harlow, *Treasury of Railroad Folklore*, pp. 249–255; and Archie Robertson, *Slow Train to Yesterday*, quoted in Botkin and Harlow, *Treasury of Railroad Folklore*, pp. 258–264.

15. Beebe, *Mixed Train Daily*.

16. Botkin and Harlow, *Treasury of Railroad Folklore*, pp. 241–242.

17. Beebe, *Mixed Train Daily*, quoted in Botkin and Harlow, *Treasury of Railroad Folklore*, p. 242.

18. *Ibid.*, pp. 242–243.

19. Morse, *West River R.R.*, quoted in Botkin and Harlow, *Treasury of Railroad Folklore*, pp. 249–255. For the quotation, see *ibid.*, p. 249.

20. The best description of an overland immigrant railroad journey may be found in Stevenson, "Across the Plains," the record of a trip taken in the early 1870s.

21. Woodward, *Strange Career of Jim Crow*, pp. 23–24.

22. *Ibid.*, pp. 27–28, 38–39.

23. *Ibid.*, pp. 37–41. For the legal case, see *Louisville and Nashville Railroad vs. Commonwealth*, 99 Ky. (1896), 663.

24. Louise Fisk Bryson, *Every-Day Etiquette: A Manual of Good Manners* (New York, 1890), p. 95. John A. Ruth, *Decorum: A Practical Treatise on Etiquette and Dress of the Best American Society* (New York, 1879), p. 142. Bryson, *Etiquette*, pp. 95, 94, 90, 89. Florence Hartley, *The Ladies' Book of Etiquette and Manual of Politeness* (Boston, 1875), pp. 38–39.

25. Johnston, *Twenty Years of Hus'ling*, pp. 73, 123.

26. "Travelers Aid" (n.p., n.d.), a publication of the Travelers Aid Society of Metropolitan Chicago. The Immigrants' Protective League of Chicago was founded in 1908. See Henry Leonard, "The Immigrants' Protective League of Chicago, 1908–1921," *Journal of the Illinois State Historical Society* 66 (1973), 276.

27. Willard, *Glimpses of Fifty Years*, p. 390; *ibid.*, p. 247. Lucretia Hale, *The Peterkin Papers* (New York, 1963), was first published in 1880. Lucretia Hale to Edward Hale, September 23, 1875, Lucretia Hale Papers, Smith College, Northampton, Massachusetts.

18. PRIVATE PROPERTY IN PUBLIC PLACES

1. *Railroad Gazette* 5(1873), 401.

2. John B. McEwan, *The Story of Baggage* (Chicago, 1924), pp. 36–37.

3. *Railroad Gazette* 15 (1883), 754.

4. McEwan, *Story of Baggage*, pp. 33–38.

5. All U.S. patents of this period were written in a standard format which stated at the outset that the inventor had patented certain "new and useful improvements."

See, for example, U.S. Patent No. 476-598. See, for example, U.S. Patent Nos. 645,085; 791,506; 530,599; 185,372; 114,818; 657,463; 602,494.

6. U.S. Patent No. 114,818. U.S. Patent No. 185,372. U.S. Patent No. 303,859.

7. See, for example, J. J. Warren Luggage Company Catalog, 1892 (Worcester, Mass., 1892), pp. 6–107; and Sears, Roebuck Catalog No. 114 (1904), pp. 897–899.

8. U.S. Patent No. 476,598. U.S. Patent No. 495,448. J. J. Warren Catalog, 1892, pp. 6–107. On pockets or envelopes, see Montgomery Ward Catalog No. 55 (1894), pp. 514–517.

9. Montgomery Ward Company Catalog No. 19 (1877), pp. 101–116. On hand-held traveling bags, see *ibid.*, No. 23 (1878), p. 142. On the cheapest and the most expensive bags, see *ibid.*

10. On Sears, Roebuck travel bags for the 1890s see, for example, Sears, Roebuck Catalog No. 107 (1894), pp. 570–571. On Montgomery Ward bags, see Montgomery Ward Catalog No. 55 (1894), p. 517. On Gladstone bags, satchels, and telescope bags, see *ibid.*

11. On Sears's 1901 line, see Sears, Roebuck Catalog No. 110 (1901), p. 915. See also *ibid.*, No. 114 (1904), pp. 1037–1038.

12. J. J. Warren Catalog, 1892, pp. 6–107.

13. On toiletries and picnic items, see *ibid.*, pp. 10–29, 33, 43–44, 49–50. On specialty bags for physicians and others, see *ibid.*, pp. 45–55. On hand luggage, see *ibid.*, pp. 30–42, 59–70.

14. On the Jenny Lind trunk, see "From Carpet Bags and Gladstones to Modern Wiltshire Cases" (n.p., n.d.), a publication of the Charles T. Wilt Luggage Company, Chicago, Illinois. On the Gladstone bag, see, for example, Montgomery Ward Catalog, No. 41 (1887), p. 205; *ibid.*, No. 48 (1891–1892), p. 430; *ibid.*, No. 50 (1891–1892), p. 438.

15. For trunk names associated with royalty, see Montgomery Ward Catalog No. 19 (1877), pp. 105, 110, 113. For trunk names associated with resorts, see *ibid.*, No. 27 (1880), pp. 156–157. For trunk names associated with the West, see *ibid.*, No. 19 (1877), pp. 105, 112; No. 27 (1880), p. 157; and No. 41 (1887), p. 204.

16. Montgomery Ward Catalog No. 27 (1880), p. 155.

17. *Railroad Gazette* 15 (1883,) 845. *Ibid.*, 15 (1883), 312, 845.

18. Fanny Eckstorm Hardy to Smith College Class of 1888, October 24, 1900, Smith College Archives, Northampton, Massachusetts. Lucretia Hale to Charles Hales, July 1, 1864.

19. *The Travelers' Guide Containing Distance Tables to All Parts of the Country: Population United States, Stamp Duties, Telegraph Rates, U.S. Postal Laws &c.* (Buffalo, N.Y., 1871).

20. See *Railroad Gazette* 5 (1873), 234, 441; *ibid.*, 15 (1883), 564.

21. Beebe, *Mr. Pullman's Palace Car*, p. 59.

22. On the type of articles taken West, see, for example, Lillian Schlissel, *Women's Diaries of the Westward Journey* (New York, 1982).

23. H. Roger Grant, *Railroad Postcards in the Age of Steam* (Iowa City, Ia., 1994).

24. Among Brett Harte's best-known stories about the West are "The Luck of

Roaring Camp," first published in 1868, and "The Outcasts of Poker Flat," first published in 1869.

19. FROM UNION TO UNIFORMITY

1. AAPTO, *Proceedings,* September 8, 1876, p. 443.

2. Carlton Corliss, *Day of Two Noons,* quoted in Botkin and Harlow, *Treasury of Railroad Folklore,* p. 516.

3. AAPTO, *Proceedings,* March 13–14, 1855, p. 3.

4. American Railroad Association, *Proceedings of the General Time Convention and Its Successor the American Railroad Association from Its Organization April 14, 1886 to October 11, 1893 Inclusive* (New York, n.d.), p. 6. The 1872 proceedings are in this volume, despite the discrepancy in dates.

5. Railway Signal Association, *Journal,* 1895–1919, collections of Yale University Library. Forney, *Car Builder's Dictionary,* 1879, pp. iii–vi.

6. See note 14, Chapter 14.

7. Concerning uniform ticketing procedures, see AAPTO, *Proceedings,* March 13–14, 1855, p. 1. On coupon or card tickets, see *ibid.,* November 19, 1856, pp. 28–34. On ticket speculation, see *ibid.,* pp. 33, 35.

8. On the Coupon Ticket Committee, see *ibid.,* September 20, 1881, pp. 10–11. On mileage tickets, see *ibid.,* March 15, 1887, p. 8.

9. On local and regional associations, see *ibid.,* September 18, 1894, p. 202. On interchangeable mileage tickets, see *ibid.,* October 17–18 1899, p. 419.

10. On the meeting, see General Time Convention, *Proceedings,* pp. 681–682. On participating railroads, see *ibid.* On plans for standard time, see *ibid.,* p. 683.

11. *Ibid.,* pp. 684–688.

12. On number of time zones, see *ibid.,* p. 691. For Rodgers letter, see *ibid.,* p. 685. For letter from math professor, see *ibid.,* p. 686. On New London Time, see *ibid.,* p. 691.

13. On the nationwide vote, see *ibid.,* p. 694. For a list of railroad companies voting for standard time, and the track mileage of each, see *ibid.,* pp. 694–697. On total track mileage in the country, see *Poor's Manual,* 1883. Regarding God's time, see Corliss, *Day of Two Noons,* quoted in Botkin and Harlow, *Treasury of Railroad Folklore,* p. 516. Regarding the mayor of Bangor, Maine, see *ibid.,* p. 517.

14. On changing the gauges of Southern railroads, see John F. Stover. "One Gauge: How Hundreds of Incompatible Railroads Became a National System," in *Invention and Technology,* vol. 8, no. 3 (1993), 54–61.

15. Holbrook, *American Railroads,* p. 360. On specialty narrow-gauge roads, see, for, example, C. Frances Belcher, *Logging Railroads of the White Mountains* (Boston, 1980).

16. On Koch's luggage, see Koch, *Journey,* pp. 29, 30. Details from the entire journey are related on pp. 10–61.

17. On the use of accompanied baggage for commercial purposes, see, for example, AAPTO, *Proceedings,* March 8, 1865, p. 135; March 14, 1866, p. 147; October

2, 1866, p. 169; March 6, 1867, p. 187; March 8, 1884, p. 10; September 15, 1891, p. 95. On the publicity that surrounded baggage issues, see, for example, *Railroad Gazette* 15 (1883), 64, 159, 312, 582; 25 (1893), pp. 94, 436. Quotation may be found in AAPTO, *Proceedings,* October 2, 1866, p. 165.

18. For new luggage rules in 1866, see *ibid.,* March 14, 1866, p. 147. On 250-pound weight limit, see *Railroad Gazette* 15 (1883), 312. On trunks of commercial travelers, see *ibid.,* 15 (1883), 64.

19. On the editorial, see *Railroad Gazette* 15 (1883), 312.

20. On the Boston and Albany case, see *Railroad Gazette* 15 (1883), 582. On the bicycle issue, see *ibid.,* 25 (1893), 94.

21. Reed, *Train Wrecks,* p. 27, is one of numerous sources that note the increased speed of trains after the Civil War. *Ibid.,* p. 56, mentions the *Railroad Gazette* report. On p. 26, Reed notes that the *Gazette* counted 1,201 railroad accidents in 1875, but that the National Census Report on Transportation counted 8,216 railroad accidents in 1880. He concludes that neither figure can be accepted without qualification. Kirkland, *Men, Cities and Transportation,* vol. 2, 350–397, recounts the story of the safety movement that paralleled the rising number of train wrecks after the Civil War. An exposé of the risks to employees and passengers may be found in James O. Fagan, *Confessions of a Railway Signalman* (Boston, 1908).

22. Recommended parts for railroad cars were listed in *The Car Builder's Dictionary* (New York, 1879), republished in 1971. *The Car Builder's Dictionary* for 1888 has also been reprinted. See *Railroad Gazette* 5 (1873), 267–268, for an article describing the results of a Master Car-Builders' Association questionnaire on the best method of lighting, heating, and ventilating train cars.

23. See *Railroad Gazette* 5 (1873), 54, 267–269; *ibid.,* 15 (1883), 25, 85, 528, 858; *ibid.,* 25 (1893), 139, 854. See also Beebe, *Mixed Train Daily.*

24. A number of books exist on the history of motion study. A good one is Sigfried Giedion, *Mechanization Takes Command: A Contribution to Anonymous History* (New York, 1948), especially pp. 96–127.

25. Regarding jumping on and off moving trains, see *Railroad Gazette* 5 (1873), 157. On conductors getting on and off moving trains, see *ibid.* On death of a passenger, see *ibid.,* p. 281.

26. See *ibid.,* p. 234, for quotation on news agents.

27. On boisterous behavior, see *Railroad Gazette,* 15 (1883), 815. In the 1880s the *Gazette* wrote about some of the implications of Supreme Court decisions regarding the Civil Rights Act of 1875 for setting arrangements aboard trains. See, for example, *Railroad Gazette* 15 (1883), 695, 713, 726.

28. *Railroad Gazette* 15 (1883), 564–565.

29. Charles D. Learned to George Davis, Esq., September 24, 1878, in Martha Elvira Stone Papers, collection of Patricia Gordon Pollock, North Haven, Connecticut.

30. On "exhalations," see *Railroad Gazette* 5 (1873), 8. On remarks in the Pittsburgh press, see *Railroad Gazette* 15 (1883), 8. The writer of these remarks was Jane Swisshelm. On cholera epidemic, see *ibid.,* 25 (1893), 367. On the search for new systems of ventilation, see note 23 above.

31. *Railroad Gazette* 25 (1893), 367, 674.

THOMAS COOLEY AND THE GHOST OF WILLIAM SEWARD

1. Thomas Cooley, Introduction, in Thomas Curtis Clarke, et al., *The American Railway* (New York, 1976), pp. xxi–xxviii.

20. CITIES FIRST AND FOREMOST

1. H. G. Wells, *The Future in America: A Search After Realities* (New York, 1906), p. 54.

2. Chandler, *Visible Hand.*

3. U.S. Department of Commerce, *Statistical Abstract of the United States, 1920* (Washington D.C., 1921), pp. 397, 854.

4. Victor S. Clark, *History of Manufactures in the United States*, vol. 3, 1893–1928 (New York, 1949), pp. 141–146. U.S. Treasury Department, *Quarterly Report of the Chief of the Bureau of Statistics Showing the Imports and Exports of the United States* (Washington, D.C., 1875); *ibid.*, 1893.

5. *Ibid.*

6. Ilene Susan Fort, *Childe Hassam's New York* (San Francisco, 1993), pp. 6–15.

7. Wells, *Future in America*, p. 59.

8. *Ibid.*, p. 66.

9. Edward A. Steiner, *From Alien to Citizen: The Story of My Life in America* (New York, 1914), pp. 70–71.

10. Calculations from U.S. Department of Commerce, *Historical Statistics*, p. 12, indicate that despite settlement of the West and reconstruction of the South, approximately half the population still lived in the North in 1880, 1890, 1900, and 1910. U.S., *Statistical Abstract, 1920*, p. 49, shows that between 1900 and 1920 all states of the Union except Colorado, Montana, and Wyoming experienced a rise in the percentage of urban dwellers and a fall in the percentage of rural dwellers. The chart on p. 133 shows the percentage of change in the number of farms by state for 1900, 1910, and 1920. During this interval either the rate of change in the number of farms or the absolute number of farms declined in twenty-five states, including Illinois, Indiana, Iowa, Kansas, Maine, Massachusetts, Michigan, Missouri, Mississippi, New Hampshire, New Mexico, Rhode Island, Vermont, and West Virginia.

11. Foster Rhea Dulles, *America's Rise to World Power, 1898–1954* (New York, 1963), pp. 27–29, 32–33; and U.S. House Naval Committee, *The Relation of the Navy to the Commerce of the United States, a Letter Written to Hon. Leopold Morse, M.C., Member of the Naval Committee House of Representatives, by R.W. Shufelt, Commodore U.S.N.* (Washington D.C., 1878).

12. George H. Douglas, *All Aboard! The Railroad in American Life* (New York, 1992), p. 222.

13. Cochran, *Frontiers of Change*, p. 41; Giedion, *Mechanization Takes Command*, pp. 96–127. See note 40, Chapter 9, and note 42, Chapter 12.

14. Based on calculations from Floyd W. Mundy and Jas. H. Oliphant and Company, eds., *The Earning Power of Railroads, 1907* (New York, 1907); and *ibid.*, 1930.

15. See note 23, Chapter 19. On replacement technology, see Maury Klein, "Re-

placement Technology: The Diesel as a Case Study," in Maury Klein, *Unfinished Business: The Railroad in American Life* (Hanover, N.H., 1994), pp. 143–154, is of interest.

16. In 1900 Charles T. Yerkes (1837–1905) had partial control of the transit systems of both Philadelphia and Chicago. In the early 1930s Samuel Insull (1859–1938) controlled the entire Chicago transit system and sat on boards of eighty-five electrical and utilities companies. See Thomas Johnson, *The Oxford Companion to American History* (New York, 1966), pp. 411, 884. For a light history of city transit, see John Anderson Miller, *Fares, Please!: A Popular History of Trolleys, Horsecars, Streetcars, Buses, Elevateds, and Subways* (New York, 1960).

17. Fred Westing, *The Locomotives That Baldwin Built* (New York, 1966), p. 86. *Youth's Companion,* November 21, 1895, p. 597.

18. Howard Loxton, *Railways* (New York, 1970), p. 113.

19. Westing, *Locomotives,* pp. 110, 121.

20. Edwin P. Alexander, *American Locomotives: A Pictorial Record of Steam Power, 1900–1950* (New York, 1950), pp. 120–256. Faulkner, *American Economic History,* pp. 501–509, 593, 607–611; and Botkin and Harlow, *Treasury of Railroad Folklore,* pp. 241–290.

21. Peter T. Maiken, *Night Trains: The Pullman System in the Golden Years of American Rail Travel* (Baltimore, 1992), pp. 23–29.

22. William Z. Ripley, *Railroads: Rates and Regulation* (New York, 1920), p. 499.

23. Faulkner, *American Economic History,* pp. 599–602.

24. U.S. Interstate Commerce Commission, Annual Report 1922, p. 219; 1923, p. 237; 1924, p. 253; 1925, pp. 263–264; 1926, pp. 285–286; 1927, pp. 293–294; 1928, pp. 297–298; 1929, pp. 307–308. The ICC records are not definitive for abandonment of track throughout the country. For national totals, see U.S. Department of Commerce, *Historical Statistics: Colonial Times to 1957,* p. 429.

21. IT'S TOO CROWDED HERE

1. Leonard Mosley, *Dulles: A Biography of Eleanor, Allen and John Foster Dulles and Their Family Network* (New York, 1978), pp. 18–19.

2. Irving Howe, *World of Our Fathers* (New York, 1976), p. 215.

3. Historic accounts of this trend may be found in Sam Bass Warner, *Streetcar Suburbs: The Process of Growth in Boston, 1870–1900* (Cambridge, Mass., 1978), pp. 46–66. Interestingly, a great many novels and stories, particularly those of contemporary mystery writer Mary Roberts Rinehart, center on large houses owned by the rich in changing neighborhoods. See, for example, *Miss Pinkerton: Adventures of a Nurse Detective* (New York, 1959, first published in 1914); and *Episode of the Wandering Knife* (New York, 1990, first published in 1943).

4. See, for example, Fort, *Childe Hassam's New York,* plates 26–29, 34–36. Jules David Prown, *American Painting: From Its Beginning to the Armory Show* (New York, 1987), pp. 125–128. See also Maria Costantino, *Edward Hopper* (New York, 1995).

5. Karl Baedeker, *The United States: With an Excursion into Mexico: A Handbook*

for Travellers, 1893 (New York, 1971), p. 56. *Ibid.*, p. 225. *Ibid.*, p. 90. *Old Colony,* p. 343.

6. *Ibid.*, p. 345. Baedeker, *United States, 1893*, p. 86.

7. Beebe, *Hear the Train Blow*, pp. 360–365. Harvey H. Kaiser, *Great Camps of the Adirondacks* (Boston, 1986), pp. 33–53. *Ibid.*, pp. 55–60, 223–225.

8. *Ibid.* Pages 71–93 provide inventory lists and general descriptions of the camps developed by William West Durant, son of railroader Thomas C. Durant. *Ibid.*, p. 40.

9. *Ibid.*, pp. 77, 134.

10. Alexis Gregory, *The Golden Age of Travel, 1880–1939* (New York, 1991), pp. 58–60.

11. Morell, *Diamond Jim Brady*, pp. 25–28.

12. Maiken, *Night Trains*, p. 11.

13. Baedeker, *United States, 1893*, pp. 57, 303, 405.

14. Maiken, *Night Trains*, pp. 6, 24, 34.

15. *Ibid.*, pp. 18, 20.

16. *Ibid.*

22. PLANS, POWER, AND POPULATION

1. Chicago, City Council Commission on Railway Terminals, *The Railway Passenger Terminal Problem at Chicago, 1933*, p. 10.

2. Alexander, *Down at the Depot*, pp. 219, 220. Condit, *Railroad and City*, p. 242. *Ibid.*, pp. 135–136. Chicago, *Terminal Problem*, pp. 10–11.

3. Grand Central, *Annual Reports, 1906*, New York Central and Hudson River Railroad Company, et al. This book is a compilation of annual reports from all the railroads using Grand Central Station, New York. Lists of boards of directors appear throughout the volume. Chicago, *Terminal Problem*, p. 10. Alexander, *Down at the Depot*, pp. 295, 285–287. Condit, *Railroad and City*, p. 218. Alexander, *Down at the Depot*, p. 295.

4. Chicago, *Terminal Problem*, pp. 23–30.

5. *Ibid.*, pp. 31–33.

6. Condit, *Railroad and City*, pp. 216, 242.

7. See Kirkland, *Men, Cities and Transportation*, I, 317–319. *Ibid.*, II, 388–389, 352–361. On the greater size, length, and speed of trains, see also Reed, *Train Wrecks*, pp. 26–27, 37–38, 77, 86, 103, 112, 144, 147, 150, 163. See, for example, Connecticut Railroad Commissioners, *Annual Report, 1909*, pp. 37, 74–79.

8. On New York's stations, see Alexander, *Down at the Depot*, pp. 260–265, and Street, *American Adventures*, p. 11; on Washington, D.C., see Alexander, *Down at the Depot*, pp. 294–297; on Baltimore's station, see Street, *American Adventures*, p. 13; on Chicago's stations, see Chicago, Railway Passenger Terminal Problem, especially pp. 7–20, 50–52, 63–65. Tracks for the proposed Randolph Street station were in fact routed underground. For Cincinnati's stations, see Condit, *Railroad and City*, pp. 272–273.

9. For a contemporary account of the construction of the New York subway system, see New York Interborough Rapid Transit Company, *Interborough Rapid Tran-*

sit: The New York Subway, Its Construction and Equipment (New York, 1904); for a historical account, see Clifton Hood, *722 Miles: The Building of the Subways and How They Transformed New York* (Baltimore, 1995). *Ibid.,* p. 13.

10. *Interborough Rapid Transit,* pp. 14, 24–25.

11. *Ibid.,* pp. 16–17.

12. *Ibid.,* p. 23.

13. Grand Central, *Annual Reports, 1906,* pp. 492–493. A foldout map between these pages shows the traction systems in each city.

14. *Ibid.*

15. *Historical Statistics: Colonial Times to 1957,* p. 429.

16. Condit, *Railroad and City,* pp. 195–196.

23. TOURING THE WEST AND THE SOUTH

1. Richard Harding Davis, *The West from a Car Window* (New York, 1903), pp. 3–4.

2. Louise Closser Hale, *We Discover the Old Dominion* (New York, 1916), p. 11.

3. See, for example, U.S. Department of the Interior, Bulletin 613, *Guidebook: Part C. The Santa Fe Route, 1915* (Washington, D.C., 1915), p. iii.

4. These points are well documented in two histories of the New South: Woodward, *Origins of the New South,* and Edward Ayers, *The Promise of the New South: Life After Reconstruction* (New York, 1993). See also W. J. Cash, *The Mind of the South* (Garden City, N.Y., 1954).

5. See note 8, Chapter 20. A good account of a family's battles with the West may be found in McKeown, *Them Was the Days.*

6. For an overview of the railroads' interest in Western tourism, see Alfred Runte, *Trains of Discovery: Western Railroads and the National Parks* (Niwat, Colo., 1994).

7. On the start of Raymond's tours, see Raymond's Vacation Excursions, *A Winter in California: Season of 1889–90* (Boston, n.d.), p. 11; on routes taken, see *ibid.,* pp. 6–7.

8. On costs of a Raymond's tour, see *ibid.,* pp. 7–11; on hotels, see *ibid.,* pp. 34–36.

9. *Ibid.,* p. 143.

10. Irving Cobb, *Roughing It Deluxe* (New York, 1914), pp. 16–17.

11. Julian Street, *Abroad at Home* (New York, 1914), p. 295.

12. Baedeker, *United States, 1893,* pp. 412–413.

13. U.S. Department of the Interior, *The Santa Fe Route, 1915,* p. 111.

14. Tyrone Campbell and Joel and Kate Kopp, *Navajo Pictorial Weaving, 1880–1950: Folk Art Images of Native Americans* (New York, 1991), pp. 53–70, 117–123.

15. Sherry Clayton Taggett and Ted Schwarz, *Paintbrushes and Pistols: How the Taos Artists Sold the West* (Santa Fe, N.M., 1990), pp. 3, 5, 47.

16. See Woodward, *Origins of the New South,* pp. 292–296; and Julian Street, *American Adventures* (New York, 1917), pp. 196–197.

17. See Woodward, *Origins of the New South,* pp. 292–296.

18. See Maiken, *Night Trains*, pp. 117–121.

19. Maiken, *Night Trains*, p. 134.

20. On black Southern music coming north, see Ayers, *Promise of the New South*, pp. 373–408; on W. C. Handy, see *ibid.*, p. 384; and see Paul Oliver, *Blues Fell This Morning* (Cambridge, England, 1994).

21. *Ibid.*

24. HOMETOWNS AND NOSTALGIA

1. James Whitcomb Riley, "The Old Swimmin' Hole" quoted in Norman Foerster, ed., *American Poetry and Prose* (Boston, 1934), pp. 1168–1169.

2. See note 3, Chapter 3.

3. Edward Everett Hale, *Memories of a Hundred Years*, 2 vols. (New York, 1902). *Ibid.*, I, 230, 231.

4. *Ibid.* Hale, *Memories*, II, 832. Despite Hale's tight equation which linked mass political conventions with the rise of railroads, the earliest such conventions were held in Andrew Jackson's 1828 presidential campaign. It is probably more accurate to say that the railroads hastened and extended the national convention as a public forum.

5. *Ibid.*

6. Henry Adams, *The Education of Henry Adams* (Boston, 1961). The book was privately printed in 1907 and first published in 1918. *Ibid.*, pp. 239–240.

7. *Ibid.*, pp. 240, 330.

8. See note 2, Chapter 24. R. L. Duffus, *Williamstown Branch: Impersonal Memories of a Vermont Boyhood* (New York, 1958), p. 247. This source must be approached with caution because Duffus partially fictionalized it to avoid embarrassing living persons. The town, the time, and the industries mentioned are all real, however, as is the railroad. And each chapter is based on a true story.

9. *Ibid.*, p. 252.

10. Willis F. Dunbar, *How It Was in Hartford: Small-Town Life in Mid-America, 1900–1920* (Grand Rapids, Mich., 1968), p. 204.

11. *Ibid.*, p. 220.

12. Chase, *Railroad Passenger Travel*, pp. 10, 20, 21.

13. *Ibid.*, p. 38.

14. Morse, *36 Miles of Trouble*, pp. 30–31.

15. *Ibid.*, p. 3.

16. Howe, *World of Our Fathers*, p. 215.

17. Steiner, *Alien to Citizen*, pp. 70–71.

18. *Ibid.*, p. 161.

19. Nancy Hale, *A New England Girlhood: An Affectionate Recreation of Things Past* (Boston, 1958), pp. 94–95.

25. LOST HOMETOWNS, LOST LIVES

1. Thomas Wolfe, *Look Homeward, Angel* (New York, 1929) p. 382.

2. Sarah Orne Jewett, *Country of the Pointed Firs* (New York, 1994, first published in 1896), p. 20.

3. Mary Ellen Chase, *The Edge of Darkness* (New York, 1957), p. 33.

4. Willa Cather, *The Song of the Lark* (1915), in Willa Cather, *Three Complete Novels* (New York, 1992). Willa Cather, *My Ántonia* (Boston, 1926, first published in 1918). Willa Cather, *O Pioneers!* (Boston, 1941, first published in 1913). Cather, *Song of the Lark*, p. 151.

5. Cather, *Song of the Lark*, pp. 270, 389.

6. Cather, *My Ántonia*, p. 368. Cather, *O Pioneers!*, p. 123.

7. Willa Cather, *Obscure Destinies* (New York, 1930).

8. Thomas Nelson Page, *Gordon Keith* (New York, 1910), pp. 3–5, 28–43.

9. Theodore Dreiser, *Sister Carrie* (New York, 1970, first published in 1900), p. 1.

10. *Ibid.*, p. 3.

11. Mary Roberts Rinehart, *The Man in Lower Ten* (New York, 1990, first published in 1909).

12. See, for example, Glen H. Mullin, *Adventures of a Scholar Tramp* (New York, 1925), pp. 3–11; and Grant, *Brownie the Boomer*.

13. Mullin, *Scholar Tramp*, p. 19.

14. See Mullin, *Scholar Tramp*, pp. 12–23; and Botkin and Harlow, *Treasury of Railroad Folklore*, pp. 221–240.

15. Mullin, *Scholar Tramp*, pp. 3–26.

16. *Ibid.*; see also Botkin and Harlow, *Treasury of Railroad Folklore*, pp. 221–240.

17. Mullin, *Scholar Tramp*, p. 8.

18. *Ibid.*; also Harry Kemp, *Tramping on Life: An Autobiographical Narrative* (Garden City, N.Y., 1922).

19. "The Bid Rock Candy Mountain," in *Railroad Songs and Ballads*, Library of Congress Recording AFS L61.

20. Cohen, *Long Steel Rail*, pp. 478–481.

21. *Ibid.*, pp. 521–523.

22. *Ibid.*, pp. 507–508, 519–520.

23. *Ibid.*, pp. 601, 630, 638–640, 602.

26. NO SERVICE WITHOUT PROFIT

1. ICC, *Annual Report*, 1921, p. 17.

2. See, for example, Duffus, *Williamstown Branch*, pp. 87–93. *Ibid.*, p. 15.

3. Lambert Florin, *Nevada Ghost Towns* (Seattle, 1971), pp. 25, 33–36.

4. *Ibid.*, pp. 33–37, 38, 39.

5. Lucius Beebe and Charles Clegg, *Virginia and Truckee: A Story of Virginia City and Comstock Times* (Oakland, Calif., 1949), pp. 7–13, 48–49.

6. Florin, *Nevada Ghost Towns*, p. 10.

7. *Ibid.*, pp. 10–39.

8. Walter Williams, *The State of Missouri: An Autobiography* (Columbia, Mo., 1904). This book gives an alphabetical, county-by-county breakdown of the population, finances, resources, manufacturing, towns, newspapers, transportation, and major products of Missouri. See, for example, Adams and Andrew Counties, pp. 316–319, and p. 321. The quality of life of the Southern rural poor during the 1930s was captured in its most extreme form by James Agee and Walker Evans, *Let Us Now Praise Famous Men* (New York, 1972, originally published in 1939). Another look at Southern rural poverty may be found in Theodore Rosengarten, *All God's Dangers: The Life of Nate Shaw* (New York, 1974).

9. Duffus, *Williamstown Branch*, pp. 77–94, 96, 98.

10. Dunbar, *Hartford*, pp. 20–21, 68.

11. *Ibid.*, pp. 68, 69.

12. *Ibid.*, pp. 183–188, 192–194.

13. *Ibid.*, pp. 193–194.

14. Connecticut Railroad Commission, *Annual Report*, 1886 (Hartford, Conn., 1886), p. xxx. ICC Annual Report, 1920, p. 26.

15. See note 29, Chapter 22.

16. ICC Annual Report , 1920, p. 26.

17. *Ibid.*, 1921, p. 19. 1924, p. 253; 1925, p. 263; 1922, p. 219; 1924, p. 253; 1926, p. 286. See note 22, Chapter 20.

18. *Ibid.*, 1923, pp. 237–238. Statistics calculated from ICC abandonments and *Poor's Manual*, 1920 and 1926.

19. *Poor's Manual*, 1926, p. 517. *Ibid.*, 1920, pp. 631, 583.

20. *Ibid.*, 1926, pp. 517, 1246, 1307.

LOOKING BACKWARD

1. Henry W. Grady, quoted in Jane Jacobs, *Cities and the Wealth of Nations: Principles of Economic Life* (New York, 1985), p. 36.

A Note on Sources

THE FOUR DISCIPLINES that provide the major sources for this book—economic history, legal history, railroad history, and social history—all share a major theme: the growth of the country from a great many small, autonomous centers of control toward regional and then national cooperation.

In the field of economic history, exclusive of railroad business history and railroad economics, I have taken most of my general information and interpretation from the works of Thomas C. Cochran, Harold U. Faulkner, and Edward Chase Kirkland. Most useful have been Thomas C. Cochran, *Frontiers of Change* (complete citations for this and other books noted here may be found in the notes); Harold U. Faulkner, *American Economic History;* Edward Chase Kirkland, *A History of American Economic Life;* and Jane Jacobs, *Cities and the Wealth of Nations.* Among the most valuable primary sources I used were *Hunt's Merchants' Magazine,* railroad company annual reports (some of which are bound separately and some of which may be found in state railroad commission annual reports), and census reports.

In the field of legal history I found materials on eminent domain, negligence, torts, and common carriers, and on major changes in American law during the nineteenth century, in Morton Horwitz, *The Transformation of American Law,* in two volumes; James Willard Hurst, *Law and the Conditions of Freedom in the Nineteenth-Century United States,* as well as his *Legitimacy of the Business Corporation in the Law of the United States, 1780–1970,* and *Law and Social Order in the United States;* Lawrence M.

Friedman and Harry N. Scheiber, eds., *American Law and the Constitutional Order;* Lewis H. Haney, *A Congressional History of Railways in the United States;* and John A. Garraty, ed., *Quarrels That Shaped the Constitution.* Among the older sources I found useful in the field of law and legal history were Isaac F. Redfield, *A Practical Treatise upon the Law of Railways;* Byron K. Elliot and William F. Elliot, *A Treatise on the Law of Railroads;* and Oliver Wendell Holmes, Jr., *The Common Law.* For information on specific laws and legal cases, I consulted statutes and session laws for most of the states and territories, supreme court reports for a number of states, federal Supreme Court reports, all congressional actions on railroads for the nineteenth and early twentieth centuries, and a number of legal digests, including West Law's *Supreme Court Digest* under railroads and common carriers.

In railroad history it is useful to categorize the sources in order to distinguish among the more popular and comprehensive histories, histories of specific railroads, and rigorous scholarly histories. Among the staples of popular railroad literature, past and present, are Stewart H. Holbrook, *The Story of American Railroads;* Charles F. Carter, *When Railroads Were New;* George H. Douglas, *All Aboard!;* Slason Thompson, *A Short History of the Railways;* Dee Brown, *Hear That Lonesome Whistle Blow;* Cy Warman, *The Story of the Railroad;* B. A. Botkin and Alvin F. Harlow, *A Treasury of Railroad Folklore;* and the many collections of pictures and anecdotes published by Lucius Beebe and Charles Clegg, including particularly *Hear the Train Blow, Mr. Pullman's Elegant Palace Car, Mansions on Wheels,* and *Mixed Train Daily.* While these are not reliable sources for purposes of historical interpretation, they contain a wealth of material on the social aspect of railroading, reinforcing the idea that human experience was profoundly affected by the historical transition from diverse local communities to one national society.

Among the many histories of specific railroads or groups of railroads, of particular value were John F. Stover, *The History of the Baltimore and Ohio Railroad;* Edward Hungerford, *Men of Erie;* James L. Kerr, *The Louisville & Nashville; History of the Old Colony Railroad;* Robert J. Casey and W. A. S. Douglas, *The Story of the Chicago and North Western System;* and Gregg M. Turner and Melancthon W. Jacobus, *Connecticut Railroads.* While the quality of corporate histories varies widely, all are useful for general background information.

Among the most useful scholarly railroad histories were Carl W. Condit, *The Railroad and the City;* James A. Ward, *Railroads and the Character of America;* Albert Fishlow, *American Railroads and the Transformation of the Antebellum Economy* (Cambridge, Mass., 1965); John F. Stover, *The Amer-*

ican Railroad; Arthur M. Johnson and Barry E. Supple, *Boston Capitalists and Western Railroads;* Edward Chase Kirkland, *Men, Cities and Transportation;* and Eugene Alvarez, *Travel on Antebellum Southern Railroads.* And, though I disagree with his conclusions and wished for footnotes, Albro Martin, *Railroads Triumphant,* is an up-to-date synthesis of railroad history.

Among the most useful scholarly studies on specialized topics were John H. White, Jr., *The Railroad Passenger Car;* James A. Ward, *Southern Railroad Man;* Marilyn I. Holt, *The Orphan Trains;* H. Roger Grant, *Railroad Postcards in the Age of Steam;* Peter T. Maiken, *Night Trains;* H. Roger Grant, *Brownie the Boomer;* and Robert G. Athearn, *Union Pacific Country.* Other useful railroad books on special topics include Alfred Runte, *Trains of Discovery;* Peter Lyon, *To Hell in a Day Coach;* and George Edgar Turner, *Victory Rode the Rails.* Special mention should be made of Norm Cohen, *Long Steel Rail,* a wonderful and scholarly collection of railroad songs.

Among a number of photographic histories of railroad stations, the key titles are Carroll L. V. Meeks, *The Railroad Station;* Walter Berg, *Buildings and Structures of American Railroads;* and Edward Alexander, *Down at the Depot.*

Key primary sources in railroad history include the *Travelers' Guide; Poor's Manual of Railroads; The American Railroad Journal;* the proceedings of the American Association of Passenger Traffic Officers; the proceedings of the General Time Convention; and the records of the Interstate Commerce Commission. On luggage, the catalogs of Sears, Roebuck and Montgomery Ward were useful.

Important books on transportation in general include Seymour Dunbar, *A History of Travel in America;* George Rogers Taylor, *The Transportation Revolution;* Charles H. Ambler, *A History of Transportation in the Ohio Valley;* and Oscar O. Winther, *The Transportation Frontier: Trans-Mississippi West, 1865–1900.* An important contribution to the cultural aspects of American tourism is John F. Sears, *Sacred Places.*

For information on the social aspects of railroad travel, I used many travel diaries and letters. Key among these were those of Frederika Bremer in *America of the Fifties;* William Chambers, *Things as They Are in America;* Albert C. Koch, *Journey Through a Part of the United States of North America in the Years 1844–1846;* Michael Aaron Rockland, trans., *Sarmiento's Travels in the United States in 1847;* Anthony Trollope, *North America;* William Fraser Rae, *Westward by Rail;* Robert Louis Stevenson, "Across the Plains;" and Frank Leslie and Richard Reinhardt, *Out West on the Overland Train,* to name only a few. The most important collections of travel diaries include Allan Nevins, *American Social History as Recorded by British Travellers;* and H. Roger Grant, *We Rode the Train.*

On the Northeast, Edward Everett Hale, *A New England Boyhood,* and the papers of Martha Elvira Stone, a collection in the possession of my family, were critical to understanding the period before the Civil War.

On the American West, numerous railroad guides, travel accounts, and accounts of settlement were useful. Martha Ferguson McKeown's *Them Was the Days* is excellent, and so is Isabella Bird, *A Curious Life for a Lady.* Also useful were the titles in the Western Frontier Library series, including Charles L. Martin, *A Sketch of Sam Bass, The Bandit,* and General D. J. Cook, *Hands Up.*

On the South, state histories were helpful and informative though biased, since many were written to attract business and settlement. Also excellent and indispensable are C. Vann Woodward, *Origins of the New South,* and Edward Ayers, *The Promise of the New South.*

Index

A NOTE ON THE AUTHOR

Sarah H. Gordon was born in Philadelphia and grew up in North Haven, Connecticut. She studied history at Smith College, where she received an A.B. degree, at Cambridge University, and at the University of Chicago, where she was awarded M.A. and Ph.D. degrees in American history. She has worked as an archivist, writer, and photographer, and now teaches American history at the Tikvah High School for Girls and at Quinnipiac College, both in Connecticut. Ms. Gordon's articles and reviews on aspects of nineteenth-century American social history have appeared in a variety of books and journals. She lives in North Haven.